DEVELOPMENT and STRUCTURE of the BODY IMAGE

Volume 1

DEVELOPMENT and STRUCTURE of the BODY IMAGE
Volume 1

Seymour Fisher
Upstate Medical Center
State University of New York

LEA LAWRENCE ERLBAUM ASSOCIATES, PUBLISHERS
1986   Hillsdale, New Jersey   London

514 02954

Lawrence Erlbaum Associates, Inc., Publishers
365 Broadway
Hillsdale, New Jersey 07642

Library of Congress Cataloging-in-Publication Data

Fisher, Seymour.
  Development and structure of the body image.

  Bibliography: p.
  Includes index.
  1. Body image. I. Title
BF697.5.B63F67 1986   155.2   85-16182
ISBN 0-89859-700-5 (set
ISBN 0-89859-684-X (v. 1)
ISBN 0-89859-699-8 (v. 2)

Printed in the United States of America
10 9 8 7 6 5 4 3 2 1

To my wife

Contents
Volume 1

Acknowledgments   ix

Introduction   xi

Preface   xiii

I. Critical Analysis of Research Concerned with Body Perception and Body Attitudes

1. The Body Stimulus   3

2. Developmental Aspects of Body Perception   47

3. Body Appearance, Prowess, and Camouflage   123

4. Body Size Experiences   159

5. Stressful Body States in Normal Persons   223

6. Pathological Phenomena   273

7. Integrative Conclusions   315

Acknowledgments

This book evolved while I was a member of the Faculty of the Department of Psychiatry of the State University of New York Medical School in Syracuse, New York. I wish to express my appreciation for the support I have received by way of facilities, computer services, and a general ambiance conducive to scholarly work. Special thanks are in order to the Upstate Medical Center library, which can apparently locate anything that has ever been printed. Also, grants from the National Institutes of Health have from time to time been of real assistance to my research.

I owe much to my wife, Dr. Rhoda Fisher, for innumerable conversations in which we explored body image issues. My daughter, Ms. Eve Fisher, and my son, Dr. Jerid Fisher, aided in the collection of data for several studies, and I thank them.

My secretary, Ms. Mary McCargar, has now seen me through ten books. Her superb typing and common sense helped to keep the whole enterprise moving.

Special acknowledgments are due to the publishers listed below for permissions to quote extensively from various of my published papers.

Williams and Wilkins:

Theme induction of localized somatic tension, *Journal of Nervous and Mental Disease,* 1980, 168: 721–731.

American Psychological Association:

Boundary effects of persistent inputs and messages, *Journal of Abnormal Psychology,* 1971, 77: 290–295.

Influencing selective perception and fantasy by stimulating body landmarks, *Journal of Abnormal Psychology,* 1972, 79: 97–105.

Academic Press:

Anxiety and sex role in body landmark functions, *Journal of Research in Personality,* 1978, 12: 87–99.

Introduction
Volume 1

This is volume 1 of *Development and Structure of the Body Image*. It contains a detailed review and analysis of the body image literature from 1969 through 1985. Volume 2 provides an overview of the extensive work that has been done to appraise a number of my major theoretical concepts concerning body image functioning. It deals with such topics as the organization of the body image boundary, assignment of meaning to specific body areas, general body awareness, and distortions in body perception. The bibliography and indexes for the two volumes are contained in volume 2.

Preface

More than a decade has passed since my last book, *Body Experience in Fantasy and Behavior,* in which I analyzed what had been learned about body image and body perception in the preceding decade. Many new studies and observations have accumulated. They need to be reviewed and assimilated. I have tried to put them into a theoretical frame that will energize their significance. We are slowly and laboriously beginning to understand how people make psychological sense of their unbelievably complex body experiences. It has been interesting to watch the expansion of interest in body experience. Starting out as a relatively parochial scholarly focus for a few neurologists and psychiatrists, body perception has increasingly recruited investigators concerned with such diverse phenomena as development of identity, adaptation to body illness and injury, obesity, sex role, territoriality, response to drugs, sexual behavior, and self awareness. Congruent with the prediction Cleveland and I made in 1958 (Fisher & Cleveland, 1958), body image constructs have proven to have considerable potency in explaining behavior. I marvel that, nevertheless, important segments of the scholarly community continue to regard people as disembodied. They give lip service to the fact that each human being is a biological object but refuse to factor into their behavioral equations the powerful impact of the immediate experience of one's own body in every situation. I firmly believe we will eventually find that measures of body perception are among our most versatile predictors of how people will interpret and react to life situations.

As research information has accumulated, it has become obvious that many of our previous notions about body perception are too simplistic. It no longer makes sense to talk about a simple unitary Body Image or Body Schema. The organization of body experience is multidimensional. At any given moment an individual may be simultaneously monitoring such different aspects of his body as its position in space, the integrity of its boundaries, its relative prominence in the total perceptual field, changes in its apparent size, and so forth. Each of these aspects may or may not be relatively independent of the others. To complicate matters further, we know that modes of body perception may shift markedly at certain developmental points and may also be quite different, even polar opposites, in males as compared to females. Consider, too, that some aspects of body experience are immediately observable and accessible by way of direct questioning of the individual, but others are either so automatized or obscured at unconscious levels that they can be observed only by means of highly sensitive indirect techniques. Approaches to the study of body perception that seek to squeeze it into a few narrow dimensions are really not defensible. It does not make sense to sample some convenient limited aspect of body experience and to assert it is The Measure of Body Image. Investigators should no longer be surprised when they administer several different measures of body experience and find that they do not correlate with one another. This does not mean, as some have asserted, that "body image" is not a valid concept but rather that it is far more multidimensional than our early models envisioned.

I have set four major objectives in this book: (a) to review and make sense of the overall body perception research that has been completed since 1969; (b) to analyze in special detail the many studies that have looked at the functioning of the body image boundary; (c) to probe and integrate my own considerable accumulation of data bearing on how meaning is assigned to the major sectors of one's body; and (d) to develop a working model of how the meanings linked to specific body areas become a matrix of signals that shape behavior.

My own studies indicate that we turn to our bodies for guidance not only with regard to matters like whether we are tired or thirsty, but also whether to get close to a particular person, or to avoid certain social situations, or to cultivate specific kinds of fantasies. I suggest that our earliest meaningful contacts with the world are strongly body oriented. Some of the most important aspects of children's relationships with their parents revolve about the satisfaction, incitement, or inhibition of body feelings. Children construct a model of their relationships with others that is heavily phrased in a body vocabulary. They learn to make judgments in body image terms about such basic issues as what is good and bad, attractive or threatening. Although adults often trace their important life decisions to logical cognition, it is probable that such decisions occur within an influential nonverbal framework of "body standards" for the way things should be. I anticipate that we will eventually be able to show that most judgments are affected by coded messages from the body "sounding board." Perceived events are constantly being translated into patterns of feeling at pertinent body sites and these patterns, in turn, feed back to and modulate central perspectives.

The issue of sex differences is constantly before us in this book. Although research in other areas has found fewer and fewer psychological distinctions between women and men, the body image literature reveals quite the opposite. The two sexes have very different modes of perceiving their bodies. They organize their body experiences in unlike ways. They differ with respect not only to the broad stylistic attitudes they adopt toward the somatic self, but also to the meanings they assign to its specific parts. This is true even with respect to parts that have no obvious sex-linked functions. There is fairly good evidence that women and men have contrasting perspectives about the role of the somatic self in their total identity. They also have different amounts and kinds of somatic anxiety. It has become commonplace in our research to find that, if a particular pattern of body perception typifies one sex, the opposite will prove to be true of the other sex. Most of the differences probably reflect the divergent ways in which boys and girls are socialized with reference to their bodies. However, it will be no surprise if some turn out to be the result of obvious biological factors like body structure and hormonal output. As will be seen, there are uniquely feminine body experiences, like menstruation and pregnancy, that do shape the average woman's images of her body. It puzzles me that most of the standard texts on sex differences (e.g., Maccoby & Jacklin, 1974) have ignored those that lie within the realm of body perception; it is just such differences, linked to one's feeling about one's body, that are basic to sexual identity and probably to identity in its broader sense.

Finally, I stress my intent to integrate findings from the psychological laboratory with observations from other disciplines that have been curious about body image events. Historians, anthropologists, and sociologists, among others, have published a good deal of information bearing on how people conceptualize their bodies. Such information often fits surprisingly well with the results coming out of artificial experimental contexts. For example, anthropologists (Needham, 1973) have described fine distinctions in the masculine-feminine meanings of the right versus left placement of bodies during burial that correspond to similar distinctions in the right versus left sides of the body revealed in perceptual judgments. Sociologists have reported defensive uses of tattoos by prisoners that are analogous to boundary defense maneuvers in psychosomatic patients (Fisher, 1970). Architects have pointed out certain connotations of the interior living space of one's home that are reminiscent of meanings ascribed to specific interior areas of the body (e.g., the heart). Historians have pictured mechanized views of the body arising during periods of economic stress that remind one of feelings of depersonalization exhibited by persons confronted by conflictual perceptual cues.

What we are learning about the organization of body experience not only is theoretically exciting but also facilitates our understanding of very practical problems like why people delay in seeking medical treatment, how they adapt to body disablement, and why they are so vitriolically biased against others whose body appearance differs from their own.

Critical Analysis of Research Concerned with Body Perception and Body Attitudes

This section embraces an analysis of the scientific literature concerned with body perception that has appeared since 1969. A review of the earlier literature up to 1958 may be found in Body Image and Personality *(Fisher & Cleveland, 1958); and a review of publications from 1958 to 1969 was presented in* Body Experience in Fantasy and Behavior *(Fisher, 1970).*

What does one include in an analysis of studies of body perception? Broad definitions and categories have been applied. Any observations pertinent to the terms body image, body concept, body scheme, body attitudes, and body experience fall within the province of the review. In short, any study qualifies for inclusion if it even remotely deals with how individuals view and assign meaning to their own body. The analyses presented are quite detailed, with sufficient information so that the reader is free to arrive at independent judgments concerning the studies that are evaluated. Greater brevity might be preferred, but, without pertinent details, judgments cannot be truly meaningful. Special effort is devoted to summarizing material, detecting similarities and contradictions, and formulating general principles. It is not the intent of this review to dissect out all the minute defects of the studies considered. Rather, criticisms are directed only at what appear to be major shortcomings.

A word is in order concerning the terms that are employed in referring to body perception phenomena. Some people urge that we should carefully limit the ways in which we use references like body image, body schemata, and body percept. For example, Shontz (1969) would refer to "body image" only when one has in mind "the personal body as a dynamic component of personality" (p. 6). He would confine "body schemata" to the cognitive aspects of body perception. Such distinctions seem to be premature. It is doubtful that any aspect of body experience can be said not to be significantly affected by personality vectors. Thus, even the simplest of judgments about one's body size are probably touched by personal values. With this perspective, terms like body image, body concept, and others are used loosely and occasionally interchangeably at a general level of discourse. However, as the book unfolds, a number of new terms with rather precise technical meanings are spelled out in the context of empirical findings.

1 The Body Stimulus

It is by now well documented that a person becomes uncomfortable when made increasingly aware of his or her somatic self. Such augmented awareness may result from looking in a mirror,[1] hearing a recording of one's voice, or just being exposed to an audience (Fisher, 1970; Holzman, 1964). Heightened response has been detected even when people are unknowingly confronted with their self-representations. For example, if shadow profile pictures are obtained from people without their knowledge, a considerable percentage of the individuals will fail to identify themselves when they later encounter their pictures mixed in with the shadow profiles of others. Interestingly, when they are asked to describe or evaluate their own unidentified profiles, they usually do so in exaggeratedly flattering terms that suggest a self-protective strategy (Huntley, 1940; Reitz & Thetford, 1967; Schnitzer, 1961; Wolff, 1943;). However, they may also at times respond in a markedly self-depreciatory fashion. Fisher (1970) noted:

> There is plenty of evidence that when an individual is confronted with his body or some representation of it as a perceptual object he gets stirred up in fairly unique ways. He is surprised, puzzled, autonomically activated, and motivated to take various kinds of defensive strategies. It is even a bit astonishing to learn that he does not have a precise patent against which to compare his mirror image and may have difficulty in deciding precisely how he looks. (p. 14)[2]

Apparently, as suggested by Holzman, Berger, and Rousey (1967), self-representations contain information that is ordinarily shut out, but that becomes threatening when it cannot be avoided, as in the context of the direct confrontation of one's mirror image or recorded voice.[3] There may be expressions and postures that reveal unconscious attitudes that are largely ego alien. Support for such a view comes from studies (e.g., Rogers & Walsh, 1959) demonstrating that, when persons are asked to describe self-representations (e.g., pictures of self) under conditions where they are not aware of the self-reference involved, they exaggerate just those qualities about which they are especially defensive. For example, persons inhibited about being aggressive unknowingly rated their self-representations as more aggressive than those of others (Rogers & Coleman, 1959).

3

Researchers continue to be curious about how well people can identify their own bodies and about the nature of their reactions when they unknowingly encounter self-representations. Gellert, Girgus and Cohen (1971) probed the ability of male (N = 97) and female (N = 69) children between the ages of 5 and 13 years to recognize their own bodies. Their photographs were taken from the front, back, and side while they wore brief bathing suits. The children were later asked to select their own photographs from a set consisting of their own and those of a number of same-sexed age mates. Selections were made under different conditions: with heads and necks covered and uncovered; with the accompanying pictures of other children varying in their degree of similarity to the self pictures. There was almost perfect accuracy in identifying self when the head was visible in either side or front views. Accuracy for the back view improved with age, from 52% (5–9 years) to 88% (9.5 years). When the head was concealed, accuracy was low but still greater than chance at all age levels. No sex differences in ability to identify self were detected. Interestingly, fat children made significantly more errors in self-recognition than did thin children. By and large, accuracy in self-perception, even among children as young as 5 years of age, was high when adequate cues were provided.

Nash (1969) obtained photographs of seventh- (N = 26) and ninth-grade (N = 20) boys and cut them into strips in such a fashion that 11 different isolated body parts were depicted (e.g.,forehead, eyes, chest, legs). Within each grade group, the boys were mutually acquainted. Subjects were asked to pick from each series of pictures of a given body part the one representing self and any others they recognized. In both grade groups, self-recognition was greater than chance, and the older subjects did better than the younger ones. Self-identification was most accurate for the forehead and second best for the mouth. There was also reasonably good recognition of the chest and eyes. However, self-recognition was particularly poor for hand, leg, nose, and ear.

In a second phase of the study, Nash asked 10 psychiatric residents who had had pictures of their heads taken to render a series of judgments similar to those obtained from the children just described. In this judging situation, larger photographs were used and a larger variety of perspectives was employed (e.g., profile views). It was found that self-recognition exceeded chance expectation for almost every part of the head (except hair and ear). Those parts of the face that were most successfully identified for self were also those most often correctly identified for others. The mouth and the eyes were among the most recognizable of the entire head. Self-recognition was greater for a silhouette of one's face than for any other type of facial photograph. Nash doubted that one's degree of familiarity with various parts of one's body could explain differential success in identifying pictures of those parts. He wondered if the explanation was more likely to involve how interested persons were in specific areas of their bodies as a function of their "membership in a stigmatized group, or occupation, or biological changes associated with particular phases of development, or 'incorporation' of parental concern about body surface appearance" (p. 338).

Collins, Harper, and Cassel (1976) examined the ability of adolescent boys ($N = 55$) and girls ($N = 94$) who averaged 18 years of age to identify their own bodies when facial and clothing cues were eliminated. Subjects were photographed from three different perspectives (front, side, rear) while wearing a standard brief costume and with facial features concealed by a hood. A week later they were asked to pick out their own photographs, which were presented along with six photographs of others of similar height and weight. The identification of one's own body proved to be rather accurate: about 85% correct for front view; 65% for side view; and 76% for rear view. The girls required significantly more time than the boys to render their self-identification judgments. Collins et al. speculated that this might be due to the girls' "greater ego involvement" with their bodies.

Collins (1981) photographed 17 male and 17 female Australian subjects in the nude. Their mean age was 19. One month after the photographs were taken, the subjects were asked to identify front, side, and rear views of themselves from an array of seven photographs grouped according to height and linearity. Judgments were similarly made with reference to individual body parts: head, thorax, abdomen, arms, and legs, as well as the torso and top and bottom half of the body. The front view of the full body was correctly recognized by 94% of the males and 100% of the females. The respective correct identifications for the rear view were 63% and 92%; and for the side view, 81% and 100%, respectively. The males correctly identified 100% of the pictures of the front view of their bottom half, whereas the females had only 92% success. This sex difference was reversed for the front view of the top half of the body: males, 94% and females, 100% success. The difference is noteworthy in view of previous data (Fisher, 1970) indicating that males have relative difficulty in perceiving aniseikonic change in the upper body region and that females display such difficulty in relation to the lower body region. It should be noted, though, that the difference Collins found between males' and females' ability to identify their upper versus lower body regions changed when side or back views were involved; then, females' accuracy was superior for both regions. Women were 100% accurate in identifying their own breasts, whereas men correctly identified their chests in only 88% of their judgments. Males correctly identified their own genitals in 94% of judgments; the comparable percentage for woman was 75. It is interesting that both sexes were more successful in identifying their right arm than their left (viz., 81% versus 50% for males, and 67% versus 58% for females). Overall, the females tended to be more accurate in their identifications than were the males. However, no formal significance test of this difference was provided. Collins determined the speed with which subjects rendered their judgments; and he was particularly impressed with the relative quickness with which the females could correctly identify their breasts and the males their genitals. He speculated about the special prominence of these body parts in the respective female and male sexual identities. As in a previous study (Collins et al., 1976), the females were observed to take significantly longer than males in rendering their body identifications.

Collins and Propert (1983) examined the role of menarcheal status in the ability of Australian girls (N = 175) to identify photographs depicting their body (clad only in briefs and with the head occluded). Each subject was presented with an array of five photographs (one of which was of herself) and asked to indicate which one was her own. There was a steady and significant trend for identification to improve as one proceeded along the continuum from premenarcheal to menarcheal to postmenarcheal stages, but only if the front view of the subject was involved. When subjects judged side and rear view photographs, the postmenarcheal girls were most accurate, but the menarcheal girls were surprisingly less accurate than the premenarcheal girls. Collins and Propert speculated that the body changes linked with adolescence are most quickly and systematically recognized for the front of the body, and less so for other body areas not so easily amenable to inspection. Postmenarcheal girls were able to identify the front view photograph of their body with 84% accuracy, and this matches well the judgmental accuracy found in the earlier Collins et al. (1976) study. Accuracy in postmenarcheal girls was 74% for identifying the side view and 71% for the rear view.

Nolan and Kagan (1980) looked at the ability of 61 boys and 61 girls (ages 2½ through 5½) to recognize photographs of their hands and faces. Subjects viewed each of their photographs in the context of three similar foils and had to identify which was self. Besides the usual full-face pictures, there was also one of the eyes and nose only and another with the eyes blackened out. Ninety-five percent of the children were able to identify correctly their full face photographs[4] as well as those in which the eyes were blackened out. Pictures of the hands in a palms up position were significantly better identified by the older half than by the younger half of the total sample (45% versus 26% correct). But only the girls showed improvement with age in identifying their faces from which all but the eyes and nose had been omitted. Correct identification rose from 33% for the younger girls to 59% for the older girls. Similarly, only the girls showed improvement with age in identifying pictures of their hands with palms down (44% correct under age 4 to 79% correct over age 4). Nolan and Kagan did not offer an explanation for the fact that the girls showed significant improvement with age, whereas the boys did not.

Solhkhah, Heller, and Aderman (1979) explored the ability of 46 male and 42 female children (ages 11–13) to define correctly their facial proportions when confronted with a mirror that systematically distorted their features.

They were given the task of adjusting the mirror so that the distorted images would be "back to normal." Personality scores from the High School Personality Questionnaire (Cattell & Cattell, 1969) and teachers' ratings were also available for the subjects. A generally high level of accuracy was found in the mirror judgments. However, it should be emphasized that the subjects were first shown an undistorted image of self before being exposed to the distorted versions. This provided an anchor that enhances accuracy. Previous work (Schneiderman, 1956) has shown that, if adults are not provided with such an anchor, they may make considerable errors when attempting to correct distorted mirror images of self. In the Solhkhah et al. study there were no sex differences[5] in the accuracy of the facial judgments, but the girls tended to overestimate more than the boys. There were scattered findings involving personality measures that did not add up to much. For example, "relaxed" boys made the most distortion errors. Boys who were low in "social interaction" perceived themselves as smaller, whereas "sociable boys" tended to enlarge their facial features. Girls "rated as average in sociability enlarged their facial images, where those extreme in sociability view themselves as small or perhaps more 'feminine'" (p. 249).

As already mentioned, the special arousal elicited by confrontation with one's self can be detected (e.g., by increased autonomic response) even when the individual is apparently unaware that the confrontation is taking place. A number of studies have continued to document this fact. Gur and Sackeim (1979; Sackeim & Gur, 1978) have done some ingenious work in this area. They sought to demonstrate that an active, defensive process of "self-deception" is involved in misidentification of self in self-confrontation situations. They have used primarily reactions to one's own voice as the basis for their investigation. In one study, they exposed 30 male and 30 female college students, individually, to tape recordings of voices of self and others. Subjects were to indicate in each instance whether the voice was their own or that of a stranger, and furthermore to rate their confidence in their judgments. GSR was simultaneously recorded. Inasmuch as a high level of GSR arousal has been found to typify people exposed to their own voice, even when the voice is incorrectly identified as not self, Gur and Sackeim (1979) assumed that GSR response could be used as a rough index of whether identification of self had, at some level, actually occurred. They relied heavily on this idea to construct a paradigm for demonstrating that motivated deception and contradiction enter into self confrontation responses. Gur and Sackeim considered that (p. 150), "If subjects hold contradictory beliefs when they incorrectly identify voices, then their levels of GSR reactivity should be high when they misidentify voices of self as others (false negative responses) and low when they misidentify voices of others as self (false positive responses). This would indicate that when subjects committed such errors, at some level of processing correct identifications had been made."

The results conformed significantly to this pattern. There was also evidence that those subjects who made errors in identifying self were particularly likely to score high on a "measure of individual differences in tendencies to engage in self deception."[6]

In another phase of this study, Gur and Sackeim had subjects (30 male, 30 female) judge for a series of recorded voices whether they were hearing themselves or others. Half of the subjects had first had a success experience and half had had failure. It was expected that the failure experience would make self-confrontation more aversive and that success would have the opposite effect. As expected, the subjects who were primed with failure had more difficulty in recognizing their own voices, but not in identifying the voices of others. Interestingly, while the failure subjects made more errors in identifying self, the success subjects made more errors that involved incorrectly judging the voices of others to be one's own. Gur and Sackeim (1979) succinctly noted: "In short, when people are made to feel good about themselves, they tend to 'project' and see themselves in places where they are not. When people are made to feel bad about themselves they tend to 'deny' seeing themselves in places where they are" (p. 165). In a general review of the self-confrontation literature, Gur and Sackeim concluded that self-confrontation is threatening because it makes persons aware of their "internal discrepancies" and negative attributes.[7] This awareness presumably produces increased physiological arousal, negative affect, and defensive constriction in ideation. Gur and Sackeim were particularly impressed that even during sleep persons respond selectively to hearing their own recorded voices. It has been shown in two studies (Castaldo & Holzman, 1967, 1969) that when persons are exposed to tape recordings of their own voices during sleep, they are especially likely to have dreams in which they play active, assertive, and independent roles. This contrasts with the more passive roles sleepers take in their dreams when they are exposed to the recorded voices of other persons. Two aspects of this work are especially noteworthy. First, it is striking that even during sleep people react in a fashion that indicates they can identify self versus nonself stimuli with considerable accuracy.[8] Second, whereas the response to one's own voice in the conscious state is often negative and defensively constricting, the response in the sleep state can be said to be positive and active. It is possible that in the sleep state people are less defensive and more accepting of their blemishes and failings,[9] which they are ordinarily so sensitive to during self-confrontation.[10]

MIRROR CONFRONTATION: ABILITY TO IDENTIFY ONE'S BODY

Since 1970 there has been a dramatic increase in research concerned with the effects of being directly confronted with a mirror image of one's self. Most of this research was stimulated by social psychological theory rather than by body image concepts. More will be said about this shortly. One interesting line of inquiry has focused on the reactions of animals and young children when they perceive themselves in a mirror. Gallup (1968, 1970, 1977) pioneered the systematic study of how various species of animals behave before their mirror images. He demonstrated that chimpanzees and orangutans can learn to relate their mirror images to their own bodies. If a red dot is placed on a chimpanzee's head so that it is visible only in a mirror, the chimp soon responds to his mirror image by increasing his rate of touching of the red dot area on his head. Only the chimpanzee and the orangutan have been found to exhibit such self-awareness. Apparently, only they and humans meaningfully link their mirror images to the unique areas of space occupied by their own bodies. Only they perceive a link between their mirror representations and their kinesthetic experiences of separate being or identity. Gallup, McClure, Hill and Bundy (1971) have shown that in the chimpanzee such sense of identity is somehow related to having had interactions with members of its own species. If a chimpanzee is reared in severe isolation, it fails to manifest recognition of its own mirror reflection.

Previous, largely impressionistic, reports (e.g., Dixon, 1957; Zazzo, 1948) concerned with the responses of human babies to their mirror images have differed in their accounts of when self-recognition occurs. More carefully controlled studies (Amsterdam, 1972; Amsterdam & Greenberg, 1977; Brooks-Gunn, 1975; Lewis & Brooks-Gunn, 1979; Schulman & Kaplowitz, 1977) concluded that such recognition typically takes place in the last few months of the second year. Illustratively, in her observations of 88 children ranging from 3 to 24 months. Amsterdam (1972) found an age-related mirror behavior sequence of the following character: from about 6 to 12 months, infants reacted to their reflections as if to they were sociable playmates; during the second year, withdrawal and wariness appeared along with signs of self-admiring and embarrassed behavior; from 20 to 24 months, 65% of the babies recognized their mirror images.[12]

The importance of the 20–24 months period in the self-awareness process is well supported by the work of Kagan (1981). He studied self-awareness in children from different locales in the United States and also in a sample from the Fiji Islands. The studies were longitudinal and involved objective analyses of observed behavior. Several different criteria for self-awareness were utilized: signs of distress at not being able to imitate the acts of a model; smiling in a "masterly" fashion upon mastering a task; goal-directed action designed to alter the behavior of an adult; and self-descriptive utterances. It was found that: "The central psychological victories of the last half of the second year appear to include both the appreciation of standards and the emergence of awareness of the self's actions, intentions, states, and competences" (p. 118). Kagan pinpointed self-awareness as blossoming between 15 and 23 months.

Levine (1979) has provided an interesting analysis of the relationship of mirror recognition behavior to other measures of self-definition in young children. She studied 78 boys in the 2-year-old range. A battery of tests was administered that included a mirror-recognition task; an assessment of ability to understand the possessives "my" and "your" and also to use self-referring pronouns correctly; and measurement of ability to take another's perceptual perspective. Ability to recognize self in the mirror was found to be positively and significantly correlated with the ability to use self-referring pronouns correctly. However, mirror recognition was not significantly correlated with pronoun recognition or with perceptual role taking. Those children who did recognize themselves in the mirror obtained higher vocabulary test scores than did those who failed to recognize self, but only at a borderline level of significance. One of Levine's conclusions was that children develop the ability to identify their mirror images earlier than they do other aspects of self-definition (e.g., "me" versus "you"). She also demonstrated that those children who seemed to be most self-aware had greater closeness to mother. They had had briefer past separations from mother, particularly during the first year of life. Interestingly, they were also less likely to have siblings, and their mothers displayed more positive attitudes about reciprocal interaction with them. In another report, Levine (1983) indicated that the most self-aware children were also most concerned in defining the boundaries between self and non-self in their interactions with peers. For example, they were particularly likely to claim ownership of any toys that were present.

Bertenthal and Fischer (1978) administered a battery of mirror recognition and object permanence tasks to 48 infants (24 male, 24 female) ranging in age from 6 to 24 months. The researchers were testing a theory that self-recognition develops gradually, over a series of stages, rather than appearing suddenly at a given age. A gradual increase in ability to recognize self was indeed observed, beginning with rudimentary reaching gestures toward one's mirror image to the final ability to give one's name when someone points to the mirror image and asks, "Who's that?" Bertenthal and Fischer suggested that previous disagreements in the literature concerning the age at which self-recognition occurs resulted from differences in the stringency of definition. In addition, a moderately high correlation was found between degree of ability to recognize self and stage of object permanence attained.[13]

Lewis and Brooks-Gunn (1979) carried out extensive research with multiple samples to ascertain when and how self-recognition develops in the first few years of life. They used not only responses of infants to mirror images but also their reactions to video images and pictures of self. They found that before the age of 15 months infants "never" responded to mirror-reflected marks that had been placed on them; the modal positive response to such marks was 21 months. Experiments in which infants were exposed to pictures of self indicated "pictures of self are responded to as such by 21–24 months of age and are probably responded to even earlier" (p. 140). It was found too that the earlier infants show signs of self-recognition, the more likely they are to exhibit specific negative emotional responses when they encounter a stranger. With respect to this point, it was said

> The well-known phenomenon of stranger fear that occurs in many, if not all cultures . . . must be related to the developing knowledge of the self. That is, as infants differentiate between familiar and unfamiliar objects and people and learn about the permanence of these objects and people, they are also learning about themselves. As infants learn that their mothers and fathers are different people, they also learn that they are neither mother nor father but unique persons. (p. 197)

EFFECTS OF INCREASED SELF-AWARENESS

An impressive surge of research concerned with the impact of being exposed to one's mirror image grew out of the efforts of Duval and Wicklund (1972). These investigators became interested in the question of how self-awareness affects behavior. They originally theorized that when persons focus their attention upon themselves, they become self-critical and typically highlight their own defects and deviations from the ideal. Duval and Wicklund often used a mirror to intensify self-awareness. The typical design involved having subjects perform a task while sitting near a mirror in which they could perceive their own images. The presence of the mirror was usually treated as incidental and not requiring an explanation. Voice recordings and apparent exposure to television cameras have also been employed to magnify the individual's focus on self. The numerous studies carried out by Duval and Wicklund and others have consistently shown that enhancing awareness of that spatial (bodily) area called the "self" influences a number of aspects of behavior. As might be expected, one of the prime effects of being exposed to a mirror is the enhancement of the centrality of self. Individuals react to their mirror images by becoming more aware of "I." A number of researchers have documented this fact. For example, Davis and Brock (as described by Wicklund, 1975) created a task that called for subjects to read a passage written in a foreign language. There were periodic blanks in the passage, and the subjects were led to believe that a pronoun was always the missing word. They were asked to guess what the correct pronoun might be in each instance. The frequency with which first-person pronouns were offered as guesses was significantly greater during a mirror than no-mirror condition, although this effect was obtained only when subjects had been primed in advance to feel good about themselves.

In a related experiment, Duval and Wicklund (1973) demonstrated that exposure to a mirror increases the perception of self as a causal agent, that is, as a central source of influence. Subjects were presented with a series of hypothetical situations in which they had to judge the degree to which either they or another might have caused various positive and negative consequences. The following is an example of one of the hypothetical situations: "Imagine that you have selected and purchased a race horse. You enter the horse in a major race and hire a good jockey to ride him. The horse wins first place. To what degree did your actions cause the victory and to what degree did the actions of the jockey cause the victory?" (p. 26). Subjects expressed their judgments as percentages indicative of the relative degree to which self versus the other was regarded as the causal agent. It was shown that those who were exposed to their mirror images were significantly more likely than those in the nonmirror condition to judge themselves as responsible for what had occurred. This was true whether the situation implied good or bad consequences. In another phase of this study, it was found that when awareness of self was decreased by asking subjects to perform a distracting motor task, their attribution of causality to self decreased.

The self-centrality induced by the mirror experience shows itself too in a greater awareness of one's own emotions and inner feelings. During mirror feedback, people perceive their own emotional states with special vividness. This may result in their experiencing emotions more intensely; and, interestingly, it may permit heightened accuracy in their reporting about themselves. Pryor, Gibbons, Wicklund, Fazio, and Hood (1977) found that when persons with enhanced bodily awareness rated their degree of sociability, their ratings proved to be more highly correlated with measures of their actual sociable behavior than was true for subjects with limited bodily awareness. In another study (Gibbons, Carver, Scheier, & Hormuth, 1979), it was discovered that persons with mirror-induced self-awareness were particularly resistant to a "placebo" suggestion that a "drug" they ingested would produce certain arousal symptoms. Their heightened awareness of their own body sensations facilitated detection that the placebo drug was actually producing no bodily effects.

A second apparent major effect of the mirror experience is a decrease in self-esteem. Although there are definite exceptions, the experience tends to induce negative attitudes toward oneself. This was suggested by early work (Fisher, 1970) noting that people become upset when they hear recordings of their own voices or are called upon to respond to other stimuli with self-connotations. A number of studies of self-confrontation have documented its negative impact. Ickes, Wicklund and Ferris (as described in Kleinke, 1978) reported that during exposure to a mirror persons rated themselves as unusually low in self-esteem. Relatedly, Wicklund (1975) outlined an experiment in which persons' degrees of positive feeling toward self were lower when the individuals were exposed to a television picture of themselves than when they were exposed to television pictures with no self-implications. One may add that several studies (Wicklund, 1975) have demonstrated that in situations in which people feel disapproved, they are likely to avoid exposure (e.g., to a mirror) that intensifies self-awareness. On the other hand, when persons are given positive, laudatory information about themselves, mirror exposure may magnify positive effects on self-esteem[14] (Wicklund, 1975).

The third and perhaps most important consequence of magnifying self-awareness through a mirror experience is increased conformity to the prevailing standard. People who are confronted with their mirror images seem to become sensitized to whether they are deviating from the salient values or rules. They become critical of their possible deviations from the standard. Numerous studies have documented the increased conformance and moralism brought on by intensified self-awareness. A few illustrations follow: Diener and Wallbom (1976) were able to show that, in a situation where college students were tempted to cheat on an examination, there was markedly less cheating by those who could see their mirror images than by those not so viewing themselves. Duval, Duval, and Neely (1979) dramatized the moralistic sense of responsibility of self-aware persons by creating an experimental situation in which they were exposed to images of themselves on a TV screen and then were asked to help unfortunate disease victims. In this context they were more willing to take responsibility for and assist the victims than were subjects in a control condition who had not been confronted with their own TV images. Diener and Srull (1979) reported that persons with heightened self-awareness (produced by exposure to their own TV images) while judging the number of dots in a series of slides were particularly likely to evaluate how well they were performing by comparing themselves to the prevailing social standard of performance.[15] Persons who had not been made self-aware were more likely to judge their own performance by their personal standards rather than by the standards of others. Diener and Srull noted: "Self-aware subjects were more concerned with their social selves and felt more pressure to comply with the social standard" (p. 419). One is tempted to conclude that accentuated self-awareness usually leads to guilty scrutiny of self.[16] It is as if mirror type experiences strengthen a person's alliances with superego values.[17] In this vein, it is striking that Fisher (1970) found evidence that persons who become sick, and who would therefore presumably experience intensified bodily awareness, are inclined to feel increased guilt. Perhaps illness and body injury, by intensifying focus on one's own body, produce some of the effects of mirror feedback.

VIDEOTAPE FEEDBACK

As one reads the self-confrontation literature, one is surprised to learn that most of the research carried out in the Duval and Wicklund social psychological framwork ignored related work in other areas. It is fair to say that a large proportion of the Duval and Wicklund-type research concluded that the special awareness created by encounters with self has negative consequences. As already noted, this self-awareness has been depicted as uncomfortable and evocative of a sense that one is not up to par. It is true that a few positive effects have been ascribed to self-confrontation (e.g., reinforcing the enhanced self-esteem resulting from a positive success experience, becoming more realistically aware of how one feels internally), but such positive effects have been treated as being uncommon. On the contrary, numerous positive effects of enhanced self-awareness have been reported in a variety of studies carried out from perspectives that differ from those of Duval and Wicklund. For instance, Fisher (1970) reported that augmented body awareness in women is linked with well-articulated body boundaries, although this was not true for men. A considerable array of projects have shown that people often react in positive ways to videotapes of their own behavior. Most of these projects involved measuring subjects' responses to videotape recordings of themselves as they performed tasks or interacted with one or more other persons. Studies have demonstrated that videotape self-confrontation improves self-concept (Blount & Pedersen, 1970; Rezler & Anderson, 1971; Roberts, 1972; Truss, 1972). Others have variously shown that self-confrontation increases the number of positive statements about self (Jonassen, 1979a, 1979b); augments self-aggrandizement (Goldman, 1969; Smith, 1970); and results in more accurate self-awareness (Braucht, 1970; Walz & Johnston, 1963). There have also been frequent observations indicating that videotape feedback of their own image has therapeutic effects on maladjusted persons (e.g., Griffiths & Hinkson, 1973; Mermelstein, 1968; Spire, 1973; Spiro & Silverman, 1969). It is striking that two studies (Ammerman & Fryrear, 1975; Fryrear, Nuell, & Ridley, 1974) have even shown that both normal and delinquent children develop increased self-esteem simply by being repeatedly exposed to still pictures of themselves. Of course, there are a fair number of studies that have not been able to detect positive results of videotape self-confrontation; and some have shown a negative impact. But, overall, the positive effects of videotape self-confrontation are evident.

The question immediately arises why such positive effects have so infrequently been reported in the literature based on the Duval and Wicklund perspective. To begin with, most of the Duval and Wicklund-type research is based on putting individuals in a room where they perform a task while sitting alone in front of a mirror or a TV camera; when a mirror is used, there is often little or no explanation of why it is present in the room. That self-confrontation is occurring is addressed largely at a covert level. On the other hand, in most of the self-confrontation work involving actual videotape feedback, subjects are introduced to the videotape as an active, purposeful procedure that has centrality. Often the tape is viewed while the experimenter is present or shortly after it has been linked to some meaningful objective. One may speculate that the somewhat covert and deceptive mode involved in the Duval and Wicklund approach may encourage subjects to lean toward a negative view of their self-confrontation experience. That is, they might see the experience as embedded in a vaguely suspect context that would impel them to focus on the negative aspects of their own self-perceptions. It has been shown in several studies (Wicklund, 1975) that persons who are somehow made to feel they are negatively regarded have magnified guilt and anxiety during self-confrontation. By way of contrast, many of the videotape playback studies convey the implicit or explicit message, "You are being asked to view yourself because this is a meaningful procedure that will help you to make certain judgments or to facilitate insights about yourself." They seem to encourage looking at one's image with the intent of extracting as much positive information as possible. The self-confrontation context in the Duval and Wicklund-type studies highlights being alone and even isolated; whereas the typical videotape self-confrontation has more "we," or social connotations. One cannot escape the implication that different modes of self-confrontation may have quite different effects. Passive exposure to a mirror and active scanning of videotape feedback are simply not equivalent.

Another issue raised by the videotape confrontation work concerns the role of mediating personality variables. In the experiments carried out under the usual Duval and Wicklund paradigm, there was little interest in whether self-confrontation effects vary as a function of personality attributes.[18] There are, though, a considerable number of videotape confrontation studies that have clearly established the importance of personality mediators. For example, Cundick and Rose (1976) found that low defensive persons were more likely than high defensive persons to respond negatively to their videotaped images. Kipper and Ginot (1979) noted that accuracy of persons evaluating videotapes of their own behavior was influenced by the nature of their customary defense mechanisms. Those most inclined to projection manifested the greatest distortions in self-evaluation, and those typified by a turning-against-self orientation evaluated their images most negatively. Alker, Tourangeau, and Staines (1976) reported that people with humanistic values were able to respond with particular sensitivity to self-confrontation information. Cohen (1974) discovered that level of trait anxiety plays a role in how dissatisfied people feel when they see their videotaped images.

The findings from the videotape feedback studies argue that one cannot safely make sweeping generalizations about the impact of self-confrontation. Not only do personality variables mediate, but also the significance attached to the self-confrontation experience is the result of definitions either implicitly or explicitly offered by the experimental ambiance. If the experimental context implies that self confrontation is being secretly imposed and therefore that the experience is somehow linked with deception, subjects may perhaps approach their own images with a more negative set than if they can see the self-confrontation as a goal-oriented, task-accomplishing act. Indeed, as the original Duval and Wicklund concepts have been tested in a wider range of experiments, it has become apparent that these concepts were far too simplified. Increasingly, we are learning that although self-confrontation does often intensify self-criticism, it can also lead to greater realism, less suggestibility, more intense emotion, and greater openness to valid information.

MEASURES OF BODY AWARENESS

A number of attempts have been made to devise measures that directly or indirectly pertain to an individual's overall degree of body awareness. These measures have usually been based on the implicit assumption that there are trait-like individual differences in body awareness. Fisher (1970) reviewed the pertinent literature up to 1970. He considered what was known about the following measures:

1. MMPI Hypochondriasis scale, which attempts to evaluate degree of preoccupation with one's body as a "sick" or "ailing" object. It does not concern itself with bodily self-awareness in normal, healthy states.
2. An index developed by Van Lennep (1957) based on the number of references to body themes introduced into stories about Thematic Apperception Test type pictures.
3. The Secord (1953) Homonym test, which requires subjects to give their first associations to a series of homonyms, each having a body and also a nonbody meaning. Illustratively, the word "beat" might stimulate the association "heart," which has obvious body connotations or the association "win," which does not have a body reference. Examples of other homonymns included in the Secord series are: swell, trunk, mole, nail, gag. Scores are based on the total number of associative responses with body connotations.
4. The Mandler, Mandler, and Uviller (1958) self-report questionnaire (Autonomic Perception Questionnaire), which systematically inventories the amount of autonomic arousal one consciously experiences in a variety of situations.

Fisher (1970) could find little consistent research support for the validity of these measures as indices of general bodily awareness. He therefore introduced a new measure of body awareness (Body Prominence), which gave more promise of being directly linked to the prominence of one's body in the total perceptual field. Body Prominence is based on the frequency with which people refer to their own bodies when a sample is taken of what lies within their immediate awareness. The actual procedure for obtaining a Body Prominence score involves asking subjects to list on a sheet of paper "Twenty things that you are aware of or conscious of right now." All direct or indirect references to one's body are scored and summed. Considerably more material concerning the validity of the Body Prominence measure is presented at a later point.

Since 1970 little work has been done to really augment our knowledge of the validity of the Van Lennep (1957) index or the Mandler et al. (1958) Autonomic Perception Questionnaire. Those papers that have been published concerning the Autonomic Perception Questionnaire have been concerned largely with whether it can predict actual physiological arousal in specific organs like the heart. The results have usually been negative and, in any event, have little pertinence to the issue whether the questionnaire taps general body awareness.

Numerous studies have employed the Secord Homonym Test. The overall results have not been promising with regard to whether the Homonym Test measures some form of body awareness or anxiety. Eichler (1973) found that it did not correlate with body anxiety as judged from an interview. Sanger (1978) indicated that it did not differentiate women who had had radical breast surgery. Dines (1982) reported that it did not distinguish adolescent amputees from normal adolescents. Mitchell (1970) noted that it was not correlated with good versus poor adjustment in paraplegics. Newey (1976) found it unrelated to scores on the Embedded Figures Test. Djalali (1978) discovered that it was not affected by exposure to a body oriented therapy and found, further, that it did not distinguish drug addicts from controls. Three studies found the Homonym Test unrelated to the Fisher-Cleveland (1958) Barrier score (viz., Mermelstein, 1968; Saltaformaggio, 1979; and Dines, 1982).

There were several instances in which the results were more positive. Daoud (1976) observed that Homonym Test scores were elevated in women just before a scheduled hysterectomy. Saltaformaggio (1979) indicated that Homonym scores were positively correlated with indices of body image disturbance derived from figure drawings. McCuistion (1973) observed that women who attended a self-help, feminist-oriented clinic decreased their Homonym scores. Jupp, Collins, McCabe, Walker, and Diment (1983) demonstrated a decline in Homonym scores in obese women who had lost weight. It is probably fair to say that the validity of the Homonym Test has yet to be demonstrated in any consistent fashion.

Since 1970 other new instruments have appeared that are concerned with specific forms of self-awareness and are therefore potentially pertinent to body awareness.[19] One, developed by Snyder (1974), is referred to as the Self-Monitoring scale. It is a self-report questionnaire that seeks to measure: "individual differences in concern for social appropriateness, sensitivity to the expression and self-presentation of others in social situations as cues to social appropriateness of self expression, and use of these cues as guidelines for monitoring and managing self-presentations and expressive behavior" (p. 529). Studies have shown that actors obtain significantly higher scores and psychiatric patients significantly lower scores than do various control

groups. Also, persons with high self-monitoring scores were found to communicate affective states more accurately than did those with low scores.[20]
Further, they were relatively more concerned with finding out what is socially appropriate. However, no direct studies have been undertaken of the
relationship between Self-Monitoring scores and degree of awareness of one's
own body.

A Self-Consciousness scale was devised by Fenigstein, Scheier, and Buss
(1975). It taps two major factors relevant to self-consciousness: (a) private
self-consciousness, which concerns habitual attendance to one's thoughts,
motives, and feelings, and (b) public self-consciousness, which is defined by
a general awareness of self as a social object. The scores from this questionnaire have very low correlations with Self-Monitoring scores. Previous studies have shown that private self-consciousness is positively linked with length
and veridicality of self reports, reflectiveness, and more intense reactions to
transient affective states. Public self-consciousness scores are positively
correlated with sensitivity to peer group rejection. They are also positively
correlated (Turner, Gilliland, & Klein, 1981) with physical attractiveness and
readiness to evaluate one's own physical appearance.

Another pertinent technique was fashioned by Exner (1973). It involves a
30-item sentence completion task in which most of the stems contain a self-
reference (e.g., I, my, mine). Responses were scored primarily in terms of
whether the sentence completion was self-focused or external world oriented. It has been shown that the self-focus score is positively and significantly correlated with the use of self-referring pronouns in an interview
situation and also with amount of time spent looking at self in a mirror (in a
context where there was no awareness that the mirror behavior was being
observed). There were also findings suggesting that psychiatric patients show
larger differences between self-focused and external-world-oriented responses than do normal persons. Schizophrenics, involutionals, psycho-
paths, homosexuals, and adolescent with behavior problems were
particularly likely to offer a relative excess of self-referring responses.

Miller, Murphy, and Buss (1981) have developed a Body Consciousness
Questionnaire specifically intended to measure how aware people are of their
body. It contains 15 items, and a factor analysis has revealed three factors:
private body consciousness, public body consciousness, and body competence. The private versus public distinction refers simply to the difference
between self-directed awareness of one's own body and awareness of one's
body as a social object. In studies involving large samples of subjects, one
sex difference appeared: Women obtained significantly higher scores for
public body consciousness. Interestingly, no such sex difference appeared for
a nonbody measure of public self-consciousness, as defined by the previously
described Fenigstein et al. (1975) Self-Consciousness scale. The private body
consciousness scores correlated only moderately (.30–.45) with the private
self-consciousness scores from the Fenigstein et al. Self-Consciousness

scale. However, the public body consciousness scores correlated substantially (.66–.71) with the Fenigstein et al. public self-consciousness scores. When the body consciousness scores were related to a questionnaire measure of hypochondriasis, only inconsequential correlations appeared. However, quite noteworthy, hypochondriasis was significantly and negatively (– .32) correlated with body competence scores in males (but not in females). The construct validity of the Body Consciousness Questionnaire was evaluated at one level by determining whether it could predict sensitivity to sensations induced by the ingestion of caffeine. It was found in both men and women that the higher the private body consciousness scores, the greater were the number of body changes reported. Mueller, Heesacker, and Ross (1984) have gone on to demonstrate that public body consciousness scores are significantly and positively predictive of better memory for facial photographs that have been compared to self. Presumably, those high in public body consciousness are more oriented to using self appearance (socially defined) as a schema in organizing their experiences.[21]

FALSE BODY INFORMATION

Unique forms of self-confrontation have been employed in studies dealing with the behavioral effects of false body feedback. Typically in such studies, subjects are exposed to information that they have been convinced represents events occurring in their bodies, and the impact of the feedback is measured. This line of research was originally inspired by the work of Schachter and Singer (1962), who reported that when states of physiological arousal are induced, persons search their environment for an explanation. If the search suggests a particular cause, the state of arousal will be labeled accordingly. For example, if there are anger cues present, arousal will be labeled as anger; whereas if funny cues are present it will be labeled as a humorous state. Schachter and Singer concluded that, in effect, the meanings persons ascribed to their emotional arousal could be cognitively manipulated.

Valins (1966) went a step further and proposed: "Once it is granted that internal events can function as cues or stimuli then these events can now be considered as a source of cognitive information" (p. 400). He suggested that the cognition that one is aroused takes on significance aside from the actual arousal itself. He proposed that people would respond to the cognition of being aroused even if arousal was only apparent and not real. He hypothesized: "If cognitive representations of internal events are important for emotional behavior, then, . . . non-veridical representations of physiological changes should have the same effect as veridical ones" (p. 401). He tested the hypothesis by exposing male subjects to slides of nude women. While the subjects looked at the slides, they heard clicks they were told represented their own heartbeats. The clicks were actually tape recorded and were presented in such a fashion that heart rate seemed to increase during inspection of certain of the nude slides, but not during others. When the subjects were asked to rate the attractiveness of each of the nudes, they gave higher ratings to those they had viewed while their "heart rates" increased. This was interpreted by Valins as supporting his idea that it is the cognitive information about internal body events rather than the event itself that helps to define an emotion. Although considerable criticism[22] (e.g., Goldstein, Fink, & Mettee, 1972; Harris & Katkin, 1975) has been directed to the Valins' findings, they have been reasonably well replicated (Barefoot & Straub, 1971; Zillmann, 1978). False feedback for body areas other than the heart also has been provided in various studies, for example, GSR (Lick, 1975; Piccione & Veitch, 1979) and alpha (Lindholm & Lowry, 1978). Such studies confront subjects directly with fictitious data (usually depicted as coming from a physiograph) about their bodies.

In addition, a number of more indirect modes for misleading people about the nature of their body responses have been developed. These are often based on having subjects ingest a placebo whose properties are mislabeled. For example, Storms and Nisbett (1970) administered a placebo to one group of insomniacs and persuaded them that the placebo would produce physiological arousal in them when they retired to go to sleep. They also administered a placebo to a sample of insomniacs who were led to believe it would result in relaxation of their bodies. They predicted, and the results verified, that the insomniacs who thought the placebo would increase their physiological arousal were able to fall asleep more quickly than the insomniacs with the opposite expectation of the placebo. Presumably this happened because the former were less disturbed by the arousal linked with apprehension over not being able to go to sleep. The latter had to cope with the upsetting fact that, even having ingested a "relaxing" substance, they experienced their usual emotional arousal as they tried to sleep.[23] An analogous manipulation of "physiological" information was used in a study by Dienstbier and Munter (1971). Subjects in two groups were administered a placebo. The message was given that in one group the ingested substance would produce emotional arousal and that in the other it would have minimal effect. In both of these conditions subjects were given the opportunity to cheat on a test. Dienstbier and Munter reason that those persons who believed the placebo would produce emotional arousal could attribute to it any sympathetic upset linked to fear or guilt about cheating. Thus, the affect aroused by the intent to cheat could be linked (displaced) to the placebo and would be weakened in its inhibitory effect on cheating behavior. As predicted from this formulation, the subjects who expected the placebo to be arousing cheated significantly more than did the subjects without such an expectation.

In both examples just cited, important bits of behavior were shaped by convincing people they were experiencing physiological states that were in actuality largely fictitious. Numerous other analogous studies could be enumerated. Consider just a few. In one context subjects were cleverly led to believe that body excitation they were experiencing (which actually was left over from doing exercise) was tied to a subsequent response to stimuli designed to instigate aggression (Zillmann & Bryant, 1974; Zillmann, Katcher, & Milavsky, 1972); as such, it augmented the aggression. A similar process has been demonstrated for residual excitation from exercise as an energizer for responses to erotic stimuli (Cantor, Zillmann, & Bryant, 1975). The excitation from the exercise was manipulated by the experimenter to create the illusion that it was a component of a different response system. Another study (Hendrick & Giesen, 1976) found that persons increased or decreased their beliefs about certain issues as a function of being exposed to a meter that seemed (fictitiously) to be registering in physiological terms how much they believed or disbelieved arguments pertinent to that issue. The meter's arbitrary message indicating one's physiological response as "believing" or "disbelieving" was typically accepted as real and was sufficient to affect attitudes significantly. In still another study, Henning (1975) trained subjects to make accurate estimates of their blood alcohol levels after drinking various liquids in a laboratory setting. He found that, when subjects were given false feedback about what they had drunk, their estimates of their blood alcohol levels based on body sensations were accurate in relation to the false feedback but inaccurate in terms of the amount of alcohol that had actually been put into the body. In other words, the subjects were manipulated so that they thought they were experiencing body sensations indicative of particular blood alcohol levels, which were actually nonexistent.

As one scans the accumulated research in this area, it is inescapable that persons' perceptions of what is happening within their bodies are surprisingly manipulable. Recall, for example, that individuals can be persuaded they are experiencing sensations of excitement when they are actually calm, and vice versa. Or recall that they can be convinced they are experiencing sensations of an elevated blood alcohol level, even though their alcohol intake has, in reality, been minimal. From a commonsense view, findings of this sort are quite unexpected. One would assume that after making infinite observations of their own bodies, people acquire great expertise in registering and interpreting such body events. People would seem to be so knowledgeable about their own body sensations that it should be hard to mislead them in this area. However, the empirical findings cited earlier indicate quite the opposite.[24] This is perhaps not so surprising if one considers previously discussed studies in which subjects sometimes failed to identify front view pictures of themselves or could not accurately correct errors in their appearance that were introduced by a distorting mirror (Fisher, 1970). Despite repeated everyday acquaintance with their own most obvious exterior body attributes, people do at times evidence considerable error in their definitions of these attributes. If this can happen with respect to the most obvious external features of the individual, there should be a greater probability of error when less visible and more hidden aspects of the body are involved.

With regard to falsifying body information, the question can be raised as to the degree to which such falsification is employed by people in coping with their own body experiences. Ross, Rodin, and Zimbardo (1969) suggested, "Perhaps thrill seeking and the use of drug stimulants are to some extent maintained by the misattribution opportunities they provide" (p. 28). They speculated that people who are motivated to deny or escape certain threatening body feelings may do so by linking them with intense but artificially created body arousal that does not have negative connotations. One form of body arousal may be used to mask the origin and even the existence of another threatening form. This paradigm was suggested to Ross et al. by a variety of previous studies in which misattribution diminished the apparent intensity of unpleasant body sensations. Illustratively, they performed a study (involving 40 female college undergraduates) in which they showed that, if prior to exposure to a frightening stimulus (viz., electric shock) subjects could be made to feel that any anxiety they experienced was due to the impact of an extremely loud noise, they felt less anxious than subjects exposed to the frightening stimulus but who did not have the opportunity to misattribute their anxiety to the noise. Ross et al. cited an analogous study by Nisbett and Schachter (1966) in which it was shown that subjects who were given a placebo that presumably produced "side effects" paralleling fear sensations were able to tolerate a higher level of electric shock than were subjects who were not given the opportunity to attribute their shock-induced anxiety of the placebo. That is, when subjects could deny their anxiety feelings by perceiving them as "side effects" to the placebo they had ingested, they could perceive the total situation as relatively less threatening. It is certainly conceivable that at specific times people learn to create specific body feelings that will help them to mask body experiences that are particularly disturbing. Whenever they know they are about to deal with a problem that stirs up severe anxiety feelings, they might, for example, ingest enough food or alcohol to produce discomforting body feelings. The anxiety sensations could then be attributed to the food- or alcohol-induced sensations. Not only would this camouflage the anxious body feelings but it would create the impression that any body discomfort that did occur was under voluntary control, since the ingestion of substances like food and alcohol are, except in extreme cases, usually regarded as voluntary acts. Another illustration of such a camouflaging maneuver occurs when someone who is experiencing a great deal of vague, unexplained concern about body vulnerability and fragility seeks out situations that are full of body threat (e.g., driving high speed racers, parachuting). The sense of body threat can be linked to the risky activities the individual has "chosen" to undertake and would not have to be experienced in the probably much more threatening sense of being overcome by a nameless fear of body dissolution (as can be seen in some hypochondriacal persons). It is likely that other maneuvers, like ingesting drugs or exhausting oneself through overwork, can also be used as techniques for falsifying the real nature of one's body feelings.

PERCEIVING BODY EVENTS

Obviously a person's body is a source of innumerable sensory experiences. Sensations converge from multiple body sites and organs. We know that there are considerable individual differences in how such sensations are received; they may be magnified, reduced, or ignored. Fisher (1970) has shown that there are fairly consistent tendencies for individuals, especially males, to distribute their attention selectively to the various sectors of their bodies. One person may be highly aware of sensations from the back of the body, moderately aware of the stomach, and minimally attentive to the legs. Another may show just the obverse pattern. Body sensations also differ in the accuracy with which they can be defined. For example, those originating in the viscera are usually more vague[25] and difficult to localize than those arising in the skin or striate masculature. Body perceptions may vary too with regard to such other parameters as how well they mirror actual physiological changes and the degree to which they are influenced by variables like sex, age, and personality. There have been scattered studies concerned with understanding better the process of perceiving body sensations. Actually, there was a period from about 1910–1930 when such sensations were minutely studied and attempts made to relate their occurrence to particular emotions, attitudes, and modes of judgment (e.g., Hunt, 1932; Nafe, 1927; Nakoshima, 1909; Warren, 1922; Yokoyama, 1921; Young, 1927). However, interest in this area subsequently declined rather steeply; and only in recent years has it been renewed.

That previous studies involving false body feedback have been so successful in their deceptive intent offers little encouragement that people are able to perceive accurately what is happening in major sectors of their bodies. In numerous instances, persons have been led to accept as accurate false heart rate information that had only chance relationships with their actual heart rates. Apparently, people who are asked to make judgments about events in the interior of the body space can behave with considerable uncertainty. This has been a typical finding in the biofeedback literature, where subjects seldom are able to make accurate estimates[26] of the activity levels of organs like the heart or stomach until they have received special training.

Heart Perception

Direct appraisals of accuracy in tracking one's own heart rate over time have not yielded very promising results. In a typical study, Ashton, White and Hodgson (1979) asked subjects (6 males, 6 females) to decide in which of two brief time periods their heart rates had reached the highest point. There were 110 such decisions obtained. Overall, the judgments attained only chance accuracy. However, with feedback to correct their errors, subjects were able to average 90% to 100% accuracy. Almost equivalent results were obtained by Brener and Jones (1974) in a study of 30 males who had to distinguish vibratory stimuli that matched their heart rates from those that did not. Before training, the accuracy rate was at a chance level. After training, accuracy averaged in the 80% range. These data indicate that the potential for a high level of accuracy exists, but it may not typically be functional when people are left to their own judgment devices. It is pertinent to this issue of training that Jones and Hollandsworth (1981) were able to verify their hypothesis that persons who cultivate a sensitivity to their own physiological functioning (e.g., distance runners[27]) would display superiority in accurately perceiving their heart rate, even at rest. The study involved 36 males and 36 females who fell into three categories of physical fitness: distance runners group (high fitness), tennis players group (intermediate), and sedentary group (low). Only the distance runners did better than chance in their heart rate judgments during rest. After induced exercise the tennis players and sedentary subjects significantly improved their judgments, but the distance runners did not. The Autonomic Perception Inventory (Mandler et al., 1958) was administered to all subjects, but was not significantly correlated with heart rate judgment accuracy. House (1983) and Morgan and Pollack (1977) also have provided data corroborating the superior ability of long distance runners to judge their own physiological arousal.

Katkin, Blascovich, and Koenigsberg (1984) have analyzed in some detail the literature concerned with perception of one's own heart responses. They concluded that at resting levels the average person does little better than chance in judging his or her own heart rate. But they pointed out that on the basis of the evidence provided by Jones and Hollandsworth (1981), accuracy in such judgment does increase to a better than chance level at higher activation levels. Further, they cited data (Katkin, Blascovich, & Goldband, 1981) indicating an interesting sex difference: Although both sexes are poor judges of their own heart responses before they have any special training, males do significantly better than females after the training. Katkin et al. emphasized the importance of determining just how well persons can perceive their own visceral responses because a number of theories of emotion (e.g., James, 1892; Schachter & Singer, 1962) make use of the notion that the experience of emotion is secondary to the perception (and labeling) of visceral arousal.

Pennebaker (1982) conducted several projects that provide additional information about heart rate perception. In one experiment 18 male and 13 female college students estimated their heart rates while they were watching a series of slides. Just prior to being exposed to the slides, half the subjects were allowed to take their own pulse for 20 seconds, and half were not given such information. Subjects were asked to make heart rate judgments by pushing a button as rapidly as they perceived their heart to be beating. Correlations between judged and actual heart rates were negligible. They were no higher in those who had monitored their own pulse rates than in those who had not. Subjects were also asked to estimate the accuracy of their heart rate judgments. Overall, they felt they were "moderately accurate." However, the correlation between perceived accuracy and actual accuracy was inconsequential. A second experiment with 11 male and 11 female college students roughly duplicated the procedure of the first experiment, except that subjects were exposed to a variety of other conditions like listening to loud noises and viewing a sexually arousing scene. The results were essentially the same as those obtained for the first experiment. It is remarkable that an analysis of the data indicated that the various conditions to which subjects were exposed had a significantly greater influence on their heart rate judgments than on their actual heart rates.

Muscle Tension

Studies of ability to judge tension in one's own musculature also have suggested a limited degree of accuracy. Sime and DeGood (1977) obtained largely negative results in their evaluation of how well female subjects (N = 30) could discriminate changes in the tension levels of the frontalis muscle. Subjective reports of tension changes had chance correlations with actual EMG measures, except at the highest levels of change. Similar negative findings have been published with regard to the relationship between subjective estimates of tension and muscle relaxation effects on EMG (e.g., Alexander, French, & Goodman, 1975; Lader & Matthews, 1971; Shedivy & Kleinman, 1977).[28] Widmer (1975) did find that normal subjects (in multiple samples) could judge the tension levels in a number of different muscles better than chance, but still at a low level of success. Alcoholics and schizophrenics did not exceed chance expectancy. Further, it was possible to demonstrate that procedures (e.g., massage and body-oriented training) that made normal subjects more aware of their bodies increased their accuracy in judging muscle tension.

Symptom Reporting

The difficulties of interpreting one's own body events have been highlighted by Pennebaker (1982) in a series of ingenious investigations concerned with symptom reporting. He systematically probed various conditions that affect both the number and the kinds of body symptoms persons perceive in themselves. The details of this work will not be reported here, but it can be noted that Pennebaker established that symptom reporting is influenced by suggestion, by amount of attention individuals direct to their body, and by the arbitrary hypotheses or fantasies they entertain about their own physiological processes. It is apparent that people frequently magnify body sensations and misperceive them as indicating body pathology. At the same time, they also ignore body cues that are true manifestations of body malfunctioning. Pennebaker found that people show generalized tendencies to be high or low reporters of body symptoms. High reporters are people who chronically attend to their internal states. They are more self-conscious, more self-monitoring, and more anxious; they have lower self-esteem and feel less in control of their environment. Interestingly, they were found to be particularly sensitive about their appearance. Pennebaker remarked: "symptom reporters place a very high premium on self-presentational concerns. This finding is consistent with the fact that [they] also tend to be high on the trait of public self-consciousness" (p. 144).

General Arousal

A number of projects have examined the relationship between self-estimates of *general* emotional arousal and actual measures of it. One frequently employed mode of self-estimate is based on the Autonomic Perception Questionnaire (APQ). This consists of a number of graphic rating scales dealing with the frequency and intensity of bodily perceptions under conditions of anxiety, as well as several scales dealing with perceptions during states of pleasure. In two original studies (Mandler et al., 1958; Mandler & Kremen, 1958), significant but rather low positive correlations[29] were demonstrated between self-reports of autonomic activity and actual degrees of autonomic activity measured during stress. Autonomic reactivity was represented by a composite index involving five different parameters: galvanic skin response, heart rate, respiration, temperature, and blood volume.

These two early projects were followed by a succession of studies dealing with the degree of correlation between experienced arousal and actual physiological activation, often with more negative results. Puente, Beiman, Doom, and Young (1980) observed that APQ scores[30] were not predictive of muscle tension, respiratory rate, or heart rate during stress. The scores did, however, predict skin conductance responses. The subjects (44 male, 44 female) represented extreme high and low APQ scorers. Feldman (1974) also reported that APQ scores and specific estimates of heart and respiration response (in a sample of 63 male and female subjects) were largely not significantly correlated with either actual heart or respiration responses in a variety of situations. Boggess (1976) could not detect a significant link between subjects' (12 female, 8 male) reports of their degree of arousal to affective visual stimuli (e.g., nudes, tragic scenes) and actual measures of physiological response (skin conductance, pulse volume, heart rate). Paquette (1973) found no relationship between subjects' (27 males, 28 females) awareness of body cues and accuracy in estimating either their heart or breathing rates. The body awareness index was based on the frequency with which body cues were mentioned in spontaneous descriptions of one's own emotional states. Paquette noted that the sample was in general characterized by extremely high rates of inaccuracy in the estimates of body activation. Weinstein, Averill, Opton, and Lazarus (1968) found no consistent correlations between self-reports of emotional distress and anxiety (during stress conditions) and parallel measures of autonomic response. Six different samples (all males) were studied and the physiological measures involved either skin conductance or skin conductance and heart rate.

The negative findings were congruent with previous studies that observed minimal correlations between questionnaire measures of anxiety and presumed physiological indices of anxiety (Chambers, Hopkins, & Hopkins, 1968; Johnson & Spielberger, 1968; Katkin, 1965; Sarason, 1960). Morris and Liebert (1970) employed a brief questionnaire to obtain self-estimates of emotionality (from 106 male and female subjects) and reported such estimates had only an inconsequential relationship with pulse rate in a situation designed to elicit emotional response. Rappaport and Katkin (1972) examined (in 64 males) the possible presence of a link between reports of "emotional feeling" or "nervous sensations" during stress and parallel autonomic arousal, as defined by GSR. No such link could be established. It was shown, though, that subjects with high manifest anxiety displayed more GSR response during a mild stress than did those with low anxiety. Gerdes (1979) asked subjects (48 male, 48 female) to rate their degree of autonomic arousal after receiving or not receiving an injection of epinephrine in a stress situation. She noted that females reported experiencing significantly more arousal during the epinephrine condition. However, this could not be shown in a male sample. Ikeda and Hirai (1976) could detect no differences between subjects (20 male, 22 female) with high autonomic awareness (measured with a modification of the APQ) and those with low awareness in their number of nonspecific GSRs. Schandry (1981) showed in a group of 16 females and 23 males that State Anxiety and Emotional Lability were not related to actual heart rate. But these two measures of arousal were significantly and positively linked with being a "good" versus "poor" perceiver of one's own heart beat. Schandry remarked: "it seems that higher self-reported anxiety is due to better perception of physiological processes rather than to actual level of autonomic arousal" (p. 487).[31]

Sexual Arousal

Considerable work has also been done with reference to the relationship between subjective estimates of sexual arousal and physiological measures of genital organ activation in women. Almost all the studies in this area have made use of a vaginal photoplethysmograph to measure vaginal response. Typically, vaginal recordings were obtained during baseline conditions and also during exposure to various kinds of erotic stimuli (e.g., films of sexual intercourse, sound recordings of sexual encounters). Subjects were variously asked to rate their degrees of sexual arousal by marking rating scales, punching buttons indicative of different levels of sexual excitement, and so forth. Most subjects were college students without significant sexual problems; some had special difficulties in being sexually responsive. A range of pertinent studies has been reported. A considerable number (Geer, Morokoff, & Greenwood, 1974; Hoon, 1980; Hoon, Wincze, & Hoon, 1976; Morokoff, 1981; Morokoff & Heiman, 1980; Osborn & Pollack, 1977; Schreiner-Engel, Schiavi, & Smith, Jr., 1981; Wincze, Hoon, & Hoon, 1976) have reported largely negative or unstable results. That is, they have concluded that subjective reports of sexual arousal and actual measures of vaginal arousal have low, shifting relationships. In the same negative vein, Wilson and Wilson (as reported in Heiman, 1976) found that while ingestion of alcohol decreased vaginal activation, it simultaneously increased subjective arousal.

Although these studies seem negative, there were interesting qualifications and exceptions. First, in the Wincze et al. (1976) investigation, although self-ratings of sexual arousal in the experimental situation were not related to vaginal response, there was a significant positive correlation (.75) between vaginal response and self-ratings of how arousing erotic experiences in real life usually are and also a significant positive correlation (.41) with ratings of the degree to which a number of different physiological changes (e.g., breast swelling, pelvic warmth) are typically noted to occur during sexual activity. That is, vaginal response in the experimental context was not linked with the immediate degree of experienced sexual arousal but was significantly correlated with recall of how aroused one becomes in real life sexual encounters.

Comment should also be made about the Morokoff (1981) study. Morokoff concluded from her overall data that subjective ratings of arousal and measures of vaginal activation were correlated at only a low, inconsistent level. She had studied one group that successively viewed an erotic videotape, imagined a sexual fantasy, and wrote out the fantasy. Another group went through the same procedure, except that the videotape did not contain any erotic material. In the group exposed to the erotic videotape, there were only chance relationships between self-ratings of arousal (based on a 7-point scale) and the vaginal arousal measure. When the subjects in this group were asked, in addition, to push a lever that registered their self-perceived levels of erotic arousal at intervals during the film, an average (significant) correlation in the .30s was found with vaginal activation. As for the group that was not exposed to the erotic videotape, there were significant positive correlations (ranging in the .40s) between vaginal response and self-ratings (7-point) of arousal, but only during the erotic fantasy condition. The positive findings just cited are interesting, but in view of the limited sizes and shifting character of the coefficients one would have to agree with Morokoff that, if there was a link in this study between self-rated arousal and measured vaginal arousal, it was limited and fluctuating.

Several studies have found relatively low correlations of penile activation (as measured with a strain gauge) with reports of sexual arousal in heterosexual males (Farkas, Sine, & Evans, 1979; Schaefer, Tregerthan, & Colgan, 1976) or with reports of arousal in homosexual males (Barlow, Agras, Abel, Blanchard, & Young, 1975; McConaghy, 1969). However, several studies have reported just the opposite. Spiess (1977) obtained a correlation of .87 between self-ratings of sexual arousal (based on a psychophysical technique) and penile activation in a sample of 10 premature ejaculators and 14 controls. Premature ejaculators were not less accurate than the controls in judging their levels of penile activation. Abel, Blanchard, Murphy, Becker, and Djenderedjian (1981) observed average correlations of .74 and .67 between self-reports of sexual arousal and two different measures of penile arousal. The self-reports were in the form of ratings on a scale ranging from 0 to 100.

Let us consider a number of other promising observations. Heiman (1977) carried out a project that included both female ($N = 59$) and male ($N = 39$) undergraduates. The photoplethysmograph was utilized to measure vaginal arousal and penile tumescence was determined by means of a strain gauge. Subjective arousal was ascertained with a 5-point rating scale. In both males and females, moderately strong significant correlations (range .40–.68) were found between subjective arousal and genital arousal. In a subsequent study (Heiman & Hatch, 1980) involving 16 men and employing a similar methodology, correlations in the .70s were found between subjective and physiological arousal. Heiman (1980) further utilized the photoplethysmograph technique to explore the relationships between subjective arousal and vaginal activation in samples of married ($N = 27$) and unmarried ($N = 28$) (but sexually active) women. Correlations were less impressive, averaging in the low .40s in the unmarried sample, and were not at all significant in the married sample. This difference may be due partially to the fact that the unmarried subjects manifested greater vaginal response to the erotic stimuli than did the married subjects. It is possible that the unmarried subjects found the erotic stimuli more interesting or novel and that as a result they became more genuinely engaged in the task of judging their own levels of sexual arousal. Incidentally, inspection of these data in the present study indicated that the range of vaginal photoplethysmograph scores was not smaller than that found in the first Heiman project, in which the correlations of subjective and physiological measures were strikingly high. It is noteworthy too that in the present instance the degree of vaginal responsiveness was not consistently positively correlated with self-reports of previous sexual responsiveness, as defined by such indices as orgasm consistency and intercourse frequency. Heiman did observe an interesting phenomenon that points up the complexity of relating subjective reports of sexual arousal to actual arousal. She found that some of her subjects were especially likely to feel offended by the mere act of being asked to report their degree of sexual arousal. This reaction to the reporting process itself could conceivably affect the level of vaginal physiological activation independent of the impact of the erotic stimuli.

One of the most successful studies, carried out by Korff and Geer (1983) merits a detailed analysis. Thirty-six female college students serving as subjects were exposed to a series of 10 erotic slides; vaginal activation was measured with the photoplethysmograph. Subjects registered their evaluation of how sexually arousing each slide was (by means of a 5-point rating scale) while viewing the erotic stimulus. They also used a novel psychophysical technique to express their subjective evaluations. This technique involved acquainting the subjects with a range of sounds and brightness levels that could be produced to represent either visual or auditory scales of intensity. They were then to respond to each erotic slide by producing either a sound or brightness equivalent to its apparent arousal impact. Fifteen subjects used the sound to register their impressions, and 21 used a light source. The design of the study also called for the subjects to be divided into three groups: one was instructed to focus on the "changes that may occur in your genital area" (viz., vaginal lubrication, pelvic warmth, and muscular tension), as each erotic slide was presented. A second was told to focus on "changes that may occur in your body" (viz., heart rate increase, nipple erection, breast swelling, and muscular tension). The third group was not given any instructions to attend to particular body cues of sexual arousal.

When the data were analyzed, large correlations between the subjective and objective indices of arousal were observed. The Likert type ratings of subjective arousal correlated .82, .99, and .97 respectively with vaginal activation in the control, nongenital focused, and genital focused groups. The arousal judgments expressed as light intensities correlated .73, .89, and .94 respectively with vaginal activation in the control, nongenital focused, and genital focused groups. The arousal judgments expressed as tone intensities correlated .85, .91, and .88 respectively with vaginal activation in the control, nongenital focused, and genital focused groups. In addition, correlations for subjects who had not been given instructions about focusing their attention on specific areas of their bodies were significantly lower than those in the groups that had been instructed to focus either on genital or nongenital body locales. Korff and Geer speculated that they obtained higher correlations between subjective and physiological indices than previous studies had for the following reasons: (a) a variety of stimulus levels was included to insure that a large continuum of physiological and subjective responses would be sampled; (b) subjects' reports of arousal were obtained while they were actually watching the erotic stimuli, rather than, as was true of most previous studies, after the stimulus presentation; (c) the experimental design was relatively uncomplicated and thus subjects were less likely to be confused or to misunderstand their roles. This was said to contrast with most other studies that combined many tasks (such as fantasizing and rating films) that presumably cause confusion and thereby decrease accuracy of self reports.

Further successful efforts have emerged from a series of studies that employed labial temperature instead of the vaginal plethysmograph to measure sexual arousal (Henson & Rubin, 1978; Henson, Rubin, & Henson, 1978; Henson, Rubin, & Henson, 1979; Henson, Rubin, Henson, & Williams, 1977). These studies have determined changes in labial temperature during the viewing of an erotic film as compared to changes during the viewing of a nonerotic one. Ratings of subjective levels of sexual arousal were typically secured every 3 or 4 minutes, except during the showing of the films. Ratings were taken just before, after, and (retrospectively) at the highest level of arousal during the film. Subjects indicated their arousal on a 7–point scale (1 = no genital sensations to 7 = orgasm). Correlations between the ratings and the labial measures of activation were uniformly high (often in the .60–.80 range). In one study (Henson & Rubin, 1978) both labial temperature and vaginal photoplethysmograph readings were taken; although these two sets of readings were significantly correlated, only the labial ones were significantly correlated with the subjective ratings of arousal. Henson and Rubin (1978) speculated:

> It is possible that labial temperature was more highly correlated with subjective ratings of arousal because the labia minora and the clitoris to which it is juxtaposed are more highly supplied with nerve endings than the vaginal wall. . . . Thus, physiological changes of the labia might be more easily perceived than changes of the vagina and consequently might be more likely to be utilized in a subjective judgment of the amount of arousal. (p. 149)

It should be added that outside of the erotic film context correlations between subjective and physiological indices of arousal usually dropped off to low, nonsignificant levels.

Steinman, Wincze, Sakheim, Barlow, and Mavissakalian (1981) published a study that focused particularly on sex differences. They compared the responses of 8 male and 8 female heterosexuals to a variety of films of homosexual and heterosexual activity. Male penile changes and female vaginal changes were recorded. Throughout the experiment subjects indicated their levels of sexual arousal by moving a lever over a ten–point scale. High correlations (roughly .80–.90) between subjective and actual arousal were obtained for the males. The equivalent correlations for the females were significant but of lesser magnitude (roughly .50–.60). Steinman et al. were particularly impressed with the higher level of correlation in the male sample and remarked: "Overall, the literature suggests that for most males there is relatively strong correspondence between physiological and subjective measures of sexual arousal but that this relationship is far more variable for females" (p. 543). This statement exaggerates the clarity with which the literature demonstrates such a sex difference. In fact, as earlier cited, there are a number of studies that have found low correlations between judged and actual sexual arousal in male subjects.

Overall, the results just reviewed indicate that under the right circumstances people are capable of accurately perceiving their levels of erotic arousal.[32] Many of the studies came up with negative results, but a sufficient number produced high positive coefficients to be impressive. Even a careful analysis of the studies that were positive and those that were negative does not provide a really satisfying explanation for the differences in results. They do not seem to differ consistently with respect to the ages or backgrounds of the subjects involved, the types of stimuli employed to elicit erotic feelings, the methods used to measure subjective arousal, or the ranges and distributions of the subjective and physiological scores. However, it is worth pointing out that Korff and Geer (1983) did find the highest correlations between subjective and physiological indices of arousal when subjects were instructed to focus their attention on the body areas that were likely to register the effects of erotic stimuli. A particular kind of preparatory tuning to the target body locale may be an important ingredient of accurate body perception. It is also pertinent that, in the two studies reporting the highest correlations (Korff & Geer, 1983; Spiess, 1977), the self-reports of arousal were obtained by means of psychophysical measures that eliminated some of the stereotype biases said to be linked to the more customary use of number scales to express magnitude. At the risk of being repetitive, a few other highlights pertaining to the perception of sexual arousal will be mentioned again. First, it is possible that some persons (e.g., unmarried) may find erotic stimuli more novel than do others (e.g., married) and therefore may become more engaged with the task of self-observation, which, in turn, could heighten accuracy of the observational process (Heiman, 1980). Second, some aspects of the activation of a body locale like the female genitals may be more easily perceived than others. That is, the greater consistency of measures of labial temperature as compared with vaginal photoplethysmograph measures in their correlations with estimates of arousal may reflect the fact that the former involve areas of the genitals more available (as a function of density of nerve receptors) to being perceived.

Accurate Visceral Perception

Except for the promising studies in the area of sexual arousal just reviewed, there are only a few scattered others that have come up with promising results concerning the ability of people to assay their own body responses accurately.[33] Consider the following. Thayer (1967, 1970, 1971) and Thayer and Cox (1968) completed several projects involving multiple samples that showed reports of feelings of activation versus deactivation in exciting versus relaxing conditions to be significantly linked with physiological indices of activation. Specifically, the changes in experienced arousal from one condition to another correlated with the changes in physiological activation (skin resistance, heart rate). The correlations were substantial (viz., .41, .50, .60, .68). It is of special note that subjects high in authoritarianism[34] evidenced the largest discrepancies when their subjective estimates of arousal were compared with the corresponding physiological measures of activation. The authoritarians had the greatest difficulty in accurately perceiving their own body events. This confirms previous reports by Bookbinder (1963) and De-Soto, Kuethe, and Wunderlic (1960) concerning the special problems that high authoritarians have in accurately defining their own body states.

Fisher (1967b), too, obtained positive results when measures of relative awareness of the heart and stomach (as compared with other body organs) were related respectively to heart rate and stomach contractions during stress and rest. Sixteen males and 30 females were studied. Subjective awareness of the heart and stomach was determined by means of the Fisher (1970) Body Focus Questionnaire, which calls for subjects to make a series of paired comparisons of their degrees of awareness of different sectors of their bodies. The experienced prominence of the heart and of the stomach was positively and significantly correlated with the physiological activation of each of the respective organs. The Body Focus Questionnaire was not administered at the same time that the physiological measures were taken. Rather, it was administered at time intervals ranging from 30 minutes to 7 days distant from the period in which the physiological measures were obtained. Thus, it parallels the way in which the APQ measure is typically secured. It is more a trait index than a state index. Apropos of the significant positive correlation between stomach awareness and stomach motility observed by Fisher, previous studies have found subjects to have rather low (although better than chance) ability to judge correctly various quantities of liquids introduced into their stomachs (e.g., Coddington & Bruch, 1970; Stunkard & Fox, 1971; Whitehead & Drescher, 1980). Training with exteroceptive feedback greatly improves the accuracy of the judgments.

Edelman (1972) used a questionnaire developed by Landy and Stern (1971) that evaluates subjects' perceptions of their own bodily arousal in terms of their reports of the frequency of various bodily reactions (e.g., sweating palms, increased heart rate) in stress situations. In a study of 16 males and eight females, it was found that those who perceived themselves as developing heart symptoms during stress were significantly more likely to respond by heart rate increase in an imagined stress context than did those who portrayed themselves as likely to manifest reactions implying they are GSR responders. Avowed "GSR responders" did not, however, display greater GSR responses than avowed "heart rate responders" in an analogous imagined stress context.

OVERALL PERSPECTIVES

It is not sharply apparent why the Edelman, the Fisher, the Thayer, and the previously described studies of sexual arousal discerned a higher level of accuracy of body perception in untrained subjects than have the great majority of other observers. In a number of these successful instances, the methods for measuring body experience were different from those utilized by other researchers. The Thayer method calls for subjects to choose specific, carefully selected adjectives that depict how activated or deactivated they feel. The Fisher method involves a systematic series of paired comparisons of the perceptual prominence of specific body locales. The Edelman approach is based on reporting body reactions that appear in particular organ systems during stress. Some of the most impressive studies of perception of erotic arousal in self make use of a novel psychophysical method for obtaining estimates of self-arousal. Most of the previous approaches to measurement of subjective feelings (outside of the area of sexuality) were based on the Autonomic Perception Questionnaire or similar questionnaires, which provide a gross overall index of how aroused the individual feels in various situations. A number of other approaches have called for self-ratings of such vague entities as "emotional feeling," "emotional distress," and "nervous sensations." It is true that several studies (e.g., McFarland, 1975[35]) employed very precise techniques for measuring heart perception. However, these techniques typically asked subjects to make an extended series of complicated cognitive decisions. Subjects would, for example, be requested to discriminate stimuli contingent on their own heart beats from stimuli triggered by a pulse generator set to produce a frequency equal to the subject's mean heart rate. It is possible that the more positive findings of the Thayer, Fisher and Edelman studies derive from the fact that they not only call for focused judgments but also make it possible for the subjects to express those judgments in a simple, easily understood context.

There is a curious inconsistency to the shifting levels of accuracy in perceiving events in such organs as the heart under different conditions. If one were to take the majority of pertinent studies at face value, one would have to conclude that people are ordinarily capable of only a low level of accuracy in visceral perception. But, as one analyzes the available data, one notes variations. First, although accuracy is low in the resting condition, it tends to increase when activation is heightened. As already indicated, Jones and Hollandsworth (1981) discovered a small but significant improvement in accuracy of heart rate perception when subjects were activated beyond a resting level by having them perform exercise. Second, as Jones and Hollandsworth also showed, when persons have engaged in athletics (e.g., distance running) that would chronically heighten cardiac awareness, they are more accurate perceivers of heart activity than are those who lack such an athletic background. That is, one's degree of previous investment in activities that increase body awareness seems to play a role in one's expertise in perceiving visceral responses.

Relatedly, there is some suggestion that simple massage or training in learning how to become more body aware may have a similar facilitating effect (Widmer, 1975). Indeed, a study by Korff and Geer (1983) concerning perception of vaginal arousal indicated that just giving subjects a message about the proper anticipatory tuning to a body locale may improve the accuracy with which it is perceived when activated. Third, special training that provides individuals with exteroceptive feedback concerning the accuracy of their visceral observations can dramatically enhance accuracy. Numerous studies have documented this fact. The degree of improvement resulting from repeated exteroceptive feedback involves shifts from low, largely chance correctness to 80% to 90% levels. This is, indeed, striking. It is intriguing that such improvement, as defined by heart perception, is found primarily in males and hardly at all in females (Katkin et al. 1984). Fourth, there is evidence that factors linked with an antiinteroceptive orientation, e.g., authoritarianism, can negatively affect visceral perception. Fifth, it appears that some methods are better than others for eliciting realistic body observations. Techniques that call for vague, diffuse judgments or that involve very elaborate and artificial cognitive distinctions seem to interfere with focused accuracy in evaluations. There are obviously many factors that mediate how accurately persons judge body experiences at such diverse sites as the heart, stomach, vagina, penis, and muscles.

There are no simple generalizations for determining whether persons can or cannot correctly perceive their own body events.[36] The puzzling aspect of most of the visceral perception literature is that it portrays average people as having little better than chance ability in the quiescent state to identify their own visceral experiences, yet, paradoxically, as becoming highly accurate after relatively brief periods of receiving corrective feedback information. It is true that in, activated states, accuracy is significantly better than chance but still relatively poor. Can visceral perception be as inadequate in real life as the research findings imply? It seems to be incredibly maladaptive for the average person to be so out of contact with his or her visceral events. If, as the literature suggests, practice and feedback in a laboratory context can so quickly transform people into expert visceral perceivers, why would the infinite body experiences that people have not provide them with comparable opportunities to learn? People do have repeated experiences in which they are exposed to activating or deactivating stimuli and observe increases or decreases in the responses of organs like the heart and stomach. Would they not learn to attain better than chance level accuracy with regard to such phenomena? One could ask whether there is simply a lack of motivation for acquiring visceral perception skills.

There is research evidence (Marshall & Zimbardo, 1979; Maslach, 1979) that unexplained visceral arousal is disturbing.[37] There seems to be a strong need to understand what is happening within one's body. Studies have shown that when unexplained arousal is elicited, either by injection of epinephrine or by hypnotic techniques, subjects interpret it negatively. They do not like things to be occurring in their bodies they cannot define or understand. This implies they would have real motivation to cultivate the skills necessary for maintaining articulated body awareness. That is, in order to feel secure about what is going on in the body realm, they would have good reason to avoid ambiguity by learning how to scan their own body experiences in sensitive, dependable fashion. This seems to be a reasonable line of logic. Why, then, do so many studies not fit with this expectation?

There is a striking similarity between the discrepancies in the area of visceral perception and those observed in other aspects of the self-confrontation literature. It will be recalled that several studies (Fisher & Mirin, 1966; Wolff, 1943) have shown that a surprising number of persons did not recognize shadow profile views of their own faces when they unexpectedly encountered them. Even more remarkable, a not inconsiderable number did not recognize front views of their own faces when they came upon them in an unexpected context (Lefcourt et al., 1975)! Schneiderman (1956) reported that, when subjects were confronted with distorted mirror images of self and were provided with a mechanism for correcting the distortions, they frequently had difficulty in reconstructing the true mirror images. This was especially so if they encountered the distorted images without first having been given the opportunity to view undistorted versions of self. Relatedly, there are studies (e.g., Gur & Sackeim, 1979) in which frequent nonrecognition of one's own recorded voice has been observed. If people have difficulty correctly identifying their exterior, visible features, is it surprising that they should inaccurately perceive inner, less visible aspects of their bodies?

But, even as one acknowledges this point, one recalls again that people can also, under special conditions, demonstrate great acuity in body perceptions. For example, as already indicated, they can, with just a bit of special training, become extremely accurate in detecting small changes in their heart rates. Schumacher, Wright, and Wiesen (1968) have shown that subjects can be very sensitive in detecting their own tachistoscopically presented pictures. Shontz (1969) has demonstrated that, whereas most persons are less accurate in estimating the sizes of various parts of their bodies than they are of nonself objects, their degree of error is only moderate. Furthermore, Gur and Sackeim (1979) and others have presented data suggesting that, even when people seem to be making errors in identifying stimuli linked with self, they may, at a level out of awareness, be processing the stimuli with exquisite sensitivity.

The available data certainly indicate that body perception is typified by difficult-to-explain shifts from one level to another. In tracing likely causes for this shifting quality, one needs to look at some past pertinent findings. Wolff (1943), Huntley (1940), Fisher and Mirin (1966), and others who have studied misidentification of pictures of different parts of oneself have typically found that it lends itself to defensive purposes. Strong positive or negative feelings about self are linked with the misidentification process. Gur and Sackeim (1979) and Castaldo and Holzman (1967) have suggested that misidentification of one's own voice serves to block awareness of information that is ego alien. Holzman, Berger, and Rousey (1967), in a study of bilingual persons, discovered that only when these individuals heard recordings of their voices in the native tongue did they react defensively. The recording in the second, later-learned language did not elicit such defensiveness. It was concluded that when learning one's native language one learns not only vocabulary and grammar but also a complex "paralanguage" that expresses unconscious intentions and attitudes, some of which are ego alien and unacceptable.

Fisher (1970) has shown in considerable detail that degree of awareness of body areas is influenced by defensive needs. Persons may tune specific body locales in or out of awareness as a function of sensitivities to the dynamic themes associated with them. For example, men who have particular anxiety about possible loss of control and "letting go" are unusually sensitive to stimuli from the back of the body. Similarly, men who are especially conflicted about incorporating and "taking in" manifest an heightened focus on their eyes. The manner in which body areas are perceived has proved to play a role in the individual's personality defenses. As is described in considerable detail later, intensity of awareness of a body locale may itself serve as a persistent signal suggesting approach to, or avoidance of, certain classes of objects.

Fisher has also shown that when persons view their own bodies (in a mirror) through aniseikonic lenses, which produce distortions in the perceptual field, they are quite selective in how they see different parts of the body altered by the lenses. If there is unusual anxiety linked with a particular body locale, it is especially resistant to perceptual alteration. It is as if uncertainty about a body area mobilizes a defensive need to enhance its stability by increasing its rigidity to change. This rigidifying process was apparent in one study (Fisher & Richter, 1969) in which it was shown that the closer a woman was to menstruating (and therefore had intensified anxiety about her pelvic region), the less likely she was to perceive changes in her pelvic area when she viewed her body through aniseikonic lenses. Relatedly, in another study (Fisher, 1973a), the smaller the actual size of a woman's breasts (and therefore presumably the greater her anxious dissatisfaction with them), the less likely she was to perceive aniseikonic alterations of the breast region. Similar selective defensive responses to potential aniseikonic lense changes in body perception have been reported by other investigators (e.g., Uddenberg & Hakanson, 1972).

The close asociation between body perception and personal needs could not be better illustrated than by the research dealing with intensified body awareness. It is clear that the mere act of looking in the mirror affects degree of body awareness, and this, in turn, can reverberate through many levels of behavior. The increased self-focus set off by mirror feedback can increase guilt, intensify self-dissatisfaction, and affect mood. Obviously, when subjects are asked in a laboratory context to tune into their own visceral events and try to report them as accurately as possible, they are made more self-aware and this may trigger all kinds of responses that may be experienced as unpleasant and which would then interfere with the self-perception process. Also, under special circumstances, augmented self-focus can increase the accuracy of visceral perception (Gibbons et al., 1979).

This brief review is intended to bring home the fact that when people begin to scan their own bodies, they become unusually involved with emotional issues that can affect their perceptions.[38] The total body and its major aspects have special ego-involving connotations; and attention focused on any body target may elicit defensive responses that affect how they will be perceived. Let us consider concrete examples of this process. Perception of the heart has been studied probably more intensively than has perception of any other body locale. Typically, subjects are asked to turn their attention to the heart and to estimate its rate under different stimulus conditions. However, there are a number of studies that indicate that the mere act of focusing attention on the heart immediately triggers attitudinal changes that could, in unpredictable ways, affect the very act of heart observation. Fenigstein and Carver (1978) demonstrated that subjects who are made more aware of heart beats become more self-focused.[39] It is well established that becoming more self-focused may result in feelings of decreased self-worth, increased anxiety, and even counter-defensive turning to nonbody stimuli that will decrease body awareness[40] So, it is probable that subjects who are asked to estimate their own heart rates may find that their ability to do so is impeded by such factors as anxiety or the sudden defensive need to shift their focus away from their bodies. Of further pertinence is Fisher's (1970) finding that male subjects who were asked to monitor their own heart rates for brief periods exhibited different responses to stimuli with guilt connotation than did subjects who performed nonheart control tasks. This work grew out of Fisher's observations that men who are inclined to be unusually aware of their hearts also tend to be religious and guilt oriented. This suggests that an increase in guilt may result from being instructed to monitor one's heart rate; and it is conceivable that such increased guilt could diminish heart monitoring efficiency. Additionally, general variables such as authoritarianism and defensiveness have been linked with sensitivity to one's own body sensations.

Perhaps highly authoritarian subjects who direct their attention to, say, the heart in order to estimate heart rate, will experience negative feelings capable of interfering with the rate estimation task.

As Fisher (1970) suggested, one's body is psychologically closer to self than any thing else; and, thus the body is a prime target onto which one projects intense feelings. The body seems to be a maze of landmarks and prominences that are charged with meaning. When people scan their own bodies, they encounter an array of stimuli, many of which have powerful, often negative, emotional connotations. The research into self-awareness has demonstrated that the close inspection of one's own body is an undertaking laden with meaning.[41] There must be strong and persistent motivation for people to turn an objective eye upon their own body geography. One wonders whether experimental subjects who are asked to scrutinize their own body responses have been given sufficient motivation to devote themselves seriously to such a trying and perhaps at times even alarming task. This is an especially pertinent question when the task calls for a close examination of low level sensations and feelings whose contours are vague and have to be separated from an overlapping context of other body experiences. This examination calls for a relatively broad and also intensive sweep of the total body experiential field and consequently increases the possibility of encountering body stimuli that have a threatening impact.

The task may become more acceptable if the scrutiny of one's own body can be sharply narrowed by a focus on body sensations that are of larger magnitude (e.g., as a result of high body activation) and therefore easily separated from the total body context. Or the task might become more feasible if procedures were used that magnify the rational cognitive aspects of the operation. For example, providing quantitatively corrective exteroceptive feedback across a series of visceral judgments could frame the task as an intellectual one and minimize the emotional implications of what is being pursued perceptually within one's body. At still another level, the body judgment process may be facilitated by techniques that quiet and soothe the individual's fears about body exploration. This effect can be seen in studies (e.g., Widmer, 1975) that have improved visceral judgments by preceeding them with a period of reassuring body massage or messages that dramatize the virtue of being honestly in contact with one's own body. It is possible that the few studies that have reported good correlations between subjective estimates of body events and physiological indices of such events just happened to mobilize conditions that minimized interfering body anxieties. Theoretically, it should be possible to demonstrate a good correlation between perceived and actual body activation if one were to recruit nonauthoritarian subjects; provide them with reassurance that it is safe to explore one's own body experiences; place the body judgment task in a context that defines it as strictly cognitive and intellectual; and maximize the likelihood that the body sensations to be judged ranged into at least moderate and high intensity levels.

NOTES

[1]Schwarz and Fjeld (1968) found that persons who were asked to focus on their mirror images for a period of time in a darkened room often experienced gross distortions in their apparent appearance, unusual kinesthetic sensations, and even unpleasant physical symptoms (e.g., vomiting).

[2]Lefcourt, Hogg, and Sordoni (1975) reported that 10% of samples of college students did not recognize their own front-view photographs when they encountered them in an unexpected context!

[3]Zeitner and Weight (1979) reported that the greater a woman's pupillometric constriction when viewing a photograph of self, the higher her self-esteem. Such a relationship did not appear in a male sample.

[4]Collins and LaGanza (1982) discussed the unusual difficulty that subjects have in identifying inverted views of their own face. They found that young adolescents (ages 13–14) could identify tachistoscopically exposed inverted pictures of their face significantly faster than could late adolescents (ages 18–21) or adults (ages 25–35). It was speculated: "It seems that the young adolescent at the height of preoccupation with his body and its transformation is sufficiently egocentric to have a clear image of his face, as a complete gestalt, which is not lost on inversion of an external image such as a photograph" (p. 327).

[5]Although there is no consistent pattern of sex differences in ability to recognize one's face or body straightforwardly, two studies have revealed greater accuracy for females under special conditions. Yarmey (1979) and Yarmey and Johnson (1982) found that when subjects were asked to recall which of several photographs of themselves they had previously equated with specific attributes ("real self", "most sociable self"), the females were significantly superior in their recall. Yarmey (1979) speculated: "It is possible that women gaze more frequently at their mirror reflections and overpractice self-perceptions more so than do males" (p. 456).

[6]Schlicht (1967) and Schlicht, Carlson, Skeen, and Skurdal (1969) explored the possible relationship of personality disturbance to the manner in which persons respond to their own pictures tachistoscopically presented at speeds too fast to permit conscious recognition. No consistent results emerged.

[7]Douglas and Gibbins (1983) have questioned the significance of the Gur and Sackeim findings concerning GSR response to one's own voice. In a study of 30 women, they did "replicate Gur and Sackeim's findings of high GSR when a person's own voice was present, irrespective of whether recognition was reported." However, they noted: "The same result was also obtained when the voice to be recognized was not the subject's own" (p.592). The substitute target voice they employed in their experiment was that of an acquaintance of each subject. If others can duplicate the Douglas and Gibbins work, this would raise some doubt about the Sackeim data.

However, it would still fail to explain why Gur and Sackeim obtained such meaningful results in showing that an experience of failure makes the response to one's own voice more aversive and also in demonstrating a relationship between the inclination to engage in self-deception and the number of errors in identifying one's own voice.

[8] Indeed, if one uses the degree of activity of the central dream figure as an index of "recognition" of one's own recorded voice, the results indicate about 90% correct identification. This is definitely higher than the amount of correct recognition persons in the conscious state show when listening to a series of self and other voices.

[9] It is parenthetically pertinent that Weston and Rousey (1970) found that persons with speech defects have more intense responses to their recorded voices than do persons without speech defects.

[10] Wolff (1943) and others (Huntley, 1940) have already shown that self-confrontation that occurs at an unconscious level often results in exaggeratedly positive depictions of self.

[11] However, Dickie and Strader (1974) did find evidence that as early as 12 months of age children seemed to be unusually aroused by the perception of their mirror image.

[12] Mirror self recognition, although markedly delayed in autistic and retarded children, does eventually occur in all except the most profoundly primitive states (Harris, 1977; Hill & Tomlin, 1981; Mans, Cicchetti, & Sroufe, 1978; Neuman & Hill, 1977; Pechacek, Bell, Cleland, Baum, & Boyle, 1973).

[13] Bigelow (1975) found that the opportunity to observe concurrence between self and mirror movements plays a significant part in learning mirror recognition of self.

[14] Steenbarger and Aderman (1979) have raised the possibility that the negative self-ratings linked with mirror exposure are more likely to occur with a negative self-discrepancy that seems to be permanent and unalterable.

[15] Lefcourt, Hogg, and Sordoni (1975) found that those whose locus of control is external (i.e., who generally see themselves as controlled by outside forces) are more comfortable with intensified self-awareness than are the internally oriented. Lefcourt et al. suggest that this may be due to the fact that externals are more concerned than internals with how they appear to others: "Internals might be less aware of themselves as perceivable objects and consequently less ready to recognize their own physical images" (p. 26).

[16] Klein and Wolitzky (1970) noted the curious fact that when masking is used to prevent people from hearing their own voices, there is an increase in number of references to morality themes (e.g., expressions of guilt). Is it possible that the voice-masking procedure induces a heightened awareness of oneself?

[17] Incidentally, Wicklund (1975) reported no sex differences in the effects of enhancing self-awareness.

[18] One exception is represented by the experiments of Lefcourt et al. (1975), which demonstrated that those with an external locus of control are more comfortable when self-awareness is increased that are those with an internal locus.

[19] During the course of the extensive research initiated by Duval and Wicklund concerning the effects of increasing body awareness (e.g., by exposure to a mirror), various methods were devised for detecting the intensified focus on self. For example, Davis and Brock (as described by Wicklund, 1975) employed a task that called for subjects to guess which pronouns should be inserted at various blank points in a

foreign passage. The frequency with which first person pronouns were offered as guesses was taken to be an index of how much attention was directed to self. Such measurement devices were intended to be state measures, and they were conceptualized as tapping self-awareness, rather than body awareness.

[20] Their heightened self-awareness may increase their ability to recognize their true affective states.

[21] A Physical Self-Efficacy Scale (Ryckman, Robbins, Thornton, & Cantrell, 1982) has also been developed that is at least tangentially pertinent to the measurement of body awareness. This scale was designed to measure how physically competent people perceive themselves to be. It consists of two subscales: Perceived Physical Ability and Physical Self-Presentation Confidence. The first directly concerns perceived physical ability, and the second reflects degree of confidence in one's presentation of physical skills. An example of an item linked to the first subscale is "My physique is rather strong." An example of an item linked to the second is "I am not concerned with the impression my physique makes on others." Studies have shown that persons who are high in Physical Self-Efficacy are also high in self-esteem, low in self-consciousness and anxiety, and high in sensation seeking. Also, they are high in the ability displayed in the actual performance of physical skills and in their degree of participation in sports.

[22] One of the most serious questions about Valins' (1966) results has been raised by Hirschman, Clark, and Hawk (1977). They show that in some contexts Valins' findings can be duplicated without use of the apparently increasing heart beat, but simply by playing an extraneous sound that increases in pulse frequency.

[23] Brockner and Swap (1983) have shown in an ingenious experiment that placebo manipulation has opposite effects on those who have high as compared to low levels of body consciousness. A reverse placebo effect was significantly greater in subjects with high body consciousness.

[24] It is true that manipulation of apparent physiological states is somewhat less stressful when these states are at either the high or low extreme (e.g., Carver & Blaney, 1977a, 1977b; Nisbett & Schachter, 1966).

[25] Porges and Raskin (1969) have shown that there is significantly more error in estimating the rate of occurrence of one's heart beats than in estimating the rate of a series of intermittent tones.

[26] Nowlin, Eisdorfer, Whalen, and Troyer (1971) dramatized how insensitive heart perception can be under certain circumstances when they described the responses of a series of heart patients to an experiment in which their heart rates were artificially increased by means of a pacemaker. These patients were found not to be able to distinguish when their hearts were or were not being speeded.

[27] The hypothesis was supported only for male distance runners and not for the females. This is yet another example of the repeated sex differences that have been observed in the visceral perception literature. Apropos of this issue of sex differences, Young and Blanchard (1972) reported that males displayed greater cardiac control than did females in two operant conditioning experiments. Also, Whitehead et al. (1977) observed that males were more accurate cardiac discriminators than were females.

[28] One study (Luborsky et al., 1976) examined accuracy in estimating one's own blood pressure. Mean error for such estimation was plus or minus 12.4 mm Hg. Luborsky et al. considered this degree of error to be "moderately accurate." After 15

days of blood pressure information feedback, a subsample of the subjects improved almost 100%. However, a special control group that was given inaccurate blood pressure feedback improved almost as much! A satisfactory explanation for this result was not provided.

[29] No sex differences were noted in the magnitudes of the correlations.

[30] McNair, Gardos, Haskell, and Fisher (1979) observed that psychotic patients with high APQ scores showed the least degree of positive therapeutic response to placebo treatment.

[31] Borkovec (1976) reported a series of studies involving multiple samples in which APQ scores mediated levels of anxiety in different stimulus contexts.

[32] Gerard (1982) reported that, in a sample of women who had experienced mastectomy, ($N = 13$) there was a significantly lower correlation between subjective and physiological (defined by vaginal plethysmograph) arousal than in a control group ($N = 11$) that had not suffered such body loss. She raised the possibility that "the mastectomy experience may have left these women with less ability to acknowledge their sexual arousal . . ." (p. 311).

[33] Considerable attention has also been devoted to the question whether body perception variables play a role in the ability to control visceral activity. It has been speculated (Brener & Jones, 1974) that learning such control might be mediated by the ability to perceive accurately what is occurring in specific organ systems. Most of the research in this area has involved the use of the Autonomic Perception Questionnaire (APQ) (Mandler et al., 1958). The results have been inconsistent and confusing: McCanne and Sandman (1976), Puente, Clark, and Beiman (1980), and Phares (1975) reported no relationship between APQ scores and ability to achieve operant heart-rate control. But Bergman and Johnson (1971) found that subjects with medium APQ scores attained more control over heart rate acceleration and deceleration than did subjects with extreme high and low scores when no external heart-rate feedback was supplied. Further, Blanchard, Young, and McLeod (1972) found that low APQ scorers were better at controlling their heart rates than were high scorers. Using another method for measuring body perception based on ability to detect heart rate accurately, Whitehead, Drescher, and Blackwell (1975) discerned a negative correlation between accuracy and ability to control heart rate. Neither Gannon (1977) nor Dale and Anderson (1972) could find a correlation between accuracy of heart rate perception and ability to control heart rate. At the same time, Clemens and MacDonald (1975) detected a significant positive correlation between an objective test of heart beat discrimination and ability to increase but not decrease heart rate. Interestingly, McFarland (1975), Carroll and Whellock (1980), and McCanne and Lyons (1982) reported a similar result; and this may provide a lead worth more careful exploration. However, overall, one is most impressed by the contradictions and vagueness in the results that have accumulated so far with regard to heart rate control.

It should be added that three studies (Stern, 1973; Stern & Kaplan, 1967; Stern & Lewis, 1968) have shown a clearer pattern of results with regard to learning control of GSR response. A self-report questionnaire (Somatic Perception Questionnaire), which inquires into the types of somatic symptoms one develops during stress, consistently demonstrated that people most likely to report an inclination to sweat reactions were also those most proficient in learning control of GSRs.

[34] Ancoli and Green (1977) demonstrated that authoritarianism was negatively correlated with the ability to control alpha during alpha wave biofeedback training.

Further, Weinstein, Averill, Opton, and Lazarus (1968) have discussed variables other than authoritarianism, such as defensiveness and repression-sensitization, that produce discrepancies between self-reports of arousal and parallel physiological measures. Paquette (1973) found that the greater the internal as compared to external locus of control, the more accurate subjects were in tasks involving the judgment of heart and breathing rates.

[35] Note that scores derived from the precise focused technique used by McFarland to measure ability to track heart rate had only a chance relationship with Autonomic Perception Questionnaire scores.

[36] In a study by Orta (1979), in which subjects were asked to judge changes in the activity levels of four different body systems (heart, muscle, respiration, blood flow), those who were poor judges of heart responses were also poor judges of responses in the other three systems. The ability to judge activity levels seemed to be generalized. The average level of accuracy attained in the judgments was quite low. Orta also found that subjects were significantly more sensitive to changes in muscle tension than to those in the other body systems. The generality of one's ability to judge visceral activity was supported too by the Whitehead and Drescher (1980) finding of a correlation of .51 between accuracy in judging stomach contractions and accuracy in detecting heart beats (in a sample of 11 males and 9 females.) However, Pennebaker (1982) found only insignificant correlations between ability to estimate one's heart rate accurately and the ability to estimate one's temperature accurately. He also pointed out that the biofeedback literature indicates low correlations between skill in controlling one autonomic function and skill in controlling another.

[37] Wegner and Giuliano (1980) present evidence of an increase in self-focus that goes along with unexplained arousal, and this may play a significant part in the unpleasantness associated with such arousal.

[38] Studies (Epstein & Fenz, 1965; Fenz & Epstein, 1967) of experienced versus novice parachutists have revealed that the novices are actually more accurate in estimating their degree of physiological arousal just prior to the jump. Fenz and Epstein concluded that the experienced parachutists had learned to dampen their awareness of their true physiological state and that this had adaptive value because heightened awareness of their arousal could interfere with performing the complicated maneuvers they engage in while falling. This represents a possible example in which shutting out accurate body perception facilitates adjustment. It is pertinent to this issue that Type A coronary-prone individuals have been observed (Weidner & Mathews, 1978) to pay relatively little attention to their body state when they are performing a task. Presumably, they wish to avoid the interference effects that might result from focusing on the body state. Other studies (Mathews, Carver, & Scheier, 1982) have pointed up the fact that focusing attention on one's body sensations when one is exposed to painful stimuli can be maladaptive in the sense that such focusing magnifies the pain. At the same time, the focusing probably increases accuracy of perception, which, in some circumstances (e.g., if tissue damage were produced that required treatment), could facilitate adaptation.

[39] Gillis and Carver (1980) also showed that self-aware persons are particularly likely to overestimate their heart rates.

[40] Galassi, Frierson, Jr., and Sharer (1981) reported that college students with low grade point averages seemed to be less aware of their own body sensations during an

examination than were students with a high grade point average. This difference may possibly represent a defensive shutting out of body awareness by low grade point students, who usually perform poorly on examinations.

[41] Some people do actively seek exploration of their own body experiences. Instead of being defensively distant, they immerse themselves in their body arousal. They seem to find enjoyment in encountering the unexpected within their own body realms. For example, two studies (Eisenman, 1980; Kohn & Annis, 1978) have reported a link between smoking marijuana and a desire for "internal sensation seeking."

2 Developmental Aspects of Body Perception

INTRODUCTION

This chapter is devoted to exploring what is known about how growing children organize and make sense of their body experiences. There is every reason to believe that children differ radically from adults in their body perceptions. As Piaget (1960) observed: "During this stage children believe that thinking is 'with the mouth.' Thought is identified with the voice. Nothing takes place either in the head or in the body" (p. 38). If this statement is true, it would follow that many children assign to the mouth a function and significance that normal adults do not. For such children, the mouth would be represented in the body scheme rather differently than it would for adults.

In the same vein, Gellert (1960), in the course of questioning young children about their knowledge of the body interior, encountered imagery of the following character about the heart (p. 4):

"The heart is where God lives."
"The heart makes you dream."
"The heart makes you do all the things you're supposed to do."

She found a variety of other inaccurate body ideas. Fifty percent of children below the age of 11 thought their lungs were located in their heads. Many children assumed they had two hearts, two bladders, but only two ribs. Gellert noted too that "estimates of the number of lungs ranged from 1 to 100" (p. 8). Similarly, Williams (1979) reported in a survey of Phillipine children that some referred to the lungs as being "for the storage of waste" or "to strengthen the bones"; and others conceived of the bones as places "where food passes." In addition to such anecdotal material, there is a pool of research findings that highlight differences between the body perceptions of children and adults. These differences are not always in the direction of the adult's being more realistic and accurate. For example, Wapner (1968a) has observed that in a context where the body is tilted, children make fewer errors than adults do when judging the position of the longitudinal axis of the body. Numerous approaches have been taken to tracing body image development. They have diversely involved drawings of the human figure, identifying body parts, making judgments of the body's position in space, estimating body size, adapting to lens-induced alterations in the appearance of the body, responding to one's mirror image, and so forth.

There is no detailed, well-put-together account of how children construct their body maps. Indeed, there have been few if any attempts to integrate broadly the pertinent data already available in the literature. It is fair to say that Piaget (1954) and others assume that children's early basic notions about the world grow out of their sensory-motor experiences. That is, the body in action, moving in space and reaching for objects, provides the framework for structuring the world. Presumably, early experiences are phrased primarily in body terms and organized around the spatiality of the body. We are only just beginning to acquire data about this process of organization. These data will be reviewed shortly.

Some of the dominant theories of cognitive and personality development provide at least sketchy paradigms of how children learn to make sense of their body experiences. Piaget has been interested in the role of body experience in early development, but it is difficult to capture his views. He starts with the assumption that in the beginning the infant does not have an awareness of its own body, as such. He states (Piaget, 1954):

> In other words, at first the universe consists in mobile and plastic perceptual images centered about personal activity. But it is self evident that to the extent that this activity is undifferentiated from other things it constantly assimilates to itself it remains unaware of its own subjectivity; the external world therefore begins by being confused with the sensations of a self unaware of itself, before the two factors become detached from one another and are organized correlatively. (p. 351)

Piaget's concept of egocentrism implies a high awareness of self (and one's body) in the young organism. Flavell (1963) has pointed out, however, that this involves a misunderstanding of the term:

> The concept of egocentrism is a most important one in Piaget's thinking and has been from the very earliest writings. It denotes a cognitive state in which the cognizer sees the world from a single point of view only—his own—but without knowledge of the existence of viewpoints or perspectives and, a fortiori, without awareness that he is a prisoner of his own. Thus, Piaget's egocentrism is by definition an egocentrism of which the subject cannot be aware; it might be said that the egocentric subject is a kind of solipsist aware neither of self nor solipsism. (p. 60)

But in his emphasis on the sensory-motor aspect of adaptation Piaget does ascribe basic importance to the perceived body as an organizing force. That is, he sees body action or movement as the raw material of all intellectual and perceptual adaptation; the body interacting with objects leads to the organization of schemas. During infancy the actions are overt and clearly sensory-motor. Schemata are built up by motor repetition. "Circular reactions" permit them to become solidly established. The child's earliest circular reactions, says Piaget, are to his own body. The following quote from Clapp (1969) illustrates this process: "Let us examine the reflex of grasping and how this enables the hand to become incorporated into . . . schemata. Suppose the palm of the child's one hand touches his other hand and this elicits the reflex of grasping. By circular reactions this bit of sensory-motor behavior is repeated and the grasping movements of the hand become incorporated into the postural model schemata of the body" (p. 18). As the child develops, there is an internalization of body actions. This internalization involves the creation of images that represent sensory-motor sequences. With time, the images presumably become more schematic and abstract. The image is rooted in motor activity, that is, in the movements of one's body. In this respect, Piaget's view parallels motor theories of thought proposed by others such as Jacobson and Washburn (Humphrey, 1951). He specifies the development of symbolic function as first proceeding by way of "image signifiers" that are motor acts. For example, he describes a child who anticipated the potential opening of a matchbox by opening her own mouth. Presumably, such reduced (body-phrased) imitations are forerunners of symbolic representations that become more and more reduced and internalized. Apropos of this point, Flavell (1963) notes: "Piaget's theory permits him to see adult logical operations as sensory-motor actions which have undergone a succession of transformations rather than as a different species of behavior entirely" (p. 83). Piaget seldom offers explicit accounts of body experience, as such. However, many of his raw observations of child behavior clearly relate to the development of the body scheme. This is particularly true in Piaget's (1951) detailed accounts of how his own children learned to imitate body behaviors that required a prior knowledge of their own body topography. He makes it clear that the child has to learn to treat self as an object, to learn its special object qualities, and to grasp its locomotive properties in relation to fixed object positions in space. There are numerous body image connotations in his accounts of how children develop spatial concepts (e.g., up-down, right-left) and generally acquire complex spatial coordinates in which the body is a central anchor. He also pointed out (Piaget, Inhelder, & Szeminska, 1960) that, before using an independent measuring instrument, children often employ parts of their own bodies to measure things, which suggests they learn conservation of length with their own bodies before generalizing the principle to nonbody objects.

Werner (1940) was a pioneer in explicitly assigning importance to the body as a psychological construct. He suggested that children's body experiences are central to their world and color all their perceptions. He offered innumerable examples of how body perceptions provide a framework for defining self, for organizing space, and for coding numerical concepts. With Kaplan (Werner & Kaplan, 1963) he spelled out too how strongly language is anchored in body feelings and images. The importance he assigns to the body in the cognitive development of the child is illustrated in what he has to say about the role of the body in learning to grasp number concepts (Werner, 1957):

> As is true of primitive man, the child's fundamental counting schemes are rooted in the body itself. A small boy begins of his own accord to use his fingers as a counting device, even though he can count verbally only as far as 2. For example, he has 3 stones before him. Holding out his three fingers he says: "That's more than two. . . . It's like this!" He will handle 4, 5, 6, 7 stones in the same fashion, even bringing the fingers of the other hand into use (p. 295).
>
> All these facts support the assumption that the hand area represents a natural number space. Any higher development of a number schema, however, will necessarily bring into play the optical field. In order to become dominantly optical in nature "number space" . . . must be largely stripped of the somatically oriented and motor rhythmic elements included in the more primitive activity of finger counting. Little is known of the manner in which this transition occurs. (p. 297)

Werner thought that "physiognomic perception" was strikingly characteristic of children and that it dramatically demonstrated the pervasive impact of body sensations on their interpretations of the world. Physiognomic perception involves "motor and affective elements" being "intimately merged in the perception of things" (Werner, 1961, p. 337). It is illustrated by a child's describing an object as sad when it is leaning over and quite the opposite when it is standing up, or a cup as tired when it is lying on its side. Presumably, the physiognomic response reflects a special closeness between self and objects, such that feelings usually contained within one's boundaries are projected onto the objects. Werner assumed that the attribution of self qualities to nonliving things declined consistently as children matured. His early emphasis on the importance of one's own body as a psychological force was later translated, collaboratively with S. Wapner, into the rich program of sensory-tonic research dealing with body perception that flourished at Clark University (see Wapner & Werner, 1965a).

Freud obviously assigned importance to body attitudes in his developmental constructs. He hypothesized (albeit vaguely) that body feelings are basic to ego formation, and his libido theory links personality development to a process involving the successive shifting of attention and energy investment, in the growing child, from one body area to another (viz., oral, anal, genital). He constructed a personality typology that was linked with the degree to which persons continued inappropriately to invest in certain major body zones. Thus, the "oral character" was one who as an adult continued to focus, like the young child, highly on the mouth; the "anal character" focused on the anal sector of the body. Detailed descriptions of these character types can be found elsewhere (Abraham, 1927; Freud, 1908). Fisher and Greenberg (1977a) demonstrated that the oral and anal typologies are among the best scientifically validated of Freud's formulations. However, they also indicated that there was as yet no confirmatory evidence for Freud's notion of a fixed series of developmental stages in the prominence of body zones. Freud's idea that different areas of the body vary in their psychological importance as persons mature is one we shall examine further, especially within the context that the experiential prominence of such areas may integrate associated patterns of feelings or attitudes.

Freud's descriptions of the developing child were often rich with body image implications. He commented on such phenomena as the child's learning to distinguish events in his or her own body interior from those outside; the sensations aroused in specific body areas by socialization experiences (e.g., toilet training, weaning); anxieties about potential body damage linked to parental threats; confusion about body structure related to the discovery of sex differences; fantasies aroused by the movement of materials in and out of orifices; and so forth. He invented the idea that when growing children observe or fantasy certain patterned events to be occurring in their body, such patterns may become paradigms for constructing images about what the world is like. Thus, the sense of possessing an overregulated anal sphincter may create an image of life as a place in which regulation and control are dominant themes. Throughout Freud's account of the growing up process, the body as an experienced object is always prominent.

Erikson (1950, 1959) followed Freud closely in his account of developmental shifts in the intensity of investment in major body zones. Like Freud, he elaborated the concept that "encounters" with such zones establish life precedents and expectations. Erikson (1950) speaks of experience as "anchored in the ground plan of the body" (p. 108). He formulated an elaborate developmental schema in which each fundamental life attitude was associated with attitudes toward specific body organ systems. For example, feelings of trust and distrust were linked with early evolving images of the mouth; attitudes about autonomy and shame with anal and muscle images; and initiative and guilt, with images of the genitals. Erikson was even more imbued than Freud with the role of body perceptions in shaping the child's identity. The specificity of his theories concerning body "organ modes" in development is unique. Although most of his constructs in this area have not yet been put to the empirical test, scientific support (e.g., Cramer, 1975) has emerged for his theories concerning the representation of male and female organ modes in sexual identity.

Schilder (1950) probably assigned the body image greater centrality in development than has any other personality theorist. He also speculated in much finer detail about the factors that contribute to the structure of the body concept. Like Piaget (1954), he starts with the assumption that the newly born infant really does not have an awareness of its body. He remarks: "We do not perceive our own body differently from objects in the outside world. It is, therefore, senseless to say that for the newborn child only the body exists and the world does not. Body and world are experiences which are correlated with each other. One is not possible without the other. When Freud states that on the narcissistic level only the body is present, he must be mistaken" (pp. 122–123).

Despite disagreement with Freud on this point, he did follow him closely in conceptualizing the build-up of the body scheme as centering successively on three primary erogenous zones (viz., oral, anal, genital). He also considered other body landmarks, such as the skin and the eyes, to be prominent reference points in the child's evolving image of his or her own body. Schilder (1950) hypothesized that the child's "desires" become differentially associated with such major reference points: "Individuals in whom a partial desire is increased will feel the particular point of the body, the particular erogenic zone belonging to the desire, in the centre of the body image. It is as if energy were amassed on these particular points. There will be lines of energy connecting the different erogenic points, and we shall have a variation in the structure of the body-image according to the psychosexual tendencies of the individual" (p. 124). He specified: "Two factors, apparently, play a special part in the creation of the body image. The one is pain, the other the motor control over our limbs" (p. 104). He considered motor control to be of importance because he felt that people acquire body knowledge primarily from their experiences with the body in action, in movement. ("By actions and determinations we give the final shape to our bodily self," p. 105). The motor aspect of body experience signified for him that the body image is constantly changing and shifting. He had difficulty reconciling his concept of the body image's fluidity with his assumption that there are major fixed attributes presumably linked to the structuring of primary erogenous zones.

As to his reference in the aforementioned quote to the importance of pain in body image development, it is difficult to decode what he really meant. He variously refers to pain as an experience that magnifies the importance of affected body parts and diminishes the prominence of unaffected body areas; as a signal the child learns that indicates an imminent threat to the body's integrity; and as a disorganizing element in the body image. Presumably, one of the reasons he regarded pain as important in the child's evolving body concept is that it produces stressful alterations in the body scheme that dramatically change the relative prominence of body sectors and require efforts at integration ("the aching organ becomes a centre of renewed experimentation with the body," p. 126).

Schilder (1950) also enumerated other factors he thought entered into the shaping of the child's body perceptions. He noted, for example, that self-touching with the hands may magnify the prominence of certain body areas as compared to others. Thus, the ease with which children can reach specific body areas will influence their long-term attitudes toward them. Schilder hastened to add:

But there is no question that our own activity is insufficient to build up the image of the body. The touches of others, the interest others take in the different parts of our body, will be of enormous importance in the development of the postural model of the body. . . . Pain, dysaesthesia, erogenic zones, the actions of our hands on the body, the actions of others toward our body, the interests of others concerning our body, and the itching provoked by the functions of our body are . . . important factors in final structuralization of the body-image. (pp. 126–127)

Witkin and his associates (1962) regarded differentiation as a key dimension of the body concept. They assumed that (Witkin, 1965) "achievement of a differentiated body concept is a manifestation of the child's general progress toward psychological differentiation." Witkin's definition of body concept differentiation is well depicted in the following statement concerning the development of the body image:

One may imagine that very early the child experiences himself and his body as a more or less continuous body-field matrix. Later, boundaries are formed between body and world outside, and some awareness is developed of the parts of the body and the interrelation among them. Whereas the child's conception of his body is early relatively global, later it is more articulated—that is, there is an impression of the body as having definite limits or boundaries and of the parts within as being discrete yet interrelated and joined in a definite structure. (pp. 27–28)

Witkin approached the problem of measuring body concept differentation by use of tasks that evaluated the degree to which people experience their body as clearly segregated from the surrounding field. For example, one task is based on the ability to judge the position of true vertical for a luminous rod in a dark room where the usual spatial cues have been removed and confusing visual cues (e.g., a tilted luminous frame) have been introduced. Conflict is thereby created between the apparent upright as defined by one's own body sensations and the upright as defined by the surrounding field. A second illustrative technique involves a determination of how much differentiation (e.g., detail, sex identification) is introduced into one's drawing of a human figure. Witkin et al. (1962) have shown that body concept differentiation in children and adults parallels the capacity to make such differentiation with respect to objects external to self. Witkin (1965) notes that "ability to perceive body as segregated from field goes with ability to perceive any object as discrete from organized context" (p. 38).

Witkin et al. (1962) also demonstrated that an individual's degree of body concept differentiation as of age 10 is significantly predictive of the degree of differentiation displayed in the adult years. They investigated the attributes of mothers of children with varied body concept differentiation. They concluded that mothers who interfered with differentiation in their children approached rearing in a way "which interfered with separation from the mother" and this "included giving physical care inappropriate to age, preventing the assumption of responsibility, markedly limiting a child's activities because of fears or anxieties, stressing conformity, especially pressing for adult behavior when children were very young" (pp. 312–313). Also found was a trend for the child's degree of body concept differentiation to be positively correlated with mother's degree of differentiation. Witkin and his colleagues were the first to demonstrate in convincing detail the link between an important aspect of the child's body image and the treatment received from mother. They also highlighted the similarities between how the child perceives its own body and how it perceives nonself objects.

Kohlberg (1966) was not interested in the body image of children specifically. However, he fashioned an elaborate cognitive theory of sex role development that is tied to how children perceive their body attributes. He rejects the notion that children derive their sex role concepts primarily from interactions with their parents. Rather, he portrays sex role definition as arising in the course of cognitive judgments made by children about their own bodies and those of others ("sex role attitudes" are "rooted in the child's concepts of physical things—the bodies of himself and others," p. 82). He depicts children in the 2- to 4-year age range as uncertain of the constancy of their sexual identity and arriving at some certainty about it only around the age of 5 or 6.

Children, it seems, learn to label their bodies as male or female, and, once they are certain of this categorization, they begin to think and act in ways that are congruent with it. They then value positively those objects and acts consistent with their gender category. The task of psychosexual differentiation is seen, then, as arising out of the child's ability to learn that his or her body possesses physical qualities that are labeled "boy" or "girl." These qualities embrace structure, size, and genital differences. Kohlberg (1966) boldly traces children's ideas about the differences in power and social roles of males and females to deductions they make on the basis of what they observe about their own bodies as compared with those of the opposite sex. The perception of one's own body as being of certain sex represents, in Kohlberg's theory, a primary step in becoming socialized and structuring a life role. Kohlberg attempted to document his theory by citing various studies that found little relationship between parent behavior (or the child's view of parent behavior) and the child's sex role concepts. That is, children presumably learn sex roles not by imitating their parents, but by building up ideas about what attributes are associated with male versus female bodies. Kohlberg also found support in the parallel between constancy in labeling self as being of a certain sexual identity and the development of constancy with reference to nonself objects.

Of course, many others have offered ideas and theories about the growth of the body image. There are, for example, Reich's (1949) notions about the translation of character attributes into muscular "character armor"; or the views of individuals like Cratty (1964), Frostig (1975), Barsch (1967), and Kephart (1960), who regard early adequate structuring of the body concept as extraordinarily vital for cognitive development; or the theories of Lacan (Wilden, 1972), which assign much significance to phallocentric images and the "mirror stage" in ego construction; or the work of Klein (1932), which does, after all, portray early personality development as occurring in a matrix of fantasies about body incorporation and destruction.

Although theories concerning the development of the body image are inclined to be vague, they do propose a number of interesting ideas that could be, and in some instances have been, put to the test. Let us briefly inventory some of the major ideas they have advanced.

1. As might be expected, most theories propose that the child starts out with a hazy or even zero awareness of its own body as a separate entity.

2. It is usually assumed that the body concept becomes more differentiated and complex with age and that one of the major initial steps in differentiation is to evolve a sense of possessing a boundary.

3. The body is typically portrayed as a principal frame of reference in the child's learning spatial directionality (e.g., right versus left).

4. To some extent, all theorists treat the individual's body as being, early on, a perceptual object that is uniquely different from nonself objects, especially in its degree of ego involvement.

5. A number of major theorists regard body image formation as proceeding through a fixed series of stages, with each stage focusing on a primary body area (viz., mouth, anus, genitals).

6. Patterns of experiences with major body zones during socialization (e.g., pressure to rigidly control them) are depicted as establishing paradigms for interpreting extrabody events that are experientially linked to those zones.

7. The discovery that one's body belongs to a specific sex category is often presumed to be a fundamental step in structuring the body concept. But, according to some, such awareness of sex difference also becomes a source of alarm (e.g., castration anxiety) that one's body can exist in a radically different form and therefore is susceptible to unexpected change or even mutilation.

8. Theorists are inclined, either explicitly or implicitly, to assume that body attitudes of children are strongly influenced by their parents' values and child rearing practices.

9. Certain phases of the developmental sequence are apt to be referred to as being times of special body image instability. Two that are frequently cited are (a) the so-called Oedipal period, which is said to call for attitudinal shifts in relation to the body's genital region; and (b) adolescence, with its accompanying overall radical body transformations.

10. It is typically assumed that, as children mature and move through adolescence into adulthood, their body feelings become less influential and cognitive factors more powerful in their decision making. That is, they shift to a judgmental framework in which perspectives other than those provided by one's own body sensations and cues become increasingly important.

EARLY KNOWLEDGE OF BODY

One of the first questions to arise in a discussion of the development of the body image relates to when children become aware of the existence of a unique body space representing self. As already indicated, there has been considerable theoretical speculation about this matter, and it has become possible to explore the question empirically as well. One major approach has involved children's reactions to their own mirror images. Several studies (Amsterdam, 1972; Amsterdam & Greenberg, 1977; Brooks-Gunn, 1975; Schulman & Kaplowitz, 1977) have found good evidence that self-recognition first appears clearly in the last few months of the second year. It is only at that point that full equation of the mirror image with self seems to occur. This equation is interestingly pointed up by Levine's (1979) detecting a significant parallel in 2-year-olds between ability to recognize one's own mirror image and ability to recognize and use self-referring pronouns. A more detailed account of these mirror studies is presented in the chapter dealing with self-confrontation.

There is little data concerning what children actually know about their bodies in the first few years of life.[1] We are largely ignorant of what they perceive as they scan their own corporeal space.[2] There are obvious reasons why it would be difficult to secure meaningful reports from young children. Gellert (1960, 1962) indicated that it was almost impossible to obtain dependable information about body perception from children below the age of 5. She studied 96 hospitalized boys and girls ranging in age from approximately 5 to 17. She simply asked them about the locations and functions of various body parts and posed miscellaneous questions like, "What do you have inside you?"

It was found that awareness of the existence of the bones in the body was one of the earliest accurately acquired bits of information about the body interior. Gellert (1962) speculated that this was a function of the fact that bones are easily palpable at so many different body sites. The size and location of the heart were also generally known. Thus, 60% of 4- to 6-year-olds could already locate it accurately. By age 7, most children were knowledgeable about the importance of the heart, and by age 13 there was unanimous understanding of its functions. At all ages the heart was judged to be the most essential part of the body. The size of the heart (as indicated by drawings) tended to be perceived fairly accurately, whereas the size of the stomach was usually exaggerated. Other interior body elements often mentioned by the younger children were stomach, blood, brain,[3] nerves, and intestines. Below the age of 7 the function of the lungs was generally unknown. Gellert noted that whereas previous studies (Michel-Hutmacher, 1955; Nagy, 1953) had portrayed young children (before age 8) as visualizing the body interior largely as a reservoir of blood, food, and wastes, she found more accurate differentiation. She indicated too that at about age 9 there seemed to be a significant spurt in children's knowledge about the body. The median number of items listed as being inside the body increased from 3.5 (prior to age 9) to 8.6 (at age 9). By age 11, the majority of children seemed to have generally "correct" concepts concerning stomach, lungs, skin, nerves, ribs, and heart. No sex differences were detected.

Gellert (1962) was impressed with the relatively limited numbers of ideas that children had concerning their body organs. Even the ideas that were incorrect bore a striking similarity. For example, over half the children between the ages of 7 and 11 years erroneously agreed in locating the lungs in the neck or head. It is an intriguing question as to how such uniformity arises. The agreements about blatantly incorrect concepts cannot be attributed to formal teaching sources. Gellert wondered whether the raw experiences that children have with their own bodies might not provide common misleading cues that lead to distorted conclusions.

Smith (1973) studied knowledge of the body in third- and fifth-grade children ($N = 146$). She asked them to name the contents of the body, to draw (on a human figure outline) the organs they identified, to describe the functons of the organs, and to explain the nature of body illness. She reported that children within this age range had limited knowledge about body organs and illness. The body organs most often identified were, in decreasing order: bones, brain, blood, and heart and blood vessels. Most children had an "adequate knowledge" of four to five major body organs. Degree of knowledge about body organs correlated in the .60s with adequacy of knowledge about the nature of illness. Body organ knowledge was also significantly positively correlated with the father's educational level.

Following up Smith's study, Williams (1979) surveyed the knowledge of the body and illness in Phillipine children in grades 1, 3, and 5 (229 well and 130 hospitalized). She employed the same procedure as Smith had. The ten most frequently identified body parts were: bones (81%), intestines (68%), heart (63%), brain (51%), blood vessels (48%), blood (41%), liver (34%), muscles (33%), stomach (30%), and lungs (28%). The hospitalized children seemed to understand illness better than those who were well. Males were found to be more knowledgeable about body organs and illness than were females. Such a sex difference had not been observed by Smith (1973) in her survey of children in the United States. But Williams did reaffirm Smith's observation that the higher the educational level of the children's fathers, the greater was the children's understanding of the body.

Another cross-culturally oriented study was complete by Steward, Furuya, Steward, and Ikeda (1982). Subjects were 41 Japanese children (20 boys, 21 girls) and 33 American children (14 boys, 19 girls) whose mean ages were 5.9 and 5.0 years, respectively. They were asked to complete one drawing of the outside of a child's body and a second of the inside of the body. The American children gave significantly more attention to the outside figure than did the Japanese children; the American children were more likely to include the arms, legs, facial details, and clothing elaborations. This difference was attributed to the fact that Japanese are less likely than Americans to reveal much of themselves publicly. The Americans were said to have a larger public or "outside" self. By way of contrast, few differences were found between the two cultural groups in their drawings of the inside of the body. Japanese children were significantly more likely to include the brain. The mothers were asked to predict the state of health of their children as adults. Children of both cultures whose mothers expected them to be less healthy tended to give significantly less attention (detail) to the inside body drawing. This was interpreted to mean that the mother with anxiety about her child's future health somehow communicated a repressive or "looking away" attitude with respect to the inside of one's body.

Brumback (1977) administered the Inside-of-the-Body test to 150 children (grades 1-6). This test involved drawing a picture of all the parts of the "inside of a person." The mean number of parts identified in grade 1 was 5.2; by grade 4, it was 9.6; and by 6th grade, 13.1. Younger children identified more visible parts like arms and legs. Older children referred more frequently to deeper cavity organs. The heart was the most commonly identified organ (89%). Bones were mentioned very early. Brumback concluded: "The present study demonstrates that a child initially perceives the inside of the body as composed mainly of heart and bones and such regional skeletal structures as hips, arms, and legs. As normal children become older, they begin to view the body as composed of the many other internal organs" (p. 708). Brumback was generally impressed with the accuracy of the children's organ drawings. The originators of the Inside-of-the-Body test (Tait & Ascher, 1955), who studied 22 sixth-grade children, found them to be most knowledgeable about five internal organs: heart, stomach, intestine, brain, and ribs. The children were also particularly aware of the skeleto-muscular aspects of the body, and it was their heightened awareness of such aspects that distinguished their body drawings from those of adults.

Porter (1974) asked 72 boys and 72 girls (first, third, and fifth grades) to fill in the outline of a nude child's body: "On your picture, draw everything you know that is inside your body." Analysis of the drawings indicated a pattern of organ awareness similar to that reported by Tait and Ascher (1955). At every age level, males named more body parts than did girls. Some trends were noted for girls to mention the bladder or kidneys more often than the boys, and boys were inclined to mention larynx, trachea, and tongue with relatively greater frequency.

Crider (1981) interviewed 21 children (ages 6-12) about their concepts of the body interior. Each child was requested to tell what is inside the body, to draw it, and to indicate the locations of the various organs on a schematic drawing provided by the examiner. The information obtained conformed to Gellert's (1960, 1962) observations. Crider sought particularly to demonstrate that, with increasing age, knowledge about the body becomes less global and more differentiated, as would be expected from the developmental theories of Werner and Piaget. She anticipated:

> Specifically, the initial (preoperational) conceptions of body functions should deal with relatively global states of the whole body . . . without clear differentiation of internal and external. . . . At a somewhat higher level (concrete-operational) a variety of structures and functions should be clearly differentiated. The conception of functions should be in terms of coordinated movements in space and time. . . . Higher level, more integrated (formal-operational) conceptions should posit hypothetical transformations that account for the perceived functioning of the body. Functions should be hierarchically organized in terms of organs, systems, and the interdependence of systems. (p. 53)

Crider considered that the data she obtained from the subjects roughly conformed to this paradigm. However, she pointed out that there is great individual variability at given age levels. Also, the same child may at times display more primitive concepts about one organ and more differentiated concepts about another.

Some interesting data concerning acquisition of knowledge of the genital region of the body are also available. First, children seem to be aware of their sexual classification by the age of 3 or 4 (Fisher, 1970). Conn (1940a, 1940b) and Conn and Kanner (1947) studied children's knowledge of genital sex differences in a dollplay interview. They discovered that only 50% of the children 4-to 6-years old had an accurate concept of such differences. The corresponding percentage in the 7-8 year range was 72%; and in the 11-12 range, 86%. Katcher (1955) evaluated in considerable detail the genital knowledge of 149 boys and 117 girls in the 3-9 year age range. He asked the children to identify pictures of portions of male and female bodies. A large proportion of those in the 3-4 age group made significant errors in identifying genital regions. By age 5, only 50% made significant errors in genital judgments; by age 6, 70% were without error. Katcher also reported that girls seemed to understand genital differences earlier than boys do. In general, a clear image of genital differences is still uncommon at age 4; by age 5, there is a significant increase in such knowledge; and by age 6, more than half the population of children shows awareness of genital distinctions. A variety of studies (Fisher & Greenberg, 1977a) have shown too that identification with male or female roles begins to crystallize perceptibly by ages 4-6.

A novel source of information concerning the child's body perceptions is the work of Foellinger and Trabasso (1977) and Johnson, Perlmutter, and Trabasso (1979). In these studies children 5-11 and 4-8 years respectively were presented tasks that involved learning to associate actions or words with specific parts of one's body and later recalling them. A body spatial framework was basic to the hierarchy of recall. It was consistently found that recall was significantly better for the words or actions linked to the head and leg areas than for any other body sectors. This was interpreted as being due to the fact that the head and legs are the "ends" of the body and therefore most salient and discriminable as cues. In other words, the two ends of the body emerged as most prominent in the body framework (body image?) that shaped recall.

The salience of the head and legs in the body scheme was further documented by Johnson et al. (1979) when they analyzed existing data concerning the frequency with which various body terms are used in the English language and also the most frequent serial order of depiction of parts when children draw a picture of the body. References to the head and legs were more frequent than for any other body parts; and the most typical figure drawing part sequence for children was head-legs rather than head-body-arms-legs, a drawing sequence that is typical for adults. Johnson et al. were impressed with the fact that head and leg dominance in the body hierarchy could be detected as early as 5 years of age. Fisher (1965b, 1968b, 1970) has also demonstrated in adults, as Johnson et al. did in children, that aspects of the body image may provide an organizing influence in recall.

The fact that Johnson et al. (1979) could demonstrate a clearly defined body spatial framework in children as young as age 5 is interesting in light of Story's (1979) evidence of differentiated body image attitudes in children even at age 3. Story pointed out that previous studies had observed that children in the 3-5 year range were aware of racial and ethnic differences in body form and even had preferences for certain somatotypes. In her study she surveyed body attitudes in 264 children in the 3-5 age range. The children were administered a test that "consisted of the interviewer pointing to a body part in nude drawings of a child of the same sex and race as the child being interviewed and asking, 'Do you like your _____?' " (p. 52). This was repeated for 16 body parts. With the use of the drawings, each child was also asked, "What part of your body do you like best? Why?" and "What part of your body do you like least? Why?" Story was impressed with the ability of the young children to make the differentiated body judgments requested of them. Indeed, when 38 of the children were retested after 2 weeks, a retest reliability coefficient of .91 was obtained. Also, significant sex differences emerged. Girls more often liked best their hair, eyes, nose, and mouth; boys favored their arms and genitals. No relationships were found between body part preferences and the following variables: height, weight, body build, race, education of head of household, birth order, and number of siblings. Boys were significantly more favorable in their body judgments than were the girls, and children of nudists were more favorable than children of nonnudists.

Overall, the studies just reviewed suggest that children in the early years slowly and gradually accumulate knowledge concerning their interior anatomical constructions. Until age 9 they seem not to have an articulated awareness of more than four or five internal organs. These organs are generally the heart, the parts of the digestive system, and the brain. There is also an early awareness of the bones. The heart seems to be particularly prominent in the early schema of the body interior. There are indications that exterior body parts (like arms and legs) are learned earlier than interior parts. After age 9, learning speeds up concerning body anatomy, and the understanding of organ functions becomes relatively sophisticated. That Williams (1979) found patterns of body knowledge in Phillipine children to be similar to those observed in the United States suggests some cross-cultural constancy in the process of learning about one's body. At the same time a few cultural differences did emerge. For example, Williams observed more references to reproductive organs than had been reported for United States samples. It is not apparent what it is that determines the sequence in which knowledge concerning the major internal organs is assimilated. Why is there a trend to be more aware of, and knowledgeable about, the heart than about the stomach? Children certainly have more salient daily experiences with the stomach than the heart, yet this is not reflected in the apparent prominence of the two organs. It is doubtful that parents explicitly declare, "Your heart is more important than your stomach." However, they may in more subtle and concealed ways communicate the life and death centrality of the heart. We need to learn a great deal more about the nature of such subtle and often concealed parental messages about the body.

BODY DIRECTIONALITY AND SPATIALITY

A primary operation in the construction of the body image is learning to distinguish the directional or spatial dimensions of the body. Children acquire spatial markers so that they can identify the front-back, up-down, and right-left coordinates of their bodies. They presumably go on to generalize these coordinates to the surrounding space.[4] Werner (1957) highlighted the role of the body in defining spatial coordinates by citing examples of how the language of directionality often involves body imagery. He pointed out that the Mande (African) group of languages refers to "behind" with the term "the back"; the term for "before" is the same as the word for "eye"; and "in" is defined by the word for "stomach." Relatedly, in English the terms "in back" and "to face" refer simultaneously to the body and to spatial positions.

It is well established that mastery of up-down and front-back precedes that for right-left. Children evidence a clear awareness of up-down and front-back distinctions before the age of 5 (Benton, 1959), whereas right-left discrimination proceeds more slowly. Piaget (1926) indicated on the basis of his studies that children can discriminate right from left on their own bodies by the age of 6 but are not able to make this discrimination on the bodies of others until age 8. Benton too reported that children are capable of making basic right-left judgments about their own body beginning in the 5th or 6th years of life. Belmont and Birch (1963) concluded on the basis of their studies that "the age of 7 appears to be critical for the development of the ability to distinguish left and right in relation to one's own body parts. Subsequent to this age, up to the age of 12, little significant improvement in this ability takes place. . . ." (p. 268).

Long and Looft (1972) initiated a particularly intensive probe into the development of directionality in children. They administered to 70 male and 70 female children (ages 6-12) a battery of 125 items concerned with ability to demonstrate knowledge of various spatial directionalities in relation to self and also non-self objects. On the basis of their findings they outlined the following progression:

Age 6   Children are fully aware of the vertical and horizontal reference perspective; beginning to develop a sense of laterality, but it is basically egocentric.

Age 7   Development of laterality is "more refined." Children demonstrate ability to make references to both sides of the body simultaneously.

Age 8   Laterality is becoming decentered. Children relate body laterality to other objects and are capable of utilizing body reference for directional definition of the other object (e.g., "the key is on *my* left"). However, if their position is altered by moving to the opposite side of the table, they state that the referent object is still in the same position in relation to the adjacent object. They can use body laterality as a directional reference (e.g., "draw a line to the right").

Age 9   Laterality distinctions of considerable complexity are made. "Children could perform successfully in mirroring face-to-face situations involving cross-body reference (e.g., 'touch the right ear with left hand')" (p. 379).

Age 10   "Children could indicate correctly the right and left of the opposite subject facing them. This clearly implied that the children at this age have achieved the ability to view an object from different perspectives and, in normal situations, to free themselves from using their body as reference" (p. 379).

Long and Looft and also Wapner and Cirillo (1968) indicated that the full development of skills with reference to right-left directionality is probably not attained until the age of 14 and perhaps even as late as age 16. The earlier mastery of the up-down direction as compared with right-left is considered by Long and Looft to be a function of "the influence of gravity. Perhaps the human organism's necessary change from a prone to an upright posture compels him to appreciate the pervasive nature of this frame of reference early in life" (p. 379). Piaget and Inhelder (1956) suggested that the differentiation of right and left is difficult simply because they are manifestly so similar (symmetrical).

Interestingly, it has been learned that when persons are asked to face and imitate a model making right-left movements, the imitation may proceed in two different ways. A mirror perspective may be adopted, which assumes quite simply that the hand opposite one person's right must be the other person's left. Or the imitation may involve imagining that one has rotated one's body 180° in space and occupied the body position of the other. With increasing age the strategy of transposing one's body becomes the preferred method for making right-left decisions. Gellert (1967) reported that by the age of 10 about two-thirds of children (N = 388, with approximately equal numbers of boys and girls) she studied made their right-left decisions on the basis of 180° transposition and that girls shifted to the transposition strategy earlier than boys did. Melnick (1974) wondered whether the transposition method might not be more kinesthetic, that is, body related, than the quasi-mathematical structure that "your hand must be the opposite of mine because we are facing opposite" (p. 467). The considerable skill that eventually evolves in the adult with respect to identifying the right and left sides of one's own body has been shown by Cooper and Shepard (1975) in the adeptness subjects display when judging the right or left identities of line drawings of hands presented in different versions (palm or back of hand) and orientations.

Aside from the directional parameters just reviewed, there are findings that bear on developmental changes in the organization of the body as a spatial object. These findings derive from studies of the effects of distorting lenses on body perception. When viewing the world through lenses that displace the visual field in a certain direction, people quickly adapt and learn to compensate for the displacement. For example, if the lenses shift the field to the right, they will at first aim too far to the right when reaching for an object. However, after a period of inspection not necessarily involving motoric trial and error, they are able to correct their aim. When the lenses are removed, there is an initial tendency to continue the compensatory strategy, and this is expressed in biased aiming that is too far left. This bias too quickly disappears.

Harris (1965, 1966) concluded from his examination of the pertinent literature that adaptation to visual displacement is due to a change in the perceived spatial position of one or more parts of one's body. In commenting on the compensatory response of the individual to a right displacing lens after adaptation has occurred and the lens has been removed, Harris (1966) remarks:

> Is this adaptation a change in visual perception? Does the adapted person reach farther left because he now sees things farther to the left? The answer, I think, is no; he reaches farther left because he now feels that his arm is farther to the right than it really is. While he was looking through the prism, he saw the hand to the right of its actual location; after adapting, he feels that it is to the right of its actual location. . . . His positional sense has been modified, so that a given physical position of the arm now gives rise to a different proprioceptive perception of that arm. (p. 5)

In other words, the visual experience produced by the distorting lens has resulted in a revision of the body's spatial scheme. The apparent position of one's arm in space has been modified. Harris adds: "My experiments and reinterpretations of Kohler's[5] and Stratton's[6] . . . indicate that purely visual perception does not change radically during adaptation to optical distortions. And the sense of position and movement of the body, far from providing a reliable access to reality, proves to be extremely flexible and easy to deceive. Instead of serving as a source of trustworthy information with which to rebuild reversed or inverted vision, the position sense itself becomes inverted or reversed" (p. 21).[7] Harris' theoretical position has been both affirmed and opposed to some degree by others (e.g., Putterman, Robert, & Bregman, 1969; Rock, 1966; Wallace, 1980). Rierdan and Wapner (1966) have specifically criticized it as being too simplified in the sense that it neglects changes that lens distortions also produce in object perception. Although similar criticisms have been offered by others (e.g., Quinlan, 1970; Wilkinson, 1971), there is still widespread agreement that one of the effects of lens distortion of the perceptual field is to alter body perception significantly.

Mandell (1979) conducted a fascinating study of developmental changes in lens perception. His perspective was similar to Harris' in that he assumed that lens-induced shifts would result in compensatory changes in the body scheme. Before we detail the work he undertook, it is necessary to outline some earlier findings that provided a framework for his approach. Mandell and Auerbach (1975) demonstrated that when people adapt (during prism displacement) to pointing with their right index finger to a nonbody target, the degree of adaptation is greater than when one points to a part of one's own body (viz., left index finger). That is, there is greater compensatory shift in the apparent position of the right finger when pointing to an external target than when pointing to another part of one's own body. Further, there is less compensatory shift in the left finger when the right finger is pointing to the nonbody target and more in the left finger when the right is pointing to the left.

This pattern of findings was interpreted to mean that when the right hand is simply pointing to an external target, there is conflict between the lens-induced visual distortion and the proprioceptive experience linked to the pointing finger; and that therefore the apparent position of the right hand has to be altered to integrate the conflict. But when the right hand points to the left hand, presumably a new kind of sensory input (from the left hand) is introduced; and, because of the more extensive body involvement, this input recruits the central body schema into the process of resolving the conflict (between distorted vision and accurate proprioception). The body schema is said to aim at preserving the existing spatial integrity of the body and therefore to tend to minimize potential alterations resulting from conflictual sensory input. Thus, the right finger pointing at the left is "constrained" by the body scheme to a minimal change in spatial position. However, because this situation, in contrast to the one in which the right hand points to an external target, more directly involves the left hand in the conflict resolution process, the left also shares more in the apparent shift in spatial position.

It was in the context of such findings from an adult population that Mandell (1979) studied the degree of right and left finger spatial adaptation following lens-induced visual versus kinesthetic conflict in three age samples (4.0-4.11; 5.0-5.11; 6.0-6.11), each containing 20 children (approximately equal numbers of boys and girls). In addition to the lens distortion tasks, the children were administered the Draw-A-Person Test (scored by Goodenough criteria) and a Finger Differentiation Test developed by Kinsbourne (1978), which measures ability to make judgments about the positions of one's fingers. One of the prime findings was that children in the youngest age group (4.0-4.11) did not show greater adaptive shifts in the right hand when pointing to an external target than when pointing at their own left hand. This fulfilled Mandell's expectation that: "Without the powerful, unifying impetus of a well-integrated body schema, it was hypothesized that younger children, who lack a well developed body schema, would respond and adapt to a part of their own bodies in much the same way they respond to objects in the environment" (p. 144). The same absence of a well-integrated body schema in the very young was offered as an explanation for the further finding that in the 4.0-4.11 sample there was little evidence of adaptation in the left hand when the right hand pointed at it. Mandell (1979) notes: "Without a well developed body schema, awareness of a violation of normal constraints of the body is less clearly perceived, and will not require generalization of the adaptive shift to preserve the integrity of the body schema. Thus, little adaptation is expected of the left hand, whether it serves as the target for the right hand or remains completely unexposed" (pp. 83-84). The 6-year-olds displayed an adaptation pattern similar to that found in adults, and the 5-year-olds were roughly intermediate between the younger and older samples in their conformance to the adult pattern.

What is most striking is that the data reveal a transition, such that the youngest respond to their body as if it were a nonbody object; the next older group shows greater differentiation of the body and nonbody; and the oldest group evidences an even greater sense of difference. The adaptive pattern shown during the prism distortion condition in which children pointed to the left hand with the right proved to be even more highly correlated with the two measures of body schema development (viz., Draw-A-Person and Finger Differentiation tests) than with age. It was shown that the greater the apparent maturity of the body schema, the more likely were the children to display the adaptation pattern characteristic of adults. That is, the more likely they were to respond as if a central body schema were involved in the adaptation process. That the figure drawing index was linked to the complex lens adaptation pattern in this fashion adds a special bit of support to the construct validity of the figure drawing as a measure of body concept. Mandell's work documents the increasing tendency of the maturing child[8] to respond to his or her body differently than to nonself objects. The maturing process involves the construction of a central body schema that preserves certain special perceptual conditions for one's body as against other objects in the world. This body-nonbody distinction is documented by Shontz' (1969) studies, in which size perception of one's body is typified by rather unique properties. It is pertinent that Shontz has shown that a higher level of body schema development, as represented by a comparison of normals with persons who are intellectually retarded, is accompanied by a greater distinction between how one perceives the size properties of one's body as contrasted to those of nonself objects. Retarded persons seem to apply the same judgmental frame of reference to objects "out there" as they do to their own body space.

Another major developmental study of adaptation to lens distortions was carried out by Devoe (1969). He was particularly interested in the relative degree to which alterations in body as compared with object perception occur in children of different ages as they adapt to vision rearranged through (left) displacing prisms. Ninety children were appraised, 30 in each of the age groups 6-7, 9-10, and 13-15. Equal numbers of boys and girls participated. Subjects' responses to the lenses were measured in relation to contexts that varied with respect to how much they called for using body versus object cues. The major conditions were as follows: (a) a visual measure of object perception that called for judging the position of true horizontal; (b) a kinesthetic measure of object perception that required pointing to a visual target; (c) a kinesthetic measure of body perception that involved pointing to what appeared to be the "straight ahead" (midline of one's body projected out); (d) a visual measure of body perception that required the subject to judge when an external object appeared to be "straight ahead." The overall findings were interpreted by Devoe as follows:

> Adaptation to re-arranged vision, for 6–year-olds, involves changes in body perception, but not in object perception. Conversely, for 14–year-olds, adaptation to re-arranged vision involves changes in object perception, but not in body perception. To be more specific, 6–year-olds adapt to prisms through changes in body perception . . . which serve the function of making the environment to appear normal . . . 14–year-olds . . . adapt to prisms by maintaining stability of body perception which allows flexibility of object perception. For 10–year-olds, adaptation . . . involves neither changes in body perception, alone, nor changes in object perception, alone, but simultaneoous changes in both body perception and object perception. (p. 141)

The Devoe data indicate that the Mandell (1979) findings are oversimplified in their suggestion that by the child's age of 6 the more "mature" mode of integrating visual distortions with the body image framework has been achieved. Devoe's (1969) study indicates clearly that the maturational process continues and that further changes occur, as evidenced by adaptive differences even between children in the 9-10 versus 13-15 age categories. The nature of the differences among the age groups indicates that with increasing age the response to the lens distortions moves more and more in the direction of maintaining body image stability. Children in the 6-7 range readily alter body perception in order to "balance" the discrepancies created by the distorting lenses. However, those in the 13-15 range hold fast to the existing body image framework and "balance" discrepancies by altering perception of objects "out there." This pattern is congruent with the Mandell (1979) results, which also suggested that with increasing age adaptation to lens changes was increasingly a function of restrictions imposed by the body schema. There is a developmental trend to give priority to the maintenance of the stability of the body perceptual field.[9]

BODY ATTRACTIVENESS

Children learn quickly that the attractiveness of one's body powerfully affects others' responses. Standards of body attractiveness are assimilated at an early age. Cross and Cross (1971) asked judges ($N = 300$) of various ages (7 to adult) to rate the facial beauty of facial photographs. Surprisingly, the ratings were not significantly linked with the age levels of the judges. The younger subjects were apparently using the same standards as the older ones. Dion (1973) reported that children ($N = 65$) in the 3-6 age range distinguished pictures of their peers in a fashion congruent with adult standards of what is attractive. She felt that her data indicated that the "rudimentary distinctions between 'pretty' versus 'homely' people begin very early in the child's social development" (p. 188). The children in Dion's sample preferred "attractive" peers as friends and inferred that they were more likely to behave in a prosocial fashion than would the "unattractive." Dion and Berscheid (1974) noted in a sample ($N = 77$) of children in the 4-6 age range that definite like-dislike attitudes were manifested toward peers as a function of how physically attractive or unattractive they were considered to be. Cavior and Lombardi (1973) had children ($N = 62$) in the 5-8 age range rank full-length photographs of persons (either 11 or 17) years for physical attractiveness. The rankings of the two categories of photographs had been previously judged by peers of the same ages. It was found that the rankings made by the 5-year-olds did not correlate significantly with those of the peer groups. However, by age 6 the correlations were significant, and there was an increase in such correlations up through age 8. Styczynski (1976), comparing children's (ages 3, 5, 7, 9) ratings of the attractiveness of facial photographs with parallel ratings by adults, found significant agreement, except in the case of the 3-year-old raters. The studies just enumerated suggest that children perhaps as young as age 3 are aware of the distinction between what is and what is not physically attractive. They also have fairly well-developed social attitudes toward people so categorized.

Highly structured biases, either for or against certain body types, have also been shown to evolve at an early age and to persist through life. Numerous studies (e.g., Kirkpatrick & Sanders, 1978; Lerner, 1973; Lerner & Schroeder, 1971b; Staffieri, 1967, 1972) have established that mesomorphs are most positively evaluated and endomorphs most negatively. Ectomorphs are usually assigned an intermediate position. The stereotypes of these body configurations are rather rigid and highly generalized. All kinds of pleasant, good, and rather heroic qualities are ascribed to the mesomorph. The endomorph is doomed as bad, lazy, mean, dirty, and stupid. Ectomorphs often are dismissed as lonely, sad, weak, tired, and sneaky. Girls seem to be relatively more favorable than boys toward the ectomorph.

As mentioned, sterotyping of body types begins at an early age. It has been shown to occur quite consistently in children as young as 5 and 6 (e.g., Lerner, 1972a, 1972b; Lerner & Gellert, 1969; Lerner & Schroeder, 1971b; Staffieri, 1967) and to become stronger well into late adolescence (Lerner, 1972a, 1972b). It has also been observed to occur in cultures outside of the United States (Lerner, 1972a, 1972b). If children evolve rather definite biases about the goodness-badness of various body types, how does this affect their own body perceptions? Do children of endomorphic build view their own bodies more negatively than do mesomorphic children?

Lerner and Korn (1972) approached this issue by testing two alternate hypotheses. They reasoned that children with the negative body type could either accept the prevalent negative evaluations of their body and all the associated "bad" connotations or defensively reject them. They studied three groups of males (ages 5, 15, 20). In each group there wre 30 "chubby" and 30 "average build" males. The subjects were asked to rate side-view drawings of an endomorph, a mesomorph, and an ectomorph with a series of positive and negative terms. Later they applied the same list of adjectives to themselves. In a second session, they were asked to choose from the side-view drawings the stimulus they "most looked like" and "most wanted to look like."

Analyses of the data indicated that the chubby subjects at all age levels viewed themselves at having relatively few of the qualities usually linked with the endomorph. Lerner and Korn (1972) reported "These data suggest that chubby subjects maintain a rejecting negative valence toward their body build. While showing evidence of aversion for their own build, chubby males express an affinity . . . toward a physique other than their own. Thus, in no age group do chubby subjects have their highest assumed-similarity scores associated with the Endomorph, and in all age groups their assumed-dissimilarity scores for the Endomorph are higher than that for the Mesomorph" (pp. 10-11). The chubby boys in all age groups were less accurate in identifying their true body type than were the average build boys. Lerner and Korn considered the overall results to signify:

> Having comparable knowledge of the parameters of body-build stereotypes, subjects having unfavored or favored physiques are differentially affected. The former rejects the association between the stereotype and their own behavior. . . . On the other hand, subjects having a favored physique appear to accept the relevance of the stereotype to their own behavior, prefer to have the physique they possess. . . . Thus, it appears that as an indirect effect of the body-build stereotypes a negative body concept is inculcated in chubby children, while in average children a positive body concept is formed. These indirect effects appear to be relatively stable within the age range sampled. (p. 12)

The defensive ("I am not really chubby") stance detected by Lerner and Korn (1972) in chubby boys had also been reported by Lerner and Gellert (1969), who found that chubby children were less able to identify figures matching their own chubbiness than they were to match such figures correctly with the chubbiness of peers. One wonders how much negative information about the body that is being continually communicated by others can really be defensively filtered out by children. It would be surprising if the filtering process could be even moderately effective, especially since exposure to self-perceptions (e.g., in mirrors) is inexorable in its reinforcement of what is being relayed by others. However, the research data pertinent to this matter give mixed messages. Cavior (1970) discovered that when children (5th and 11th grades) rated their own physical attractiveness, their judgments had only chance correlations with how their classmates rated them. Berscheid and Walster (1974), summarizing several other studies dealing with the accuracy of adults in evaluating their own physical attractiveness, concluded that it attains only a "trivial" level. Howitt, Stricker, and Henderson (1967) secured objective measures of the esthetic appearance of the teeth of high school students and compared them with the students' self rating of their teeth. Correlations were significantly positive but low (.25–.35 range). Berscheid, Dion, Walster, and Walster (1971) could not detect a significant tie between the physical attractiveness of men and women (as rated by outside observers) and their self rated attractiveness (as measured by the Secord and Jourard, 1953, Body Cathexis scale).[10]

These studies seem to indicate that children and adults are capable of building up and maintaining private images of their own appearance even when the feedback from others is not congruent. However, despite the demonstrated ability of people to deceive themselves in this fashion, it also is true that they are influenced negatively to some extent by undesirable body attributes. In their original studies, Secord and Jourard (1953, 1955) found evidence that men who were unusually small or women who were unusually large were particularly likely to rate their bodies negatively.

Relatedly, Oscarson (1969) classified 225 girls (5th, 7th, 9th, 11th grades) into endomorph, mesomorph, and ectomorph categories and also assessed, by means of incomplete sentence technique, how positively or negatively they perceived their bodies. The endomorphs and ectomorphs proved to have significantly more negative body perceptions than did the mesomorphs. Also, the endomorphs tended (not significantly) to be more negative in their self-perceptions than the ectomorphs. Oscarson found that children's accuracy in identifying their own body type did not vary as a function of their actual type[11] or their age. It is pertinent too that the accuracy with which subjects could identify their own body type was not significantly related to how positive their self-body appraisals were.

Blyth et al. (1981) surveyed 274 seventh-grade boys by measuring various of their body attributes (e.g., weight, height) and also their amount of dissatisfaction with such attributes. There was a significant trend for satisfaction with height to be positively related to actual height. With respect to weight, both heavy and light boys were more dissatisfied than medium weight boys and the more obese were especially dissatisfied when compared with their leaner peers. Other studies have shown that obese children have negative body attitudes (e.g., Hendry & Gillies, 1978). (Also, see the section on obesity for similar findings in adults.)

One is left with the overall impression that, although a good deal of self-protective denial of one's negative body attributes occurs in children (and adults), the possession of such attributes is eventually likely to result in negative feelings about one's body. Children who are appreciably overweight are particularly likely to encounter intense disapproval and bias, which ultimately are translated into a sense of possessing an inferior body. There is little doubt that the child whose body deviates grossly from the norm, especially in a disapproved sense, will have problems in body image construction.[12] What we know is that the disapproval from "out there" becomes interiorized and results in rejection of one's own body. However, we know little about other possible effects. For example, is body boundary formation or body concept differentiation disturbed? Do special difficulties arise from consistently labeling one's body as masculine versus feminine? Does external ridicule result in a low threshold for anticipating body damage? These are questions that require exploration.

Another matter pertinent to the issue of perceived body attractiveness is whether there are developmental trends. Do young children differ from older ones in how positively or negatively they appraise their bodies? Several studies have examined body evaluations by self in the sequence from early to late adolescence.[13] They have employed the Secord-Jourard (1953, 1955) Body Cathexis Scale. Clifford (1971) gave a modified version of the scale to 146 male and 194 female children ranging from 11 through 19 years. There was a general tendency, as there is in most studies of adults, for self-appraisals to be more on the positive than on the negative side. No real differences were observed as a function of age level. Speer (1969) evaluated 192 boys in the 10th, 11th, and 12th grades and concluded that differences in Body Cathexis scores were not linked with age. Pomerantz (1979) examined 100 males and 100 females in each of the 8th, 10th, and 12th grades. No significant age differences in their body ratings appeared. Brunn (1975) did find in a highly selected group (N = 47 male, 72 female) of neglected, institutionalized children (age range 11-18) that the older subjects were less likely than younger ones to express high approval of their bodies. In view of the special character of this sample, one should probably not give much weight to the age difference that appeared. It seems from the data obtained by the Clifford, Pomerantz and Speer studies that there are no clear age differences in how positively or negatively 11- to 19-year-olds view their body.

All four studies just cited came up with evidence that girls rate their bodies more negatively than do boys. This same pattern was found in another study involving children as young as 3-5 years of age (Johnson et al., 1979). It has also been observed in adult populations (e.g., Johnson, 1956; Jourard & Secord, 1955; Schwab & Harmeling, 1968; White & Walsh, Jr., 1965). There has been speculation that the more self-critical attitude of the female toward her body reflects the special cultural emphasis on judging women strictly in terms of their physical appearance and their conformance to standards of beauty and fashion.

STRUCTURING BODY PERCEPTIONS

Body Construction

Most of our information about how children perceive their own bodies comes from nonverbal measurement procedures.[14] Two have been most widely applied: (a) figure construction or assembly and (b) figure drawing.

The figure construction approach asks children to construct a human figure (e.g., with clay) (Golomb, 1972) or to assemble a human figure from a series of body part representations (Gellert, 1975). Researchers have been generally impressed with the accuracy of figure constructions, even for very young children. In a study of 142 children ranging in age from 2 to 4 years, Wallach and Bordeaux (1976) found that children asked to assemble the parts of a human manikin displayed high accuracy by the age of 4. This finding contradicted a previous report by Premack (1975) that none of 10 children he studied (ages 28-45 months) could appropriately assemble the photograph of a human figure that had been cut into six parts. Golomb (1972) too observed in a sample of Israeli children ($N = 125$) that children by the age of 4 could create substantially recognizable human forms with play dough.

Brown (1975) evaluated the human figure constructions of 406 children over the age range from 3 through 11. Several judges rating the figure constructions found that the greatest improvement in the construction of the figures occurred between the ages of 3 and 6. Also, girls consistently produced figures that were superior to those of the boys. The following summary observations were made.:

> Three-year-olds rarely (18%) made recognizable figures or heads. . . .
> Four-year-olds . . . made four times as many recognizable figures as did the three-year-olds. The figures began to include a noticeable trunk, forehead, chin, arms, and legs. . . . By age five there was a noticeable increase in the percentage of recognizable figures. Again, the features: eyes, nose, and mouth were drawn into the heads. The presence of a neck, shoulders, feet, and ears became noticeable at age five. (p. 51)

Brown noted that from age 9 through 11 there were few significant changes in the figure constructions.

The most elaborate investigation of children's figure constructions was carried out by Gellert (1975). She asked 250 children (ages 5-13) to use an array of body part representations to construct a figure that would be "as much like you as you can." The representations involved 35 cardboard pieces that varied from extreme diminution to extreme exaggeration of correct size. With one exception, all children were able to assemble a recognizable human form. Improvement in performance was shown until age 10, when it apparently attained an asymptote. It is interesting that the accuracy of figure constructions was not correlated with intelligence and was not linked with sex differences. There were certain patterns of error shown that Gellert thought might reflect corresponding distortions in children's body perceptions. They may be summarized as follows:

1. The head size of figures was consistently overestimated. Such exaggeration of head size by children[15] has been well documented by other approaches (Fisher, 1970).

2. There was a notable tendency to omit and misplace the arms and hands. Of the youngest children, 21% omitted the arms and 8% the hands. In about 5%, the hands were attached directly to the trunk, with no intervening arms. Forty percent in the younger age groups attached the arms near the midpoint of the trunk or below it. In the very youngest, this percentage was as high as 79. Thus, the majority of the 5-year-olds apparently perceived the juncture of the arms to be near the horizontal midline of the body. Twenty-two percent of all the children chose right and left hands that differed grossly in size and were clearly asymmetrical. Such distortions in representation of the upper extremities contrasts with a minimum of distortion in relation to the legs and feet; no child at any age omitted the paired legs. Likewise, the trunk was typically subject to only minor inaccuracies. Gellert (1975) suggested that "the incorrect or omitted representation of the upper extremities may be a developmental state . . . and . . . accurate conceptions of this aspect of the body image are often attained surprisingly late in childhood—or, perhaps not even then. The present findings . . . suggest the hypothesis that the arms and hands may not be as integral or basic to the body scheme as are the head, trunk, and legs . . ." (pp. 319-320).

3. Gellert detected one noteworthy distortion by about 10% of the children with respect to the legs. She observed a trend to locate the legs too far apart at the juncture with the trunk, as though "supporting the body from there as furniture legs usually are placed to provide stable support for the rest of the piece" (p. 321).

Of course, the question arises whether the figure construction technique used by Gellert truly measures how children perceive their bodies. To what extent are the distortions an artifact of the method used? There is no comprehensive answer to this question. One can only point to overlapping findings involving other measurement modes. For example, it has already been mentioned that the exaggeration in head size observed by Gellert (1975) has also been observed in both children and adults by Wapner and others (see Fisher, 1970) using methods that call for direct estimates of the sizes of various body parts. Similarly, the major difficulties that Gellert reported children to have with placement of the arms and the lesser but detectable difficulty with the junction of the legs with the trunk have also been noted in children's figure drawings (Freeman, 1975; Freeman & Hargreaves, 1977; Gellert, 1975; Johnson, Perlmutter, & Trabasso, 1979).

Gellert (1975) made a point of reviewing discrepancies between results obtained with figure constructions and those obtained with figure drawings. The figure drawings of young children frequently depict "spider-like representations which omit the trunk and show the extremities emanating from the apparent head region" (p. 323). Also, children frequently depict the trunk as vague and in unrealistic terms. Neither form of distortion appeared in the figure constructions. Gellert and also Golomb (1972) and Wallach and Bordeaux (1976) are inclined to see figure construction as a more direct way than figure drawing to measure children's body concepts. They suggest that specialized skills are required to create a drawing and consequently distortions that appear in drawings may merely reflect difficulties in expression rather than distortions in concept. There has been, of course, long-standing dispute as to whether a person's drawing of a human figure can be validly taken as a measure of his or her body image. Fisher (1970) reviewed the relevant literature that had appeared up to 1970 and concluded:

> The weight of the pertinent evidence that can be extracted from the literature suggests that the like-sex figure drawing produced by an individual does mirror some aspects of his feelings about his body and perhaps more broadly certain attitudes about himself as a person. Body type, age, physical appearance, and body anxiety do seem, in many cases, to find representation in the individual's drawing. However, the presence of gross body defects is apparently not usually revealed in figure drawings. (p. 72-73)

Since 1970 there has not been much new evidence that directly tests the degree to which figure drawings do tap body image attitudes. Scattered studies suggest that figure drawings are diversely sensitive to whether people are black or white (Jernigan, 1970); the effects of vasectomy (Cord, 1972); the impact of psoriasis (Leichtman, Burnett, & Robinson, Jr., 1981); the increasing masculinity or femininity linked to the maturation of children (Laosa, Swartz, & Diaz-Guerrero, 1974); and (in a limited fashion) the changes induced by pregnancy (Tolor & Digrazia, 1977). Several studies have reported that programs designed to produce alterations in the body image (e.g., perceptual-motor training) resulted in logical changes in figure drawings [David, 1975; de Chiara, 1976; Matthews, 1971; McCarthy, 1973; Potts, 1970; Sunal, 1976]. However, four studies that examined the effects upon figure drawings of "body awareness training" (Bennett, 1980), "movement therapy" (Saks, 1979; Shuman-Carpenter, 1977), and "sensory-motor training" (Maloney & Payne, 1969) reported negative results. It should be noted, though, that two of these four studies with negative results involved retarded persons, whereas none of the studies reporting positive findings included the retarded. Further, extensive work by Witkin and his associates (Witkin, Dyk, Faterson, Goodenough, & Karp, 1962) has shown some logical relationships between figure drawing differentiation and a variety of variables and may be seen as offering some support for the assumption that figure drawings tap meaningful body image dimensions. More is said later about the findings accumulated from the use of the Witkin figure drawing measures.

The strong tendency for children to distort arms and hands in their figure constructions and drawings is striking[16]. We obviously need to learn more about this phenomenon. Fuller, Preuss, and Hawkins (1970) reported that "emotionally disturbed" children were significantly more likely than normal children to distort arms and hands in figure drawings. This was especially true for the item "hand cut off." Koppitz (1966) too noted this phenomenon. Felix and Arieli (1966) studied the "hand image" in children by evaluating their performance on the Hand assembly from the Wechsler Adult Intelligence Scale and also by asking questions that called for identifying and localizing their fingers. They evaluated 197 children, including various sub-samples (e.g., normal, psychotic, brain injured). They found that 4–5 years was the period, "when the child begins to be capable of *spontaneous recognition* and at times also of *partial assembly* of the hand.[17] Age 12 was determined as a ceiling where the functions of recognizing and assembling the hand have been completed and reach their developmental peak" (p. 32). In his extensive investigations of finger localization, Benton (1959) too found that age 12 was the developmental peak. His data indicated that children's skill in identifying fingers is greatest for the two extreme fingers (thumb, little finger) and lowest for the finger next to the little finger. He noted: "The incessant play of hands and feet of the young infant, in the course of which he feels, grasps, squeezes, and gazes at various parts of his body . . . may be looked upon as providing the nervous impulses that form the sensory foundations of his first perception of his body" (p. 130).[18]

A particularly novel approach to exploring the role of the arms, hands, and fingers in the body schema was undertaken by Clapp (1969). He compared 30 normal children with 60 mentally retarded children. The children were in the 3-6 age range, and there were equal numbers of boys and girls. Clapp conceptualized the body scheme as consisting of postural and surface subdivisions: "Postural model schemata are the standard upon which all body movements, body postures, and the maintenance of postural tonicity are evaluated. That is, each new movement or posture is evaluated against, integrated with, and related to previous movements. Surfaces schemata are used in localizing touch and making tactile discriminations on the body" (p. 3). Tasks from a test by Berges and Lezine (1965) were used to measure the arms and hands postural model schemata. These tasks called for the children to imitate 20 gestures made by the examiner with his arms and hands. The children's vision was occluded by special goggles so that they could see the examiner but not their own arms or hands. To measure the finger postural schemata, 16 finger gestures from the Berges and Lezine test were administered in an analogous fashion to the children. Body surface schemata involving the arm and hand were evaluated with a procedure that called for the children (with vision occluded) to identify where a series of touches were applied to various spots on the arms and hands. The body surface schemata for the fingers were similarly evaluated by calling for judgments as to which of a sequence of fingers were touched[19].

Accuracy scores were computed for all of the procedures just listed. The normal children were found to be consistently superior to the retarded in their ability to accomplish all the tasks correctly. However, of special interest was that in all groups there was greater schema development (more judgmental accuracy) for the proximal (hands and arms) body sector than the distal one (fingers). In the normal children there was also significant evidence that the postural model schemata of the hands and arms were more developed than the surface model schemata for the same area. This difference did not occur for the fingers. For normal children the accuracy scores for the surface and postural schemata (pertaining to the hand-arms area) were not significantly correlated, whereas they were significantly positively correlated for the fingers. The findings of this study indicate there may be a differential rate of schema development even for two contiguous regions like the arms and hands versus the fingers. One can detect a difference in not only postural (motor) but also surface (skin sensation) measures. The complexity of the phenomena involved is pointed up further by the fact that, although the postural schemata were apparently more developed than the surface schemata for the arms and hands, this was not analogously true for the fingers. Similar differences in body perception as a function of body locale have been observed with respect to body size judgments (Shontz, 1969) and focus of attention (Fisher, 1970).

If one reviews the previous material indicating that children misrepresent the location of the arms, overestimate head size, and, conversely, manifest relatively less distortion when depicting lower body areas, the possibility presents itself that there may be more difficulty integrating into the body image the upper, as compared with the lower, body sectors. It is not clear why this should be the case. There are, after all, probably as many conflicts and affects associated with the functions of the lower as the upper half of the body. However, it is possible that disturbing conflicts and tensions involving the body arise earlier in relation to upper body functions. That is, the infant may have more early negative experiences with parental figures that are related to eating and oral intake than to the functions of the urinary and anal sphincters. Although control of eating is instituted almost immediately, control of eliminative functions is typically postponed for some time. If one speculates that the body image in its very early stages is, because of its hazy primitive structure, particularly vulnerable to disruption, it is conceivable that the initial problems linked to oral intake (which would involve the mouth and perhaps the hands) could result in a disproportionate distortion in the body concept encoding of the upper body areas. It is apropos to point out that previous research (Fisher, 1970) found the distinction between upper and lower sectors of the body image to be meaningful. For example, it was shown (Fisher, 1970) that when asked to view their bodies in a mirror while wearing aniseikonic[20] lenses, men manifest more anxiety about the upper than about the lower body regions, and women show the inverse pattern. Aniseikonic lenses create the potential for perceiving a stimulus as altered; but, the greater the anxiety linked with the stimulus, the less likely it is to be perceived as altered. Men are more resistant to seeing aniseikonic changes in the upper regions, and women are more resistant to apparent changes in the lower sectors. This same upper-lower sex differences was observed in children by Wittreich and Grace (1955) and Fisher (1970). Fisher conjectured that the difference might reflect a variable like the greater anxiety inculcated in females about motility and movement in space, which would be associated with the legs and therefore the lower part of the body. However, one could entertain the possibility that, in view of the culture's greater acceptance of oral receptivity (passivity and taking) in the female (Fisher, 1973c) than in the male, parents might, from the outset, be less positive and more conflicted about feeding male than they are about feeding female infants. This is, of course, pure speculation, but other unusual selective behaviors by parents toward male as compared to female children have been documented (e.g., Rothbart & Maccoby, 1966). In any case, it is worthwhile to consider that there may be an up-down body image gradient with respect to the impact of early socialization experiences.

BODY IMAGE AND COGNITIVE SKILLS

Many have urged that children cannot master cognitive skills until they have developed an adequate concept of their own body (e.g., Ayres, 1961, 1965; Cratty, 1964; Frostig, 1975). There is certainly evidence that children use body parts to mediate mastery of counting and number concepts (Saxe, 1981). A number of speculative attempts have been made to link learning disabilities with body image defects. However, the pertinent data are confusing and difficult to interpret. Hallahan and Cruickshank (1973) reported after an intensive analysis of the pertinent literature that it was still an unsettled question whether perceptual-motor training improved various kinds of cognitive functioning in children. They felt that despite the existence of numerous studies, the great majority were seriously flawed or contradictory. Inasmuch as one of the most important goals of perceptual-motor training is to strengthen the body image, the Hallahan and Cruickshank review obviously bears on the issue whether body image variables are important in the development of cognitive skills. Hallahan (1975) concluded after a literature analysis that there was little relationship between body image parameters (e.g., right-left orientation) and ability to read. However, to illustrate the contradictory perspectives that exist in this area, Croxen and Lytton (1971) presented data from their own studies and those of others (Belmont & Birch, 1965; Benton & Kemble, 1960; Lovell & Gorton, 1968; Shearer, 1968) that suggested that children with reading disabilities are relatively poor not only in right-left discrimination but also in finger localization. The matter takes an even more confusing turn with Fletcher, Taylor, Morris, and Satz's (1982) data from a large-scale longitudinal study of boys (starting at age 5) in which finger localization did predict reading achievement, but more as a function of its correlation with certain developmental parameters rather than of its body image component. They isolated a "somatosensory differentiation" factor that loaded significantly on finger tapping and right-left discrimination. Fletcher et al. felt "that there is a unique component to finger recognition performance that is related to awareness of body scheme" (p. 130).

In spite of the confused impression one gets from a broad sweep of this literature, there are a few studies that should be cited on the positive side because they are well designed and encourage further exploration of the issue whether body image factors are basic to cognitive skills.

Curcio, Robbins and Ela (1971) were interested in the role of body experience in the acquisition of number conservation. It will be recalled that Werner (1957) attributed considerable importance to the body as a frame of reference in learning number skills. Piaget et al. (1960) too noted that children use parts of their bodies to measure objects, as if they might acquire conservation of length with their own bodies before generalizing the principle to objects outside of themselves. Curcio et al. observed nursery school children ($N = 167$) as they carried out various number tasks, one of which involved number conservation with reference to both external objects and their own bodies. In the case of number conservation with reference to nonself objects, the experimenter gave the subjects and himself equal numbers of pipe cleaners and placed them in two rows, with one-to-one correspondence, and asked, "Who has more pipe cleaners, you or I, or do we both have the same number of pipe cleaners?" The experimenter then spread his own row out to twice the length of the subject's and repeated the question. When number conservation was tested on the body, the subjects were requested to hold up their hands, palms outward, fingers slightly spread; and were asked, "Do you have more fingers on this hand (left) or on this hand (right) or do you have the same number of fingers on both hands?" Then, the subjects were requested to spread apart their left hand and leave the fingers of the right hand together. Again, the subjects were asked to evaluate the equivalence of the two hands. Significantly more children passed the criteria for number conservation when their own hands were involved than when nonself objects were used. Because this finding did not reveal anything concerning causation, a second study was undertaken to determine if number conservation for nonself objects is built on learning number conservation in the body context. A complicated design was set up in which children were given special training either in number conservation with external objects or with their own hands. The body-oriented training was found to be superior in helping children to attain number conservation, but only if they were already close to the threshold for acquiring number conservation.

Fleming (1967) administered an elaborate battery of intellectual (e.g., Wechsler Intelligence Test for Children) and visual-motor (e.g., Bender Visual-Motor Gestalt) tests and also tasks with body image connotations (e.g., manikin of Wechsler Object Assembly and House-Tree-Person drawing) to children in the elementary school age range. There were 27 boys with normal hearing and 27 with serious hearing impairment. By means of factor analysis, it was possible to demonstrate that body image variables are developmentally integral to the appearance of certain skills. For example, increases of mechanical ability with age were apparently tied to maturation of body image skills. In another instance, the ability to organize "sequential relationships" was linked to body image factors. Fleming concluded that there is a "fundamental relationship of organization of the human body and organization of objects" (p. 48). Deaf children were observed particularly to lag behind hearing children with reference to maturation of the body image.

Teitelbaum (1965) examined whether providing children with the opportunity to heighten and develop their awareness of their bodies and of their functions in space would affect their cognitive skills with respect to spatial directionality. An experimental and two control groups were studied. Each group consisted of 40 boys (ages 6-8) matched for intelligence and initial performance on two tests of spatial concepts (e.g., subtests of Raven Coloured Progressive Matrices). The children in the experimental group were exposed to 15 sessions in which they received intensive training in how to respond quickly and accurately in situations requiring changes of body position (e.g., walking on balance boards, hopping). Special care was taken not to use verbal references that might provide verbal mediators for the body experiences provided to the children. The control subjects participated in a routine physical education program for an equivalent period of time. The experimental subjects showed significantly greater improvement than did the controls in tests of cognitive ability involving spatial concepts. Presumably, the body training received by the experimental subjects developed aspects of the body image, which then facilitated certain cognitive spatial skills. It bears repeating that the study took special pains to avoid giving the experimental subjects any verbal labels for their body training experiences that might serve as mediators for doing well on a cognitive test.

PROMINENCE OF BODY IN SELF-PERCEPTION

We would like to understand the role of body experience in the child's development of a self-concept. No doubt the self-concept is wrapped around the piece of space labeled as "my body." However, we know (Wylie, 1974) that the self-concept is a complex structure that embraces not only "my body," but also social roles, possessions, and personal ties. We lack adequate information as to how quickly the core body aspects of self[21] become overlaid with role definitions and other self definers. There is certainly evidence that attitudes toward self in children are correlated with body feelings. For example, Speer (1969) observed a significant positive correlation in adolescents between self-acceptance and favorableness of feelings toward their own body. Similar findings have been presented for preadolescents by Blyth et al. (1981), Oscarson (1969), Brunn (1975), and McLean (1975).[22] Dujovne (1973) reported a significant positive relationship, even as early as age 9, between semantic differential ratings of self and ratings of one's own body. The magnitude of the relationship was not different from that found in adults. However, the correlation between self and body ratings was significantly higher in girls than in boys.

Several attempts have been made to examine in detail the components of self in children. Montemayor and Eisen (1977) studied 136 males and 126 females (age range 9–18). The Twenty Statement Test (Bugental & Zelen, 1950) was administered. The children were presented with a test form with 20 spaces and asked to write 20 different answers to the question "Who am I?" The responses were scored for 30 different categories (e.g., sex, age, religion, social status). One of the categories, "physical self, body image," included such responses as "I am 5 feet 10 inches", "I am fat." Analysis of the data indicated that at age 10, 87% of the children used a body image self-description. This percentage was higher than that for any other self-descriptive category. However, in succeeding age groups (viz., 12, 14, 16, 18) there was a continuous decline in the body image references (57%, 46%, 49%, and 16% respectively). No sex differences were detected. Obviously, the importance of body imagery in the self-definitions of these children, while gradually declining, remained high through age 16.[23]

Fahey and Phillips (1981) also used the "Who Am I" technique in a study of 2610 Australian children (ages 6–12, approximately equal sex representation). "Physical appearance" was one of the analytic categories applied to the responses obtained. As age increased from 6 to 12, an almost continuous increment in references to one's body was noted (22%, 36%, 40%, 51%, 57%, and 52% respectively). The pattern of increase differs from the declining trend in the Montemayor and Eisen study just cited. However, the two studies agree insofar as both detected a substantial percentage of body references.

Keller, Ford, and Meacham (1978) used four different procedures to sample the components of the self-concept in 3-, 4-, and 5-year-old boys ($N = 24$) and girls ($N = 24$). The children were exposed to the following:

1. They were told, "I would like to write about you. What's the first thing I should put in what I write about you?" This was repeated until 10 statements were obtained.

2. In a second task, the children orally completed sentences that began with such stems as (child's name) is _____ or (child's name) is a boy/girl who _____.

3. The third task elicited from each child a series of self-descriptions. Each series was started by an experimenter self-description and then a

question to the child. The experimenter said, "Now I'm going to say some things about me. And then you can say some things about you. Like this, I can walk. Can you walk?"

4. The fourth task was presented as follows: "Now I'm going to say two things about you and you tell me which one is the best to put in what I write about you." In each instance, one statement referred to the body and one concerned an activity children can perform.

All procedures were administered twice with an interval of 6 weeks. The responses of the children were classified into various categories (e.g., actions, relationships, possessions), one being specifically designated "body image" (e.g., "I have eyes"). It was found that the percentage of body references in the total number of self-references varied a good deal, depending on which of the four procedures had been applied. The more unstructured approaches, exemplified by open-ended questions and sentence completions, elicited the fewest body references; and the other two approaches, with their structured response alternatives, elicited the most. In the 3, 4, and 5 age sequence, the averages of the unstructured test-retest scores for the boys were 9.5%, 4.0%, and 4.5% respectively. For the girls, the comparable averages were, respectively, 3%, .5% and .5%. For the more structured tasks, the comparable percentages for the boys were 22.5, 32.0, and 35.0 respectively; and for the girls, 25.0, 24.0, and 33.5 respectively. It is not apparent why there were such increases in self-references with body connotations in response to the structured tasks. It is interesting, in this respect, that when McGuire and Padawer-Singer (1976) elicited spontaneous written statements from sixth-grade students (127 girls, 125 boys) who were responding to the instruction, "Tell us about yourself," only about 14% of the statements had any body connotations, although girls gave more body references than did boys.[24]

The question whether structured or unstructured inquiry is most likely to elicit from children reports with body connotations is further complicated by the amount of body imagery in certain forms of children's spontaneous expressions. Several investigators who have collected spontaneous stories and other kinds of verbalizations from children have been impressed with the frequency with which the body is mentioned, especially as an object at risk. Pitcher and Prelinger (1963) collected spontaneous stories from 70 girls and 67 boys in the age range 2 through 5 and developed an objective, reliable scoring system for classifying the content of the stories. It was striking that at least 50% of the content directly or indirectly had body connotations, and almost a third of the material referred to the threat of being hurt or mutilated. A few extracts illustrate the flavor of the stories:

The piggie got hit by the choo-choo. He got a little hurt. He broke his neck. He broke his chin. He climbed up a tree. The leaves hurt him. He got hurt on a big cigarette lighter. He put ice on it. (p. 30)

The doggie went away. He jumped over a tree. He hurt himself. Mommy put a band-aid on. He played with his toys. (p. 37)

There was a boy. He hardly even went to the bathroom. And he thought every day and every thought he thought up his head got bigger and bigger. (p. 133)

In summarizing the trends in their data, Pitcher and Prelinger noted:

> Among the twos, the theme is largely concerned with violation of body intactness: over and over again some part of the body is broken or severed. . . . At three the theme of hurt or misfortune is expressed chiefly by objects or people falling down. Sickness and attention from a doctor are new interests at this age. Falling continues prominently at four, and the ambulance and hospital are very popular. With the fives, calamities are more likely to involve acts of God or of nature . . . the damaging force that threatens the child tends to become less personal. (pp. 184–185)

The data indicate too that boys at all ages were more likely than girls to conjure up themes involving body destruction. Themes of death increased progressively from age 2 through 5. References to clothing also showed a trend to increase progressively. However, themes of hurt or misfortune fluctuated irregularly from year to year (highest at 2 and 4).

Ames (1966) collected spontaneous stories from 135 girls and 135 boys distributed over an age range from 2 through 5. Themes of body destruction were found to be among the most prominent. Almost 9% of the children created images with castration implications. Accidents that were destructive to life and limb occurred in 40% of the stories. Harm to people occurred in about 44%, and harm to animals in another 22%. Death was a theme in 19%. Sickness was referred to in about 5%. As in the Pitcher and Prelinger study, boys were generally more likely than girls to depict "castration" themes; but, although there was a decline in such themes with boys the older they were, the opposite trend typified the girls. Death themes increased slightly with age for both sexes, except at age 5. It was further noted: ". . . all ages combined—falling down and being dead or killed or eaten up led for girls; things being broken, falling down, things smashing, pushing or crashing into other things, and being dead or killed led for boys" (p. 391).

Maurer (1965) examined a sample of 91 boys and 39 girls (ages 5–14). He asked them straightforwardly, "What are the things to be afraid of?" The great majority highlighted their fear of wild animals capable of hurting and mutilating one's body.

Gottschalk (1979a) analyzed the spontaneous speech of 41 male and 68 female children (ages 6–16). Each child was asked to speak for 5 minutes "about any interesting or dramatic life experiences you may have had"; and the tape-recorded material was scored for various content categories. Anxiety about mutilation and death turned out to be one of the major forms of anxiety expressed by the children. No significant sex differences appeared, nor did clear developmental trends emerge. Neither did the children's mutilation and death scores differ significantly from those found in adult samples.

Bauer (1976) interviewed a sample of 60 children (age range 4–12) that included equal numbers of boys and girls. He recorded their responses to the following communication: "All of us are afraid of something, but we are afraid of some things more than others. What are you afraid of most?" He found that fear of body injury and physical danger were named by 11% of the children in the 4–6 age range, 53% in the 7–8 range, and 55% in the 10–12 range. The children in the 4–6 age range were more likely to mention ghosts and monsters, rather than specific threats to their bodies. However, one could certainly raise the question whether monster images do not convey at least an implicit threat of body damage.

Gochman (1971a) presented data that apparently contradict the findings just cited. He asked 52 girls and 58 boys (ages 7–18) to talk about 11 pictures designed to evoke responses about health relevant themes. For example, there was a picture of a boy tripping over a rock, falling, and hurting himself; another portrayed a mother and a child in front of a medicine cabinet. Gochman was surprised to find that the mean number of health references elicited by the pictures was extremely low. He detected neither age nor sex differences in such references. It is not apparent why he found so little concern about illness and body damage in his sample of children. In other studies, Gochman (1970, 1971b) obtained estimates from children as to their likelihood of incurring various kinds of illnesses in the future. He discovered that the greater the expectancy of falling victim to any one illness, the greater the concern that other illnesses would occur. However, he could detect no real age or sex differences with regard to total expectancy of future illness or expectancy of specific forms of illness.

Campbell (1975) interviewed 264 hospitalized children (ages 6–12) concerning their concepts of illness. There was considerable consensus over the developmental sequence as to the nature of illness. But there were developmental differences too: "The developmental trend in thematic content represents a move away from definitions based largely on feeling states. . . . There is an age-linked increase in precision of definition (reflected in differential reference to the disease concept and specific diagnoses)" (p. 99). Younger children were more likely to include vague, nonlocalized feelings in the illness category, and older children seemed to be more aware of the social implications of getting sick. In a later paper involving the same subjects, Campbell (1978) indicated that, with increasing age, children feel they must act in a more "Spartan" (less emotional) fashion when sick. The degree of Spartan orientation was positively correlated with mother's educational level.

Apparently, the value system of the mother with the higher educational level emphasized self-control and keeping a "stiff upper lip" in the face of illness.

Apropos of the matter of illness, one must remark on the curious fact that children who become sick often feel guilty about it. Bergmann (1965) observed a variety of hospitalized children and noted: "There is in many children's minds a firmly fixed belief that illnesses are self-induced, the well deserved punishment for all sorts of badness, disobedience, disregard of rules, neglect of prohibitions, bodily abuse. Parental warnings against foolhardiness and self-indulgence, cautionary tales, and religious teachings about sin and retribution, wherever they occur, give authoritative backing to these convictions . . ." (p. 80). This guilty pattern of response has also been detected by others (Gellert, 1961; Gips, 1956; Langford, 1948; White, Elsom, & Prawat, 1978) in interviews with children and even further in children's projective responses (Cruickshank, 1951; Schneider, 1960). Kister and Patterson (1980) asked 15 children (roughly equal numbers of boys and girls) at four different age levels (pre-school, kindergarten, second grade, fourth grade) to listen to a story about a child who committed a minor transgression and subsequently suffered from an ailment. The children were then requested to respond to forced-choice questions about the possible link between the transgression and the ailment. Forty to 60 percent of the children perceived the ailment as linked to badness. The younger the children, the more likely they were to focus on such a link. White, Elsom, and Prawat (1978) observed a significant tendency for children to see death as a punishment. Brodie (1974) detected a significant trend in nonhospitalized children: those who were high in general anxiety were most likely to perceive illness as a punishment for misbehavior. The role of guilt in the child's illness experiences is striking, and there are indications that it also colors the adult's fantasies about sickness and body disablement (e.g., Janis, 1958; MacGregor, Abel, Bryt, Lauer, & Weissmann, 1953).

Generally, the data just scanned indicate that body experiences and sensations are relatively prominent in the child's self-perceptions. It is true that the percentages of body-oriented content issuing from various studies differ considerably at times. The methodology used to secure information about self-perception seems to be quite important in determining the amount of body content that is revealed. Even so, in most of the studies the body image content obtained with different approaches attained at least the 25% level.[25] No specific trends in percentage of body content could be detected in relation to age and no consistent sex differences were evident.[26] When there is minimal need for defensive concern about obvious self-reference in what children say, the body imagery in their fantasy material is heavily laden with anxiety about being hurt and penetrated. Themes of body mutilation, dissolution, and destruction are outstanding. There also seems to be a preoccupation with guilt in those who are experiencing illness or disability.

TRANSITIONAL OBJECTS

The preoccupation of children with body threat leads logically to the matter of *transitional objects*. Winnicott (1953) observed that children often pass through a phase (somewhere between 4 and 12 months of age) when they attach exaggerated value to something (e.g., blanket, diaper, teddy bear) that serves a soothing function. He used the word transitional to refer to a level of experience that is neither external nor internal, but rather is an intermediate one to which both sources contribute. A real object can transitionally become the target of internal fantasy, and a new elaborated object is thereby imaginatively produced. Thus, a child may endow an inanimate blanket or teddy bear with loving, lifelike qualities. Although transitional objects have largely been equated with blankets and teddy bears, Winnicott felt that any object, thought, or concept could become one. He stated: "An infant's babbling or the way an older child goes over a repertory of songs and tunes while preparing for sleep come within the intermediate area as transitional phenomena" (p. 89).

Until recently the information available about transitional objects consisted of clinical vignettes and speculation. However, a good deal of pertinent scientific work has begun to emerge. Careful definitions have been formulated. Busch, Nagera, McKnight, and Pezzarossi (1973) proposed on the basis of their analysis of the literature that the following criteria be applied when labeling something as a transitional object: the child's attachment should occur in the 1st year of life and last for more than 1 year; the object should help to diminish anxiety; and it should be distinguishable from objects that satisfy needs directly. Also, the object should have been "created" by the infant rather than by the parents and should not actually be part of the child's body.

Busch et al. observed 40 children in a nursery school setting and interviewed their mothers to obtain pertinent information. It was noted that the typical transitional object is a "soft, malleable object with which the child has had a close association, and which has been an integral part of certain aspects of his life *since birth*. . . . The life experience in which the object was used most, prior to the child's attachment to it, is in going to sleep, and the next most frequent, the feeding experience" (p. 200). The texture of the object seemed to be one of its outstanding discriminating features. First attachment to the object was typically reported to occur around 6 months of age. It was noted: "While the primary transitional object is being handled and fondled by the child, he is usually also sucking on something or engaged in some kind of autoerotic activity" (p. 203). The transitional object was judged to be of greatest importance to the child at the following times: bedtime, periods of stress, when passively inactive, while away on trips for an extended period.

Gay and Hyson (1976) interviewed 20 parents of children with strong attachments to transitional objects and extracted the following:

1. Age of first attachment was largely within the 1st year.
2. Blankets were most frequently chosen as objects.
3. Use of the object was often associated with oral activity like thumb sucking.
4. Loss of the object produced considerable distress.
5. The object was particularly sought when the child was tired, during separation, and when the child was playing.

Gay and Hyson also observed four children in their homes for several hours and rated various behaviors in relation to transitional object use. They found: "indicators of stress were very prevalent before contact with the treasured object, declined somewhat while the children were with the objects, and then sank to control after the blankets were given up" (p. 290). The use of the transitional object seemed to be a successful technique for reducing stress-induced tensions.

Thomas (1980) intensively observed four children (two boys, two girls) who were in the 20–30 month range and who had strong transitional object attachments. The observations took place in a naturalistic nursery setting over a period of 8 months. Limited home observation also occurred. Detailed notes were made of each child's behavior in relation to the transitional object. The data clearly suggested that use of the objects (blankets in this instance) was often triggered by stress. Thomas was impressed with the way the blanket was linked to the body: "An outstanding feature of the children's use of their blankets at times of stress was the degree to which body-connected uses were dominant. At such times, the children used their blankets in tactile exploration, fingering or fondling it, often in combination with stroking themselves with the blanket" (p. 159). She added (pp. 159–160):

> The use of the blanket in fingering and fondling, rubbing and stroking, particularly at times of stress, may relate to the experience of stress on the level of a threat to the child's ego integration, which, for the child at the end of the second year of life, continues to be in terms of body ego. . . . The primacy of body-connected uses in the children's behaviors with their blankets at times of stress suggests that the use of the blanket enables the child to restore a sense of integration and stability in his/her body-image. (pp. 159–160)

Thomas was struck with how often the transitional object became a technique for stimulating the body, creating some sort of sensory input. Presumably, such input increases body security at moments of difficulty.

The transitional object was also observed to be utilized in nonbody ways, e.g., playfully manipulated, assigned a function ("It's an airplane"). Interestingly, Thomas detected a trend for girls to be more oriented than boys to the body input uses of the transitional object and to be more inclined than boys to use the object in combination with close physical proximity to mother. Indeed, boys were said "never to initiate direct physical contact with mother at times of blanket use" (p. 162). Thomas conjectured that the girls exceeded the boys in body-connected uses of their blankets because they experience threat in body terms more than boys do. The Gay and Hyson (1976) study referred to earlier also detected a sex difference in response to transitional objects. The boys were said to use their blankets in situations where there was a battle over autonomy or mother's demands, whereas the girls did so more in situations involving sensed rejection or feelings of guilt. However, inasmuch as there were age differentials between the boys and girls in the small sample studied, it was not at all certain that the observed contrast was due to the sex difference. That a possible sex difference has been spotted in two studies, though, is deserving of special consideration.

There were previous investigations (Gaddini, 1970; Hong & Townes, 1976) that presented data indicating that transitional objects may be most common in cultures where the child receives limited stimulation from mother. But in cultures (e.g., rural Italy, Korea) where mothers stay in unusually close proximity to the young child for an extended period, where weaning is relatively late, and where closer alternate caretakers (e.g., grandmothers) are available, the use of transitional objects appears to be significantly less than in the typical urban United States home in which mother diverts her attention to many outside interests. Gaddini (1970) proposed that infants who have sustained physical contact with mother have less need to create a special symbiotic representation of it via contact with the transitional object. In spite of this implication that attachments to transitional objects are compensation for defects in caretaking, there is evidence that children who do have such attachments to transitional objects are unusually adept at coping with certain stresses. Passman and Weisberg (1975) observed 64 children (24–39 months of age) who varied in their attachments to their blankets. They found that the greater the attachment, the greater the freedom and the lower the distress shown in adapting to new exploratory situations. Several other studies (Lamb, 1976; Passman, 1976; Passman & Lautmann, 1982) have focused on the efficacy of the security blanket versus the presence of parental figures in facilitating the ability of young children to adapt to new situations. The presence of parents (especially mother) seems to have relatively greater reassurance value.

In general, the background of experience with the transitional object does create a framework of security in new contexts. From the perspective of body image theory, it is meaningful to ponder the implications of the attachment of so many children to an inanimate object that is notable for its pliable and texture attributes, that is held close to the body and provides rich sensory input, and that supplies relief from distress when things are not going well.

Thomas' (1980) theory that the transitional object reinforces body security is an attractive one reminiscent of Greenacre's (1953) speculations that adults use fetish-like objects (e.g., shoes, leather goods) in a similar fashion to reassure themselves when they experience threats to their body integrity. That the transitional object is usually held close to the skin and is so often valued by the child for its texture qualities takes on special significance in light of past work by Fisher and Renik (1966) and Van De Mark and Neuringer (1969) indicating that the body boundary may be articulated by means of stimuli applied to the skin. What the child does with the transitional object may be an efficient method for providing continuous boundary reinforcement when it is most needed. As we have already seen, young children are strongly inclined to worry about the potential body penetrating and damaging implications of what occurs in their vicinity and therefore need to develop self-protective strategies. Cramer actually (1975) conceives of the transitional object as becoming almost a phantom appendage to the body: "The infant experiences the transitional object, in fact external to himself, as being somewhat outside, but not completely separate from him. In this sense it is truly an extension of his own body, and the manipulations and 'games' he plays with it are also being played with (a part of) himself" (p. 534).[27]

BODY IMAGE DIFFERENTIATION

As earlier described, Witkin and his associates investigated the development of differentiation in the body concept. Witkin (1965) visualized the average child as starting out with a body perception that is "relatively global" and gradually developing "an impression of the body as having definite limits or boundaries and of the parts within as being discrete yet interrelated and joined in a definite structure." He used several different measures to tap the differentiation variable, but one he frequently applied to children involved measuring "articulation of body concept" (p. 28) in human figure drawings. Children were asked to draw a person and, as a second task, to draw a person of the opposite sex. Articulation was scored on a five-point scale. The most articulated drawings (Faterson & Witkin, 1970) "manifest high form level (e.g., waistline, hips, shoulders, chest or breasts, shaped or clothed limbs, etc.); appendages and details represented in proper relation to body outline, with some sophistication in mode of presentation; appropriate, even imaginative detailing (e.g., young girl in evening clothes, well-dressed man with cigarette, etc.)" (p. 430). The lowest level of articulation was represented by "most primitive and infantile drawings . . . which manifest a very low level of form (ovals, rectangles, sticks, stuck on to each other); no evidence of role or sex identity (same treatment of male and female with, at most, difference in hair treatment, no facial expression, little shaping or clothing)" (p. 430). The differentiation measure based on figure drawings has been shown (Witkin et al., 1962) to correlate well in adults and children with other measures of differentiation (e.g., Rod and Frame Test, Embedded Figures Test).

Faterson and Witkin have demonstrated a clear age progression of greater articulation in the figure drawing representations of the body. They studied two groups: one, 30 boys and 30 girls who were followed from age 10 through 24; and the second, 26 boys and 27 girls who were followed from age 8 through 13. There was increasing articulation of body concept from 8 to 14 years, but increases thereafter were relatively small. The trends were significant for both boys and girls. Interestingly, although the mean articulation level increased from year to year, individual subjects showed a high level of stability in their relative degree of articulation (retest correlations ranging in the high .70s and .80s). Surprisingly, females consistently obtained higher body articulation scores than did males. The same pattern of female superiority in articulation has also been reported by Baker (1967) and Corah (1965); by Weller and Sharan (1971) for Israeli children and by Jegede (1976) for Nigerian children. One exception occurred in a study by Dreyer, Huloc and Rigler (1971), in which 12 boys and 10 girls of adolescent age did not differ significantly in their articulation scores derived from their figure drawings. These children had been followed longitudinally, and a significant increase was noted in their articulation scores from prepubescence to pubescence.

In any case, the overall trend of the sex difference findings based on figure drawing articulation scores is surprising. It is the reverse of the sex difference pattern usually observed when degree of differentiation (also referred to as field independence versus field dependence) is measured by means of the ability to make accurate judgments of the position of vertical in the presence of conflicting cues or the ability to separate an item from a field in which it is incorporated. It is well documented in a range of cultures that adult males obtain higher differentiation scores than adult females, usually beginning at the age of 8 or 9 (Maccoby & Jacklin, 1972; Witkin et al., 1962). The reverse trend, which was found for the figure drawing articulation index, was truly puzzling, and attempts originally were made to explain it as an artifact (Faterson & Witkin, 1970):

> The unexpected reversal is likely a function of the Articulation-of-Body-Concept technique. As the scale is now formulated, details of clothing, hair treatment, special adornments such as jewelry —contribute heavily to Articulation-of-Body-Concept ratings. Such an emphasis is much more characteristic of human figures, especially female figures, drawn by girls than by boys. Thus, females may be expected to earn high Articulation-of-Body-Concept ratings on the basis of such a stylistic difference alone. (p. 433)

However, Coates (1974) doubted that the greater articulation manifested by girls in their figure drawings could be dismissed as an artifact. She reported that, when the Preschool Embedded-Figures Test, which is still another means of measuring field independence, was administered to children in the 3 through 6 age range, the scores for the girls were higher for every age except 6. Similar results were reported by Derman and Meissner (in Coates, 1974), who studied 4-and 5-year-old lower class boys and girls, and also by Weller and Sharan (1971) in an investigation of 5-year-old Israeli children. Maccoby and Jacklin (1974) reviewed all the studies in which the Embedded Figures Test had been administered to preschool children and concluded that there was no evidence that males at this age level obtained more differentiated scores than females.

One is left with the impression that, even by measures of differentiation other than figure drawing articulation, superiority in differentiation emerges slowly for the male and is not clearcut until late adolescence. The picture becomes even further complicated when one considers that a number of studies have now reported that, when differentiation is defined in terms of the figure drawing measure, adult women too obtain articulation scores either equal to or greater than those of men (e.g., Ihilevich & Gleser, 1971; Witecki, 1978). Overall prior to adolescence females definitely exceed males in the differentiation of their figure drawings; and there is also evidence that they may, at some very early ages, equal and at times exceed males in differentiation, even when other measures like the Embedded Figures Test provide the definition. In addition, during the adult years women seem at least equal to males in figure drawing differentiation. But they are definitely less differentiated[28] in terms of various other measures (e.g., Rod and Frame Test, Embedded Figures Test) used by Witkin et al. (1962) to tap the field independence-dependence dimension.

What are we to make of the different patterns of sex differences that are associated with the articulation of body concept index as compared to the Witkin et al. (1962) perceptual measures (viz., Rod-and-Frame and Embedded Figures)? First, the figure drawing index consistently correlates with the perceptual indices. The correlations are generally in the .60-.70 range. The indices do tap a common variable, but they are also obviously different from each other. There are no data suggesting that the figure drawing measure uniquely evaluates a particular pertinent differentiation parameter more or better than the others do. Witkin et al. repeatedly give the impression that the figure drawing score had to do with something called "articulation of body concept." Actually, one can find only a few scattered supportive validity studies, and they do not really add up to a solid case. There is a tacit assumption of face validity in terms of the fact that the figure drawing test calls for creating an image of the human body. However, we know that variables other than the body image variety (e.g., artistic ability) significantly affect the quality of a figure drawing. The truth is that we lack a clear picture of what the Witkin et al. figure drawing index measures. We do have empirical evidence that it correlates consistently with perceptual indices of differentiation. We also know that there is previous research by other investigators that indicates a link between figure drawing characteristics and body feelings and attitudes. As for the Witkin perceptual differentiation indices, we know that they are consistently correlated with measures indicating differentiation in function at many different levels (e.g., cognitive, experiential, personality defenses). They are also correlated (Witkin et al., 1962) with the ability to make accurate judgments about certain body experiences (e.g., two point stimulation, writing on the skin, directionality).[29] In other words, both the figure drawing and the perceptual measures probably reflect an unknown mixture of perceptual and body image factors.[30] However, the fact that they result in opposed patterns of sex differences[37] indicates that they must differ fundamentally in some way. The difference is probably an important one. If one were merely to employ the perceptual indices, one gets a picture of the female as less differentiated than the male from about the age of 8 through adulthood. But the articulation of body concept measure depicts the female as probably more differentiated than the male from early childhood through ages 14 or 15, and at least equal to the male from that point through adulthood.

Interestingly, the sex difference pattern obtained with the figure drawing articulation score corresponds more meaningfully with previous body image research findings than do those obtained with the perceptual indices. Previous research (Katcher & Levin, 1955) suggested that female children develop a clear image of their relative smallness (in comparison with the size of adults) earlier than male children do. Also, Fisher (1970) has summarized findings concerning the body boundary and shown that from the age of 3, girls tend to have more clearly articulated body boundaries than boys do. Indeed, this same pattern persists into adulthood. Other studies (Fisher, 1970) have demonstrated that adult females do not have either a more inferior or a more anxious concept of their bodies than men do. Fisher has proposed that in many ways women feel relatively more secure about their bodies. Body awareness in women has been found to be linked to well-articulated body boundaries, whereas in men it seems to be correlated with indices possibly suggestive of maladjustment. Also, changes in body apearance have been shown to be more threatening to men than to women (Fisher, 1970). In short, the relative strength and hardiness of the female body image that emerge from the body image literature match the developmental sex difference pattern depicted by the articulation of body concept index[32] considerably better than they do the one portrayed by the Witkin et al. (1962) perceptual measures.[33]

With regard to the issue of a sex difference in development of the body image, some observations of Wapner and Werner [34] (1957) should be considered. They studied 119 boys and 118 girls between the ages of 6 and 19. One of the measures they obtained had to do with the children's judging the true vertical of a luminous rod while experiencing body tilt either to the right or left. Wapner and Werner established, in the course of a series of experiments, that as children mature they are increasingly likely to respond to body tilt by displacing apparent vertical in the direction opposite to the tilt.[35] When adults are tested in primitivized states (e.g., schizophrenia), such displacement gives way to seeing vertical as pulled in the same direction as the body tilt. The "mature" response to body tilt is a compensatory[36] perception of vertical as shifted away from the direction of tilt. As Wapner and Werner traced the developmental response of boys and girls to body tilt, they found that girls manifested the compensatory pattern earlier than the boys did. Whereas the girls did so as early as age 12, the boys did not do so until 16-17 years.

A related sex difference has been noted too with respect to judgment of the position of the longitudinal axis of one's body when it is tilted laterally. A number of studies have placed subjects in a darkened room in which they were tilted laterally and asked to adjust a luminous rod so that it corresponded to the position of their body's longitudinal axis. It has typically been observed (Baker, Cirillo & Wapner, 1969; Wapner, 1968a; Wapner, Cirillo & Baker, 1971) that adults tend to perceive their degree of body tilt as greater than it actually is. That is, judgments of body position deviate in the direction of going beyond the true location of the body axis. Children are more accurate in their judgments and do not display as much overestimation of body tilt. Interestingly, there is a trend for children to show a slight decrease in errors from age 7 until about age 13, but between 13 and 15 there is a relatively sudden appearance of the adult pattern of overestimating tilt. At this time the shift to the adult pattern is of greater magnitude for girls than boys. The same sex difference has been observed in adults (Bauermeister, Wapner, & Werner, 1963). Girls are developmentally quicker than boys to adopt the adult set toward locating the positions both of vertical and of one's own body in space under tilt conditions. During such conditions, the angular disparity between perceived vertical and perceived position of the body's longitudinal axis is greater in adults than in children, and is greater for girls than boys in the 13-15 age range. Wapner et al. (1971) interpreted degree of angular discrepancy as an index of "differentiation between body and object space" (p. 175). It is presumed that the greater the degree of differentiation between body and object space the greater the developmental maturity implied.[37]

Witkin et al. (1962) were inclined, on the basis of the results, with their perceptual measures (e.g., rod-and-frame) to portray women as having an inferior body image. Witkin et al. (1954) proposed that the woman's greater "field dependence" might be explained in terms of the psychoanalytic formulation concerning the consequence of the anatomical difference between the sexes. Presumably, the female's discovery that she lacks a penis "plays a decisive role in the psychology of women; that constant unfavorable comparison between herself and the male leaves in the woman, as a sort of narcissistic injury or scar, a permanent sense of inferiority" (pp. 488-489).

This would therefore interfere with the development of a well-differentiated body image; and, consequently, when a woman is called upon to use her body in a situation in which there are conflicting visual cues, she has an inferior source of information. Obviously, the accumulated data from the articulation of body concept studies do not match such a picture of female body inferiority.[38] It is likewise true that previous body image research reviewed by Fisher (1970) and also data emanating from the sensory-tonic group not only do not match the Witkin view, but suggest just the opposite. As earlier cited, several investigations indicate that females express more overt verbal criticism of their bodies than do males (e.g., Clifford, 1971; Jourard & Secord, 1955). Females say they are more dissatisfied with their bodily appearance. It is intriguing that this reversal is specific to a measure based on conscious self-description. All the previous sex differences enumerated, which suggested relatively greater maturity and security for the female body image, were derived from behavioral tasks in which body evaluative implications were not easily discernible to the subject. One could hypothesize that males, because of their basic body insecurity, are more likely to be defensive when asked to report openly whether they have body dissatisfactions. Indeed, the measures often used to tap body dissatisfaction are quite susceptible to social desirability effects (Fisher, 1970). One could also speculate that females are more likely than males to be required by cultural standards to assign importance to their outer attractiveness and therefore to focus on their deviations from accepted norms in this respect. Perhaps both of these factors are contributory.

THE ADOLESCENT SHIFT

What happens to the body image when the developing child becomes an adolescent? There are good theoretical reasons for expecting that adolescence will be a time marked by changes in body feelings and attitudes. The fact that the body is so radically transformed during this period would justify such an expectation. But, further, from the perspective of psychoanalytic theory, adolescence represents a phase in which the child emerges from the latency plateau and experiences a resurgence of urges (especially sexual) that reflect the accelerated sexual maturity of the body. Spruiell (1971) remarked apropos of this resurgence:

> If we think about the endless testing of physical limits and prowess and endurance, of the limits of pain, of the experimental alterations of costumes, of the fascination with the extensions of the body image by way of automobiles and tools, we can see that the middle adolescent is seeking to reconstruct his body image and the images of others, to either rid himself of the representations of the other sex or to settle for them, to free himself from old images out

of his childhood, and above all, to incorporate his newly functioning genitalia as a narcissistic center of his body image. It can then become the focus of his tender contacts with the functioning genital of another, with foreplay subsuming the residual pregenitality. (p. 129)

However, there has been considerable dispute as to whether adolescents do experience a remarkable amount of change or turbulence. One could argue that change is characteristic of all phases of life. The body is constantly in the process of altering. Conceivably, the shifts in the body that occur between certain ages early in the developmental sequence could be experienced quite as radically as those occurring at adolescence. Although there is a longstanding stereotype that adolescents are significantly more disturbed and in turmoil than adults, Weiner (1970) summarized a considerable literature that simply does not fit this stereotype. There does not seem to be convincing evidence that adolescents are more psychologically upset than other age groups.

Investigators have also looked at other indices to determine if there are unusual changes during the adolescent period. The results have been mixed and at times confusing. For example, a number of investigators have looked at self-concept in prepubescents versus pubescents and found little difference. Engel (1959) followed 172 children and Carlson (1965) 49 children longitudinally from preadolescence to adolescence and could not detect real shifts in their self-esteem, as defined by self-ratings. Monge (1973) factor analyzed semantic differential ratings of self on a large sample of boys and girls ranging from grades 6–12 and found: "The evidence for a restructuring of the self concept around and after pubescence was very slight for boys and modest for girls" (p. 391). However, in contradiction to what has just been cited, Simmons, Rosenberg, and Rosenberg (1973) found in a study of children (N = 1917) ranging in age from 8 through 15 that certain self-concept attitudes particularly characterized adolescents. They observed: "To summarize, the results show a general pattern of self-image disturbance in early adolescence. The data suggest that, compared to younger children, the early adolescent has become distinctly more self-conscious; his picture of himself has become more shaky and unstable; his global self esteem has declined slightly . . ." (pp. 558–559). Montemayor and Eisen (1977) analyzed responses to the "Who Am I" test in a range of age groups (9–18). There were 136 males and 126 females. Montemayor and Eisen concluded that adolescents differed significantly from younger children in both the number and kinds of descriptive phrases they apply to themselves. They were more likely to depict themselves with terms that were abstract, interpersonal, future oriented, and psychological and were less likely to refer to self in terms of concrete qualities, physical self, and material possessions. Bohan (1973) has provided a good summary of the contradictions prevailing in many of the published reports concerning variations in self concept in younger versus adolescent individuals.

MENARCHEAL STATUS

Studies addressing body image parameters have, overall, provided evidence that adolescence is a time of altered body perception. In those studies a number of indices were used as markers of significant adolescent body alterations, which vary from the appearance of secondary sex characteristics to the occurrence of menarche (in the case of girls). Several investigations have looked at body image changes in girls as a function of whether they were pre-or postmenarcheal. Koff, Rierdan, and Silverstone (1978) obtained human figure drawings from 87 girls on one occasion when they averaged 12 years of age and then again when the girls averaged 12.5 years. Also administered was modified version of the Secord-Jourard (1955) Body-Cathexis Test, which, instead of asking subjects to rate their own bodies, called upon them to imagine that the girl in their figure drawings was a character in a story and then to imagine how she would rate various parts of her body. At the time of the first testing, 64 of the 87 girls were premenarcheal. Six months later, 34 were premenarcheal and 53 were postmenarcheal. Three groups were extracted for analysis: those premenarcheal on both occasions ($N = 34$); those postmenarcheal at both times ($N = 23$); and those who changed from pre- to postmenarcheal during the 6 months intervening ($N = 30$). The figure drawings obtained were scored for degree of sexual differentiation, as defined by a scale developed by Haworth and Normington (1961).

It was found that girls who changed from pre- to postmenarcheal status showed a significantly greater increase in sexual differentiation scores than did those whose menarcheal status did not change. This was analogously true when sexual differentiation was defined in terms of frequency with which the first figure drawn was the same sex as the subject rather than the opposite. The results from the Body-Cathexis ratings, based on three female body parts (viz., bust, waist, hips), showed the same shift toward femininity, but were of borderline significance. When all postmenarcheal girls were compared with all premenarcheal girls, a similar pattern of differences emerged. This was true even though the groups did not differ in age. Apparently, the experience of menarche initiated changes in the various indices in the direction of greater sexual differentiation and femininity.

Interestingly, Koff et al. (1978) felt their data indicated "that change in body image, rather than being a continuous process, occurs more or less sharply around the time of menarche" (p. 640). The differences linked to the onset of menstruation failed to appear in girls who possessed secondary sex characteristics (e.g., axillary hair, breast enlargement) at the time of retest, but who had not yet experienced menarche. That is, it seemed to be menarche rather than puberty that precipitated the body image alterations presumably represented by the figure drawing and Body Cathexis measures. Koff et al. considered their findings to support Kestenberg's (1961, 1967) view that menstruation is a dramatic event that initiates radical reorganization of the girl's body image around the role of being a woman. They commented on the potential contradictions posed by a previous study (Dreyer, Hulac, & Rigler, 1971) indicating that sexual differentiation of drawings was significantly greater in post- than prepubertal girls[39] irrespective of their menarcheal status. However, they felt that there was no contradiction simply because Dreyer et al. had not controlled for the fact that their postpuberty subjects were older than their prepuberty subjects. Thus, one could not validly distinguish whether the figure drawing differences obtained were due to age or pubertal alterations.

Rierdan and Koff (1980a) sought to replicate and extend the Koff et al. (1978) investigation by analyzing the human figure drawings of 94 girls (grades seven and eight). Forty-nine were premenarcheal and 45 postmenarcheal. The mean ages of the girls in the two categories were not significantly different. The figure drawings were scored for sexual differentiation as they had been in the previous study. Once again, the postmenarcheal girls obtained significantly higher sexual differentiation scores. They also significantly more often drew the first figure to be the same sex as self. There was a significant trend for those girls who had most recently become menarcheal to obtain higher sexual differentiation scores than those for whom a greater period of time had elapsed since the onset of menarche. This finding suggested to Rierdan and Koff "that awareness of sexual differentiation and identity as a focal experience may peak immediately after the onset of menstruation and diminish thereafter as the girl integrates a sense of herself as sexually mature into a broader psychosocial identity" (p. 56).

In another study, Rierdan and Koff (1980b) undertook to test the hypothesis that initial feminizing changes in a girl as she enters puberty are disruptive of the body image and that menarche subsequently provides a means for reintegration. They cited Kestenberg (1967) as theorizing that one way the early adolescent girl (premenarcheal) evidences her anxiety about the beginning changes in her body is by becoming preoccupied with her "external body parts," which presumably represent the changes in concrete form.

They went on to assume that if such is the case they should find in the early adolescent girl's drawings of a female figure an unusual preoccupation with "external" signs of sexual development. They chose as an index of such preoccupation the degree to which the breasts of the figure were depicted explicitly. Four groups of females were studied: 39 sixth graders, 70 seventh graders, 44 eighth graders, and 95 college women. No real differences in breast depiction could be established between the girls who were pre- and postmenarcheal. However, the combined group of early adolescent girls did draw explicit breasts significantly more often than the college women, who represented the late adolescent phase. Rierdan and Koff felt their results:

> . . . support speculation of developmental and clinical theorists regarding changes in body image associated with actual body changes during puberty. That explicit representation of secondary sexual characteristics decreased from early to late adolescence is consistent with our hypothesis . . . that early adolescents emphasize and are preoccupied with body parts whose changes signal the beginning of puberty, while later adolescents, being past the period of most rapid growth and change in body contour . . . have a better integrated and more coherent body image. (pp. 343–344)

This conclusion seems overstated in view of the fact that the only aspect of the figure drawings examined was the manner in which the breasts were depicted. Also, it is puzzling that while the two studies cited earlier concerning pre- and postmenarcheal girls emphatically suggested that this categorization is important in relation to body image changes in adolescents, the Rierdan and Koff's (1980b) study did not find it to be so.

Additional questions are raised concerning the implications of the three studies just cited when one considers the findings of Thorbeck (1978). This investigator applied the Witkin et al. (1962) Sophistication of Body Concept scoring procedure to the figure drawings of 94 girls who fell into three categories: those who had not yet begun to menstruate; those who had begun within the last 6 months; and those who had been menstruating for 2 years or more. No differences could be detected in the body image differentiation scores of the three categories. Neither menarche nor the recency of menarche seemed to have a detectable body image impact. Although the Witkin measure applied in the present study is not the same as the Haworth and Normington (1961) sexual differentiation measure used in the other studies cited, it can logically be expected to detect differences between the pre- and postmenarcheal, in view of the fact that the previous studies assume that the postmenarcheal girl has a more mature, and therefore presumably a more differentiated body image than the premenarcheal girl does.

Haft (1973) too failed to find major body image differences between pre- and postmenarcheal girls. She appraised 190 adolescent girls (ages 12-15). About two thirds had begun to menstruate. The age difference between those who had and those who had not yet started to menstruate was only about 6 months, but it was statistically significant. The following body image measures were secured: (a) Fisher and Cleveland (1958) Barrier and Penetration indices which are derived from responses to inkblots and reflect how clearly and definitely one experiences one's body boundaries; (b) Semantic Differential ratings (Osgood, Suci & Tannenbaum, 1957) of one's body; (c) Semantic Differential ratings of self, ideal self, and other figures. No differences in boundary articulation or body ratings were detected between the pre- and postmenarcheal girls. The girls in the two menarcheal categories could not be distinguished in terms of the body image parameters. The significant difference in age between the two groups raises an issue as to whether age and pre- versus postmenarcheal status were confounded. On the other hand that the difference was only of the magnitude of 6 months diminishes the seriousness of this point.

Warner (1982) analyzed parameters in 31 postmenarcheal and 22 premenarcheal girls (seventh and eighth grades). These parameters were derived from a self-concept scale, an anxiety questionnaire, a body cathexis scale, and a menstrual attitudes questionnaire. No differences could be demonstrated between the groups in satisfaction with female feminine parts, self-esteem, anxiety, or femininity. One significant difference did emerge. Postmenarcheal girls reported significantly fewer masculine/instrumental traits than did the premenarcheal girls. Obviously, the findings did not, in general, suggest that the two groups were really unlike each other.

The Warner (1982) study, when considered in conjunction with Haft (1973) and Thorbeck (1978) investigations cited earlier, raise real doubts about the generality of the apparent body image changes said by Koff et al. (1978) and Rierdan and Koff (1980a, 1980b) to occur as girls pass from the pre- to postmenarcheal phase. If such changes do occur, they seem to be confined to a sex role parameter uncertainly defined by a relatively unvalidated figure drawing measure of sex differentiation and the controversial index based on sex of figure drawn first. They were not detected in the Thorbeck study when the more widely used Witkin Sophistication of Body Concept index was applied to pre- and postmenarcheal figure drawings.

PUBERTAL STATUS

As one surveys other pertinent studies, there does seem to be a trend for body image changes to emerge as a function of the entrance into puberty.[40] Smith and Lebo (1956) reported significant figure drawing differences among 42 boys (ages 12–15) varying in maturity as defined by pubic hair development. The differences were also varied. The more mature boys more often portrayed hair (e.g., beards) "excessively" and also put ties on their figures; the less mature "excessively" depicted "masculine objects such as cigars, pipes, cigarettes, scars, masks, and Adam's apples" (p. 73). However, these findings, although indicating differences, did not fall into any kind of meaningful pattern with respect to a continuum of sexual or body image differentiation.

Oscarson (1969) used an incomplete sentence technique to probe feelings about one's body in 225 girls (5th, 7th, 9th, and 11th grades). Examples of the incomplete sentence stems used to get at body feelings are: My figure——;

My looks——; My clothes——. Significantly greater negative feelings about one's body were found in seventh graders (pubescent) than in any of the other grade levels (both pre- and postpubescent).[41] Also, prepubescents showed less body dissatisfaction than did any of the postpubescents.[42]

A particularly extensive investigation of body image in relation to adolescence was carried out by Harrison (1975). Twenty boys and 20 girls at four different age levels (11-12, 13-14, 15-16, 17-18) were appraised. They were classified into prepubescent, pubescent, and postpubescent categories on the basis of their reports of changes in their body size and the presence of secondary sex characteristics. The following were undertaken:

1. Subjects were asked to estimate the sizes of five different parts of their body and also of five nonbody objects. The procedure for estimation was the same as that used by Shontz (1969).

2. Subjects responded to the Rorschach Inkblots; and the Fisher-Cleveland (1958) Barrier and Penetration scores were computed.

3. Subjects indicated whether they experienced any of a variety of body distortions as defined by the Fisher (1970) Body Distortion Questionnaire.

The results obtained were complex. It was found that pubescents (both boys and girls) had significantly lower Barrier scores (indicating less definite boundaries) than either pre- or postpubescents.[43] Relatedly, pubescents reported significantly more body image distortions than prepubescents (borderline level) or postpubescents. They also underestimated their body size significantly more than prepubescents, but tended (not significantly) to overestimate more than postpubescents did. The results for the Fisher-Cleveland Penetration index indicates that pubescents obtained significantly lower scores than prepubescents, but did not differ from postpubescents; prepubescents had higher scores than postpubescents.

These data portray pubescents as special in their body perceptions, viz., having less definite body boundaries, experiencing more body distortions, and displaying selective body size judgments. Pubescents seem to be relatively less comfortable about their body image experiences. The one finding difficult to place in context is that pubescents had significantly lower Penetration scores (indicating a lesser sense of boundary vulnerability) than did prepubescents. This apparently contradicts the finding that the former have lower Barrier scores than the latter. One can only remark at this point that the Barrier index stands in a much better validated position than does the Penetration index (Fisher, 1970). The Harrison (1975) findings plus those of Smith and Lebo (1956) and Oscarson (1969) suggest that pubescence brings with it certain body image alterations. There are hints that the alterations involve a greater sense of body vulnerability. It is surprising how difficult it has been to establish with any consistency that adolescent body changes are accompanied by body image shifts of large magnitude.

Harrison (1975) also came up with findings indicative of sex differences in response to pubescence. Girls significantly exceeded boys in Barrier score during pubescence, but not during pre- or postpubescence. Surprisingly, however, girls also obtained higher Penetration scores than boys during pubescence and also prepubescence. This was reversed during postpubescence. With regard to body distortion experiences, girls significantly exceeded boys during pubescence, with the reverse holding true during prepubescence. The measure of body size perception indicated that girls consistently overestimated their body size more than boys in all three phases. It is important to add that there were no differences between boys and girls, in any of the pubertal phases, with regard to their size estimates of nonself objects. More is said at a later point about the differentiation of body from nonbody size estimates.

One cannot find a clearcut pattern in the sex differences just outlined. Harrison (1975) contrived an explanation that is so patently contradictory it is not worth describing. What needs to be underscored is that there was an apparent sex difference in the body image adaptation to pubescence. Such data raise the question whether males and females do differ in some fundamental way in how they perceive their changing adolescent bodies. Erikson (1951) administered a play construction task to male and female early adolescents (ages 11-13) and detected differences in the spatial configurations they produced, which he thought reflected differences in how they experienced their bodies. He requested the boys and girls to construct imaginary scenes with an array of standard play materials. The play scenes produced were photographed and later analyzed by means of objective scoring categories. There were marked differences between the sexes with reference to what they fashioned. The boys more often portrayed scenes involving moving vehicles, elevated structures, and settings of linear motion. The girls depicted interior settings, open structures, and static situations. Erikson interpreted these differences as analogous to the sex differentiation in the structure of the genitalia. Presumably, the boys were projecting their phallic perception of their body in their upright and moving play representations, whereas the girls were projecting their vaginal (internal)[44] concept in their depiction of areas that were open and accessible. Erikson was, in essence, assuming that the play constructions provided a measure of the degree to which one experiences one's body in the masculine or the feminine mode. Honzik (1951), Schuster (1973), and Goodfader (1982) were able, but Budd (1981) was unable, to confirm Erikson's observations concerning the differences in the ways boys and girls shape their play constructions. In any case, what has emerged from subsequent work is that the differences depicted by Erikson are not specifically linked to the pubertal body.

Cramer (1975) administered the play construction procedure to 91 children (approximately equal numbers of boys and girls). There were equal divisions into a younger group (mean age = 5.5) and an older one (mean age = 11.5). It was discovered that both the younger and the older groups displayed the same pattern of sex differences as Erikson (1951) originally reported. The sex difference was not unique to the arrival of adolescent body transformations.[45]

A similar conclusion is derivable from a line of research based on the Franck-Rosen (1949) Drawing Completion Test. This test calls for subjects to complete a series of drawings in "any way you like." In a manner analogous to the Erikson play construction technique, the completions are scored for masculinity-femininity in proportion to the degree to which they display phallic as compared to feminine qualities. Phallic is defined in terms of enlargement, expansion, sharpness, protrusion, and activity; and feminine with reference to openness, bluntness, containers, and passivity. These qualities are presumed to mirror underlying differences in the male versus female body experience. A number of investigators (e.g., Franck & Rosen, 1949; Lansky, 1964) have mustered data indicating that adult males and females can be consistently differentiated by the phallic versus feminine nature of their design completions. However, what is of immediate interest is that the differentiation does not suddenly occur at the time of adolescence. It has been shown in children as young as 7 years (Harkey, 1978). Harkey described a sex difference with reference to how scores fluctuated over the whole development sequence. She found a trend for females from early childhood through adolescence to obtain relatively similar drawing completion femininity scores, whereas males tended weakly to obtain more masculine scores as they entered puberty. Harkey also questioned whether the Franck-Rosen procedure is actually a measure of body image. She pointed to the paucity of evidence of a specific shift in the Franck-Rosen completion scores at the time of puberty. She asked why, if the body does become so clearly more accentuated as masculine or feminine at the time of puberty, is there not a corresponding representation of the process in the Franck-Rosen index? She wondered if the qualities that distinguish male and female design completions might not be due simply to the degree to which each sex is identified with aggressive power values, which, in turn, are equated with phallic versus feminine symbols. The original Franck-Rosen assumption that their technique taps into body feelings may be questionable. The issue awaits further investigation.

OVERVIEW

Developmental Trends

Much research energy has gone into exploring developmental changes in body perception. The methods used have been diverse, and it is difficult to organize the results so that they provide a flowing picture of the evolving body image in the growing child. However, we can present a schematic outline of the data that have emerged. First what have we learned about the first 3 years of life? There is good evidence that as early as the 2nd year children begin to become aware of their mirror image as a unique representation of self, and by the end of the 2nd year they usually demonstrate realization that there is a unique sector of space equated with "I." The 2– and 3–year olds are also learning to identify body parts like the legs and hands and are becoming knowledgeable about the distinction between front and back of the body and also its up and down aspects. Paralleling a grasp of such body spatial categories, there is a growing ability to perceive that the space in the vicinity of one's body shares in the categorization. Young children's considerable awareness of body attributes is revealed in the ability, even as early as age 3, to identify racial and ethnic body differences and show knowledge of the general standards applied in judging body attractiveness. At this age they also begin to achieve real awareness of the sexual identity of the body. It is impressive how far 3-year-olds have progressed in becoming experts about their own body space. Signs of uneasiness about the body also appear early. Some observers note that, in the 1st year, children make use of transitional objects to increase soothing input into the skin and mouth at times of special stress. Relatedly, it has been reported that a good third of the imagery in imaginative stories secured from children at age 3 has body-threatening connotations.

As children move into ages 4 and 5, acceleration appears in their body image development. A variety of new accomplishments show up. Knowledge of body parts expands. At age 4, 60% of children studied could locate their heart accurately. They showed themselves capable too of making fine distinctions with respect to parts of the hand (e.g., thumb, little finger). There is evidence that children in this age category have arrived at a differentiated awareness of the arrangement of upper versus lower body parts and are capable of using this schema in organizing body relevant material presented for memorization. It is during this time period that a really significant improvement in the ability to recognize and represent the human form occurs. Relatively high accuracy is shown in three-dimensional manikin constructions and in figure drawings. However, certain distortions commonly occur, such as attaching the arms at the horizontal midline of the body or exaggerating the size of the head. The increasing differentiation of the body image is manifested in the ability of children to make consistent evaluative judgments about how much they like or dislike their various body parts.

It is particularly noteworthy that by age 5 the presence of a central body schema is functionally highlighted in the way certain types of perceptual distortions are assimilated. Thus, when children use a finger to point at a target while they wear lenses that distort the apparent location of that target, their adaptation to the distortion is a function of whether the target is "out there" or a part of their own body. As soon as one's body becomes importantly involved, special defensive strategies come into play. These body oriented strategies in response to distortions are not yet detected at age 4. At the same time that the body image is taking on increased complexity, new signs of irrational body attitudes surface. Feelings of guilt about body illness and injury emerge rather strongly, although they seem to be perceptible in attenuated form as early as age 3. There are suggestions that they increase in intensity at least through age 9.

By age 6, children achieve the basic distinction between right and left within their own body space. However, they are not yet able to generalize this awareness to nonbody space. At this age they have also generally attained an understanding of the differences between male and female genitalia. Clear stereotyping of the relative desirability of various body types (e.g., mesomorph versus endomorph) also manifests itself at this time. At 7, a reasonable level of realism in estimating body size appears. At the same age, children show too that they understand the importance of the heart in body functioning, and they have some creditable knowledge of other internal organs, such as the lungs. Age 8 is distinguished by the progression from being able to identify right and left on one's own body to being able to do so with reference to the bodies of other persons. Further, body concept differentiation, as defined by the Witkin et al. (1962). Sophistication of Body Concept index, begins to increase significantly at this point and continues to increase until about the age of 14.

Evidence is accumulating that age 9 represents another point of special acceleration in the buildup of the body image. A real spurt in knowledge concerning body parts and body functions has been demonstrated. Also at 9 years, the ability to draw the human figure begins to peak; a further, rather marked increase in accuracy of body size estimation occurs; and a magnified facility for making complex right-left judgments (e.g., "mirroring" the right-left movements of another individual) shows itself. Minimal change in the body image has been observed during age 10, except for a noticeable increment in ability to take spatial perspectives independent of the position of one's own body.

At ages 11 and 12, as the adolescent phase slowly gets under way, the majority of children demonstrate an overall correct awareness of the locations and functions of the major organs of the body. Around 12 a ceiling is reached in facility for tasks that call for a discriminating recognition of the hand and fine differentiations of stimuli applied to the hand. Girls who are beginning to menstruate may experience increased feelings of body femininity, although this has not been convincingly documented. Twelve also marks the point at which girls (but not boys) begin to manifest the adult response pattern when asked to judge the vertical while they are laterally tilted. The adult pattern is typified by compensatorily shifting the apparent vertical opposite to the direction of tilt, whereas the more childlike pattern is to shift the apparent vertical toward the tilt. On the average, boys do not manifest the adult pattern until they reach the age of 16 or 17.

Beginning around the age of 13, girls (and boys later on) display the adult pattern of perceiving the longitudinal axis of the body as inordinately displaced in the direction of tilt. Before this point, the typical pattern is to minimize the apparent lateral shift of the body's longitudinal axis. The adolescent period, with its accompanying body changes, does produce body image alterations, but they are difficult to detect and may not be of the major magnitude that some have assumed. One of the more measurable effects of adolescence is the intensification of feelings of body vulnerability. Specifically, sensations of boundary diffusion and body distortion seem to be stirred up during this period. What is surprising is that various indices that tap images about the phallic versus feminine properties of the body do not suddenly increase at pubescence, as might be anticipated for each sex. Instead, rather clear differences in this regard can be detected as early as ages 5 or 6. It is true that boys show an increase in phallic imagery as they enter adolescence, but the increment is not great. Although the development of the body image seems to proceed relatively rapidly, new, more complex modes of body perception continue to enter the picture as late as ages 16 and 17.

There are three points in the age sequence that are particularly noteworthy. The first occurs in the final months of the 2nd year, when children learn to identify their body space with a unique sense of self. Then, at ages 4 and 5, a rather marked spurt occurs in mastery of body perception. There is a noticeable expansion in knowledge of the body and in the ability to produce representations of it that are reasonably realistic. The body schema seems suddenly to be capable of providing a defensive or coordinating frame when coping with confusing distortions or complex inputs (e.g., material for memorization) that need to be sorted out. A third noteworthy developmental point appears at age 9. One finds another upsurge in knowledge about the body, in the ability to create realistic depictions of the body, and in manipulating spatial concepts linked to body coordinates. One might have thought that adolescence would also emerge as a phase of unusual body image development. From a common sense point of view, this would seem to be a certainty. However, aside from the fact that there is a heightening of concern about the security of the body, little else has been empirically demonstrated. One is reminded that previous assumptions about adolescence being a time in which disturbance and turmoil flourish have also not been ratified by objective inquiry. The question arises, of course, as to why ages like 4 and 5 and 9 are so modal. We do not, in truth, have reasonable answers. One could speculatively point out that the 4 through 5 age period coincides with Freud's Oedipal phase or that age 9 is said by Piaget (1960) to be the point at which ability to coordinate different perspectives first occurs developmentally.

However, for now these are only coincidences, perhaps ripe for exploratory investigation.

Sex Differences

Another distinctive aspect of the body image developmental process is the presence of pervasive sex differences. Fisher (1970) has already reviewed in considerable detail the numerous ways in which men and women differ in their body perceptions. Similar differences appear again and again in the developmental data analyzed in this chapter. Writers like Maccoby and Jacklin (1972), who have concluded that sex differences are minimal, seem to be unaware of the multitude of differences revealed by body image research. Let us consider the major sex differences that have shown up in children. A meaningful way to approach those differences is in terms of immaturity-maturity or effectiveness-ineffectiveness.[46] The data indicate that girls more often manifest superiority to boys in their mastery of body image tasks. Quite early (age 6) girls structure their body boundaries, in terms of the Fisher-Cleveland Barrier score, more articulately than do boys. That is, they apparently experience themselves as possessing more secure body borders. It is of parallel import that beginning at age 6 girls demonstrate greater body image differentiation, as defined by Witkin et al. (1962) Sophistication of Body Concept figure drawing index. Further, girls as young as 4 or 5 are less likely than boys to be preoccupied with themes of body destruction and castration in their imaginative productions.

This does not mean that they are less body oriented. Indeed, as already mentioned, exploratory studies have shown that even in the first year of life girls are more likely to use transitional objects in direct, body-comforting ways. Also, by age 15 girls introduce more body themes into the projective stories they create when responding to pictures. This apparently greater awareness of the body on their part persists into adulthood. When they experience failure, girls do not react with as much of a sense of loss in body height as do boys. For girls, failure is not so easily translated into a sense of diminished stature. However, girls do tend to reduce their own height estimates more than boys do when comparing self with an authority figure (Shaffer, 1964).

There are skills involving mastery of body spatial coordinates in which girls display relative maturational acceleration. Girls more quickly learn to make right-left judgments with respect to the body of others by the strategy of visualizing an 180° rotation of their own body in space. They are also quicker to show the adult pattern of compensatory shift of the apparent vertical (away from the direction of tilt) during conditions of lateral body tilt and of exaggerating the apparent position of the body's longitudinal axis (toward the direction of tilt) during body tilt.

Turning now to instances in which boys are superior to girls in body image adaptation, we find the following: Boys are slightly more accurate than girls in estimating the sizes of various parts of their bodies. Boys do not overtly express as much dissatisfaction with their body appearance as do girls. In addition, by the age of 8 or so, boys rather consistently display greater accuracy when judging the vertical position of a luminous rod in a context where there is visual distraction. As noted, Witkin et al. (1954) have interpreted this finding to mean that the male is somehow superior in his ability to use his body as a frame of reference in a confusing unstructured setting.

An overall picture emerges of the female child as more quickly and more easily mastering the various developmental body image problems than does her male counterpart. It is paradoxical that she begins earlier than he to voice dissatisfaction with her body appearance and continues to do so right into the adult years. This verbal dissatisfaction is counterbalanced by the fact that she seems to feel basically more body secure when judged by such measures as boundary definiteness (Barrier) and degree of preoccupation with themes of body destruction in imaginative productions. As earlier mentioned, her readiness to express the verbal dissatisfaction may mirror the fact that she is less defensive than the male about her body. Or it may reflect the special importance ascribed in our culture to the female's being outwardly attractive.

In any case, it is apparent from the available evidence that the male child is not superior, and probably is inferior, to the female child in attaining a sense of body security and adequacy. Female inferiority might be suggested superficially in terms of the criterion of verbal self-criticism, but it becomes implausible when other probably more basic criteria are applied. That little girls cope at least as well with their bodies as little boys do obviously contradicts the positions of Freud and Witkin, who portrayed the female as suffering early on from body inferiority because she lacks the supposedly prized penis. It is interesting to speculate why the female child apparently fares so relatively well in her body image development. Some of her superiority may simply be the result of her faster rate of body maturation during the years leading up to adolescence. She may therefore learn to master certain body image "construction" tasks at a faster rate. Another, probably more important, factor is that the culturally defined sex role quite early casts the male body as being in greater danger than the female body. The male role calls for an aggressive stance and a readiness to engage in combat with competitors. Combat is linked with potential body destruction. The female child feels less obligated to visualize herself as involved in aggressive encounters that could damage her body domain. Indeed, she may get the message quite early that her body is to be prized for its potential to create new life. Perhaps it is because the male child is so imbued with anxiety about being damaged that he begins to regard his body as a disturbing source of danger. His anxiety about his body space could, of course, interfere with his ability to sort out and organize body stimuli and to conceptualize his body as possessed of secure boundaries.

Individual Consistency

How much consistency do children display in their body image development? If, at a very early age, they are high or low with reference to some body image parameter, do they maintain equivalent positions in subsequent years? Although there is not a large mass of pertinent research, previous studies suggest moderate individual stability over time. Some of the pertinent findings have been mentioned in this chapter, and some have been considered elsewhere (Fisher, 1970). As might be expected, the most revealing findings have come from longitudinal observation. Let us quickly skim what is known. Kagan and Moss (1962) followed a sample of children ($N = 89$) from birth until adulthood. Among the variables they studied was one with obvious body image significance—fear of bodily harm. They measured this variable in terms of how much fear subjects displayed about their bodies in various situations and in terms of subjects' speed of response to tachistoscopically presented pictures depicting body harm. The results indicated a moderately high level of consistency in concern about body damage over the entire developmental range studied. Retest correlations were generally in the .50 range. Witkin et al. (1962) discovered that body concept differentiation (as measured by both perceptual and figure drawing methods) showed high consistency. Correlations in the .70s and .80s were noted between scores obtained in early childhood and those secured at the time of adolescence. Other observations suggest consistency in body perception. Thomas (1980) observed babies over a number of months and reported that they made use of transitional objects in what appeared to be an individualistically consistent fashion. Story (1979) noted that when children as young as age 3 were asked to indicate their like-dislike for a number of different parts of their bodies their judgments correlated .91 with equivalent judgments obtained 2 weeks later. While the issue is far from closed, there seem to be initially promising indications that individuals show fair developmental consistency with respect to several body image parameters.

How Have Theorists' Notions Fared?

Early in this chapter the thoughts of various major theorists who have contemplated issues bearing on body image development were summarized. The views of Piaget, Werner, Freud, Erikson, Schilder, Witkin, and Kohlberg were variously examined. Following this examination, a number of the basic assumptions either explicit or implicit in their theories were teased out and stated. Now that a review of the developmental literature has been completed, let us look back and judge how well these assumptions have or have not been affirmed empirically.

1. As theorized, there is support for the notion that the child starts out with hazy awareness of its own body and gradually evolves a more complex, more differentiated, and more sharply bounded body concept. The support

comes from diverse sources: (a) increases with age in body concept differentiation reported by Witkin et al. (1954, 1962[47]); (b) progressively augmented knowledge about the body observed by Gellert (1960, 1962) and others; (c) well-documented improvement, with age, in ability to differentiate such spatial dimensions of one's body as up-down and right-left (e.g., Piaget & Inhelder, 1956).

2. Evidence is available, as theorized, that the body provides a prime frame of reference in the child's learning of spatial directionality. The work of Piaget and Inhelder (1956), Benton (1959), and others (e.g., Belmont & Birch, 1963) indicates that children learn to differentiate spatial dimensions like right versus left on their own bodies before they can make such discriminations on the bodies of others. However, Winer (1975) reported individual diffferences in children at the first grade level with regard to their preference for the body, as compared with other objects, in providing a frame of reference for making right-left judgments. The possibility that, in some instances, knowledge acquired by observation of the bodies of others may precede knowledge of one's own body is pointed up by Benton's (1959) report that the ability to discriminate body parts on a doll may occur earlier than the ability to discriminate the parts on one's own body.

3. What can one say about the assumption that children view their body as a unique perceptual object, especially in terms of ego involvement with it? Here and there are supportive data. There is the special response shown by 2-year-olds to their mirror image (e.g., Amsterdam & Greenberg, 1977). Consider too that by the age of 5 or 6 children respond differently to a distorted visual field involving their own body parts than to one consisting of nonself targets (Mandell, 1979). Children have been observed to display different patterns of size judgments with respect to their own body parts than they do in relation to nonself objects (Fisher, 1970). Similar uniqueness in responding to one's own body is suggested by the fact that it is more difficult for children wearing aniseikonic lenses to detect visual distortions in their own body mirror image than in nonself objects (Fisher, 1970).

4. No data were found to support Freud's notion that body image formation moves through a series of fixed stages (e.g., oral, anal), with each stage focused on a primary body area. In addition, there is no direct support for the notion that children's experiences as they learn to control such major body zones establish paradigms for interpreting extrabody events experientially linked to the zones. However, there have not been any serious attempts to determine if the oral, anal and genital zones are sequential foci in the development of the body image. Fisher and Greenberg (1977) did summarize some indirect evidence that particular patterns of experiences with the oral and anal zones may result in the development of corresponding clusters of personality traits (viz., oral and anal character types). This issue awaits further exploration.

5. The process of learning that one's body belongs to a specific sex

category has been said to be fundamental to structuring the body concept; and the awareness of sex differences has been said (by Freud) to bring awareness that one's body can exist in a radically different form and therefore that it is subject to unexpected change or even mutilation (castration anxiety). Little has emerged from the research literature that can be used to test these ideas. We do know that as early as ages 5 and 6 boys and girls differ in the degree to which they are identified with phallic versus feminine images, but it is not clear whether these images are equated with the body or simply symbolize certain power values. No one has demonstrated that basic parameters such as body image security or differentiation are significantly linked within each sex to degree of masculinity–femininity. On the other hand the fact that there are so many differences in body image between males and females that go beyond sexuality, as such, indicates that the sexual classification of one's body plays a prominent part in body image organization. As for the link between awareness of sex differences and body anxiety, no one has specifically shown that feelings of body vulnerability (especially castration anxiety) are intensified because children become aware of the nature of the differences between male and female genitalia.

6. Have any data accumulated indicating that the body attitudes of children are influenced by their parents' values and child rearing practices? Although one would, from a common sense viewpoint, accept as a truism that parents shape their children's body attitudes, there is only a moderate amount of pertinent documentation available. It has been shown that the higher a father's educational level, the greater his child's knowledge about the body (Smith, 1973). Witkin et al. (1962)demonstrated that mothers who are intrusive and stimulate overdependence encourage poor differentiation in body concept. In another context, Fisher (1970) has offered data indicating that parents who are intrusive and overcontrolling tend to inhibit body boundary structuring in their children, whereas an aesthetic orientation on their part has the opposite effect. Kagan and Moss (1962) reported that boys with unusually elevated body anxiety had overprotective mothers. The three studies just cited suggest that the parent who invades the child's autonomy and breaches the child's self boundaries is most likely to interfere with the development of a sense of body security. Incidentally, we know too that children who live with chronically ill parents are likely to develop elevated anxiety about their own bodies (Arnaud, 1959).

7. Are there special periods of body image instability coincident with certain phases that are presumed to be times of crisis? Do body image disturbances become prominent during the so-called Oedipal phase or the period of adolescence? The evidence does not indicate that the Oedipal period, which would occur roughly at age 5, is a time of unusual body image instability. However, there are data indicating that although no dramatic alterations in body image occur at adolescence, signs of increased feeling of body vulnerability do arise at this point. It may be that every year in the

developmental sequence is accompanied by its own special problems and that one cannot distinguish modal crest points of crisis.

8. Finally, let us look at the assumption that with increasing maturity children are less likely to rely on body feelings and more on cognitive factors when making decisions. If this assumption refers to the fact that the maturing organism takes into account a progressively wider range of cognitive information when arriving at judgments, it can be said to be well supported by a variety of research findings. However, if there is the implication that body cues decline in import, one would have to be skeptical. Indeed, it is likely that as children grow up they become increasingly adept at monitoring their body sensations and discriminating their meanings (e.g., significance of sensations in specific organs). The older child may even use more body cues in decision making than the younger one, but the ratio of body cues to nonbody cognitive information utilized may diminish. Fisher (1970) has presented studies indicating that body cues may, at an unconscious level, participate more potently in decision making than usually realized.

One may say that the theoretical assumptions did not fare badly. About half were moderately well affirmed and a few received borderline support. Little direct validation could be found for Freud's linkage of body image development with a sequence of energy investments in major erogenous zones. Likewise, almost no direct support could be mustered for Freud's hypothesis that the discovery of genital differences precipitates body anxiety. However, in both of these instances there have simply been few or no studies that have addressed themselves creditably to testing the issues in question. We need a good deal more clarifying work with respect to several issues: whether there are crisis points in body image development; whether the body becomes progressively more or less important as a frame of reference in making judgments; and the degree to which sex role definition enters into the various aspects of body image development.

Because it is of special theoretical import, let us return for a moment to what is known about the role of parents in shaping the body image. We have some hint that the educational level of children's parents may be influential. For example, we know that children whose fathers are better educated will acquire relatively more knowledge about their body functions. There are suggestions too that highly educated mothers are more likely to communicate to their children that a "stiff upper lip" attitude is appropriate when one falls ill. We have some reason to believe that children who grow up in a household in which there is a chronically sick parent will feel more than average discomfort about their bodies.[48] But the area in which we have the greatest amount of data relates to the impact of parental overprotection and intrusiveness upon children's degree of body security. As reported earlier, if parents act as if they own the child's body, if they behave as if their child cannot capably manage its own body space, the result is a perception of one's body as weak, vulnerable, and without adequate protective borders. Relatedly, as is described in a later chapter (Levine, 1979), children who are the earliest to achieve a clear awareness of body selfhood have mothers who foster "reciprocal interaction" with them.

Parental correlates of sex role definition have also been documented (Fisher, 1970). Inasmuch as the sex role ascribed to one's body is undoubtedly important in the organization of the body image, this is pertinent to the issue under discussion. What we have learned is that feelings of sex role adequacy are most likely to be present in children whose like-sex parent has demonstrated warmth, friendliness, and competent effectiveness. A more indirect indicator of the importance of parent attitudes for the development of the body image has emerged from studies that have found that some body attitudes of adults are tied to their memories of their parents. Illustratively, Fisher (1970) discovered that the amount of attention adults focus on a given body sector may be linked to their recall of having been treated by their parents in specific ways. Another example is suggested by the fact that castration anxiety in men is correlated with particular fantasies about father (Fisher & Greenberg, 1977a). Obviously, there are many issues concerning parental influence on body image development that remain to be pursued. We do not know such basic things as whether parents' behaviors can influence the speed with which certain forms of cognitive mastery of the body (e.g., discriminating right from left) proceed or whether parental attitudes affect children's ability to build up an accurate picture of their body size.

The issue of parental influence in shaping the body image bears on the more general question of how children learn about the body. How much do they acquire by observing and "feeling" the bodies of others (e.g., their parents)? How much do they learn from self-observation? Schilder (1950) speculated that the body image evolves largely from bodies interacting with bodies. That is, we form impressions of our body in the context of how others react to it. A concrete example is the fact that children with disapproved of body attributes (e.g., endomorphic) come to regard their own body space negatively as the result of the negative feedback from other people. Winer (1975) found evidence that some children may be more inclined than others to use markers outside of their own body coordinates for defining right and left directionality. Perhaps there are related individual differences in how much children acquire knowledge about the body from self-observation as compared to inspection of others. These differences might derive from such factors as the extent to which parents permit their children to witness their various body activities or whether the children experience an unusual amount of personal illness that would intensify focusing upon one's own body. If children do build up the body image, at least partially, from watching other people's bodies, the bodies of their parents and sibs may be especially important sources of information.

What are some things children might learn early on from such body watching? They would certainly find out that their parents' bodies are a lot bigger than their own and would therefore presumably be impressed with the importance of body size differences. Classification of the body and its parts in terms of relative size could become a fundamental aspect of body image organization. Children would also learn quite early from studying their mothers and fathers and opposite sex sibs that bodies come in two different sex forms, they would thus be provided with the information needed to put themselves into the appropriate category. What else might they come upon? They could witness particular styles of eating, grooming, dressing, being sick, touching, and dealing with body orifices that convey messages about the nature of bodies and by implication how to regard their own. Children could, in this fashion, assimilate images about such diverse matters as body fragility, body as a good versus bad thing, body as an object to be displayed or concealed, body as an instrument for making contact with others, and so forth. We need a research program that will examine body image changes that can be induced in children as the result of exposing them to adult models with specified ways of dealing with their own body domains.

FINAL IMPRESSIONS

What are the broadest trends in body image development that can be distilled from the material presented in this chapter? They may be summarized as follows:

1. Obviously, children become increasingly knowledgeable about the body territory. They learn a great deal about the body's spatial dimensions and the functions of its organs and subsystems. Their map of the body gradually takes on more complexity and differentiation.

2. They are able to be more and more realistic in their ability to evaluate the physical properties of the body.

3. Early mastery of certain aspects of body perception seems to contribute to later mastery of particular cognitive skills.

4. Children become increasingly aware of cultural rules and standards that define such parameters as body attractiveness, sexual classification, and guilt about body usage and defect.

5. They show progressively intensified investment in developing the ability to segregate their body from the total perceptual field and to experience it as an object with at least a specified minimum degree of stability. This investment is accompanied by a parallel concern about possible invasion of the body that could violate its separateness or constancy. There is fairly good evidence that parental attitudes and behaviors are important in determining the character of the body image differentiation and boundary articulation attained.

6. An ongoing process of sexual differentiation in the body image occurs that not only relates to obvious contrasts in male and female body structure

but also is linked to differences in male and female social roles. Male versus female socialization experiences probably have major effects on the body image (e.g., body boundary security).

7. Apparently a good deal of tension and disturbance is generated in all phases of body image development. Children have to wrestle with such seemingly endless problems as whether their bodies deviate from acceptable definitions of attractiveness, whether their parents will grant them control over their own body domain, whether dangerous forces "out there" can break through their boundaries, and whether they properly match body standards of masculinity-feminity.

8. Although there are age nodes characterized by acceleration in body image development, it remains to be ascertained whether there are unique critical phases. Generally, mastery of the body space seems to proceed gradually, with the process probably extending well into late adolescence.

NOTES

[1] However, it has been shown (Caron, Caron, Caldwell, & Weiss, 1973) that children as young as 5 months can recognize the configuration of the face. Therefore, it is conceivable that very early they develop relatively complex perceptual skills with reference to their own bodies.

[2] Johnson and Kendrick (1984) examined in detail how children (ages 3-5) learn to group their various body parts. They refer to this process as "body partonomy."

[3] Johnson and Wellman (1982) have provided a detailed account of how children evolve concepts of the functioning of the brain and the "mind."

[4] Winer (1975) raised some questions about whether, in the initial stages of learning right-left discrimination, children necessarily use a body frame of reference. He found that when children in the first grade were asked to make right-left judgments and given the opportunity to use either the body or external referents as a frame of reference, there were conditions in which the external frame was preferred. He suggested: "Children who have a deficient body image or who (perhaps because of environmental factors) direct their attention to the outer world as opposed to self, might develop an understanding of right-left relations by relying on external objects. On the other hand, children who are deficient in visualizing objects in different perspectives might rely on the body" (p. 297).

Braine and Eder (1983) have likewise concluded that there is considerable variation as to when children use an egocentric versus allocentric frame of reference when making right-left judgments. In addition, they presented evidence that children as young as 2 may be far more capable of appreciating right-left distinctions than the orthodox literature would lead one to expect. They demonstrated that children who were rewarded for finding objects hidden under boxes arranged in different spatial patterns could distinguish right-left directionality equally well as the front-back dimension. They concluded that previous research which has emphasized the difficulty of identifying right-left in the surrounding space has often utilized tasks that too much tested the ability to formulate complex judgments rather than the simple distinction between right and left.

[5] Kohler (1964).

[6] Stratton (1897).

[7] Hay, Pick, Jr., and Ikeda (1965) have shown that when one views one's hand through a displacing prism, the hand feels as if it were actually where it is seen to be.

[8] Other studies (Ishii & Wapner, 1977; Taylor, 1969) suggest that children may adapt more quickly than adults to visual rearrangement by prisms. This may reflect a smaller degree of involvement of the body schema in children during the adaptation process. Visual distortions may, in the adult, need to be more complexly integrated with the requirements of the body schema and therefore result in longer adaptation times. However, one is simultaneously confronted with the fact that when persons are asked to observe themselves in a mirror while wearing aniseikonic lenses, there is an increasing ability with age to perceive distortions in one's image (Fish, 1960; Wittreich & Grace, 1955). This does not represent a real contradiction if one considers that the fact that the child adapts quickly to the prism rearrangement indicates minimal concern with, or focus on, the discrepancies between the visual and the proprioceptive experiences that are occurring. Similarly, the child who sees few distortions in his or her mirror image while wearing aniseikonic lenses could be denying any discrepancies between the existing body image and the aniseikonic distortions that are potentially available to awareness. This last statement should be further clarified by noting that the changes produced by aniseikonic lenses are not as forced as those resulting from prism rearrangement. The aniseikonic lenses create the potentiality for perceptual alteration which may or may not be perceived, depending on the state of the aniseikonic observer (Fisher, 1970).

[9] Several studies (e.g., Kahane, 1972; Silbert, 1976) have used a related methodology to examine in detail the concept of the body as a geometrical object in space. Subjects were asked to indicate where on a contiguous blank wall the felt position of various parts of their body (e.g., right shoulder, mouth) would fall if projected straight ahead on to the wall. Judgments were rendered by instructing the experimenter where to position markers on the wall. Similar judgments were obtained after a period of adaptation that involved pointing at targets with the right index finger while wearing displacing lenses. Silbert (1976) found that: "individuals' ideas of the location of their bodies in space contain large inaccuracies . . the amount of error in the judgments of the locations of body parts varies across body parts . . . the average individual's experience of the shape of his body is different from its actual shape, and can perhaps best be described as approaching a circle centered on the navel. Subjects were most accurate in their judgments of the location of the center of their bodies and progressively less so as they approach the extremities" (p. 62). Silbert noted further: "the average experienced body converges on the center of the body. Thus, it is shorter, higher off the ground, narrower in the extremities while wider in the trunk than the actual body" (p. 34). Adaptation to prism distortion proceeded in such a fashion as to preserve a concept of the body as symmetrical. Silbert observed: "The center of the body also shifted in the same direction as the right index finger and arm. That the center of the body shifted more than the right shoulder which is closer to the index finger suggests that the midline plays a special role in the organization of the body image. In the pattern of the experienced body resulting from exposure to the displacement, we see both constraints at work, symmetry and continuity. The body is shrunk toward the center to maintain symmetry, and pulled toward the left to maintain

continuity with the left-shifting right index finger" (p. 57). As soon as one part of the body seems out of position (which is true of the index finger when pointing during prismatic displacement), adaptive shifts occur in the apparent positions of other body parts in order to maintain body image equilibrium. There seems to be a basic strategy of maintaining body image stability.

[10] However, Kaats and Davis (1970) did report that women who are rated as highly attractive by others exceed those assigned medium or low ratings in the degree to which they judge their own physical attractiveness positively.

[11] This contradicts an earlier report by Hassan (1967b) that mesomorphs are more accurate than other body types in such identifications.

[12] One encounters the curious anomaly that Dion and Berscheid (1974) observed that unattractive girls of nursery school age were unusually popular with their peers. However, with age their popularity did decline and that of the attractive girls increased.

[13] Olgas (1974) looked at the relationship of several body image parameters in children to the health status of their parents. The children were between the ages of 7 and 11. There were 30 girls and 30 boys with multiple sclerotic fathers; 30 boys and 30 girls with multiple sclerotic mothers; and 60 children with healthy parents. The children responded to the Draw-A-Person test and also rated their own bodies by means of Semantic Differential continua and a Body-Cathexis scale. The various body image scores of the children with sick parents could not be distinguished from those of the children with healthy parents. There was a significant trend for girls with multiple sclerotic mothers to show more body dissatisfaction (as defined by Semantic Differential ratings) than did girls with multiple sclerotic fathers or boys with multiple sclerotic mothers. Olgas speculated that this pattern of differences indicated: "that identification with the like-sex parent is a factor in body-image building for girls" (p. 322).

[14] Some comment should be made about various batteries of motor tests that have been devised for testing children and that contain items with obvious body image implications. For example, the tests include such tasks as identifying different body parts and discriminating directionality on one's body. In an analysis of such test batteries, Marotte (1976) concluded that several displayed excellent validity and reliability, e.g., Psychoeducational Inventory of Basic Learning Attitudes (Valett, 1969) and Lincoln-Oseretsky Motor Development Scale (Sloan, 1954). She constructed a new motor body image test by extracting the most promising tests from previous batteries. She used a procedure that particularly differentiated motor and body image item clusters. In a brief summary of some of her observations about the body image capabilities of the young child, she noted: "By the time he is 2 years old he can identify some parts of the body such as arms, legs, hands, and sometimes his front and back. At age 4, we see evidence of continuing refinement in the ability to discriminate different portions of the hand (thumb, little finger, first finger) as well as portions of body segments such as knees and elbows. Between 5 and 7 years, the child develops fairly accurate sense of left and right in reference to self" (p. 37). Strauss and DeOreo (1979) also developed an extensive battery of tests to measure "body awareness" in children. When applied to children in the 4 through 6 age range, the tests are said not to show a developmental pattern that fits Piaget's stages of spatial orientation.

[15]The developmental changes that occur in the perception of one's own body size have previously been partially reviewed by Fisher (1970) and Shontz (1969). If one scans the total available literature one can offer the following generalizations:

1) Children's body size estimates are reasonably realistic, even as early as ages 6 and 7 (Ford, 1977; Koff & Kiekhofer, 1978; Shontz, 1969).
2) Children tend to become more accurate in their body estimates as they grow older, but the trend is a weak one. Around the age of 9 there is a particularly marked increase in accuracy (Ford, 1977; Gellert & Stern, 1964).
3) Children are probably more likely than adults to underestimate body height (Fish, 1960; Gellert & Stern, 1964; Rowe & Caldwell, 1963; Woods, 1966). However, no clear pattern of difference has emerged with regard to judgments of the sizes of individual body parts (Koff & Kiekhofer, 1978).
4) There may be a slight trend for boys to be more accurate than girls in their body size judgments. This remains to be further evaluated (Gellert & Stern, 1964; Stiles & Smith, 1977).
5) Girls exceed boys in the degree to which they underestimate their own height in situations where they are comparing themselves with adults (Ford, 1977; Shaffer, 1964).
6) Boys are more likely than girls to reduce their estimates of their height when they have had a failure experience (Popper, 1957; Shaffer, 1964).

It is noteworthy that Koff and Kiekhofer (1978) were more impressed with the similarities rather than the differences between the ways children and adults perceive their body size. They speculated: "The correspondence between the children's and the adults' patterns of errors, coupled with the finding that adults consistently misjudge the sizes of certain body parts, suggests that the tendency observed among the adults may have been established at an earlier stage of development, and reflect relatively stable and longstanding cognitive predispositions" (p. 1050).

[16]Gellert, Girgus, and Cohen (1971) reported that when children refer to their bodies, they are particularly likely to mention their extremities. Wapner and Cirillo (1968) noted the unusual dual status of the hand. It is part of the body image, but it also acts in the surrounding space. It bridges between the body space and external space.

[17]An interesting controversy persists concerning the role of body image anxiety in ability to deal with cognitive tasks that have body connotations. Blatt, Allison, and Baker (1965) reported that disturbed children with unusual body concerns differed from disturbed children without such concerns in that they performed relatively poorly in the Object Assembly subtest of the Wechsler Intelligence Scale for Children. This poor performance was restricted to the Object Assembly task, which obviously calls for putting together the disassembled parts of a human form. Blatt et al. also found that adults who were high in body anxiety, as defined by Rorschach indices, also did not do well on an Object Assembly task. However, Rockwell, Jr., (1967) and Marsden and Kalter (1969) could not confirm the findings with regard to the children. Blatt, Baker, and Weiss (1970) published a paper describing several different studies that significantly affirmed a link in adults between body anxiety and difficulty in dealing with the Object Assembly subtest. But subsequently other researchers have published data that seem not to be congruent with these observations (Bassett &

Gayton, 1979; Faschingbauer & Johnson, 1974; Patrick, 1979; Stewart, Powers, & Gouaux, 1973).

Lehman and Levy (1971) looked at the relationship in children between body anxiety (as measured by the Fisher-Cleveland Barrier and Penetration scores) and degree of discrepancy between IQ as measured by the Wechsler Intelligence Scale for Children and IQ as measured by the drawing of a person. Significant correlations could not be demonstrated.

[18] Benton (1959) makes an interesting observation concerning the interplay between identifying body parts on self versus on the bodies of others:

> There is some indication from normative studies that these discriminations of one's own body parts are preceded by similar discriminations of the body parts of other people. Thus, the task of identifying one's own body parts (nose, eyes, mouth, hair) on oral command was placed on Year III of the early forms of the Binet scale. But, when the nature of the task was changed, in the revised Stanford-Binet scale, to call for the identification of body parts on a doll, the age placement dropped to Year II. So it may well be that in the seeing child the first discriminations of parts of the body are accomplished by means of vision and relate to the body parts of other persons and that this is followed by a corresponding development of the perception of the child's own body parts. The first type of discrimination is evidently based on vision while somesthetic sources of stimulation—proprioceptive, tactual, and visceral—are the primary sensory foundations of awareness of the child's own body parts. No doubt the preceding visual perceptions of the body parts of other persons play a role in the elaboration of the child's perceptions of his own body parts, perhaps in the form of a visual component which links up with the somesthetic information to crystallize the identification.(p. 131)

[19] Benton (1959) observed that the ability to localize tactual stimulation of the fingers (without eliminating visual cues) begins at about age 4, and by age 6 the average child can localize with only an occasional error. However, if finger localization is attempted without visual cues, real mastery is not demonstrated until about age 9. Kinsbourne and Warrington (1963) devised a variant method for measuring finger localization and concluded that by the age of 7.5 years 95% of children showed mastery of this localization skill.

[20] Aniseikonic lenses result in the image of an object that is formed in one eye differing in size and shape from the image of the same object formed in the other eye.

[21] Mintz (1968) discovered in a study of boys ($N = 35$) and girls ($N = 28$) (5-7 year age range) that measure of self-concept were not significantly related to accuracy of body perception, as defined by estimates of one's body size.

[22] Interestingly, in samples of Japanese adolescents (ages 12-13) Lerner, Iwawaki, Chihara, and Sorell (1980) failed to find really significant correlations between self-concept measures and ratings of one's own body. However, in older subjects the usual positive relationships did appear.

[23] Pezzella (1964) administered the "Who Am I" procedure to three groups ($N = 40$ in each) of male and female children (ages 5-6, 7-8, 8-11); but asked for only 3 instead of 20 answers. Unfortunately, the categories of analysis that were applied are

difficult to interpret in relation to frequency of references with body connotations. One can say only that there seemed to be a trend for those in the 7–8 range to produce more of the references with body implications than did either of the other two age groups. This description of Pezzella's findings is phrased vaguely because her mode of data analysis is difficult to decode. When the children who were subjects were asked to stand in front of a mirror and to "Point to yourself," the vast majority pointed to the torso. With increasing age there was a definite trend to point to the midline of the torso rather than to right or left sectors. Interestingly, boys pointed to their heads more than girls did. Also, girls seemed to make more body references than boys did.

[24] Fisher (1970) obtained an analogous sex difference. He reported that, when he scored the spontaneous statements of college students for body references, females gave significantly more body references than did males. However, the direction of the sex differences was contradicted by the forementioned Montemayor and Eisen study, which found no sex differences, and the Keller et al. (1978) investigation, which found that boys at three age levels tended to give more body references than did girls during unstructured and structured inquiries. It is difficult to pinpoint why such contradictory results concerning sex differences have emerged.

[25] Fisher (1970) found that in an unstructured setting when adults were asked to "List 20 things that you are aware or conscious of right now," about 17% of the content listed referred to their own body.

[26] Van Lennep (1957) discovered, when he scored "Body Sensations" in the context of stories given in response to pictures, that there were sex differences. Although the numbers of references to the body were approximately the same for boys and girls until age 15, from that point girls began to give more such references, a difference that extended into the adult years.

[27] Kafka (1969) described a woman who repeatedly cut her own skin and apparently derived satisfaction from so doing. He interpreted her behavior as reflecting a conversion of her own body into a transitional object.

[28] Pitblado (1976), though, has reported that under conditions of unusually extreme lateral tilting, adult women show more differentiation (field independence) than do men in their judgments of the vertical position of a luminous rod.

[29] Previous studies (Gill, Herdtner, & Lough, 1968; Klepper, 1968; Kurie & Mordkoff, 1970) showed that increasing a person's body awareness prior to the rod-and-frame test significantly decreased judgmental errors. One study (David, 1975), however, reported negative results in this respect.

It is also pertinent that Barrett and Thornton (1967) compared two methods of scoring the rod-and-frame test, one specifically designed to get at "body sensitivity" and the other based simply on total error and found the two measures were not significantly related. The "body sensitivity" score was developed by Benfari and Vitale (1965). It classifies subjects as "body oriented" or "frame oriented." Body-oriented subjects are those who place the rod opposite the direction of body tilt and frame when both are tilted in the same direction. Frame-oriented subjects position the rod so that it is tilted in the same direction as the frame. Whether the rod-and-frame test significantly taps into body image variables remains an open question.

[30] Cohen (1974) presents data indicating the diversity of possible interpretations of the various Witkin differentiation measures.

[31] Witkin et al. (1954) noted:

. . . there is an important difference between men and women as to the basis of their performance in our orientation tests. Since, in the men's group, scores for the orientation tests are related to scores for other tests which involve body activity dependent on structural and physiological factors, it appears that utilization of the kinds of body factors, as such, is an important factor in men's performance in the orientation tests. The absence of such a relation in scores for women indicates that their performance in the orientation situations does not involve utilization of these factors to a very great degree. From the high correlations reported earlier for women between the body-adjustment, and – – – tests which require simply the separation of an item from its context and do not involve reference to the body, we may surmise that for women more than for men the perception of body position tends to be a matter of separating the body as a *visual item* from its visual context". (pp. 108–109)

32 As one surveys the work of Witkin et al. (1962) concerning the attributes of mother that are predictive of the child's level of body concept differentiation, it is striking that mother's own figure drawing differentiation score is considerably more successful in such prediction than is her ability to adjust a luminous rod to the vertical. It is also pertinent that although mother's inclination to foster differentiation (as determined by interview) was correlated positively and substantially with her child's degree of differentiation, as defined by the perceptual tests (e.g., rod-and-frame, embedded figures), it had relatively low correlation with the child's level of body concept differentiation. Such a pattern of findings suggests that different aspects of mother's behavior contribute to her child's differentiation when defined by perceptual measures, as compared to her child's differentiation as depicted by the figure drawing index.

33 Weller and Sharan (1971) proposed that girls are particularly likely to manifest more body concept differentiation than boys in cultures that "emphasize verbal-intellectual achievement, with a concomitant neglect of skills in the use of and perceptions related to the body" (p. 1554). They offered validation of this idea in data indicating that girls were most likely to obtain higher body articulation scores in samples of Israeli children that came from subcultures in which verbal-intellectual attainment was most prized. Presumably, in such subcultures the pressure to move toward intellectuality and away from the body is communicated significantly more strongly to male than to female children.

34 A review of a number of the major body image implications of the sensory-tonic research initiated by Wapner and Werner has been presented by Fisher (1970).

35 Blane (1962) reported a related developmental phenomenon. Children 9 to 12 years of age who had suffered unilateral paralysis displaced the apparent vertical position of a luminous rod toward the side of the paralysis, but children in the 15-19 year range with unilateral paralysis displaced vertical in the opposite direction.

36 Similar compensatory responses, which involve shifting in a direction opposite to the pull of an experienced tension, have been demonstrated in judgments of the location of the "straight ahead" and in directionality of autokinetic movement (Wapner et al., 1971).

37 Wapner et al. (1971) cited work indicating that schizophrenics differentiate poorly between object and body space, as evidenced by small angular disparities

between their judgments (during tilt) of the position of vertical and their body positions.

[38] Witkin et al. (1954) failed to maintain a proper perspective concerning the limited body image implications of their findings. They knew from their own data that women could utilize body cues in a variety of situations just as effectively as men. Thus, when women were allowed to make spatial judgments on the basis of kinesthetic information alone they did as well as men. Only in the presence of conflicting visual cues did women turn in a performance that was relatively inferior. Their so-called body image defect was limited to a specialized type of situation involving visual cues. With respect to such visual cues, it is apropos to add that a study (Witkin, Bernbaum, Lomonaco, Lehr, & Herman, 1968) of blind and normal subjects (ages 12-18) in which disembedding of perceptual stimuli was limited to touch, there were no sex differences for three of the four tasks; and the girls were actually superior in performance of a fourth. Relatedly, Walker (1972) could discern no sex difference in a situation where judgments of the vertical were made that depended upon tactual sensations.

[39] The same result was also obtained for a group of male subjects.

[40] Considerable attention has been focused on whether speed or delay in developing adolescent secondary sex characteristics has an impact on personality structure. If a child is an early or late maturer, does this affect his or her adaptation? Numerous studies bearing on this issue have been published (e.g., Blyth et al., 1981; Clausen, 1975; Elder, Jr., 1968; Dwyer & Mayer, 1968; Mussen & Jones, 1957, 1958; Weatherley, 1964). There has been some disagreement concerning the characteristics of early versus late maturers. Several studies (e.g., Mussen & Jones, 1957, 1958) suggested that late maturing boys have more adaptation difficulties than early maturers. However, Peskin (1967) presented data indicating that the opposite may be true. He concluded that the late maturing boy has more time than the early maturer to adjust to the upsurge in sexual impulses accompanying the sexual maturation of the body. The late maturer is therefore presumably the more comfortable with his impulses, more able to integrate them into his personality economy. There are some indications that girls may be less affected than boys by the fact of early or late body maturation (Elder, Jr., 1968).

An extreme form of delayed maturity is encountered in children who suffer from endocrine, genetic, or chronic illnesses that grossly inhibit growth and can eventually result in a dwarf-like body. These children are slow to mature and are grossly smaller than their peers. They are conspicuously deviant in body size. Many clinical and anecdotal observations of growth-inhibited children may be found (e.g., Krims, 1968; Kusalic, Fortin, & Gauthier, 1972; Lewis, Money, & Bobrow, 1973; Money & Pollitt, 1966; Spencer & Raft, 1974). These children are frequently described as unhappy, depressed, and retarded in their psychosocial maturity. However, they are also often depicted as unusually friendly, humorous, and clever in their ability to adopt strategies that permit them to adapt to their deviant position. Few systematic studies of their psychological attributes have been carried out. Several have employed figure drawings and have largely shown that the growth-inhibited child is not typified by radical distortions in body perception (Drash, Greenberg, & Money, 1968; Drotar, Owens, & Gotthold, 1980; Money, Cohen, Lewis, & Drash, 1968). There are data suggesting that, despite their deviant body structure, dwarfs tend to adapt rather well. Brust, Ford, and Rimoin (1976) studied 7 men and 9 women who were dwarfs.

Intelligence level and personality traits were evaluated, and the Draw-A-Person was administered. The male dwarfs deviated significantly from normal on the personality tests, but largely in the direction of being less masculine and more conforming. Female dwarfs did not differ from normals at all in their personality scores. Intelligence in both males and females was above average. The figure drawings suggested that the dwarfs see themselves not only as small, but perhaps even smaller in proportion to normal persons than they actually are. It was concluded: "The degree of psychological well-being and confident self-identity of these adult dwarfs was striking. Their positive adjustment to life despite the stress of a major physical deformity was demonstrated by their ability to maintain productive lives including employment, marriage, and parenthood. Psychological testing confirmed the clinical impression of a relative lack of psychiatric symptoms, excessive anxiety, or depression" (p. 163).

[41] Rierdan and Koff (1980b) also found girls in the seventh grade to be unusually negatively aware of their bodies and unusually tuned into the sexual changes they were experiencing.

[42] Speer (1969) examined differences in Body Cathexis (Secord & Jourard, 1953) in postpubescents ranging in age from 15 through 17 and could not detect significant variations as a function of age.

[43] Support for this observation is provided by Megargee (1965), who reviewed data collected by several investigators and concluded that low Barrier scores typify "early adolescents."

[44] Wolman, Lewis, and King (1972) questioned boys and girls (ages 5-13) about the body locations of various emotions. They observed that females were significantly more likely than males to ascribe emotions to interior as opposed to exterior body sites. The tendency to link emotion with interior sites was also significantly and positively correlated in both sexes with chronological age.

[45] May (1971) devised a technique for getting at masculine versus feminine attitudes that is based on the degree to which fantasies depict action patterns that initially surge upward and are then followed by downfall (masculine) or that are down and then move to an upward enhanced position (feminine). Presumably, the up and then down pattern of the male mirrors the basic male sequence of phallic tumescence and detumescence. The reverse pattern of the female is said to reflect the fact that women have (Cramer, 1975) "recurring experiences of menstruation, intercourse and childbirth" that are "experienced . . . as pain or discomfort followed by joy or relief" (p. 538). In other words, the male versus female fantasy patterns are assumed to be derived from body experiences. Scores based on the relative frequencies of these two patterns in stories created by subjects indicate that adult males and females differ rather consistently (May, 1966) in the anticipated direction. There are conflicting reports about what is true at earlier ages, with sex differences verified and also not verified in 5-year-olds (Cramer & Bryson, 1973; May, 1971). But sex differences have been fairly substantially shown to be present in early adolescents and even in children as young as 10 (Cramer, 1975; Cramer & Bryson, 1973).

[46] Other sex differences have been observed that have no apparent superiority-inferiority implications. For example, boys are more likely to produce images with body connotations that are phallic (Erikson, 1951). Fisher (1970) found that boys are more likely to be inhibited about perceiving aniseikonic changes in the face than girls; and girls are more inhibited about perceiving aniseikonic changes in their legs. Kagan

and Moss (1962) discovered that boys who early exhibited high body anxiety were, as adults, highly invested in intellectual pursuits, whereas the opposite was true for women who had heightened body anxiety during childhood. There are also instances in which sex differences have not been detected. Thus, no solid differences between boys and girls have shown up in their knowledge of the locations and functions of the various body parts.

[47] The Barrier score seems to increase throughout childhood and adolescence.

[48] It is also true that parents who live with a severely disabled child evolve defensive body image responses (Centers & Centers, 1963).

3

Body Appearance, Prowess, and Camouflage

Since the human body represents the individual's unique base of operations in the world, it is not surprising that endless energy is devoted to polishing and strengthening it. Each culture has its own ideas about what it takes to make a body "right." All cultures have their own notions about how the body properly should be shaped and sized and decorated. The images of what a "good" body should look like are unbelievably varied. The modal body appearance in one group may seem to be not at all human to a representative of another group. Apropos of this point, Darwin said in one instance (Vlahos, 1979): "I believe in this part of South America, man exists in a lower state of improvement than in any other part of the world . . . their hideous faces daubed with white paint, their skins filthy and greasy, their hair entangled . . . one can hardly believe they are fellow creatures and inhabitants of the same world" (p. 27).

Vlahos has reviewed many of the more radical body "improvement" practices around the world. She describes the elaborate body tattooing practiced in Polynesia, body scarring prominent in Africa, genital organ mutilation (e.g., circumcision, clitoridectomy) characteristic of many locales, lip enlargement found in Brazil, and teeth filing popular in Africa. She points out that analogous body reshaping is current in Western culture in such practices as rhinoplasty, ear piercing, circumcision, and breast augmentation. Of course, tattooing also is still popular on the modern scene. The idealized images of the body proclaimed by each culture are translated into clothing fashions, preferences for certain body builds, health and exercise regimens, and a thousand body camouflaging strategies. This chapter examines what is known about experiencing one's own body in relation to its appearance, camouflage, and conformance to idealized standards.

BODY APPEARANCE

Standards and Self Judgments

As indicated previously, at any early age individuals develop standards of body attractiveness fairly similar to those they will adhere to as adults. The chubby physique of the endomorph is universally looked upon negatively; and at the other extreme, the thin ectomorph is also typically disapproved, although the disapproval is considerably greater in relation to the male than the female. Actually, Staffieri (1972) found that elementary school girls considered the ectomorphic feminine body type as quite attractive. Generally, the mesomorph or some variation of it represents the most favored physique. There is evidence that being large (but not fat) is preferred by the male, and body smallness (except for breasts[1]) is favored by the female (Fisher, 1970). Numerous investigators have tried to map modal evaluative attitudes toward various sectors of one's own body. They have sought to find out which body areas are typically regarded most positively and which most negatively. The methodology has usually involved asking persons to rate how much they like or dislike each of their many body parts.

A major study (Berscheid, Walster, & Bohrnstedt, 1973) was based on responses to a "body image" questionnaire that readers of *Psychology Today* were invited to fill out. Of the more than 60,000 responses, 2000 that duplicated national age and sex distributions were selected for analysis. The questionnaire called for ratings of degree of satisfaction with 25 different aspects of one's body.[2] It also contained items pertinent to such matters as self-esteem, sexual preference, marital status, and early body experiences. About 55% of the men, as compared to 45% of the women, indicated they were "quite" or "extremely" satisfied with their overall appearance. This trend for females to express less overall body satisfaction than males has, as already noted, been observed in a number of other surveys.[3] Only 4% of the men in the study said they were "quite" or "extremely" dissatisfied with their overall body appearance, but 7% of the women fell into this category. Both in this study and most others of a similar nature in which persons were explicitly asked if they like their bodies, positive rather than negative evaluations predominate.[4]

With respect to specific body parts, women expressed their greatest dissatisfaction with the following: upper thighs (22%), size of abdomen (10%), buttocks (17%), teeth (11%), muscle tone (9%), and weight (21%). Males were more dissatisfied with: size of abdomen (11%), teeth (10%), and weight (19%). Greatest negativity was displayed by women toward the hip area and by men toward the abdominal regions. A number of other studies (Clifford, 1971; Lerner, Orlos, & Knapp, 1976; Snyder & Kivlin, 1975) have documented the unusual amount of dissatisfaction that females, beginning even in adolescence, feel with respect to the waist-hip-thigh region and, relatedly, to their overall weight. In the Berscheid et al. (1973) study, 25% of the women expressed some degree of dissatisfaction with their breasts and 18% of the men with their chests. Fifteen percent of the men expressed some dissatisfaction with their genital size, but only 3% of the women did so. Homosexual men were significantly more likely than exclusively heterosexual men to feel dissatisfied with their genitals and also with their bodies in general. Such differences did not obtain in comparisons of female homosexuals with heterosexuals. Generally, there was a positive correlation between liking one's body and stating that sexuality is satisfying. Married men said they felt more positively toward their bodies than did unmarried men. However, marital status was not linked with degree of body satisfaction in women.

Berscheid et al. (1973) explored their data to find out if one's feelings about self were linked to one's feelings about specific body parts. They concluded that degree of satisfaction with one's face was most highly correlated with feelings about self. Surprisingly, no gross differences in body ratings could be discerned over the age range represented (25–45 or older) in the sample.[5] Older people did not express more body dissatisfaction than did the younger. There were trends for older persons to show greater negativity toward their teeth than the younger persons, but to be more satisfied with their complexion. Women showed a sharp drop with age in satisfaction with their hands; and it was suggested, "hands are more central to a woman's beauty than we had thought" (p. 122). It is also interesting that 38% of the subjects indicated that at some time in their lives they had experienced a sudden dramatic change in body appearance (e.g., due to rapid weight gain or loss, accidents). Those who had had more than one such experience, even if the change was a positive one, were inclined to rate their bodies more negatively.

Schwartz (1982) asked 307 males and 368 females to rate 25 different aspects of their body. The subjects ranged in age from 16 to over 55. There were whites, blacks, and Puerto Ricans represented. As in the Berscheid et al. (1973) study, there were generally high levels of body satisfaction. Only 5% indicated "extreme dissatisfaction" with overall appearance. Fifty-nine percent stated they were "extremely satisfied." The body parts evoking greatest dissatisfaction were pretty much the same as those reported by Berscheid et al. (1973) There was a slight trend for people over 55 to rate their body more negatively than did those in the 16–24 range. The younger age group was significantly more satisfied with eyes, ears, appearance of sex organs, hands, teeth, and size of abdomen, whereas the older group was significantly more satisfied with complexion and nose. The results for teeth and complexion duplicate those obtained by Berscheid et al. All the differences between younger and older subjects were actually very small. The younger and older samples were more alike than different.

Schwartz (1982) was puzzled by the fact that aging was not associated with relatively greater body dissatisfaction. Women were significantly less satisfied than men with most body parts except the face. The differences were particularly large in the youngest subjects. The one body part the women were significantly more satisfied with was size of sex organs. Few real differences in body satisfaction were tied to social class. However, older subjects in the working lower class were particularly dissatisfied with their body parts. Blacks were found to be substantially more satisfied than Jews with their body. There were significant differences for 23 of the 25 body parts rated. The differences were especially pronounced for size and appearance of sex organs, complexion, arms, voice, chin, and general muscle development.

A large part of the literature dealing with evaluation of one's own body is based on the Jourard-Secord (1955) Body Cathexis questionnaire.[6] This questionnaire calls for self-ratings (5-point scale) of 46 different body parts and attributes. Studies have shown that it has reasonably good split-half (Jourard & Remy, 1957; Weinberg, 1960) and test-retest (2 weeks intervening) (Tucker, 1981) reliabilities. Relatedly, Padin, Lerner, and Spiro (1981) have also reported high test-retest stability for self-ratings of body attractiveness. However, it has been found that social desirability sets can significantly affect body ratings of the type called for by the Jourard-Secord scale (Berez, 1976; Noonan, 1966; Pantleo, 1966). With few exceptions, studies that have used the Body Cathexis questionnaire have ignored the role of social desirability in the results obtained.

Studies have been undertaken to determine how important people consider the various body areas listed in the Body Cathexis questionnaire to be in defining their own physical attractiveness. In one instance (Lerner, Karabenick, & Stuart, 1973) involving college students (118 males, 190 females), it was found that males assigned highest importance to face, facial complexion, teeth, weight, and body build. The males ascribed lowest importance to ears, ankles, hair color, and neck. The females judged as most important: face, facial complexion, teeth, weight, body build, and shape of legs. They ascribed lowest importance to ears, ankles, shoulder width, and neck. There was almost total agreement between the judgments of the two sexes. In a second study (Lerner & Karabenick, 1974) involving 70 male and 119 female college students, the observations of Lerner et al. (1973) were largely substantiated.

It will be recalled that Berscheid et al. (1973) could detect no consistent differences in body ratings across an age range from the mid-20s to beyond 45; and Schwartz (1982) observed only a slight trend for older subjects to be more dissatisfied than younger ones. Howe (1973) explored this same issue. She secured body ratings from males ($N = 75$) and females ($N = 73$) in three different age categories: 25-35, 45-55, 60-70. No overall significant differences in body ratings emerged among the three age groups. However, there was a trend for females in the oldest age group to rate their bodies more favorably than did the women in the middle to youngest groups, and the difference between the oldest and the middle age group was statistically significant. Incidentally, the females in all three groups rated their bodies less favorably than did the males, and the results were statistically significant in the 25-35 and 45-55 age categories. There was an increase in the body satisfaction of the oldest women that cancelled the male superiority found in other age categories. Howe speculated that when women reach an advanced age, they become less concerned about meeting the culture's high standards of beauty for women and therefore judge their own bodies less stringently and negatively. An analysis was undertaken to determine if socio-economic or educational status[7] played a role in the body ratings, and the findings were entirely negative. One other finding of particular interest was that the relationship between body satisfaction ratings and self-esteem was signifcantly greater in the middle and oldest groups than in the youngest.

Body Cathexis and Self-Concept

Jourard and Secord (1955) originally demonstrated a significant, moderate, positive correlation between ratings of satisfaction with one's body and ratings of satisfaction with self. The relationship has since been corroborated by numerous investigators (e.g., Berscheid, Walster, & Bohrnstedt, 1973; Gunderson & Johnson, 1965; Johnson, 1956; Lerner, Karabenick, & Stuart, 1973; Mahoney & Finch, 1976a; Nelson, 1967).[8] Further, Mendelson and White (1982) have shown the same positive relationship to hold true in both normal weight and obese children (ages 7-12). Kurtz (1971) was able to demonstrate a positive link between body satisfaction ratings and a measure of self-esteem based not on self-ratings but rather a semiprojective index of self-esteem.

There has been a good deal of musing and puzzlement about the implications of these findings.[9] In the process of trying to clarify their implications, a variety of special analyses have been undertaken to determine what aspects of the body are most highly linked with self concept ratings.[10] Mixed results have emerged from the analysis. Lerner et al. (1973) obtained ratings of body parts and also of self from 110 male and 190 female college students. They reported that in the male sample the ratings of the following specific body parts were highly correlated with self-esteem:[11] facial complexion, waist, nose, face, thighs, shape of legs, teeth, and hair texture. In the female sample, the analogously highly correlated body parts were: facial expression, waist, nose, face, thighs, profile, eyes, height, ankles, hips, chin, and hair color. Lerner et al. described the ratings of the following body parts as moderately correlated with self-ratings in males: width of shoulders, profile, eyes, mouth, neck, and hair color. The moderately correlated parts for the females involved width of shoulders, ears, and shape of legs. There was a fairly high degree of overlap between the males and females with respect to the body parts that are significantly correlated with self-esteem.

In another study, Lerner and Karabenick (1974) obtained body and self-ratings from 70 male and 119 female college students. They found that for the males only the ratings of satisfaction with two specific body parts were highly correlated with self-ratings: nose and face. The analogous body parts for the females were thighs, shape of legs, waist, ankle, profile, and neck. Body satisfaction ratings that correlated moderately with self-ratings in the males included only two: facial complexion and mouth. For the females, the moderately correlated parts included facial complexion, chest, teeth, and chin. Comparing results of this study with the previously described Lerner et al. (1973) study, one finds only limited agreement as to which body parts in the male samples were significantly correlated with self-concept ratings. Four specific parts appeared on both lists: facial complexion, nose, face, and mouth (all involve the face). For the females, the agreement between the two studies was greater. The specific body parts appearing on both lists were facial complexion, waist, thighs, chest, profile, ankles, and chin. These parts, in contrast to those listed for the males, involve not only the face, but also a number of other body sites. The cross validated parts for males and females showed almost no overlap.

Interpretation of the findings just reviewed is complicated by the fact that Mahoney and Finch (1976a) criticized the use of zero order correlations in determining the relationships of ratings of each body part with the self-concept index. They suggested: "If . . . satisfaction with body aspects is intercorrelated between various body aspects, it is impossible to ascertain the relative contribution of any given body aspect of self-concept by the use of the zero order correlation coefficients alone. Since it is reasonable to assume that the perception of body aspects takes on some gestalt characteristics, intercorrelation is quite possible" (p. 252). They considered that the most reasonable statistical approach to the issue would be to employ multiple stepwise regression. They studied 103 male and 136 female college students. Subjects rated their degree of satisfaction with each of a number of body aspects. Self-esteem was measured with the Rosenberg (1965) Self-Esteem Scale.

When initially exploring the results that would emerge as the result of employing zero order correlations, Mahoney and Finch (1976a) found that "for both sexes, face is the most important body aspect with regard to self-esteem" (p. 253). For the males, the body part with the second strongest influence on self-esteem was the chest, and for females it was the mid-torso sector. However, when Mahoney and Finch shifted to a stepwise regression mode of analysis, the results were quite different. For males, the following body aspects accounted for variance in self esteem: voice, chest circumference, teeth, nose, leg shape, facial features. For females, the significant body aspects were teeth, hair color, voice, calves, height, and hips.[12] Mahoney and Finch noted:

> "the conclusions of previous research are somewhat in error. First, the conclusion . . . that body aspects which contribute to self-esteem are generally the same for both sexes is seriously questioned. Even though the zero order correlation coefficients in the present data quite closely replicate those (previously) obtained . . . , the results of the appropriate regression analysis indicate that different body aspects contribute to explaining variance in self-esteem for males and females. Secondly, the importance of facial aspects, and face in general . . . is clearly not supported. (p. 257)

It is interesting that despite the negative attitude taken by Mahoney and Finch (1976a) toward previous related findings, there is a fair amount of overlap between the results of their regression analysis and those of the two previous major studies (viz., Lerner et al., 1973; Lerner & Karabenick, 1974) reviewed earlier. Four of the body areas (viz., teeth, nose, leg shape, facial) identified by Mahoney and Finch as important for males in relation to self-esteem appeared as significant correlates in at least one of the previous studies. This was true also for five of the body areas listed by Mahoney and Finch (1976a) as significant in the female group: teeth, hair color, shape of legs (calves), height, hips. It is striking that teeth and shape of legs showed up for both males and females as importantly linked with self-esteem. It is particularly surprising that teeth seem to be so important. If future work affirms the findings just reviewed, more intensive exploration in this area would seem to be called for.

A possible sex difference concerning the relationship between body ratings and self-ratings seemed to emerge from the work of Lerner, Orlos and Knapp (1976). They asked 124 male and 218 female college students to rate the attractiveness of a series of their body parts and also to rate the "physical effectiveness" of the parts (how well they make activities engaged in turn out successfully). Self-concept ratings were also obtained. It had been anticipated that since women are "oriented toward viewing their bodies' utility in terms of interpersonal physical attractiveness" (p. 314), their self-concept would be more linked with their perception of their body's attractiveness than with its effectiveness. Just the opposite had been anticipated for men since "to the extent males can feel that they effectively push out into their environment an appropriate, positive sense of self will develop" (p. 314). The data obtained in the study indicated that, whereas body attractiveness and body effectiveness ratings were significantly positively correlated with self-esteem in both sex groups, the correlation between attractiveness ratings and self-esteem was significantly higher in the females than in the males. The reverse pattern was found between the sexes for the correlation of body effectiveness ratings with self-esteem. A subsequent study (Lerner et al., 1980) that included 796 Japanese students (approximately 50% of each sex), substantiated the greater correlation between body effectiveness ratings and self-esteem in males, as compared to females. However, the study failed to confirm the greater correlation in females between body attractiveness ratings and self-esteem. Indeed, the results for this relationship tended to be the opposite of what was expected. Another study (Padin, Lerner, & Spiros, 1981) involving 56 male and 96 female college students detected no sex differences in the patterns of correlations pertaining to body attractiveness ratings, body effectiveness ratings, and self-esteem.[13] Overall, there appears to be only a weak trend for women's self-esteem to be more closely linked with their perception of body attractiveness and men's esteem to be more closely correlated with their perceived body effectiveness. If a sex difference in this respect exists, it is a fragile one, easily shifted by changes in sample characteristics.

Another rather complex form of sex difference with regard to the relationship between body satisfaction and self-esteem has been investigated by Lerner and Brackney (1978). They studied male ($N = 72$) and female ($N = $

107) college students to determine whether there were sex differences in feelings about internal versus external body parts. Their work derived its theoretical impetus from Erikson's (1951) observations suggesting that the female is oriented toward her "inner space" (because of her biologically dictated reproductive role) and the male toward the "outer space" (because his anatomy dictates an intrusive mode of dealing with the outer world). Subjects rated how attractive they considered each of 24 external parts (e.g., arms, face) of their bodies. They also rated these same body parts with reference to "how *important* each part was in making the subject an attractive, effective, and appropriately functioning person" (p. 229). Twelve internal body parts were added to the list of parts to be rated. Nine were non-sex-internal parts (e.g., lungs) and three were sex-internal parts (e.g., prostate gland for males, ovaries for females). Subjects were also administered a modified form of the Tait and Ascher (1955) Inside-of-the-Body Test, which calls for drawing in and labeling the internal organs of an asexual frontal outline of a human figure. A self-rating measure of self-esteem was also secured. It was found that: "Consistent with the Eriksonian idea that 'inner space' is more salient for females than males" (p. 230), females drew significantly more internal body parts than did the males. Females attached significantly greater importance than the males did not only to their internal body parts, but also to their external parts.

A particularly striking sex difference emerged when ratings of outer versus internal body parts were correlated with self-esteem. Contrary to a prediction based on Erikson's view, attitudes toward inner body parts significantly predicted self-esteem in males but not in females, and more external than internal body parts were predictors of female self-esteem. These findings introduce a new and intriguing complexity into the exploration of sex differences in body perception. The apparent association of self-esteem with the outer body in females and the contrasting association of self-esteem with the internal body sector in males bears an interesting analogy to Fisher's (1970) observation that females have better articulated body boundaries than do males. The body boundary is conceptualized by Fisher as involving the same body areas that Lerner and Brackney (1978) included in their category of "external body parts."

Diverse Studies of Body Cathexis

Since Jourard and Secord devised the Body Cathexis scale, various versions of it have been widely used and applied to a surprising range of problems. Let us briefly survey what has been done.

Attempts to Increase Body Satisfaction

All kinds of techniques have been evaluated as possible approaches to making people feel more positively toward their bodies. A fair number have reported success in doing so. Thorpe (1976) found that after a month's experience with yoga patients ($N = 11$) in a psychiatric drug unit showed more increase in body satisfaction than a control group of patients ($N = 10$) who received only a standard reality-based treatment. Zamarin (1976) showed that a personal development course (providing instruction on how to increase physical attractiveness via nonsurgical means) improved body satisfaction in 17 women; a control group of women ($N = 14$) involved in an office skills training program improved significantly less than the experimental subjects. Schneider (1977) examined the impact of an 8-week course in movement exploration and mime on 102 boys and 81 girls in a junior high school. The boys increased significantly more in body satisfaction than a control group of comparable boys ($N = 54$) who simply pursued the regular physical education program. However, the girls in the experimental group did not show greater improvement than the control girls ($N = 64$). Clance, Matthews, and Joesting (1979) demonstrated that college students ($N = 22$) who took part in an awareness training class manifested a significantly greater increase in body satisfaction than a control group ($N = 45$) that simply participated in an introductory psychology course.

A number of studies could not produce alterations in body satisfaction. Loftis, Clance, and Joesting (1978) discerned no greater change in body cathexis in persons ($N = 24$) during 8 weeks of individual psychotherapy than in controls ($N = 25$) not receiving psychotherapy during the same period. Harris, Nolte, and Nolte (1980) did not find significantly greater increase in body satisfaction in a group of teenagers ($N = 19$) who received Structural Awareness therapy (designed to improve awareness and alignment through the use of movement patterns and exercises) than in controls ($N = 6$) who simply went on a chaperoned field trip. McCuistion (1973) failed to produce a greater change in body satisfaction in women ($N = 20$) who attended a "Self-Help Clinic on body ownership" than in control women ($N = 20$) who did not participate in any special therapy program. Sussman (1977) compared changes in body cathexis in three groups: One ($N = 12$) participated nude in the activities of a nudist camp for a day; a second ($N = 12$) went on an outing for a day; a third ($N = 8$) received no special treatment at all. Sussman found no significant differences in change of body satisfaction among the groups. It is not apparent why some experimental conditions resulted in body cathexis alterations and others did not. There are no gross differences among the positive and negative studies with reference to such variables as the directness with which body experience was manipulated, reasonableness of the experimental designs, ages of subjects, and sizes of samples.

Correlational Studies

At one time or another attempts have been made to correlate body satisfaction with almost every conceivable variable. Many of the studies have sought to link body satisfaction with indices of adjustment, adaptability, and health. As might be expected, people who are physically ill have relatively low body satisfaction. Kurtz and Hirt (1970) showed this in a comparison of 40 hospitalized women with 20 normal women. Schwab and Harmeling (1968) also found relatively negative body appraisals in 124 medical patients. Interestingly, the body ratings were not correlated with the severity of illness. Johnson (1956) demonstrated that body satisfaction was significantly negatively correlated with number of somatic complaints.

With respect to maladjustment, Apfeldorf, Smith, Peixotto, and Hunley (1974) found a significant positive correlation (in 114 college women) between degree of body satisfaction and emotional adjustment, as defined by the MMPI. Jaskar and Reed (1963) had earlier observed that body satisfaction was significantly lower in hospitalized psychiatric patients than in normal controls. Goldberg and Folkins (1974) observed that body satisfaction was negatively correlated with such negative affects as anxiety and depression in 113 male and 135 female college students. Nelson (1967) reported a significant positive relationship (in 78 college women) between body satisfaction and self-actualization.

Pauly and Lindgren (1976–77) discovered that a sample of pretreatment transsexuals (16 male, 14 female) had significantly greater body dissatisfaction than normal nontranssexuals (53 male, 12 female). Transsexuals reported a significant increase in body satisfaction after sex change surgery. Duchow (1980) observed in 63 transsexuals and transvestites that, contrary to prediction, amount of body dissatisfaction was not correlated with the degree to which dissatisfaction with one's sexual identity took the form of wanting surgical sex change. Transvestites and transsexuals reported significantly more distortions in body experience than normal subjects.

Gunderson and Johnson (1965) found that body satisfaction was significantly positively correlated (in 743 Navy enlisted men) with reported past school adjustment and negatively with reported past delinquency behavior. However, it was not correlated with an index of Military adjustment. Schomburg (1974) obtained data indicating that body satisfaction was significantly and positively correlated with gradepoint average (in college males and females) and also with level of aspiration. (A subsample of blacks was found to have higher body satisfaction than whites.) The link between body satisfaction and grade point average was not, however, supported by an earlier study (White & Walsh Jr., 1965) that observed only a minimal relationship between body satisfaction and grades (in 42 male and 32 female college students).

. Grodner (1981) discerned a significant negative relationship (in 71 women) between fear of success and body satisfaction. Schultz (1973) noted that the greater the body satisfaction (in 100 male and female college students) the significantly better they performed on a gross motor task (stabilometer). However, Leahy (1967) found nonsignificant results in relating body satisfaction to a similar motor task (in 79 college males). Also, White (1971) could not detect (in 60 boys) a relationship between body satisfaction and "motor creativity." Levine (1976) established in a sample of 98 women that the more democratic they perceived their mothers' childrearing practices to have been, the greater the body satisfaction they personally felt. However, Riffle (1972) found in 83 mother-daughter pairs only a chance correlation between body satisfaction scores.

There is some evidence that body satisfaction is correlated with certain aspects of sexual and reproductive behavior in women. Young (1980) reported that sexually active and less sexually active women (N = 82 college students) were distinguished by the fact that the former obtained higher body satisfaction scores. Eichler (1973) demonstrated that in 100 college women the greater their body satisfaction, the more significantly sexually active they were. Body satisfaction was also positively correlated with low levels of menstrual discomfort, low sexual guilt, and a role definition that was career rather than conventionally feminine oriented. Young (1981) demonstrated in a sample of 83 women that body satisfaction was significantly linked with certain preferred modes of contraception. An attempt to find a tie (in 138 married women) between body satisfaction and difficulty in adapting to pregnancy did not fare well (Gordon, 1976).

Numerous other miscellaneous observations could be cited. Studies diversely indicate that chiropractors have higher body satisfaction than physicians (Lasser, 1976); that androgynous women have more body satisfaction than masculine or feminine women (Kimlicka, 1978); that degree of masculinity-femininity of vocational choice in women is not significantly related to body satisfaction (Becker, 1971); that in female but not male drama students the ability to perform pantonimic movement is positively and significantly correlated with body satisfaction (Bahs, 1969); that body satisfaction and self-disclosure are linked in contrasting ways in males and females (Cash & Soloway, 1975); that those who have favorable attitudes toward blacks (Eichholz, 1975) are higher in body satisfaction; that bias against the disabled is correlated with negative body attitudes (MacRae, 1972); that compliance with a prescribed medical regimen in post-myocardial infarction patients is tied to high body satisfaction (Bille, 1975); that women who regularly examine their breasts for lumps display significantly greater body satisfaction than women who do not do so (Scilken, 1977); and so forth.

Overview

What are some of the primary findings that emerge? First, people more frequently say they generally like than that they dislike their bodies. But[14] although they have an evaluative attitude toward their overall body space, they also have different feelings toward its major regions and specific parts. The major regions, as defined by body satisfaction ratings, that have been consistently differentiated in factor analyses are the face, the extremities, and the torso. Interestingly, age differences in body evaluation either for the body as a whole or for specific body sectors have been difficult to demonstrate. Although some sex differences have emerged, there is also considerable similarity in the way the two sexes evaluate and assign importance to body regions. There does seem to be a consistent and significant trend for females to express less body satisfaction than males, but the difference is not great. Women seem to be especially negative toward the waist-hip-thigh region. With certain reservations, it appears that body satisfaction and self-esteem are moderately highly linked. However, causality in this link has not yet been established. Degree of satisfaction with three particular body aspects (voice, teeth, and shape of legs) has turned out to be most highly correlated with self-esteem. There is, as yet, no solid explanation as to why these body aspects should emerge so significantly in this respect.

The information that has accumulated concerning how people evaluate their own appearance is, with minor exceptions, based on self-ratings. As noted, these self-ratings are significantly influenced by social desirability. It comes as no surprise that defensive responses are aroused when judgments are elicited about something with such basic ego significance as one's own body. But it is surprising how few researchers consider social desirability when interpreting their data. They assume that they are dealing with a relatively pure body image measure. The uncomplicated directness of the Jourard-Secord Body Cathexis questionnaire, which has made it so popular as a tool for studying body image, is probably also its greatest weakness. Subjects are able to manipulate their responses at will. If one simply looks uncritically at the numerous correlates of degree of body satisfaction, it appears that those who like their own body space feel better and behave more effectively than those who regard that space negatively. To name only a few of the correlates, one could say that persons who report being well satisfied with their bodies are also likely to be in good health; to be well adjusted emotionally (as defined by measures like the MMPI); to have done well in school; to enjoy sex; to be favorable toward blacks; and to be relatively accepting of body disabilities in others. However, it should be kept in mind that aside from the social desirability influences inherent in the body satisfaction ratings, many of the measures apparently linked with body satisfaction are themselves based on questionnaire responses that are influenced by social desirability sets. One may be looking at a commonality derived from shared defensiveness in response.

It is instructive to examine the frequencies with which specific body areas showed up prominently in the studies cited earlier. Some body areas were found to be particularly correlated with self-esteem, and various body sectors were particularly likely to be judged as important or to be prominent in verbalizations about the body. The face is an area that was especially prominent on lists of importance and a frequent significant correlate of self-esteem. In women, the hip, thigh, leg areas were also prominently mentioned; but this was much less true for men. Strangely, the teeth were the most frequently and consistently referred to by both sexes. In Mahoney and Finch's (1976a) study involving multiple stepwise regression analysis of the relationships of body part satisfaction to self-esteem, the teeth were one of only two body variables that accounted for significant variance in both sexes. The other body variable was the voice.

The voice is often overlooked as a prominent part of one's body presentation and therefore probably of one's body image. Because voice and teeth are both associated with the oral region, it is possible that feelings about that region and its functions play a paramount role in evaluative attitudes towards one's own body space. One could speculate, as have Freud and others (Abraham, 1927), that early oral experiences are fundamental in relating to the world and therefore are of central import in personality development. By the same token, they might be of special significance in determining positive or negative attitudes toward one's body and oneself. It is pertinent that in the earlier mentioned large-scale Berscheid et al. (1973) study, the only body part that reflected a decline in body satisfaction in the elderly were the teeth. Surprisingly, although teeth and voice have been prominent in various rating contexts, the mouth has not. One could speculate that teeth and voice involve more aggressive aspects (viz., biting, verbally controlling others) of oral functioning, whereas the mouth, as such, may be associated with less aggressive oral functions like sucking. Perhaps it is the aggressive element that somehow magnifies the relative prominence of teeth and voice.

A totally surprising point that emerged from the research data was that people do not express a real decrease in body esteem as they move into middle and old age. This certainly contradicts popular stereotypes. It is generally assumed that the elderly, who usually experience a general decline in health, come to view their bodies more and more negatively. Perhaps this assumption is true, and research techniques like the Jourard-Secord Body Cathexis scale (1955) have failed to confirm it only because they are so vulnerable to the defensive denial that the elderly might be expected to manifest when confronted with a task that calls for evaluating one's body. However, it is interesting that Fisher (1970) could not detect any decline in body boundary articulation or security in very elderly persons (ages 70-80) whose Barrier scores were compared with those of younger representatives of their own families. Relatedly, Plutchik, Conte, and Bakur-Weiner (1973a) and Plutchik, Weiner, and Conte (1971) were unable to demonstrate inferiority in the body concept of elderly persons. There may be a surprising amount of resilience in maintaining body image integrity in the face of aging.

COVERING AND DECORATING THE BODY

It seems fairly obvious, from a commonsense point of view, that body attitudes influence the character of the clothes people choose to wear. Presumably, choice of attire would be tied to the image of how one looks or would like to look. Theoretically, it should be possible to determine the kinds of assumptions people make about their appearance by analyzing their clothing styles. One could decode fine nuances of the individual's body scheme by examining the magnifications and de-emphases of specific body areas that predominate in the garments typically worn. But few serious studies of such possibilities have been undertaken. Only a handful of investigations have examined clothing behavior from the perspective of body image theory. Those completed before 1970 have been summarized by Fisher (1970). They focused entirely on the relationship between the body boundary and such variables as amount of clothing worn (Fisher, 1970), the visual intensity of clothing designs (Compton, 1964), and openness to new clothing fashions (Kernaleguen, 1968). They indicated that insecurity about one's boundary may lead to wearing clothing that artificially helps to increase boundary articulation (e.g., by use of fabrics that are highly visible because of color, design, or novelty).

Since 1970, only a few scattered studies linking body image and clothing behavior have been reported. Several, which concern the role of boundary articulation in clothing choices, are detailed in the chapter dealing with body boundaries.

In addition Williams (1974) carried out a project, involving 140 college women, that failed to demonstrate a correlation between ratings of body satisfaction and the degree of closeness-looseness of clothing worn. Larsen and White (1974) reported that male college students ($N = 60$) who differed with respect to whether they wear their hair at "normal" as compared to "deviantly long" length also differed in field dependence-independence. Those with long hair were significantly more field independent. White and Kernaleguen (1971) found that college women ($N = 40$) who varied in their deviance with respect to skirt length differed sigificantly in field independence; those most deviant were also most field independent. Brett and Kernaleguen (1975) observed only a chance correlation between being a fashion leader (one whose advice is sought about fashion in clothing) and field dependence-independence in 102 college women. Karhoff (1979) examined (in a sample of 190 women) a large array of correlations between body satisfaction and clothing attitudes, as measured by a questionnaire. Those women who were most interested in wearing clothing that was distinctively feminine and providing of change experiences were the most satisfied with their body. Fashion leaders and fashion conformists were particularly satisfied with their body attributes, whereas the women who were independent of fashion felt less fortunate about their body. Obviously, not a great deal has been learned in recent years concerning the role of body image in clothing behavior.

A number of inquiries have been launched to determine if clothing choices are somehow a function of personality. Most of the studies (Compton, 1962; Conrad, 1973; Knapper, 1969; Ollinger, 1974; Reeder, 1977; Roach & Eicher,

1965; Rosencrantz, 1962; Rosenfeld & Plax, 1977; Taylor, 1977; Yadav, 1978) involved administering questionnaires or scales to tap clothing preferences and values and correlating this information with various standard measures of anxiety, personality, values, and defense mechanisms. As one scans this literature, it becomes apparent that no links between personality and costume have been consistently demonstrated. Attempts have been particularly made to show that secure and insecure people differ in how they dress, but no solid data have emerged. Also, there has been a focus on the dimension of dominance-submission, but it has not been possible to demonstrate that dominant people dress differently from the nondominant (Fisher, 1970).

Despite the confusion in the current research literature concerned with the psychological correlates of clothing preferences, the dimension of individuation-deindividuation appears to be prominent in clothing behavior. The power of changing fashions to motivate vast numbers of people to transform their perfectly adequate wardrobe, at considerable expense, testifies to the need to use clothing to make one's body conform to cultural stereotypes. If one's body or one's appearance does not fit roughly with accepted standards, there are serious penalties to pay in the form of rejection by the group. Studies of responses to persons with deviant appearance or identity have documented this fact well. On the other hand, there is a good deal of evidence that modes of body appearance may also be used to exalt one's individuality and to announce independence of group norms. This was obviously true in the 1960s, when long hair in a state of disarray was a signal of intent to fight the Establishment. Extreme costumes, nudity, and self-mutilation have often been used as forms of personal protest.

However, there are powerful forces in every culture that aim to bring the individual's body under control. These forces are expressed not only in elaborate rules about when and how various body functions can be exercised, but also in detailed prescriptions about how the body should be displayed. Many pubertal rites really amount to a demand that individuals radically revise parts of their anatomy to fit specified patents. There are cultures where the anatomical revisions demanded are so extreme (e.g., gross mutilation of the penis) as to cause death with fair frequency. The culture may particularly require that the body be normalized by controlling its surface qualities, e.g., by covering a large part of the skin with scar insignia or tattoos. It seems to be generally true that body decoration and clothing are used to deindividuate. This deindividuating strategy can have significant psychological effect. It undoubtedly fosters conformity and permits persons to act in behalf of the collective group while experiencing a limited sense of personal responsibility.

Watson (1973) found that the more that men in various cultures deindividuate themselves before they go into battle, the more likely they are to torture and mutilate the enemy. Data from cross-cultural files were obtained for 84 different cultures and coded for the presence of deindividuation procedures like body painting, face painting, and wearing masks. The greater the use of such procedures in a culture, the more likely were the following to be practiced: taking prisoners specifically for torture, killing all enemies on the spot, sacrificing prisoners. Presumably, a decrease in self-consciousness resulting from deindividuation permits the easier expression of extreme acts of aggression and cruelty. The individual can feel absolved of personal blame. It is certainly pertinent to this point that the considerable body of research dealing with the effects of making people aware of their own bodies (e.g., by observing self in a mirror) has demonstrated that such individuated awareness increases guilt and feelings of personal responsibility for one's acts. On the other hand, the Hasidic sect (Roach & Eicher, 1965) requires its members to wear distinctive garb as a continual reminder to them of their religious obligations and the need to refrain from deviant behavior. This raises the paradoxical possibility that body painting for supposed deindividuation purposes referred to in the Watson study just described may have actually focused attention on the body and therefore enhanced individual guilt about one's duty to the group and the need to fulfill the group's definition of a warrior. We need to learn a good deal more about the balance between individuation and deindividuation that results from various body adornment strategies.

One of the basic dynamics underlying body adornment is evident in Turner's (1969) detailed account of how a central Brazilian tribe (Tchikrin) requires that every major change in an individual's status be documented by suitable paintings of designs on his or her skin. Turner remarked: "Body painting at this general level of meaning really amounts to the imposition of a second, social 'skin' on the naked biological skin of the individual. This second skin of culturally standardized patterns symbolically expresses the 'socialization' of the human body—the subordination of the physical aspects of individual existence to common social values and behavior" (p. 70). Turner noted that "our own culture's elaborate array of clothing and hair styles, makeup, and jewelry" (p. 70) is comparable to the body painting among the Tchikrin and concluded that "the decoration of the surface of the body serves as a symbolic link between the 'inner man' and some of his society's most important values" (p. 70). Studies in the United States have empirically shown a correlation between clothing styles and values, particularly with reference to wearing fashionable versus unfashionable clothes (e.g., Kness & Densmore, 1976).

One of the most provocative and ingenious explorations of the relationship between clothing modes and cultural structure was presented by Schwarz (1979). An anthropologist, he observed a tribe (Guambianos) in Colombia for a number of years. He detected an apparent complex relationship between the shapes and spatial arrangements of male versus female clothing items and values in the culture that pertain to sex role. Although his analysis is too complex to duplicate here, some hint of what he did is provided by the following example. Schwarz observed in the Guambianos tribe a dichotomy between up-down that signifies superior-inferior. He also noted a contrast between the role of the hat (upper) and the role of clothing worn on the body (lower). The hat is associated with masculine functioning and the other body garments with the feminine realm. This up-down distinction in clothing was said to mirror an analogous up-down placement of the male versus the female in the power structure. Other more complex connections between clothing patterns and cultural values were also described by Schwarz. He remarked: "In short, the items of Guambiano clothing and their relationship to parts of the human body exhibit a pattern similar to that which characterize the structure of their social relationships. The result may be considered as a transformation of the principles of Guambiano social logic to the level of clothing" (p. 39). What is particularly fascinating about Schwarz's perspective is that he presents us with the possibility that cultural patterns may be translated into a language of space and contour that finds precise expression in the way people organize their own body spatiality, as defined by clothing choices.

BODY PROWESS

Effects of Muscular Arousal on Body Perception

Muscular movement in the form of athletic activity is one of the prime approaches to shaping the body to an idealized image. To get in shape through vigorous muscular exercise has become a popular goal. Jogging, weight lifting, calisthenics, and a myriad of related techniques have been fervently embraced to reconstruct what are considered to be weak, flaccid bodies. In all likelihood, florid body image fantasies take root in the potential profits of muscularly perfecting one's body. One can speculate that athletic regimens are often expected to provide protective body benefits not unlike those linked to various forms of body adornment. Schilder (1950) assigned utmost importance to movement and kinesthetic experience in the determination of body imagery. He regarded the perceived changes in body shape and mass that accompany movement as registering continuously on one's body concept. Attention is devoted in this section to exploring what is known about the effects of muscular arousal and movement on body perception. Also, consideration is given to the possible body image implications of the literature that has accumulated which deals with the psychological aspects of athletic activity. It has, of course, been established that shifting levels of muscular tension affect learning (e.g., Shaw, 1956) and sensory (e.g., Goldwater & Zirul, 1973; Smock & Small, 1962) processes significantly. Muscular activation is known to play a prime role in alertness and states of consciousness (Malmo, 1959). There are also studies (e.g., Heath, Oken, &

Shipman, 1967) suggesting that specific personality traits may be correlated with habitual levels of muscular arousal.

What is known about the effects of muscle movement and activation on body perception? A straightforward answer would be not much. Fuhrer and Cowan (1967) reported that the judgment of body size is affected by the degree to which the body has been in movement. Hester (1970) was not able to verify this observation. Further, Shontz (1969) found that in normal subjects kinesthetic and movement variables play a minimal part in body size judgments. But he did note that parts of the body that are paralyzed (i.e., not moveable) may appear to be shrunken in size and parts that are "extraordinarily used," as would be the case for paraplegics, who must compensatorily depend on shoulder and arm muscles, take on a magnified size. Rossi and Zoccolotti (1979) found that athletes, who presumably have more experiences than nonathletes with muscular movement, are also superior in their accuracy of body size evaluations. Fisher (1970) could not demonstrate any effects on body boundary articulation of procedures designed to affect muscle sensations and muscular activation. Thus, marching to rousing music did not produce a significant change in the Barrier score (based on the properties ascribed to the boundaries of inkblot responses). Similarly, intense vibratory input did not alter the Barrier score. However, several studies (Fisher, 1970; Van De Mark & Neuringer, 1969) have shown that persons specifically asked to focus their attention on the body periphery, defined as including muscle and skin, manifest a significant increase in Barrier score. Since the focus of attention was on both muscle and skin, it is not possible to specify how much of a contribution muscle awareness, as such, made to the increased boundary articulation. More recent studies, which are described in the section dealing with body boundaries, have found that a period of strenuous exercise does increase the Barrier score in schizophrenic persons. This is due to the augmented awareness of muscles that constitute a prominent part of the bounding structures of the body. It is not apparent why exercise should be effective in augmenting boundary articulation in a schizophrenic sample, whereas vigorous marching did not appreciably affect the boundary in Fisher's study of normal subjects just referred to above.

There is some evidence that degree of field independence–dependence (Witkin et al., 1954, 1962) may be influenced by body experiences that involve the musculature. Svinicki, Bundgaard, Schwensohn, and Westgor (1974) reported that physically active males and females ($N = 10$) were significantly more field independent (as defined by the rod-and-frame test) than those ($N = 10$) who were habitually inactive. Jones (as reported by Whiting, Hardman, Hendry, & Jones, 1973) noted that women ($N = 140$) dedicated to athletic activity were unusually field independent. Indeed, they matched the average degree of field independence of American men. In an early study, Gruen (1955) noted that professional dancers were not more field independent than a nondancer control group. However, Bard (1972) observed in a group of female college students (N = 20) that there was a significant positive correlation between field independence and dancing skill. Interestingly, degree of skill for certain team sports (e.g., volleyball) was significantly negatively correlated with field independence. Bard concluded that body skills that are internally oriented (such as dancing) are more likely to be cultivated by those who are field independent, whereas externally oriented body skills (that involve a group context) attract the field dependent.

Klepper (1968) discovered that he could increase field independence in a sample of 60 women by focusing their attention on their musculature. But focusing their attention on the body interior did not enhance field independence. Ruggieri and Mazza (1980) observed in a sample of 25 males and females that autogenic training, which modifies muscle tone, significantly improved performance on the Embedded Figures Test, which is a measure of field independence–dependence. Kurie and Mordkoff (1970) observed that merely intensifying body experience affects the field independence–dependence dimension. They found that spending a period of time concentrating on bodily sensations and experiences produced in subjects more improvement in rod-and-frame judgments than did a period of sensory isolation or a control period of nonfocused relaxation. Although Witkin and his associates have, more and more, minimized the link between the field–independence dimension and body experience and instead focused on the cognitive aspects of the dimension, the data just cited suggest that the body experience link is at least a significant one.

The Jourard-Secord Body Cathexis scale (1955) and similar self-ratings of the body have generally differentiated those who are and those are not athletically inclined. Joesting (1981) observed in a sample of 66 men and women that those who participated regularly in physical activities, such as basketball and running, rated their bodies significantly more positively than did inactive individuals. Joesting and Clance (1979) observed a parallel significant difference in Body Cathexis when comparing male and female runners (N = 80) respectively with male and female nonrunners (N = 45). Snyder and Kivlin (1975) established (in a total sample of 603 subjects) that women athletes had significantly higher body esteem scores than did women nonathletes. Darden (1972) reported that a sample of male athletes (N = 145) representing diverse sports had significantly elevated feelings of body esteem. But Shochat (1970) did not find significant differences in Body Cathexis among male high school participants and nonparticipants in sports. Overall, athletes seem to experience higher body esteem[15] than do nonathletes. Of course, the very act of participating for long periods of time in an athletic program may introduce demand characteristics that require one to say good things about one's body.[16] It is apropos to add that Ryckman, Robbins, Thornton, and Cantrell (1982) found in a number of different samples of college students that those who perceived their body as "physically self-efficacious" had high self-esteem and a tendency to engage in adventurous physical activities.

Interestingly, the Body Cathexis scale has given mixed results in its sensitivity to the effects of experimentally initiating exercise programs. Henderson (1974) showed (in a sample of 59 women) that 6 weeks of physical conditioning produced a greater increment in positive feeling about one's body than did a control condition. A similar increase in positive body feeling as the consequence of an exercise program was described by Stroble (1965) in a sample of 12 women and by Hawkins (1981) in a sample of 19 women. A negative result was obtained by Jette (1975), who could not discern a change in body attitude in women ($N = 108$) exposed to a program of training in modern dance. Relatedly, Puretz (1982) reported a negative effect of a modern dance program on body feelings in women ($N = 62$).[17] Folkins (1976) asked 40 males to participate in an extended exercise program and could not detect any real changes in their body self-ratings. In addition, Cerrato (1976) did not observe a significant change in the Body Cathexis ratings of 120 male and female college students who participated in a physical conditioning program. Davis (1980) found a nonsignificant change in body satisfaction in a sample of 25 women who were provided with physical conditioning.[18]

Obviously, simply engaging in a limited period of vigorous body activity may not be sufficient to increase body esteem. It is of related interest that Heaps (1972) has presented evidence, in a study of 56 males, that persons' perceptions of their physical fitness have only a low correlation with their actual empirically determined fitness. Their degree of body anxiety (as measured by the MMPI Hypochondriasis scale) was significantly negatively correlated with their perceived body fitness but was not significantly linked with their actual fitness. Roberts (1977) reaffirmed this relatively low relationship between perceived and actual body condition. He found that subjects with high body fat percentages were just as likely to rate themselves as being "in shape" as were subjects with normal body fat percentages. These two studies support the notion that attitudes and expectations may powerfully mediate how one interprets the actual changes produced in one's body by athletic activity.

A number of other sources of data strongly suggest that vigorous body movement does have psychologically salutary effects. Baekeland (1970) found in an exploratory probe of 14 male subjects accustomed to regular exercise that when they were deprived of exercise for a month, they reacted with considerable discomfort, impaired sleep patterns, intensified anxiety, increased sexual tension, and an elevated need to be with other people. Other studies have shown that bodily exercise may decrease anxiety and elevate mood (e.g., Bahrke, 1977; Folkins, 1976; Layman, 1974; Nowlis & Greenberg, 1979; Popejoy, 1967). It has also been reported that exercise may improve self-concept in disturbed children (Johnson, Fretz, & Johnson, 1968; Bonniwell, cited in Layman, 1974); make aged men feel more self-sufficient (Buccola & Stone, 1975); and increase body security in schizophrenics (Layman, 1974).

With regard to the effects of exercise, special attention should be given to some results obtained by Schwartz, Davidson, and Goleman (1978). These investigators pursued a formulation that differentiated anxiety into cognitive and somatic components. The cognitive would be exemplified by a statement like "I imagine terrifying scenes" or "I can't keep anxiety-provoking thoughts out of my mind." The somatic is represented by reports like "I feel tense in my stomach" or "I become immobilized." Schwartz et al. measured anxiety parameters in male and female subjects (N = 44) who were in a physical exercise program and compared them with those of subjects (N = 33) in a meditation program. They found, as predicted, that subjects practicing physical exercise reported relatively less somatic and more cognitive anxiety than did the meditators. They speculated that bodily exercise was specifically potent in relieving somatic or bodily localized anxiety, but not effective in nullifying anxiety that expressed itself largely in thought and fantasy. These findings await further validation. If they continue to be supported, they would suggest not only that there is a specific species of anxiety tied to the body as an object, but also that putting the body into vigorous action, in the context of an athletic program that has body improvement significance, counteracts such negative body sensations. Of course, this immediately raises the question whether one of the motivating forces in athletic participation is to nullify body-focused anxiety. Perhaps people who choose to become highly involved in athletics do so, at least in part, for defensive purposes. This issue is explored in the section that follows.

BEING AN ATHLETE

When people are systematically questioned about why they engage in vigorous body activity, such as athletics, they offer a range of explanations. Kenyon (1968b) has developed a questionnaire that groups the major motivations into six categories: social, health and fitness, vertigo, aesthetic, catharsis, and ascetic. Illustratively, people may be variously attracted to vigorous activity because it provides an opportunity for team associations, because it permits the venting and release of unpleasant tensions, or because it stimulates novel, exciting body sensations (vertigo). Application of the Kenyon questionnaire to various populations (e.g., Schutz & Smoll, 1977) has failed to turn up gross sex or age differences in attitudes toward physical activity. Interestingly, exercise not only provides a way for releasing body tensions that are unpleasant, but also produces body experiences that can energize apparently unrelated motivational systems. Zillmann, Katcher, and Milavsky (1972) have shown that, when muscular excitement is induced in people by means of strenuous exercise, it will increase their subsequent aggressive behavior if they have already experienced special instigation to be hostile. The residual excitation from the exercise seems to intensify the response to a provocative hostile stimulus. Zillmann et al. did not find any evidence to support the common supposition that vigorous body movement reduces aggressive tensions, and Hornberger (1959) too failed to find such evidence. That the residual excitation from vigorous body movement can energize aggression raises the possibility that it can energize other forms of expression. If so, it is possible that participation in athletics may attract some people because it enhances excitement, which can be transferred into reinforcement for feelings that are normally inhibited. That is, athletes might find that arousing the body through a sports activity permits them to express themselves in areas in which they are normally inhibited.

There is a large research literature dealing with the attributes of the athlete. With minor exceptions, this literature is based on administering standard personality inventories to athletes and either comparing their scores with those of nonathletes or comparing scores of those involved in different types of sports. A reading of a number of reviews of this work (e.g., Alderman, 1974; Carron, 1980; A. C. Fisher, 1976; Whiting et al., 1973) does not leave one with a clear image of what the athlete is like psychologically. Studies variously assert the athlete is unusually stable, conscientious, tough minded, sociable, extraverted, and so forth. They generally convey the impression that the athlete is a psychologically superior being. In particular, it has been reported that outstanding champion athletes are typified by superior psychological functioning.

However, there are also reviews (e.g., Hardman, 1973) that portray the average athlete as having a not very favorable psychological profile. Hardman, after analyzing 42 studies, concluded that athletes are probably more anxious than nonathletes. He stated: "This result of the many recorded results . . . suggests that it would be rash to generalize that games players and athletes are stable; in fact, there is more evidence to suggest the opposite view"[19] (pp. 90–91). It is still an unsettled matter whether athletes involved in different sports can be reliably distinguished from one another in terms of psychological test scores.[20] There have been claims that athletes who participate in team sports (e.g., football, basketball) are more sociable than those who prefer individualized sports (e.g., track, gymnastics). But conflicting studies concerning this type of formulation continue to appear.

A question keeps reasserting itself concerning the motivations of athletes who devote themselves seriously to attaining superior prowess in a sport and who endlessly seek body perfection. Are they interested primarily in shaping the body to some powerful ideal? Are they trying to maximize body experiences that will enhance body security? Or is the body merely an incidental means for gaining prestige and superiority? It is likely that some fusion of body image and social factors shapes the athlete's agenda. We do know that athletes as a group score high on general measures of competitiveness and achievement drive. So, they probably do, to some extent, use sports as a vehicle for their general achievement strivings. We also know from several studies that their interest in sports is linked to having grown up in families in which mother and father were often sports oriented and encouraged athletic activities. That is, being an athlete is in part a function of having been socialized by one's parents to perceive athletic activity as important.

Unfortunately, we know little about the role of body image factors in becoming seriously devoted to athletic prowess. There is evidence, already cited, that vigorous body movement makes people feel more positively toward their own body space. It seems reasonable to assume that one element in the motivation to be an athlete is the resultant increased sense of body worth. As noted, (e.g., Snyder & Kivlin, 1975), athletes do, indeed, rate their bodies more positively than do nonathletes. Further, a few studies have found athletes to be more field independent than nonathletes, and this could signify a more clearly differentiated body concept.

However, here and there in the literature are hints that athletes may also seek enhancement of the body to compensate for feelings of vulnerability. There is the report (in Ogilvie, 1976) that athletes have elevated MMPI Hypochondriasis scores. One recalls too Hardman's (1973) observation that athletes are probably more anxious than nonathletes. In other instances, projective tests have been interpreted as indicative of heightened body concern in athletes. Johnson and Hutton (1970) found indicators of negative "heightened body consciousness" in a small sample ($N = 8$) of male collegiate wrestlers who had been evaluated with the House-Tree-Person drawing test. Harlow (1951) reported that males ($N = 40$) who were serious devotees of weightlifting were unusually insecure about their masculine identity. Conforto and Marcenaro (1979) observed a significant elevation in number of anatomy percepts in the ink blot responses of 10 male and 10 female tennis players and speculated that it was indicative of a tendency to "enact . . . conflicts" through a "narcissistic representation of the corporal scheme" (p. 226). They were impressed with the degree to which in the athlete the "body becomes . . . object of ambivalent investment, loved as a carrier of success, of 'good things', but at the same time opposed as a continual source of worry and alarm about its functioning. . . . This explains through a mechanism of 'fluctuation' the athlete's sensation of emotional fusion with his body when he feels 'in form' —— and the easy depressions when the body betrays the athlete" (p. 227). Of course, the few projective studies just cited are insubstantial and, at best, merely offer some speculative hints. However, Adler and Fisher (in an unpublished exploratory study that is described in more detail later) found that male athletes had more poorly articulated body boundaries than did nonathletes. Such a difference did not appear in comparisons of female athletes and nonathletes.[21] One can say only that there are some tentative clues that suggest the possibility that anxiety about body vulnerability may play a part in the athlete's devotion to making the body powerful and better than all other bodies.

RESHAPING THE BODY

Dissatisfaction with one's body can be so extreme that it leads to surgical revisions. These revisions may vary from slight changes in the curvature of the nose to radical amputation of sex organs. They may be initiated in response to grossly mutilating accidents or fancied defects that few observers can detect. Fisher (1970) reviewed the literature dealing with the psychological impact of plastic surgery and concluded that relatively little was scientifically known at that time about the motivations for, and adaptations to, cosmetic surgery. A number of impressions could be drawn from the somewhat uncontrolled studies then available:

1. It appeared that of those persons who undergo plastic surgery for cosmetic purposes, a considerably greater proportion are pleased than displeased by the outcome in the long run.
2. Reactions to surgical reshaping are often quite emotional and exaggerated in the immediate postsurgical phase.
3. It is difficult to predict reactions to cosmetic surgery in terms of the seriousness of the body defect involved.
4. Males who present themselves for cosmetic surgery seem to be more psychologically disturbed than women who do so.
5. There were hints that the revision of a body part defect may represent an unconscious effort to solve a psychodynamic conflict that is symbolized by that body area. Indeed, certain body parts like the nose seem to be especially good body targets upon which to project conflicts.
6. Specified attitudes toward life apparently characterize women who ask for particular plastic procedures. Illustratively, it was observed that the modal woman who requests a face-lift to remove signs of aging is married, Protestant, upper middle class, oriented toward accomplishment, socially poised, and distant in relations with others.

Again, these were largely anecdotal impressions that awaited further study. Note too that until 1970 there were no controlled investigations of how body image variables mediate interest in, and response to, surgical reshaping.

What has happened since 1970? Well, to begin with, there have been a few attempts to probe whether cosmetic surgery effects and body image measures are linked. Burk (1975) theorized that women who seek cosmetic surgery do so because of an unpleasant sense of disparity between their self-concept and body concept. Presumably, negative feelings about a body part considered to be inadequate or disfigured spread to the overall body concept and result in it's being viewed more negatively than the self-concept. The cosmetic patient is said to be seeking a means of reducing this disparity. Burk discerned significant support for her hypothesis in a study of female cosmetic surgery patients ($N = 55$) who rated specific body parts, the overall body, and the self-concept. Both body-part esteem and physical self-esteem were significantly lower than general self-esteem in these patients. Within 2 months following cosmetic surgery, the disparity was significantly reduced.

West (1973) evaluated 152 patients (males and females) with severe facial disfigurements after cancer surgery and attempted to predict their subsequent adaptation. He used a questionnaire designed by Litman (1961) to determine how negatively they viewed their bodies. He also obtained measures of self-concept and a variety of background variables (e.g., education, length of illness). His data indicated that the best predictor of subjects' adjustment to their disfigurement was the degree of negativity of their body ratings. The more critical they were of their bodies, the greater the disturbance and adaptation difficulties manifested.

Pauly and Lindgren (1976–1977) obtained ratings of body satisfaction-dissatisfaction from male ($N = 16$) and female ($N = 14$) transsexuals prior to sex change operations and also postoperatively. Nontranssexual controls (male, $N = 53$, female, $N = 12$) were also included in the study. The transsexuals were, in the presurgical phase, significantly more dissatisfied with their bodies than were the controls. The male transsexuals were also significantly more dissatisfied than the female transsexuals; this was a difference that disappeared postsurgically. Also, the postsurgery transsexuals increased their body satisfaction to such a degree that they could no longer be differentiated from nontranssexual controls. Fleming, MacGowan, Robinson, Spitz, and Salt (1982) administered the Jourard-Secord Body Cathexis Scale to 22 postsurgical female-to-male transsexuals who had undergone various stages of sex-reassignment surgery. The more radical the surgical transformation, the greater was the degree of body satisfaction. That is, those who had been most reshaped to the male image were the most satisfied.

In the studies just reviewed the only body image technique applied to exploring cosmetic surgery effects involved questionnaire self-ratings of body satisfaction-dissatisfaction. A few other studies that have considered body boundary aspects of plastic surgery are reviewed in the chapter dealing with the Barrier score. In any case, it is sensible to approach the impact of plastic surgery in terms of a satisfaction-dissatisfaction dimension; one of the major purposes of cosmetic surgery is to enable people to perceive their own bodily appearance more positively. There seems to be evidence that cosmetic surgery increases body satisfaction, and this corroborates earlier anecdotal studies in which the great majority of patients who underwent cosmetic facial surgery said they were pleased with the result. Numerous new reports have emphasized the consistency of positive outcomes (e.g., Crowell, Sazima, &

Elder, 1970; J. M. Goin & M. K. Goin, 1981; Jensen, 1978; Kalick, 1978; Lavell, 1980; Lefebvre & Barclay, 1982). This is in contrast to the earlier literature concerned with cosmetic surgery (e.g., MacGregor & Schaffner, 1950), which showed an alarmist concern about its potentially disruptive psychological effects. However, more recent studies (e.g., Hay, 1970b; Hay & Heather, 1973) have detected few such harmful consequences. They have also not corroborated previous reports that the male seeking optional cosmetic surgery is extremely maladjusted, even psychotic. There is now a general enthusiasm in the literature about plastic surgery outcomes. Druss (1973) depicted the satisfaction of women who have had augmentation breast surgery:

> All the women were delighted with the cosmetic result and stated that they would gladly go through the surgery again. They expressed these feelings with enthusiasm and without reservation. They no longer harbored a sense of self-consciousness about others seeing or touching their breasts. They were now pleased to wear bathing suits or the kind of low-cut clothes they had always wished to wear. . . . During the six weeks or so after breast augmentation, there is not only much self-scrutiny of the new breasts in the mirror, but also a great deal of self-handling . . . often in the dark . . . there is an attempt to integrate a new body image tactilely as well as visually. (p. 252)

There are scattered reports suggesting that women who seek optional cosmetic surgery may have an exaggerated image of how bad they look.[23] Beale, Lisper, and Palm (1980) found that in a sample of women ($N = 64$) seeking augmentation mammaplasty, 10% had normal sized breasts but were convinced that their breasts were abnormally small. Perhaps this is not surprising in view of the fact that in the Beale et al. control group ($N = 28$) of patients admitted to a hospital for general surgery two thirds of the women considered their breasts too small. Previous studies (e.g., Berscheid et al., 1973) have established that as many as 25% of women feel dissatisfied with their breasts. Hay (1970b) showed that in a sample of 45 women seeking rhinoplasty, the subjective ratings of their degree of disfigurement were significantly more negative than the evaluations of their disfigurement as determined by independent judges.

The dramatic subjectivity of response to plastic surgery is pointed up by the fact that at least two studies (Hay, 1970b; Hay & Heather, 1973) could not detect a significant relationship between measured psychological changes linked with cosmetic surgery and either the original objective degree of facial defect or the actual amount of change in the defect as the result of surgery.[24] Patients with minor defects were found to improve as much as those with larger defects. On this basis, Hay and Heather speculated that cosmetic surgery may be a useful tool for providing psychological aid to those who are chronically unhappy about an apparently minor facial deviation. They concluded from their data that correcting a minor deviation makes the patient happier and does not lead to symptom substitution. That is, they did not observe a tendency for the patient who focused dissatisfaction on a facial area to develop a new focus of complaint when that area was surgically changed. But it should be added that their methods for detecting symptom substitution seemed to be rather impressionistic.

Previous clinical reports concerning applicants for cosmetic surgery have focused on their psychopathology. The final word on this matter is not yet in. On the other hand, higher than average maladjustment in those seeking cosmetic change has been documented in some studies. Beale et al. (1980) found that women applying for augmentation mammaplasty obtained significantly elevated scores on a personality questionnaire for variables like neurotic self-assertion and feelings of guilt. Also, they reported that these women had significantly more negative relationships with parents and spouses than did controls and had more often felt the need to consult a psychiatrist. Similarly, Hay (1970b) discovered that women who wanted rhinoplasty surgery were significantly more psychologically disturbed than controls in terms of measures derived from a personality questionnaire. Hay noted that there was no correlation between degree of psychological disturbance and seriousness of the nose defect. This suggests that the defect itself was not a primary factor in the etiology of the disturbance. J. M. Goin and M. K. Goin (1981) reported that older patients who have a rhinoplasty that drastically alters their appearance may respond with a catastrophic sense of loss of identity. Younger patients are said not to respond in such a drastic fashion to gross alterations in their facial structure.

In contrast to the results just reviewed, a number of studies have found little psychopathology. Goin, Burgoyne, and Goin (1976) administered the MMPI to 20 women seeking "face-lift" operations and stated: "Some 80 percent had normal scores on the MMPI . . . 20 percent had mildly abnormal MMPI's" (p. 274). Baker, Kolin, and Bartlett (1974) reported no gross deviations in the MMPI profiles of 10 women who were candidates for mammary augmentation. Knight (1982) administered the MMPI and several other questionnaire measures of self-concept, anxiety, and body evaluation to 40 women seeking mammary augmentation and 84 controls. No differences between the groups were detected. Shipley, O'Donnell, and Bader (1977) secured a wide variety of measures (e.g., California Psychological Inventory, questionnaire concerning past history, index of self esteem) from women seeking breast augmentation and a control group. There were no indications of greater maladjustment in the breast augmentation group. Similar findings have been reported by J. M. Goin and M. K. Goin (1981). Furlong (1977) reported that in a sample of women seeking cosmetic surgery, the level of neuroticism (as defined by the Gryzier Personality Scale) was within normal limits. These women were noted too not to differ from normal controls in their body size judgments. Reich (1975) has suggested that as cosmetic surgery becomes more popular and acceptable, it is less likely to attract disturbed persons selectively.

Unfortunately, there has been no progress in exploring the possibility that the concern focused on a body defect, especially if the defect is actually minor, represents the symbolic expression of a psychodynamic conflict. For example, one earlier clinical paper (Meyer, Jacobson, Edgerton, & Canter, 1960), proposed that women seeking rhinoplasty identified the nose with father and were seeking through surgical revision to deny an identification that was interfering with taking on a feminine role. If such symbolic projections upon body defects could be demonstrated, they would reinforce Fisher's (1970) findings that showed that normal persons link meanings and conflictual issues with specific body landmarks. In any case, the problem awaits systematic investigation in various populations of patients who come for cosmetic surgery. What are needed are well-controlled designs in which candidates for plastic surgery with exaggerated concern about one body area are compared with those who have equivalent concern about another area. One could ascertain whether differences in focus of concern are linked with differential sensitivities to, or conflicts about, specific psychological themes. However, there increasingly has been an inclination on the part of those studying the psychological aspects of cosmetic surgery to play down symbolic and psychodynamic formulations. The prevalent view seems to be that people seek such surgery simply because they feel they deviate from the acceptable norm and can regain normal membership in their subcultures only by transforming their appearance.

OVERVIEW

The major topics considered in this chapter have in common the fact that they all touch on satisfaction-dissatisfaction with one's body. Whether the topic is appearance or body prowess or cosmetic surgery, the focus is on the presentation of the body as an admirable object. It has already been documented that people will submit to almost any extremes in their pursuit of body approval. What are the consequences for the body image of such pursuit? One obvious consequence is that the body is cast in the role of an instrument of social impression. As people make repeated perceptual sweeps of their bodies, they are actually sensitized to questions like, "Am I attractive?", "Is my body impressing others and winning their approval?" Among the many different roles that can be assigned to the body that of social mediator or instrument for winning approbation is often predominant. This, in turn, probably results in magnifying the importance of those body aspects that are visible and subject to immediate public scrutiny. We have already reviewed studies showing that persons' feelings about their face and voice are particularly highly correlated with their level of self-esteem. It is not mere coincidence that face and voice are two bodily foci that are among the most closely monitored by others in the course of social interaction. Presumably, individuals become sensitized to how aspects such as these are evaluated, and they attach special import to them in defining their own self-worth. It is worth speculating about the meanings that become associated with such body aspects as a result of their special mediating role. Certainly, they would come to represent the public as compared to the private body territory and therefore would be in need of special monitoring and control. They would presumably be major foci in one's distribution of body attention. Further, they might be expected to take on particular connotations as one conceptualized the process of gaining bodily approval. If, for example, the process were experienced as an act of submission, then the body aspects in question would be linked with submissive values. If it were experienced as an act of deception, the body aspects would be associated with deception. The fact that body areas take on different attributes and perceptual qualities in relation to the tasks assigned to them has been well documented by sensoritonic researchers. They have shown, for example, that, when one assigns one's arm the task of pointing to a particular target, it is experienced as significantly longer than when it is simply extended without purpose into space (Wapner, 1960). Relatedly, Fisher (1970) has shown that there are sex differences in the connotations ascribed to a particular body part, like the head or the heart, that reflect psychological differences in the role of that part in male versus female adaptation.

Implicit in the role of the body as an instrument for enhancing self is that it also becomes a medium for concealment and denial of defects. That is, the body is conceptualized as a facade with camouflaging functions. The "best face" is put on. There are certainly observations suggesting that people invest a great deal of energy in embellishing their bodies so that defects will be covered over. Much use of clothing, cosmetics, and cosmetic surgery is intended to hide real or fancied body deviations. The concealment may frequently be directed not only at others but also at oneself. People seek to cover their defects so that they can minimize their own anxious awareness of them. Studies by Holzman and Rousey (1966) and others have demonstrated that people will even avoid recognizing their own voice in order to evade certain negative, unpleasant cues about self that the voice may convey. One wonders whether "dressing up" the outside of the body may not in some instances serve to draw attention away from the body interior. We know from several studies (e.g., Tait & Ascher, 1955) that the body interior represents to many persons a mysterious, uncharted region with threatening connotations. Perhaps by dramatizing the attractiveness of the facade dimension of the body space, one can look away from the unsettling interior. Such a strategy of "looking away" is typical of many other defensive maneuvers that predominate in our transactions with our bodies. There is little doubt that concern about possessing an admirable body contributes significantly to the defensiveness typifying body perception.

The idea that an admirable body is essential to an acceptable identity leads to painful discordance in those whose bodies are defined culturally as defective. To be ugly or crippled or otherwise bodily deviant represents an onslaught upon one's self-esteem. There is some evidence that this may result in significant splitting between self and body. Two studies cited earlier (Mayer & Eisenberg, 1982a; West, 1973) indicated that the correlation between self-rated body esteem and self-esteem may be reduced to practically zero in those who have serious body faults. The body and the self are distanced from each other in order to minimize the downgrading impact of the first. There are hints that in some instances such distancing may be triggered too by having an unusually attractive body. There are anecdotal reports that attractive women may become concerned that men are drawn to them only because of their body assets and that men are unappreciative of the separate, nonbody aspects of their identity. This duality is, in a sense, similar to that observed in persons with body defects because in a paradoxical way the fact of body attractiveness takes on the significance of a defect. Attractiveness is equated with an inferior, unacceptable kind of feminine role.

These extreme forms of splitting between body and self provide glimpses of a system in which there may be varying relationships between body perceptions and perceptions of other types of self-representations.[25] There is a fair amount of evidence that most people do separate, and also conjure up, interconnections among different levels of self-representations. It is common to entertain fantasies about how transforming one's body will change some other level of self. Using the body to transform one's identity is seen dramatically in the inflated hopes of patients who seek plastic surgery for minor physiognomic deviations. The apparent intent is to acquire a different and better self by reshaping some body part, like the nose or the breast, to a more admirable configuration. There are, of course, untold examples of somatic rituals that are intended to better the inner self. In this vein, numerous largely unfounded beliefs flourish about how being an athlete can improve the inner personality. Generally, one gets the impression that there is a good deal of magical thinking about the ways in which altering one's appearance can lead to Pygmalion-like rebirth.

A noteworthy finding of an earlier cited survey by Berscheid et al. (1973), which dealt with the body concerns of a large sample of *Psychology Today* readers, relates to the impact of sudden changes in body appearance. This survey found that as much as 38% of the sample had at some time in the past experienced a sudden dramatic alteration in appearance (e.g., due to rapid weight gain or loss, injuries, cosmetic surgery). Interestingly, persons who experienced either one or multiple change episodes were particularly likely to describe themselves as unhappy. They did so irrespective of whether the changes had improved or worsened their appearance. Berscheid et al. also found that these people rated body attractiveness as more important in their life than did persons who had never had a dramatic shift in appearance.

These findings raise several provocative questions. Does the experience of radical change in appearance, even if it is a positive one, pose a threat because it undermines one's general stability and therefore is translated into feelings of "unhappiness"? Perhaps so, but, if sudden body changes create this sort of threat, why have investigators of cosmetic surgery not discerned a greater proportion of unhappy reactions in those who have had themselves reshaped? Of course, there may be a special protective readiness for change in those who selectively volunteer for cosmetic surgery. A further point is whether body transformations upset an equilibrium between the body image representation and other self-representations. Feelings about self probably evolve in relation to an equation in which level of body esteem is an appreciable factor. Altering the body esteem factor, whether up or down, calls for a rewriting of the equation and therefore a transition period of uncertainty. In view of the Berscheid et al. observation that people who have had body "transformations" ascribe unusual significance to the role of the bodily self in their lives, another question worth pondering is whether the transformations do not magnify one's overall awareness of one's body. Might not such awareness, in turn, be threatening simply because it renders one more aware of self as a biological object that inherently has somatic vulnerabilities and limitation in life span?

One catches glimpses of sex differences in the multiple facets of body appearance and prowess that have been examined in this chapter. We have learned that men are probably to a small degree more satisfied with their body appearance than women are. We have learned too that women are particularly dissatisfied with the hip, waist and thigh area and men with the abdominal region. There have been suggestions that self-esteem is linked more with feelings of body attractiveness in women, whereas in men the link is more with feelings of body effectiveness. Some small sex differences have been spotted with reference to degree of correlation between self-esteem and attitudes toward specific body parts like chest and hips (Mahoney & Finch, 1976a). One investigation even observed a trend for self-esteem in men to be linked relatively more with attitudes toward inner body areas, and in women relatively more with attitudes toward outer body aspects. Although past studies concerned with body prowess and athletics have indicated that men are more inclined than women to cultivate high levels of body strength, agility, and speed, no consistent psychological differences between male and female athletes have been demonstrated. Further, it is obvious from everyday experience that there are marked sex differences in how males and females deal with clothing and body decoration. But little is scientifically known about the possible body image origins of these differences. Finally, should be mentioned the greater probability that more women than men will seek cosmetic surgery. At present one cannot offer informative generalizations about this array of differences. It is hardly informative to extract some of the more obvious possible deductions, for example, that women are more likely than men to utilize clothes, body decoration, and cosmetic surgery to attain body ideals, whereas men prefer techniques that enhance body strength and prowess. We need to find out more about such issues as why women are more flexible than men about transforming their appearance (e.g., via cosmetic surgery), or why they are more disapproving than men of their own appearance, or why they differ from men with respect to the degree of correlation of general self-esteem with attitudes toward a number of specific body areas (e.g., internal versus external).

The set to extract approbation of one's body from others implies a kind of dependence on them.[26] So many cosmetic and other body camouflaging procedures are designed to win approval—the status of acceptibility of one's body becomes a function of the good will of others. A possible consequence could be a diminished sense that one's body belongs to self. Insofar as persons look to others to validate their body, this means loss of its exclusive ownership. It might be expected that this would register differentially as a function of the personality needs of the individuals involved. Persons dedicated to being independent or dominant or "in complete control" could experience even a small loss of body ownership as a serious frustration. On the other hand, those who seek dependent support might enjoy sharing their body ownership. Certainly, too, the reliance on others for body validation revives childhood feelings about the special relationship between the child's body and the child's parents. During the first year of life the young organism's body is, indeed, largely "owned" by its parents, and it survives only by virtue of symbiotic attachment to them. Relationships later in life that in any way mimic this paradigm could stir up the affects originally clustered about it. To be in situations where one is expecting and searching for approval of one's body is a unique re-creation of important elements of the child's dependence on its parents.

NOTES

[1] Kleinke and Staneski (1980) found that both female and male college students prefer that women's breasts be of moderate rather than large or small size.

[2] The self ratings of the various body parts were factor analyzed, and the following five factors emerged: face, extremities, mid-torso, breast/chest, sex organs. Berscheid et al. noted, however: "The five (factor) scores . . . were fairly well interrelated, showing that people tend to have an overall sense of their appearance as well as specific reactions to parts of their bodies" (p. 120). Factor analyses of the widely used Jourard-Secord (1955) Body Cathexis questionnaire have revealed similar, but also at

times quite different clusters. For example, Mahoney and Finch (1976b) factor analyzed the Jourard-Secord questionnaire scores of 98 male and 128 female college
students. For the males, they found six clusters: leg, face, weight, height, torso, voice/
hair. In the case of the females, there were five: face, weight, height, legs, extremities.
Tucker (1981) factor analyzed the responses of 83 male college students to the
Jourard-Secord questionnaire and reported the emergence of these four factors:
health and physical fitness (e.g., energy, resistance to illness), face and overall appearance, subordinate and independent body features (e.g., chin, ears, hands), physique and muscular strength (e.g., muscular strength, chest, arms, width of shoulder).
Franzoi and Shields (1984) reported a factor analysis of the responses of 366 female
and 257 male college students to the Jourard-Secord questionnaire. Three factors
emerged for the males: upper body strength, physical attributes pertinent to the
appearance of balanced body proportions, and general health. There were also three
factors for the females: weight control and body proportion, facial features, and
general health. The analyses cited are not particularly revealing, but their variable
results suggest considerable instability in the factor structures under examination.

[3] An exception to this trend occurred in two studies by Kurtz (1969, 1971), who
used a Semantic Differential approach (Osgood, Suci, & Tannenbaum, 1957) to
measure feelings about one's body. He found in both studies that college women
evaluated their body more positively than did college men. It is not clear why the use
of the Semantic Differential technique should produce such a reversal from the
pattern usually obtained with the Body Cathexis questionnaire. One possibility is that
the Semantic Differential Evaluative ratings are relatively more subtle and less
susceptible to social desirability effects. This would mean that the usual Body
Cathexis sex difference reflected a difference in defensiveness rather than true self
feelings. Kurtz found that the males rated their body as more active than did the
females. An interesting sidelight of the study was that men with large mesomorphic
builds (which are most socially desirable) judged their body as most potent, but
women with the least desirable body type (large endomorphs) assigned the highest
potency to their body. Males with high self-esteem perceived their body as high in
potency, but women with high self-esteem perceived their body as low in potency.

[4] Dissatisfaction is greater in individuals who compare themselves with some ideal
standard. Tucker (1982b) approached the issue of body satisfaction in terms of how
much persons feel their bodies deviate from their own ideal norms. He found that
about 70% of a sample of male college students indicated there was a discrepancy
between their perception of their own somatotype and an idealized somatotype.

[5] However, Schwab and Harmeling (1968) reported that body satisfaction was lower
in older male medical patients than in younger patients. This was not true in a sample
of female medical patients.

[6] Roger (1977) has constructed two parallel forms of the Body-Cathexis scale.

[7] Schwab and Harmeling (1968) reported significant negative correlations, in a
sample of physically ill persons, between body satisfaction and both educational and
income levels.

[8] Berscheid et al. (1973) found that persons who recalled being unusually attractive
as teenagers rated themselves as happier than average until middle age. Beyond
middle age their happiness level was equal to the average.

[9] An interesting disjunction between self-concept and body ratings has been observed in persons who have suffered serious body damage. For example, Mayer and

Eisenberg (1982b) found that when spinal-cord injured males rated self-concept and body concept, the two sets of ratings were minimally linked. Similarly, West (1973) noted that in disfigured cancer patients self-concept and body concept measures were not significantly correlated. West speculated that this disjunction might be a "protective mechanism on their part to protect their self-concept from being downgraded by their negative body images" (p. 165).

[10] Rosen and Ross (1968) originally reported that the correlation between rating of body satisfaction and self-concept could be increased by weighting the body ratings in terms of the importance subjects ascribed to the various body areas. This finding was subsequently supported by Watkins and Park (1972), but it was not supported by three other studies (Lerner et al., 1973; Lerner & Karabenick, 1974; Mahoney, 1974).

[11] Only correlations pertaining to specific body areas are mentioned. Some variables like "general appearance" and "distribution of weight" were not included.

[12] A nonspecific body aspect, overall physical attractiveness, was also of major import for the variance in self-esteem.

[13] Although some studies (e.g., Lerner et al., 1973; Lerner & Karabenick, 1974; Vivino, 1970) suggest a higher correlation in female than male subjects between body satisfaction and self-satisfaction ratings, other studies (e.g., Howe, 1973; Lerner, Iwawaki, Chihara, & Sorell, 1980; Mahoney & Finch, 1976a) do not concur.

[14] Bruchon-Schweitzer (1981-1982) reported a similar trend for positive body evaluation in French adolescents.

[15] The possibility that measures of body image that are not so easily manipulable by the subject may give different results than the Jourard-Secord self-report measure in evaluating the impact of athletic participation is pointed up in a report by Belzer, Jr. (1963). He had elementary school boys participate in physical development sessions and found that the sessions had no significant effects on perceived alterations in one's own mirror image, as viewed through aniseikonic lenses. Several studies (Fisher, 1970) have shown that the ability to perceive aniseikonic alterations in one's mirror image is linked negatively with how much body anxiety is being experienced.

[16] Largely nonsignificant correlations have been found between body esteem and actual measures of body strength and endurance (Layman, 1974).

[17] Eickhoff, Thorland, and Ansorge (1983) reported that an aerobic dance program (involving 39 women) did not produce any significant changes in feelings about self or body, as defined by the Tennessee Self Concept Scale.

[18] Hellison (1969) found, for males, that a "physical conditioning" program increased positive body feelings as defined by Semantic Differential ratings of one's body. However, this occurred for only a sample that had received intensive training and not for a sample on a less strenuous schedule.

[19] One negative report with particular body image implications found that high school athletes were more hypochondriacal (as defined by the Minnesota Multiphasic Personality Inventory) than were high school nonathletes (in Ogilvie, 1976).

[20] Darden (1972) obtained some preliminary data suggesting that there might be body image differences among those engaged in various types of sports. For example, basketball players displayed greater body esteem (as defined by the Jourard-Secord Body Cathexis scale) than did gymnasts. However, the findings were confusing because another measure of body satisfaction developed by Darden, which is based on selecting pictures that resemble oneself, gave results contrary to those obtained with the Jourard-Secord measure.

[21] Armstrong, Jr. and Armstrong (1968) also found a sex difference with respect to the correlation of the Barrier score with physical fitness in 111 high school girls and 71 boys. Thus, the Barrier score was positively and significantly correlated with fitness in the females but not in the males.

[22] Owens (1968) reported in a follow-up study of males ($N = 109$) who experienced radical surgery in the head and neck region that their anxiety, introversion, and "subduedness" continued to increase during the postsurgical period (up to 6 months).

[23] Several researchers (J. M. Goin & M. K. Goin, 1981) have reported that within a few weeks after cosmetic surgery, most patients could not remember their original appearance and verbalized surprise when shown their preoperative photograph.

[24] West (1973) reported only a negligible relationship between cancer patients' ratings of their facial deformities and interviewer ratings of the deformities.

[25] Dujovne (1973) described a study involving male and female children and adults who rated various aspects of self and body on Semantic Differential continua. She detected a sex difference: females experienced self as closer to body than males did.

[26] Preoccupation with whether my own body is admirable signifies, at one level, that there is heightened concern with the relationships of my body to other people. The concern centers on whether people regard my body favorably or unfavorably. This means that I am chronically tuned into the connection between my body and persons who are in my vicinity. This sensitivity can be viewed within the context of previous research by Werner and Wapner (1952) dealing with polarized versus depolarized attitudes toward perceptual objects. The Werner and Wapner research indicated that when people perceive objects, they vary in the degree to which they experience those objects as psychologically linked with or separate from their own bodies, that is, how involved they feel with the objects. Feeling psychologically "connected to" another object is defined as a "depolarized" attitude, whereas feeling clearly unconnected (separate) from the object represents a "polarized" attitude. A preoccupation with how people evaluate one's body signifies a depolarized attitude. One feels less separate, as if there were a blurring of boundaries between one's body and those who are judging it. A consequence of a depolarized stance is that people experience themselves as less firmly bounded in relation to target objects. A good deal of research (Fisher, 1970) suggests that such a decrease in boundary articulation arouses sensations of vulnerability; people are inclined to feel less protected and more open to intrusion. Therefore, investing in one's body as an object to be admired may very well intensify feelings of body fragility, as a result of the depolarization process and independent of any threatening effects of the body's eliciting negative evaluations from others.

4

Body Size Experiences

NORMAL PERSONS

Research into the size aspects of body experience has continued to thrive vigorously. A major part of the energy devoted to studying body image phenomena has been channeled into an analysis of why people differ in their perceptions of how big or small they are. It has long been obvious that size variables are importantly involved in persons' feelings about their bodies. Young children have to cope with the contrast between their own tiny body and the hulk of adults. Adolescents have to adapt to changes in magnitude of key body organs such as the penis and the breasts. Adults are forever fascinated with whether their size specifications match cultural norms. People wonder whether they are too short or too tall, whether specific body parts like the nose or the ears are too big, whether sexual parts are up to par, and so forth. A good deal of clinical observation and theorizing has been cast in body size terms. Adler linked certain compensatory behaviors with being too short. Freud thought significant aspects of feminine behavior could be traced to having genitals he thought were inferior in size to those of males. The clinical literature is full of accounts of unusual size distortions experienced by schizophrenics, amputees with phantom limbs, persons under the influence of drugs like LSD, and those who have suffered brain damage. Strange body size sensations have been linked with special subjective states presumably typical of being hypnotized, falling asleep, waking up, feeling anxious, and losing one's usual spatial markers (Fisher, 1970).

Summary of Literature (1958–1968)

Before analyzing the literature of body size perceptions, let us set the stage by quoting Fisher's (1970) brief summary of the pertinent work published in the period 1956–1968. He noted:

> What has emerged from the mass of observations concerning the individual's perception of his own body size?
>
> 1. There does seem to be a consistent trend for that which is large (or mesomorphic) to be labeled as masculine and that which is small to be linked with femininity. But one cannot say that there are consistent sex differences in over- or underestimating the size of one's body or in the accuracy of such estimation. . . .

2. To generalize about the accuracy of the average individual in judging his own size dimensions is difficult. First of all, the fact that the method of estimation itself strongly influences amount of error and also over- versus underestimation complicates comparisons across studies. But, generally, one gets the impression that with conditions of good illumination and when the method of estimation is not too indirect, the majority of individuals are quite accurate. This is also true of children by the time they reach the 9–11 age range.

3. In most studies the correlations between estimation of body size and size of non-body objects have been non-significant. Even when significant, they have been low. There do seem to be different factors participating in body as compared to non-body judgments, and they are reflected in differences in variability and degree of over- versus underestimation. The nature of the differences remains obscure.

4. Few dependable relationships have been demonstrated between size estimation and personality or trait variables. One can only make a few disconnected statements. Failure or the sense of being depreciated apparently results in feelings of smallness. Field dependence is linked in adolescent boys with perceptions of self as small. Men who are particularly competitive with women and who are aggressively oriented seem (perhaps defensively) to exaggerate their height.

5. The sensori-tonic theory concerning the function of the boundary in perception of body size has stood up well to a variety of tests. One major failure to support it has been described by Epstein (1957). But otherwise it has successfully predicted the effects[1] upon size judgments of stimuli applied to the body periphery, the nature of response distortions produced by LSD, and certain overestimation trends observed among the immature. . . .

6. An individual's perception of his body size is not related to how aware he is of his body, . . .

7. There are findings which indicate a trend for body parts in the vicinity of the lower extremities to be underestimated and those in the region of the head to be overestimated.

The total findings are not impressive. They suggest a few promising leads; but one can see that there is still a long way to go. One major obstacle to progress on this problem has been the paucity of theoretical statements (with the notable exception of the sensori-tonic concepts). Another relates to the unbelievably diverse methods of measuring body size perception which have been used. Some of the methods have resulted in consistent overestimation of body size and others when applied to similar populations have led to underestimation! Comparisons across studies have consequently lacked meaning. In ways which are not yet clear, it is apparent that body size estimates can, at times, be strongly influenced by non-body variables, such as the subject's individualistic concept of the judgment units used. His definitions of a unit like an inch or his general concept of what looks 'big' versus 'small' on the measuring rod provided him for his judgment may be quite idiosyncratic. This is a highly important and complicating matter because one is left with the dilemma of not knowing what part of the variance of body size judgments mirrors the subject's actual perception of his body size. We also know from Singer and Lamb's (1966) study that just knowing that one's size judgments will later be checked by actual body measurement is enough to make them significantly more realistic. That is, there may be a special kind of social desirability effect with which one has to reckon. These and other complicating phenomena raise serious questions about whether we will be able in the near future to develop reliable and meaningful ways of determining how the individual experiences the size aspects of his body. (pp. 49–50)

Determinants of Body Size Perception: Shontz's Work

As will be seen, Fisher's perspective turned out to be overly gloomy. There has been appreciable progress; investigators have begun to use more uniform modes of measurement. Also, a good deal has been learned about the conditions that do and do not shape body size judgments. Major credit must go to Shontz (1969) for the progress that has occurred. He reported a remarkable series of studies of body size perception. These studies set out to clarify the differences between size judgments involving the body and those pertaining to non-body objects. They were directed too at ascertaining the various measurement conditions that influence size judgments.

Shontz showed convincingly that persons experience the size aspects of their bodies differently than they do the size attributes of nonbody objects. Unique attitudes are stirred when people become judgmentally involved with their body space. Shontz performed most of his studies with an apparatus that called for subjects to estimate sizes by setting distances between two "collars" on a horizontal rod. The subjects, typically college students, were covered with a drape so that they could not see their own body. Their body estimates involved standard body sites: head width, forearm length, hand length, foot length, waist width. For control purposes, they were asked to judge the size of a variety of simple, cylindrical wooden rods about the same length, respectively, as the body sites just enumerated. Shontz found the following to be true with regard to judging body size versus judging size of nonbody comparison objects.

1. Body distances are usually overestimated, whereas nonbody distances are underestimated.

2. There is a significant trend for body estimates to be less accurate than the nonbody ones.

3. Variability of judgments across a range of body objects is greater than across a range of nonbody objects.

4. Body size judgments are clearly more likely than nonbody judgments to display part–whole effects. Barton and Wapner (1965) originally discovered that the lengths of combinations of body parts, judged as a unit, are underestimated in relation to the sums of estimates of the parts comprising these combinations. Shontz probed this phenomenon and found that although it tends to appear in judgments of nonbody objects of high contour complexity, it is particularly intensified by stimuli with human body connotations.

5. Several experiments demonstrated that body size judgments are less influenced by the intensity of the sensory input in the immediate situation

than are size judgments of nonbody objects. For example, providing both kinesthetic and visual experience with the stimulus resulted in nonbody objects' being perceived as larger than when they were experienced only visually. But no such difference in effect was detected with respect to the apparent size of body parts.

6. Perhaps most important of all, it was discovered that there are patterns of over- and underestimation that apply to specific areas of the body. Head width and forearm length are most often overestimated; hand and foot lengths are underestimated. Shontz also observed that women typically overestimate the width of their waist more than men do, and he attributed this to their "concern over conforming to American standards of feminine beauty, which required a small waist as strongly as they do an ample bust" (p. 196). There is apparently a specificity in body size judgments linked to the geography of the body.[2] These observations have been supported by other investigators (Fuhrer & Cowan, 1967; Hester, 1970; Predebon, 1980a, 1980b). Shontz felt that the pattern of specificity he had identified could not be explained either within the context of simple cephalo-caudal or central-peripheral distinctions or in terms of the real differences in the size or shapes of the body sites themselves. He did not, in fact, come up with a focused explanation of his own. When he looked at his overall findings, he suggested that:

> Body perception is more reliant on central cognitive standards than is the perception of environmental objects. The function of the stimulus in body perception is not to provide data which can be converted more or less directly into a judgment or estimate of object properties. The function is, rather, to reactivate central schematic organizations and to identify specific segments of these organizations. These segments then acquire figural properties and serve as standards for determining response magnitudes. (pp. 140)

In other words, Shontz theorized that people react directly (and more accurately) to the properties of nonbody objects; but when they respond to a sector of their body, their judgments are more circuitous and involve activating pre-existing central attitudes or feelings or concepts pertaining to that sector. Presumably, body size judgments call into play central biases to a greater degree than do the nonbody objects employed as controls.

It is to Shontz's (1969) credit that he probed in depth the effects on size judgments of reacting to objects that differ in their degree of similarity to the human body. He obtained judgments of plywood representations of face, arm, and leg regions, masks depicting the face region, and other body representations defined by articles of clothing (e.g., cotton-knit tights) stuffed to look like parts of average proportions. These body-like objects did elicit some responses not usually elicited by nonbody objects, but they did not, in general, match the patterns typifying judgments of one's own body.

In later studies, Shontz and McNish (1972) explored the effects on size judgments of perceiving body areas in a number of special conditions. In one condition (Mirror-Object-Oriented), subjects judged the sizes of their body areas and also nonbody objects while viewing them in a mirror and with the instruction to base their judgments entirely on what they saw in the mirror. In a second condition (Mirror-Self-Oriented), subjects judged the sizes of their body areas while looking in a mirror, but with the instruction that they consult the mirror image merely for information and to estimate the distances directly on their own bodies as they were actually experiencing them. During the Mirror-Self-Oriented condition, subjects continued to display the special patterns of body size judgment that occurred when a mirror was not involved. However, the Mirror-Object-Oriented condition reduced the typical body-oriented size judgment pattern.

In further studies, Shontz and McNish (1972) asked subjects to estimate distances on their own bodies and on the bodies of male and female persons, both when directly perceived and when viewed in a mirror. The subjects also estimated distances on full-sized drawings of male and female figures and on a "robot-like drawing with a contour of straight lines, but having only vaguely human characteristics." Essentially, the findings indicated that the patterning of the size judgments on one's own body did not differ from that for others' bodies. In turn, the size judgments involving human bodies were significantly distinguished from the judgments evoked by the "robot-like" figure that was not perceived as a human body. Shontz and McNish concluded that their results "disconfirm the hypothesis that response characteristics, typical of estimates of distances on the personal body, occur only as a result of direct body experience. They also appear in estimates of distances on mirror images of the personal body, in estimates of distances on the bodies of others (viewed directly or in the mirror) and in estimates of distances on two-dimensional drawings of the human figure" (p. 24). In other words, Shontz's original observations of what seemed to be aspects of size judgments unique to one's own body turned out to apply to judgments of any recognizable human body. Shontz and McNish do suggest that the special response evoked by the human form is "probably derived from personal body experience." Presumably, people attribute qualities to the bodies of others that mirror their experience with their own bodies. This is a presumption that remains to be verified. It could be proposed with some logic that early perceptions of the bodies of others provide a framework for perceptually organizing one's own body.

Interpreting the Shontz and McNish (1972) findings is complicated by the results of two studies by Predebon. In one, (Predebon 1980b), subjects judged the sizes of various parts (face width, forearm length, hand length, foot length) of the robot-like figure that Shontz and McNish had found was seldom, if ever, perceived as a human figure. However, he used subjects who for special cultural reasons largely recognized the figure as being human. He found that despite their identification of the figure as human, they did not display the specific pattern of over- and underestimation of parts (e.g., head overestimated, hand length underestimated) that typically appeared in judgments of clearly defined human figures. Predebon did not use the same apparatus to measure size judgments as Shontz and McNish had employed. But he had previously duplicated their findings regarding judgment specificity by means of his own measurement procedure, which involved verbal size estimates. In conjecturing why the "robot-like" figure did not elicit the size specificity response pattern from his subjects, even though they identified it as human, he appealed to the concept of "strength of recognition" of the human body form. He proposed that the stronger the recognition, the more clearly the response specificity pattern that emerges. Because the "robot-like" figure was only vaguely human, it could, from his perspective, be expected to elicit only weak "human body" recognition and therefore a negligible size specificity pattern.

In another investigation, Predebon (1980a) obtained verbal size estimates of four body parts (head width, forearm length, hand length, foot length) and four nonbody stimuli from 60 female college students. However, the body parts were defined in terms of specified distances on the body of the experimenter rather than on the subject's body. The nonbody stimuli were cardboard figures approximating the shape features of the body-part stimuli. Predebon found that the judgments of the body stimuli differed significantly from the nonbody judgments. For body stimuli, the mean ratio of forearm and face-width judgments was significantly greater than the mean ratio of judgments of foot length and hand length. This was not true for the nonbody stimuli, which roughly resembled the body stimuli but which were not recognized by any of the subjects as having human body connotations. This, of course, is congruent with Shontz's findings concerning the specificity of over- and underestimation linked to the geographical location of body parts.

However, what is most important to note is that once again, as was true for the Shontz and McNish (1972) study, the specific judgmental pattern linked to body locale emerged in estimates of someone else's body. Predebon (1980c) was struck with how small the differences were between the body and nonbody judgments with respect to conforming to the over- versus underestimating specificity pattern. The nonbody stimuli did, to some degree, produce the over- and underestimation patterns typical of body stimuli. Since the nonbody stimuli Predebon employed had roughly the same shapes as the judged body parts and yet were not recognized as such by the subjects, he raised the possibility that there are other "areal configuration" factors, aside from the human identification one, that play a role in the pattern of over- and underestimation errors. Predebon's two studies affirm and yet raise questions about the Shontz and also the Shontz and McNish (1972) observations. On the one hand, they affirm that the human body elicits distinctive patterns of size perception and that these patterns apply whether people are judging their own bodies or the bodies of others. On the other hand, they raise a question about the magnitude of the over- understimation pattern differences for body versus nonbody stimuli. They point up too the fact that the distinction between body and nonbody stimuli lies on a continuum and is not a simple dichotomy. Apparently, if a configuration only weakly suggests the human form, the input may not be sufficiently potent to activate selective size estimate biases.[3]

Shontz's (1969) volume is a veritable treasure-trove of information about body size judgments. He devoted particular attention to analyzing how different measurement conditions affect such judgments. He pointed out four basic techniques for obtaining body size estimates:

1. The most commonly used is the linear method, which calls for subjects to convert their judgments of distances on the body into estimates of distances on a linear scale. It is typified by setting two markers on a rod so that the space between them matches a defined distance between two points on the body.

2. The configurational method[4] secures body judgments by having subjects respond to stimuli that have the form of the body part to be judged. An example is subjects' selecting from a series of photographs of hands (of increasing size) the one best matching the size of their own hands.

3. The pictorial technique asks subjects to draw pictures of their bodies or body parts.

4. The verbal questionnaire approach elicits verbal judgments about whether the body or any body part feels unusually small or large (Fisher, 1970).

Little is known about the comparability of these various techniques. However, Shontz did find evidence that linear judgments are relatively larger than pictorial judgments, such as those exemplified in drawing lines to represent body-part size. He also observed more uncertainty about configurational than about linear judgments. He noted that when subjects were allowed to estimate body distances verbally, their estimates were smaller than when they registered linear judgments by setting markers.

Shontz performed a series of methodological experiments demonstrating that a number of variables and conditions have minimal effects on body size linear judgments. He showed that such judgments are largely unaffected by the body postures (e.g., sitting versus standing) persons adopt or by whether the body distance to be judged was defined verbally or by touching specific points on the body. They are relatively unaffected by repetition and practice, although it is true that estimates of some body areas are more influenced than others. For example, estimates of forearm length become more realistic and foot length judgments become more extreme. Surprisingly, body size judgments are not appreciably influenced by whether subjects can or cannot see their bodies. However, subjects do render larger judgments when they can see the linear apparatus by which they register their estimates, as compared to when they manipulate it with their eyes closed. Also, body size judgments are not significantly affected by whether subjects adjust the linear markers on the measurement apparatus with their own hands or whether the experimenter does it for them.

Body size judgments proved to have considerable stability over a two-week span. The one exception involved judgments of hand length. Although errors of estimation of hand length are reliable from trial to trial within a given testing session, they are not reliable with a 2-week retest interval. This is an intriguing finding because the hand is a body part that is in almost constant use, and one might expect it to be perceived with unusual accuracy and stability. Shontz speculated that it is precisely because the hand is so much in use and therefore constantly changing in shape and apparent size experientially that one would evolve a concept of it within wide rather than narrow "cognitive boundaries."

Two aspects of the linear measurement procedure proved to be more influential in shaping estimates of body size than of estimates of nonbody objects. Thus, Shontz (1969) observed that the starting position of the size judgment continuum had relatively more effect on the body size estimates. He showed that the difference between ascending and descending sequences of body size judgments was greater than the difference for nonbody objects. These findings represent still another aspect of Shontz's demonstration that size judgments involving the body evoke modes of response different from those involving nonbody objects. Body judgments are more influenced by the anchor effects introduced by the starting position of the judgment sequence.

Shontz thought this reflected a relatively greater range of uncertainty about the size aspects of one's body than about nonbody stimuli. He pointed out that previous studies (e.g., Orbach, Traub, & Olson, 1966) had found people to be uncertain about the way they look. When asked to examine themselves in a mirror that distorts their image, they are willing to accept a wide range of distortions as accurate representations of self. Shontz proposed that this kind of uncertainty about how one really looks means that when subjects make judgments by moving a marker on a linear scale, each decision of "This is it" occurs at the edge of a zone of considerable uncertainty. Subjects move on the linear scale until they reach the first point of acceptable response. Shontz reasoned: "Because responses in the linear mode are always near the limit which is close to the initial position of the markers, and because the range of acceptability is larger for personal body parts than for comparison objects, responses display a broader spread of estimates for body stimuli than for comparison stimuli when the starting position of the apparatus is varied" (p. 143). He pointed out that the uncertainty persons feel about their body dimensions is most likely experienced when they are making complex judgments in the configurational mode (e.g., when choosing which of a series of pictured hands varying in size best approximates their own hand size). But in a linear judgment situation "the subject experiences no sense of uncertainty because he merely sets the markers to the first subjectively acceptable marker and has no reason to question further the adequacy of his response. Subjective uncertainty is more likely in the configurational mode, because a number of physically different but still psychologically acceptable alternatives are exposed to the perceiver" (p. 143).

Shontz speculated that the wide range of alternative size possibilities acceptable to most people as truly representing their bodily dimensions (particularly in a configurational context) reflects the changing size experiences one has with body parts in everyday life. He noted:

> The contour of much of the body is flexible. The chest may be expanded and the stomach pulled in; the arm may be stretched out beyond its normal length when it is relaxed. Developmental changes require the person to adjust his perceptions of the sizes of his own body parts. Positional changes alter distances on the body; the hand is close to or far away from the shoulder, depending upon whether the arm is flexed or extended; the distance between the head and the feet changes when one moves from a sitting to a standing position. Quite the opposite is true of rigid environmental objects. They are experienced as stable and constant in size (pp. 143–144).

That is, each body part is probably experienced as varying in size and cannot validly be fixed into one rigid size definition.

Shontz conceives of the body size judgment process as guided by "central schemata" ("mental pictures") of various body sectors. He was interested in what would happen to the size judgmental process if information discrepant with the schemata was introduced. He devised an experiment in which subjects estimated the sizes of various body areas while they viewed drawings of the areas that were either twice as large or half as large as they are in reality. Analogous drawings of nonbody objects were viewed when subjects judged the sizes of control nonbody objects. Size judgments were also made of body and nonbody stimuli without representational drawings being present. To Shontz's surprise, the input of the drawings was generally to increase the perceived size of objects, whether body or nonbody. Indeed, both the larger than and smaller than real life drawings had the same enhancing impact. Shontz speculated that the size judgmental process is somehow influenced by sheer amount of "relevant visual informational input." In subsequent experiments, Shontz found that other inputs have a greater influence on size judgments of nonbody objects than on body objects. For example, nonbody size judgments are significantly more influenced than are body judgments by whether there is an opportunity for visual inspection of the stimulus object in question.

Shontz analyzed the size judgment literature, which includes a number of his own studies, and concluded that perception of body size is, in part, a function of the extent to which a body area is used or not used.[5] It has been documented that patients who have paralyzed extremities are inclined to underestimate the size[6] of these disabled members. Also, it has been noted that, when individuals make extraordinary use of a body area (e.g., paraplegics, who rely on their shoulders more than most people) they tend to overestimate its size.[7] Shontz referred to such size under- and overestimation as constriction and expansion respectively. He suggested that constriction may also occur in body areas that are perceived as in a state of threat or in danger. He reported too that constriction or expansion may be produced by forces that intensify or decrease awareness of the boundary of a region. Originally, it was the sensori-tonic researchers who observed such boundary effects. They found for example, that increasing the boundary articulation of the head (by touching it) decreases its apparent size. Shontz performed studies that confirmed the effects of such articulating maneuvers. However, he proposed that it is not so much the absolute degree of articulation of a body area that produces constriction or expansion as it is the change in articulation.

In the process of exploring body size judgments in various groups, Shontz discerned several differences that are noteworthy. He discovered that intellectually retarded persons less clearly differentiate body and nonbody objects in their judgments than do persons of higher levels of intelligence. He observed also that males and females generally do not differ in their body size estimates, but that there are several exceptions. First, females more often overestimate waist size than men. Second, when women make body estimates verbally (e.g., in number of inches) rather than on a linear rod, they underestimate body distances more than men do. They do not, however, display this pattern of underestimation when providing verbal size estimates of nonbody objects. Third, there is a weak tendency for women's body estimates to be less accurate and more variable than are those of men.[8] This is interesting in view of the fact that no sex difference in accuracy was found with respect to judgments of nonbody objects.

Shontz devoted considerable effort to appraising possible personality correlates of body size estimates. He examined the correlates of both general tendencies to over- or underestimate body size and inclinations to magnify or minimize the dimensions of specific body parts. He related body size judgments to a variety of questionnaire and projective measures (e.g., Cattell, 1965, 16 PF Test; Fisher & Cleveland, 1968, Barrier and Penetration inkblot scores; & Machover, 1949, Draw-A-Person Test). He detected significant relationships in some samples, but they did not hold up to cross-validation. It did impress him that where significant findings appeared they were more frequent in the female than male samples. But, generally, he concluded that personality factors probably play a minimal role in body size perception. This conclusion was premature inasmuch as he had sampled only a narrow range of possibly meaningful personality measures. A subsequent study by Harrison (1975) demonstrated in a sample of 160 children (equal numbers of boys and girls) that the higher the Fisher-Cleveland Penetration score, the greater the overestimation of the sizes of a number of body parts (head width, waist, arm, hand, leg). In two samples, Shontz had observed shifting correlations between the Penetration score and waist size estimates but dismissed them because of their apparently instability. In view of Harrison's findings, the whole matter remains open for further investigation.[9]

Shontz has made a solid contribution to the body image literature. He introduced order into an area of research full of ambiguities and uncertainties. He systematically probed the reliability of linear body size estimates and teased out the measurement conditions that appreciably affect such estimates. He observed that measurement conditions will shape body size estimates in one direction or another, although they rarely eliminate the patterns that seem to be unique to the perception of the body as such. Body size judgments differ from judgments of nonbody objects in being relatively less accurate, more variable, and specifically biased in relation to the spatial locales of body parts. The finding that different patterns of over- versus underestimation apply, for example, to the head as compared to the hand or the forearm as compared to the foot is striking and one that particularly puzzled Shontz. It is suggested later that such specificity may reflect, in part, special personal or symbolic meanings ascribed to localized sectors of one's body. Although Shontz doubted the involvement of personality variables in body size judgments, he was the first to document the special tendency of women to overestimate the size of a specific body locale, the waist, and to explain it in terms of an attitude toward the waist area of the body that derives from being a woman with certain feminine values.

Shontz's essential contribution lies in his being the first to demonstrate convincingly that size perception of one's own body differs from size perception of nonbody objects. He went on to establish that this difference applies not only with reference to one's own body but also to size judgments of any human body as compared to those of nonbody objects. He ascertained that the unique elements in perceiving magnitude on the human body cannot be attributed to the intricacies of its contours. The geography of the human form, independent of its complexity, calls forth special sets to minimize or magnify. It remains to be seen whether such sets when the size aspects of other persons' bodies are being judged, derive originally from encounters with one's own body. There are certainly precedents in the literature for the view that individuals' own body experiences affect their perceptions of other persons' bodies. It has been shown, for example, that one's own height and weight influence one's judgments, respectively, of the height and weight of others (Berkowitz, 1980; Fillenbaum, 1961; Hinckley & Rethlingshafer, 1951). It has also been shown that the degree of insecurity one experiences with regard to one's own body boundaries affects one's perception of defects in the bodies of others (Cormack, 1966). There is good theoretical reason to examine in more detail the nature of the correlations between how persons perceive the sizes of specific areas of their own bodies and their corresponding perceptions of such areas on the bodies of others.

Other Variables Influencing Normal Body Size Perception

In addition to Shontz's work, which stands as the major achievement in the study of body size perception in the last decade, other investigations merit review. Furlong (1977) examined the impact on body size judgments of a considerable number of variables. She studied normal women ranging in age over the entire adult life span; males in a narrower age range (25–26); and also samples of women seeking cosmetic surgery. She obtained size judgments of the head, hips, hand length, and foot length. Two nonbody control stimuli were also judged (viz., Canadian dollar bill, telephone). The size estimates were given in the context of a configurational technique. For each body part or control object to be judged, the subject was shown a series of 12 pictures of graduated size, and the task was to choose the one in each case that appeared to be the most accurate representation. Degree of error and amount of over- or underestimation were determined. Furlong found no decline in accuracy of body size estimates in women as they moved into their 50s and 60s. However, the older women were more inclined toward underestimation (as if they felt "shrunk"). Middle-aged women were most inclined to overestimate, and women over 55 made the smallest estimates. Women made relatively more errors with respect to body stimuli (but not nonbody stimuli) than did the men. However, most of their errors derived from their inaccuracy with respect to one body dimension, waist width. Indeed, the men were less accurate than the women on foot length. Furlong concluded after complex analyses that her female subjects showed a definite bias in their body size judgments to compensate for feelings that specific body parts were either too small or too big in relation to an ideal. She commented that they tried to "flatter" themselves and their judgments reflected a form of "perceptual defense." Several other of her findings are:

1. Socio-economic status may significantly affect women's body size judgments.
2. Educational level may influence women's body size judgments. For example overestimation of the head may be positively correlated with educational attainment.
3. Men showed a trend to be more stable over time in their body size

estimates, but not in their estimates of nonbody objects. Furlong remarked that the lesser stability over time in women's body size judgments parallels Fisher's (1970) observation that women are less consistent than men over time in their relative degree of awareness of various parts of their bodies.

4. The greater a woman's *general* dissatisfaction with her body (as measured by a questionnaire), the more she overestimates her waist width. However, no consistent correlations occur between degree of dissatisfaction with *specific* body parts and the size judgments made with reference to those parts. Furlong proposed that a woman's overall feelings about her attractiveness become somehow linked with the waist area of her body.

5. Women awaiting cosmetic surgery (viz., rhinoplasty, augmentation mammoplasty) do not differ basically from normal women in their body size estimates[10] (at least within the range of body sites sampled in this study).

Hester (1970) sought to follow up on findings published by Fuhrer and Cowan (1967) indicating that active movement of a body part increased its apparent size, with the effect being stronger in females than males. He obtained from males linear measures of the following body parts: lower right arm, upper right arm, top of the hand, head width, and waist width. Also, he obtained control estimates of nonbody objects (foot ruler, length of dollar bill). These measures were secured under three conditions: active movement of a joint-bounded body part prior to making an estimate of that part; active movement of a different body part prior to making an estimate of joint-bounded and non-joint-bounded body parts and also of the nonbody objects; and no movement prior to making an estimate of joint-bounded and non-joint-bounded body parts as well as nonbody objects. The results did not support the Fuhrer and Cowan finding that movement increases apparent body part size. However, whereas Fuhrer and Cowan obtained size estimates while moving specific body parts, Hester's subjects responded after the movements were completed. Also, Fuhrer and Cowan obtained their clearest results with female subjects; Hester's subjects were all men. In any case, Hester felt that his findings were more congruent than Fuhrer and Cowan's with those of Shontz (1969), who studied the effects of certain proprioceptive experiences on size estimates. Shontz found that size estimates were not influenced by whether subjects were standing or sitting or whether the markers on the linear estimation apparatus were moved by subjects or by the experimenter. Shontz did not discern any differences in body size estimates as a function of whether the distances on the body were defined verbally or by touching specific parts (which would presumably produce some kinesthetic input).

Two other studies bear directly on the kinesthesia issue. Rossi and Zoccolotti (1979) noted the contradiction between Fuhrer and Cowan's (1967) findings and those of Hester. They wondered if the impact of kinesthetic experience could not be more sensibly approached by comparing the body size estimates of people who differ with respect to their long-term history of kinesthetic experience, rather than relying on a brief laboratory-induced difference. Using the linear method, they compared 20 male athletes with 20 male nonathletes in their estimates of various body areas (e.g., head, forearm length) and nonbody objects (wooden rods). They found that the athletes were generally more accurate in both their body and nonbody estimates. However, they also observed that the athletes were relatively more accurate for body than nonbody stimuli, whereas the reverse was true for the nonathletes. No differences emerged between the groups with respect to over- or underestimation of body size. Incidentally, both athletes and nonathletes displayed the geographic specificity, viz., overestimating head and forearm and underestimating foot and hand, that Shontz had demonstrated. One is left with a provocative bit of evidence that habitual athletic experience increases accuracy of judgments of linear distances and perhaps results in a pattern of relatively greater accuracy for body as compared to nonbody estimates. However, the findings do not support Fuhrer and Cowan because they do not indicate that long-term athletic and presumably intensified kinesthetic experience with one's body results in magnifying its apparent size.

Another pertinent study was undertaken by Hart (1971). She was interested in whether estimates of shoulder width, based on a linear estimation procedure, would differ when subjects were standing still as compared with when walking on a treadmill. She did not find a significant difference. Since the two conditions were roughly equivalent to a static versus dynamic movement context, the results can be viewed as not supportive of the Fuhrer and Cowan data. One of the novel things Hart did was to photograph and measure the amount of side-to-side sway by each subject while walking on the treadmill and to relate it to the difference between static and dynamic size estimates. There was an absence of significant relationships. Hart noted that the average estimate of shoulder width during the dynamic condition was larger than actual shoulder width, but smaller than the average side-to-side sway distance while walking. This finding stimulated her to speculate that the perceived boundary of the body is some average point intermediate between the real boundary surface and the edge of a "buffer" space around the body that, among other possible factors, might be defined by one's image of one's body in the dynamic condition when its typical movements (e.g., side-to-side sway) create a larger sense of personal body space.

Whether dynamic and static conditions differentially affect body size judgments was appraised by Stiles and Smith (1977) in a sample of children (20 boys and 20 girls, age range 6-10). They obtained pictures of the children in a static position and while running in place. The children then estimated their height and shoulder width by adjusting, for each condition, a zoom lens so that it projected images of self apparently equal to their actual body dimensions. There was a borderline trend for both height and shoulder estimates to be more accurate when judgments involved the picture of self running (dynamic). This borderline difference finding is not impressive. It becomes even less so if one considers that not only could Hart not detect a difference in dynamic versus static estimates, but also Shontz detected no effect of body position or activity on size estimates. It seems reasonable to conclude that moving or not moving one's body in a laboratory situation has little or no effect on one's body size judgments.

A novel approach to the determinants of body size perception was taken by Schlater, Baker, and Wapner (1970). Their experiment derived from an original observation that when the hand is in active contact with an object, the perceived length of that outstretched arm is greater than when the hand is in passive tactual contact with the object. Wapner (1960) also cited work showing that arm length is perceived as longer when the arm is actually pointing at something than when it is simply extended without purpose. Such judgmental differences were theorized to reflect the difference between an active attitude toward the object (indicating, in sensori-tonic terms, an attitude of greater differentiation between self and object) and a passive one (denoting lesser self-object differentiation). It has been shown that the less the perceived differentiation between self and an object, the closer the object appears to be to self.

At another level, Baker (1968) demonstrated that, when persons enter into a sequence of estimates of the positions of objects in space, the initial judgments in the sequence are shorter ("undershooting") than those later on ("overshooting"). He interpreted this pattern in the context of an active versus passive schema (degree of self-object differentiation). Presumably, subjects first approached the task in a curious (active) fashion, and with repetitious trials their attitude became more passive (less self-object differentiated). With this contextual background, Schlater et al. hypothesized that if one obtained repeated estimates of arm length from subjects, their attitude would become more passive toward the arm; and its distal part would appear to be closer, thereby creating the feeling of a shorter arm. This hypothesis was well supported in their study of 48 male college students whose initial estimates of arm length proved to be larger than later ones. The design of the study ruled out fatigue as a reasonable alternative explanation of the findings. Previous work by sensori-tonic researchers (Wapner, 1960) had already shown that estimates of the size of a body part such as the arm are influenced by multiple variables: spatial context (open versus closed space), boundary articulation (being touched versus not being touched), and function (e.g., holding versus not holding a tool) (Fisher, 1970).

Schlater, Baker, and Wapner (1974) went on to appraise the changes in perceived arm length that occur developmentally. They considered too the differential effect on such perception of whether the arm is active (viz., pointing at a target) or is being extended passively. They studied 36 boys and 36 girls aged 7-18. They used the same measurement procedures as in their other study described earlier. Their data indicated that subjects tended to underestimate arm length and that the underestimation decreased with age. By way of contrast, they pointed out that head size judgments in children were typically overestimated. However, here, too, there was a steady decline in overestimation (up to ages 9-10) as chronological age increased. The act of using one's arm actively to point did not seem to result in length estimates different from those when the arm was in a passive mode. This last finding differs from the McFarland, Wapner, and Werner (1960) observation that there is a tendency for adults to perceive an active pointing arm as relatively longer than an inactive one.

More pertinent data emerged from two experiments by Schlater, Baker, and Wapner (1981). In a first experiment subjects (24 male college students) estimated arm length while their hand was held against an oscillating disc. During one condition, the disc moved as the fingertips made passive contact with it; in another, the fingertips actively oscillated over the stationary disc. There were also control conditions in which both hand and disc were stationary and in which both were moving. As predicted, the arm was perceived as longer when the hand was actively touching the disc than when it was passively being touched by the disc.

The first experiment addressed the question whether the directionality of action of touch affects perceived arm length. A second experiment (involving 12 male college students) dealt with the role of directionality of touch versus the role of contact (touch versus no touch). There were three conditions: no touch, active touch, and passive touch (as defined in the first experiment). The data indicated that under the active touch condition the arm was judged to be significantly longer than under the other two conditions. However, there was no difference between the passive touch and no touch conditions. Schlater et al. (1981) noted that the results were not congruent with a body boundary interpretation. That is, previous studies by the sensori-tonic group, in which touching of a body area, such as the head, had produced an apparent decrease in head size, were interpreted within a framework that portrayed the touching as articulating the boundary of the head and thereby decreasing its perceived extent. Schlater et al. pointed out that only active touch, not passive touch, reduced the apparent length of the arm. Therefore, a simple articulation of boundary explanation would not suffice. Schlater et al. also analyzed their data to see if apparent arm length could be linked with the amount of movement or kinesthetic feedback available to the subject and concluded that movement, as such, seemed to have no effect. They suggested that this was not congruent with the Fuhrer and Cowan (1967) finding that body movement increases the apparent size of body parts. They concluded:

> The findings of both studies appear to be entirely in keeping with a direction-of-action hypothesis. When a person stretches his arm out to touch an object, the focus of that action is outward, away from the toucher's body, and this is assumed to be correlated with an increase in judged arm length. In contrast,

when the outstretched arm of a person is touched by some other object or person, the focus of that action is inward, toward the body of the person being touched, and this is presumably correlated with judged decrease in length of the extended arm. (p. 153)

A variety of other studies, largely without theoretical rationale, have taken a look at the role of this or that individual variable in body size judgments. For example, Cremer and Hukill (1969) reported that the more overweight a woman is, the more likely she will either over- or underestimate her true body proportions. Engelhardt (1972) found that the fact that a woman had been pregnant, with the consequent opportunity to experience radical changes in the volume of her body, did not result in her judging the size dimensions of her body differently from women who had never been pregnant. However, Slade (1977) reported that pregnant women overestimate their body size more than nonpregnant women do. Bowers and Van der Meulen (1970) indicated that hypnotic induction produces vague feelings of change in the apparent size of parts of one's body. Barber and DeMoor (1972) found that merely sitting quietly with one's eyes closed was sufficient to create sensations of changes in one's body size.

Scattered attempts have been made to demonstrate that the actual body size attributes of persons influence their judgments about other people. For example, Ward (1967) found that one's own height influences one's estimate of the height of the average American male and female. The effect is stronger with reference to same sex than to opposite sex. Rapoport (1975) observed that short men attribute more positive qualities to tall men than tall men do. Osborn (1973) noted that subjects judge persons whom they like to be similar in height to self, and the obverse is true for those whom they dislike. Prieto and Robbins (1975) reported the interesting observation that the self-esteem of adolescent males is not correlated with their actual height but rather the height attributed to them by others (e.g., peers, teachers).

Overview

It would be impressive if one could declare that persons' perceptions of the size attributes of their own bodies are distinctly different from their perceptions of nonself objects. This would clearly establish, at least in one mode, that there are unique processes involved in the experience of one's own body. There is little doubt that size judgments of one's own body differ in several ways from equivalent judgments of simple non-self objects (e.g., wooden rod, vase, baseball). However, as described, the differences start to fade as one introduces nonself objects of greater complexity and that resemble the human form. They fade even more when the nonself object is another human body. It is probably fair to say that a stimulus that even vaguely suggests a human configuration begins to elicit selective size perceptions (e.g., patterns of over- and underestimation, part-whole effects, influence of ascending versus descending judgment starting points). The selective response becomes stronger as the stimulus is more patently that of a human form and it occurs on a continuum rather than being an all-or-none phenomenon.

The empirical findings at this point are not encouraging that size judgments of other people's bodies differ from those pertaining to one's own body. However, the human form probably elicits selective size judgments that go beyond the mere geographical complexity of that form. It is not unreasonable to suppose that the person's original experiences with his or her body are the prototype for such selective responses. There is good evidence that responding to one's own body does call forth unique biases. This has been well documented in the self-confrontation literature (e.g., Fisher, 1970). The size perception research documents the manifestation of such biases in one particular area of judgment. But it also suggests that the selective attitudes involved may, in some circumstances, spread so that they affect not only the perception of one's own body but also the bodies of others.

One of the most intriguing forms of selectivity in body perception relates to the fact that some body areas are typically overestimated and others underestimated. As already described, head width, forearm length, and waist width are usually overestimated. Contrastingly, hand and foot length are usually underestimated. Shontz (1969) also reported biases in relation to other areas: the distances from the nose to the chin and from shoulder to elbow are overestimated. Why should there be such over- and underestimating tendencies for different body areas? Shontz (1969) pondered this matter and was puzzled by it. However, he offered several directly and indirectly pertinent speculations. He wondered whether the underestimation of hand length might somehow reflect the fact that the hand is the least dominant of body parts, as determined by the double simultaneous stimulation technique (Bender, 1952). He wondered too if the overestimation of head width was linked with the unusual sensory prominence of the head (Cohn, 1953). In another context, when discussing the consistent trend for women to exceed men in overestimating waist width, he suggested, "Women's tendency to overestimate waist width may reflect concern over conforming to American standards of feminine beauty, which require a small waist" (p. 196).

Shontz's speculations all link the specificity of over- or underestimation of a body region to its experiential prominence or its psychological connotations. In other words, he seems to feel that the over- and underestimation reflects qualities or values ascribed to the particular body locale. However, he questions his own speculations when he points out that, although hand length is underestimated, hand width is not; and that head width is overestimated, but head length is not. If a body area is over- or underestimated because of the significance ascribed to it, why would the bias disappear simply because the axis of judgment had changed from the horizontal to the vertical or the vertical to the horizontal?

As an initial step in considering whether the size ascribed to a body area may be tied to the meaning or value ascribed to that area, let us take up the question of whether specific body areas differ with reference to the values or significances ascribed to them. The answer is clearly in the affirmative. Fisher (1970) documented in considerable detail that not only do various body sectors differ in their perceptual prominence, but also that each sector is linked with specific values or concerns. Two examples are: degree of eye awareness in males is associated with specific attitudes about incorporation and "taking in"; and degree of awareness of the back of one's body is associated with particular attitudes toward dirt and anality. Special values have been shown to be linked with other body areas such as the mouth, heart, right versus left sides, and so forth.

The next question is whether the size ascribed to the body in general or to specific body areas have ever been demonstrated to be correlated with particular values or meanings. The answer, again, is in the affirmative but more hesitantly. One may mention the Shaffer (1964) report that a failure experience results in persons perceiving their total height as shorter. That is, the sense of having failed presumably makes the individual feel psychologically inferior, and this is reflected in a perception of the total body space as smaller.

Cleveland, Fisher, Reitman and Rothaus (1962) found a tendency for those who are more intellectually oriented and who therefore may be presumed to attach special importance to the head (as the supposed seat of intellectuality) to be unusual overestimators of head size. Relatedly, Furlong (1977) noted that overestimation of head size was positively correlated with amount of education (and presumably the importance of intellectuality) in a female group. She also reported that women who have a low opinion of themselves as objects of feminine attractiveness are inclined to overestimate their waist width. This takes on meaning in the context of Shontz's (1969) earlier mentioned hypothesis that overestimation of waist size in women reflects the intensity of their concern about whether they conform to the usual standards of feminine pulchritude.[11] Thus, the overestimation of waist ("It is too big and fat") could be conceptualized as an expression of dissatisfaction with a specific aspect of self as defined by the meaning symbolically ascribed to the waist.[12] Although the overall evidence concerning the influence of the psychological meaning linked to a body area on the size attributed to that area is still limited, it is nevertheless encouraging. There are some solid initial findings. This does not mean that one can account for all differences in over-underestimation of sizes among specific body locales simply in terms of the psychological meanings or values associated with the locales. Indeed, studies have detected significant correlations between the size ascribed to a body area and such simple functional factors as how disabled the area is or how much it is pressed into compensatory use because some other area is disabled (Shontz, 1969). There are probably other functional parameters pertinent to each body area that will turn out to be important in estimating its size, such as motility, degree of muscularity, contiguity to joints, and so forth.

It is logical that the apparent size of an area will be influenced by its usual use or function. Sensori-tonic researchers have shown that the perceived length of one's arm may vary in relation to its immediate function. For example, in one study (cited by Wapner, 1960) the arm was perceived as longer when used to point at a target than when simply extended into space. Obviously, various body areas are employed for different purposes. It is not readily apparent how the patterns of body part over- and underestimation that have been observed would match the respective functions of the parts.

However, there is a coincidence of interest. The two body parts that are most consistently underestimated are hand and foot length. Such underestimation contrasts with the tendency to overestimate the sizes of other body areas. It is striking that both hand and foot represent parts that are linked to appendages particularly instrumental in making direct contact with the substantiality of things "out there." They are our principal "touch points" with the outer world. The repeated experience of being in contact with nonself objects, when attention is relatively more concentrated on the object than on the body part, may result in a set to minimize the prominence and therefore the apparent size of the part. Of course, this idea is already implicit in observations that the hand is low in sensory dominance, as measured by the double simultaneous stimulation technique (Bender, 1952). Linn (1955) has speculated that the hands are subordinated (that is, low in sensory dominance) in order to facilitate their role as efficient helpers in various transactions. The head, which is the most overestimated sector of self, is, in contrast, one of the least used by adults to hold and manipulate other objects.

There still remains the puzzling question as to why, as reported by Shontz (1969), a body area may be overestimated with reference to its horizontal dimension, but not overestimated in another axis. If an area were overestimated because of its psychological valence, why would this evidence itself in relation to only one axis and not another? There is no good direct answer at the moment. However, previous studies have shown that the perceptual properties of a figure can be altered by such maneuvers as rotating it or interchanging its right-left aspects. Even the degree to which an object occupies a particular vertical or horizontal position in space may influence the value ascribed to it (De Soto, London, & Handel, 1965; Ziller, Hagey, Smith, & Long, 1969). We are accustomed to viewing the various sectors of the body from certain perspectives, and these perspectives may highlight one spatial dimension more than another. The accustomed view may be equated with one specific spatial axis. To shift one's perspective to another axis may involve pulling away from the particular stereotyped image of an area that has accrued a special meaning. It may be that an individual's usual image of the head focuses on its horizontal properties. Conceivably, the right-left symmetry of the eyes exerts such an horizontal pull. It might be the unique horizontally defined image of the head that is particularly associated with the significance assigned to the head region. But estimating head length rather than head width may introduce a shift in perspective that causes the head image to lose its familiar connotations. The shift could mean that the individual would no longer be judging the size of the same psychological object. Overall, it does seem worthwhile to pursue further the idea that some of the biases people display in their judgments of the sizes of various of their body regions mirror values or meanings they associate with such regions.

Another aspect of the body size over-/underestimation judgment pattern relates to the possible existence of a cephalocaudal gradient. Most judgments of the size of the total head or separate parts of the head (e.g., head-nose, nose-chin) are in the direction of overestimation. This is true too for forearm length and for chest width and waist width. At the same time, most judgments of the lower body region (e.g., ankle to floor, knee to floor, crotch to floor) are in the opposite direction (underestimation). Even hip width tends to be slightly underestimated. This contrast between the upper and lower body size judgments suggests a cephalo-caudal pattern. However, the matter is complicated by the fact that hand length and shoulder to finger length, which are upper body areas, tend, in contrast to the head, to be underestimated. A further complication is that at times experimental conditions (e.g., amount of illumination) may radically alter the amount of over- or underestimation characteristically evoked by a particular body site.

Shontz (1969) felt that such exceptions and variations negated the existence of a cephalo-caudal gradient. But this seems to be an extreme conclusion. The fact is that across multiple studies there are trends for size judgments of upper body areas to be in the overestimating direction and those for the lower body areas to be underestimating. What might the existence of a cephalo-caudal pattern mean? It could simply reflect the relative importance of upper versus lower body areas to the average individual. Overestimation might be an expression of the unusual psychological prominence of the head end of the body. Studies have shown that people equate their head with the location of self (Fisher, 1970). Another possibility is that socialization practices in our culture convey the message that the lower body area is bad and dirty, and it may therefore be perceived as relatively depreciated (diminished in magnitude) in comparison with the upper body.

It is a beguiling finding that people are less accurate in estimating the sizes of various dimensions of their bodies than of nonself objects. Shontz (1969) found, in one fairly representative study, that the error for normals in judging their own bodies was 14.5%. For nonself objects (like wooden rods) the error was 5.5%. One explanation for such a difference is that nonself objects employed in experiments are typically less complex in shape and therefore easier to appraise. However, in the typical Shontz experiment subjects first looked at the nonself objects and then turned their attention to the size estimation apparatus; they made their size estimates from memory. But when judging their own body sizes, they were, of course, capable of experiencing their bodies quite directly (kinesthetically) throughout the judging process and did not have to make their estimates from memory. Presumably this would provide a counter-balancing advantage when judging one's own size. Further, people have an infinite number of opportunities to see and otherwise experience their particular bodies, whereas they have never before perceived the particular nonself objects they are asked to judge during an experiment.

There is no good empirical data to explain the paradoxical difficulty in accurately grasping the size dimensions of oneself. However, at least two speculations can be offered. First, the average person would have more emotional and ego-involving feelings about the body than about the average nonself object. We also know that ego-involved attitudes increase the likelihood of adopting selective, biased, and inaccurate attitudes toward objects. Shontz (1969) linked such biasing effects to "central cognitive schemata."

Second, the very density of persons' experiences with their body may foster an ambiguity about its real dimensions. As earlier noted, when people move their body and adopt various postures, their body parts actually change in shape and magnitude. Their bodies have some of the properties of a flowing mass and, thus, are difficult to categorize within tight size definitions. People arrive at approximations of body size that are actually more realistic than a narrowly defined judgment would be in the context of a freely changing system. Even fairly rigid body structures like the head and the forearm change their apparent size as the individual moves muscles while eating, talking, and grasping; gains or loses weight; responds to marked temperature changes; and feels the constricting and then expanding effects of clothing put on and taken off. The supposed inaccuracy of body size perception may paradoxically register accurately the average of the chronically experienced changes in body size.

This point may be important in explaining the minimal effect of informational input on body size concepts. As already noted, Shontz (1969) and others discovered that, when people are asked to estimate their body size dimensions and are given the opportunity to gain objective information (e.g., by looking in a mirror) about those dimensions, they do not really use that input. They do not, in response to accurate input, become more accurate in their body judgments. Shontz found that neither visual nor kinesthetic updating about one's body had much effect. Is it possible that this apparent rigidity actually reflects the fact that the body size concepts held by most persons are highly realistic averages of how they have experienced their bodies in an infinite range of situations? That is, the average size concepts they have evolved of each body part may be more realistic than the information available from brief relatively static inputs provided in a laboratory context. The existing size concepts may be more valid in an overall life experience sense. Therefore, the lack of revision of size concepts that result from laboratory inputs, like the opportunity to see oneself briefly in a mirror, may represent not rigidity, but rather an appropriately realistic decision.

We know that males and females have contrasting attitudes about their body size. Typically, males want to be large and females want to be relatively small[13] (except for their breasts) (Fisher, 1970). Despite this contrast in their size expectations with regard to self, most studies have not detected that men and women differ much in how they judge their own body size. In Shontz's (1969) review of a number of studies concerned with sex differences in body size perception, he identified few of consistent significance. Such studies failed to detect sex differences in the reliabilities of size judgments over time or in the effects of various kinds of visual inputs (e.g., exposure to an enlarged picture or a specific body part). Shontz concluded on the basis of his own work with the linear size judgment technique that women are probably a bit less accurate than men in judging their body size.[14] Shontz reported that the two sexes do not differ in the accuracy of their judgments of the sizes of nonself objects. Furlong (1977) too detected a slight trend for males to be more accurate in their body size judgments. As mentioned earlier, Shontz found that when subjects were requested to make verbal estimates of their body size, women underestimated significantly more than men do. In addition, he discovered that there was one specific body dimension (viz., waist width) among the many that were sampled that was consistently more overestimated by women than by men.

These are certainly not dramatic differences. However, the slightly greater accuracy of males in estimating self size is puzzling from one perspective. Previous work (Fisher, 1970) has demonstrated that women are less anxious about, and more aware of, their bodies than men are. The female seems generally to be more comfortable with her body experiences than the male is with his. Then why is she apparently less accurate in judging the size attributes of her body? One cannot link her inaccuracy to some general deficiency in making size judgments; according to Shontz (1969), she does as well as her male counterpart when called upon to estimate the sizes of nonself objects. No satisfying explanation presents itself. It is conceivable that in view of cosmetically acceptable body size standards that appear to be stricter for women than for men, women have a heightened sensitivity to tasks that call for focusing on their body size dimensions. Perhaps such a sensitivity would introduce increased error into their body size judgments. When Shontz asked subjects to express their body size judgments in direct verbal terms rather than by manipulating a marker, he found that women more often underestimated than men did. That is, they were pulled in the direction of the cosmetic ideal of being small. Having to express the size judgments verbally rather than nonverbally may have accentuated the sense that their body dimensions were being publicly exposed and therefore evoked the defensive underestimation.

ANOREXIA NERVOSA

It is only in the last 10 years that interest has evolved in the body perception of persons with symptoms of anorexia nervosa, a syndrome characterized by self-starvation. Most frequently, this syndrome occurs in young women who become obsessed with the feeling that they are too fat and proceed to starve themselves into emaciation and occasionally death. But even in their emaciated condition they often continue to insist that they are too fat and need to lose more weight. Because of their extreme weight loss they typically cease to menstruate. There has been some exploration of the personality traits of anorexic women and of their early socialization experiences (e.g., Bruch, 1973; Palazzoli, 1978; Vigersky, 1977). Because of the anorexic's blatant insistence that she needs to lose further weight, even when she is skeleton thin, it has been concluded that she suffers from a gross "defect" in body image. Bruch (1962), one of the first persons to study patients with anorexic symptoms from a psychological perspective, asserted that they have a "disturbance in body image of delusional proportions" (p. 188). She noted

> What is pathognomonic of anorexia nervosa is not the severity of the malnutrition per se—equally severe degrees are seen in other malnourished psychiatric patients, but rather the distortion in body image associated with it: the absence of concern about emaciation, even when advanced, and the vigor and stubbornness with which the often gruesome appearance is defended as normal and right, not too thin, and as the only possible security against the dreaded fate of becoming fat. . . . Anorexic girls are haunted by the fear of ugliness and are forever concerned with their appearance, while denying the abnormality of their starved bodies. (p. 189)

She felt that unless the anorexic patient can revise her body image toward greater realism, various forms of treatment will produce only "temporary remission."

The search for a "body image defect" in anorexic patients stimulated studies to find out how they actually perceive the size dimensions of their bodies. Slade and Russell (1973a) reported that anorexic women overestimate the width of their bodies to a significantly greater extent than do normal controls. They compared 14 female anorexic patients with 20 normal females who were "mainly postgraduate psychology students and secretaries." There were no data about comparative educational or socio-economic levels. Each subject estimated the width of her face, chest, waist, and hips by means of

linear judgments (in a darkened room) of the space between two lights, one
of which was stationary and the other could be moved either toward or away
from it. Judgments were transformed in terms of the following formula:

$$\frac{\text{perceived size}}{\text{real size}} \times 100$$

Slade and Russell (1973a) found that whereas the normal women manifested
"fairly accurate body perception, with a slight tendency, if anything, toward
underestimation" (p. 191), this contrasted with a "marked tendency toward
overestimation" in the anorexic women. However, the anorexics did not
overestimate the sizes of two nonbody objects (10 in. and 5 in. wooden
blocks) and were not distinguished from the normals in this respect. Slade
and Russell interpreted these findings to mean that anorexics suffer from a
"body image disorder" that cannot be accounted for in terms of a general
perceptual tendency to overestimate size. They also carried out an experiment in which they demonstrated that anorexics did not significantly overestimate their height. They found that when anorexics made size judgments
with regard to the bodies of other women, they were significant overestimators, but not to the same extent as they were in relation to their own
bodies. In a follow-up study of 10 of the anorexics who were treated in a
hospital setting and whose size estimates were obtained weekly, it was
observed that there was a decrease in body size overestimation as body
weight increased. Those who showed the greatest body size overestimation
during hospitalization were most likely to relapse after discharge from the
hospital.

In 1977 Slade tried to find out more about the nature of the "body image
defect" apparently linked to anorexia, which had been reported in his 1973 a
paper with Russell. He wondered whether the "defect" might be a response
to a "failure to adapt." He noted reports that the majority of anorexics are
actually overweight before their precipitous weight loss, and he considered
the possibility that their overestimation of their horizontal emaciated dimensions might represent a lag in changing their perceptions of their new reduced
size. He also considered an "abnormal sensitivity" hypothesis, which conceptualized the anorexic's body size overestimation as directly reflecting her
"fear of being or becoming fat." He thought that studying pregnant women
would provide a direct test of these alternate perspectives. He reasoned as
follows:

It was predicted that if the 'adaptational failure' explanation of the perceptual
disorder is the correct one, then pregnant women should demonstrate a tendency to underestimate their physical size, i.e., they will tend to perceive their
bodily size as that obtaining prior to becoming pregnant; that if, on the other

hand, the 'abnormal sensitivity' explanation is correct, pregnant women should evidence a tendency to overestimate their size, especially in regard to the crucial area of their waist and stomach (p. 246).

With this perspective, Slade (1977)secured body size estimates from 40 pregnant women (mean age 26.5) whose mean length of pregnancy at time of testing was 4.0 months. The measurement procedures were essentially the same as those used in the Slade and Russell (1973a) study. However, no judgments of nonbody objects were obtained. Comparisons were made between the pregnant subjects' body judgments and those of the anorexics and normal controls described in the 1973 work. The pregnant women were found to overestimate their body size significantly more than the nonpregnant normals, but significantly less than the anorexics. These findings were considered to favor the "abnormal sensitivity" explanation of body size overestimation. In a further analysis, the pregnant women were subdivided into those who had maintained a stable weight level during the 12 months prior to becoming pregnant, those who had gained weight, and those who had lost weight during that 12-month period. It was found that those with a history of stable weight overestimated their body size more than either the weight gainers or losers. On the basis of the adaptation hypothesis, one would have anticipated a different pattern of findings. One would have expected the weight losers to overestimate their augmented pregnant proportions the most and the weight gainers to go in the opposite direction. The degree of overestimation by the stable weight group should probably have been intermediate between that of the other two groups.

Sixteen of the pregnant subjects were retested at approximately 8 months of pregnancy. Although their real body size had increased considerably, their judgments of their body size had decreased significantly. Slade (1977) interpreted this to mean that by the 8th month they had adapted to the fact that their body size was changing, and therefore they were less pulled in the direction of expressing an exaggerated sense of body size increase. He saw a parallel between this and the fact that anorexics decrease their body size overestimation as they are restored to normal weight levels. Presumably the anorexics similarly adapt to the major alteration in their body size and become able to react less extremely to it.

Slade (1977) viewed his overall findings as meaning that body size overestimation is not unique to anorexics but occurs also in pregnant women. He concluded: "It would seem, therefore, that pregnant women of approximately 4 months' duration exhibit a perceptual disorder similar to that of anorexia nervosa patients, albeit of smaller proportions" (p. 251). It is striking, though, that he continued to refer to the size overestimation of the anorexics as a perceptual disorder.

Fries (1977) explored the issue further by studying women who varied widely in their amount of weight loss. He recruited 21 women whose symptoms strictly matched formal criteria of the anorexia syndrome. Also, he formed a second group of women who also manifested symptoms of weight loss, but in less extreme forms. There was a control group of 22 normal women who were hospital personnel. The body estimates were obtained in the same fashion as in the previous two studies just described. No size judgments were secured with regard to non-body objects. Both the strictly anorexic and the less severe weight loss groups overestimated their body size significantly more than the controls. However, the anorexics and the less severe weight loss group did not differ significantly from each other. It was also found that, when the subjects in these groups were combined and assigned scores to indicate the severity of their anorexic symptoms, there was a significant positive correlation between their scores and degree of body size overestimation. Despite these positive findings, Fries was skeptical about whether the overestimation was specific to anorexia. He was particularly impressed with the fact that about a quarter of his normal subjects overestimated their body size by 21% to 33%.

Mixed findings were reported by Wingate and Christie (1978) with regard to size estimation in anorexics. They studied 15 hospitalized anorexic women (mean age = 21) and a control group of 15 normal women (mean age = 21) comparable in socio-economic class and age. They also recruited a second control group of normal girls who were not only younger (mean age = 17), but also obtained ego strength scales on the MMPI comparable to the rather low scores previously found for the anorexic women in this study. Body size estimates were obtained by means of a technique developed by Askevold[15] (1975). This technique involves the subject's standing before a large piece of paper taped to a wall, then imagining herself as facing her mirror image, and marking on the paper her shoulder, waist, hip, and total height dimensions. No judgments of nonbody control objects were required. The anorexics overestimated their width dimensions significantly more than the controls of their own age. But they differed from the younger control group only in their overestimation of the waist. Neither of the control groups differed from the anorexics with reference to perceived total height. It will be recalled that Slade and Russell (1973) also failed to find a difference between anorexics and normals with regard to height estimates. Within the anorexic group, the lower a woman's ego strength score, the more she overestimated her shoulders, waist, and hips. No comparable significant relationships appeared in the older normal control group. In the younger normal sample, ego strength was correlated significantly (negatively) only with the waist size estimates. Overall, this study indicated a trend for anorexic and other women who have experienced considerable weight loss to overestimate their body size. However, their degree of overestimation was essentially no greater than that shown by adolescent girls with lower than average ego strength (but no overt symptoms of psychological disturbance) who did not have weight loss problems.

A clearly positive result emerged from the data of Pierloot and Houben (1978). They compared 31 female patients with anorexia symptoms and 20 female neurotics. Three sets of body size estimates were obtained with reference to the width of the following areas: face, shoulders, waist, hips. One set of estimates involved the Slade and Russell (1973a) procedure. Then the subject was told that she had overestimated her sizes and was asked to give "more correct" estimations. Simultaneously, a mirror was provided so that she could check her appearance as she made her estimates. Half of the subjects made another set of body size estimates prior to the procedure just described and half did so subsequently. This set was based on the Askevold (1975) procedure described earlier (which involves the subject's marking her own perceived dimensions on a large sheet of paper as if she were seeing herself in a mirror). Subjects were not dressed as they rendered their judgments in this context.

The overall findings indicated that the anorexics exceeded the neurotic controls in degree of overestimation. This was significantly true for the Slade and Russell (1973a) measurement technique. When the subjects were told to correct their estimates and to observe themselves in a mirror, there was a trend for the anorexics to show greater overestimations for all the four body sites, but only the difference for the waist was statistically significant. Incidentally, whereas the anorexics tended under these conditions to decrease their size estimates, the neurotic controls were inclined to go in the opposite direction. The estimates made by the anorexics during the Askevold (1975) procedure also revealed a fairly consistent pattern of greater overestimation by the anorexics. Further, although the anorexics were more variable than the neurotic controls in their judgments for the Slade and Russell procedure, they did not differ significantly in the Askevold series. The MMPI, the Rorschach test[16], and a measure of internal–external control were administered to the subjects. Various scores derived from these tests failed to correlate consistently with the body size estimates.

Another positive result emerged from the work of Garfinkel et al. (1983). This study was based on an evaluation of 23 anorexic women (14 bulimics, 9 restricters) and 12 normal control women who were recruited by means of newspaper advertisements. Body size estimates were secured by means of a technique developed by Glucksman and Hirsch (1969), which calls for the subject to adjust (via anamorphic lenses) the projected photographic image of herself (starting from smaller than and larger than levels) "so that it looks exactly the way you see yourself." It involves a judgment of total body size. No control judgments of nonself objects were included in the procedure. The anorexics were found to overestimate their total size significantly more than did the controls. (It should be noted that the 12 controls were significantly younger than the 23 anorexics.) Questionnaire measures of degree of satisfaction with one's body and amount of enjoyment obtained through one's body indicated that the anorexics were significantly less positive about their body. Another interesting aspect of this study was that the mothers and fathers of the anorexics and of the controls (with the sample size increased by families of anorexics and controls recruited in Ireland) were also asked to render judgments about their own body size, and no differences between the two sets of parents could be detected. They did not differ in their accuracy in estimating their daughters' size. Further, they could not be distinguished with respect to the questionnaire measures of body satisfaction.

Finally, there is a positive report by Freeman, Thomas, Solyom, and Miles (1983), which involved 15 "abstaining" anorectics, 27 bulimics, 15 normal weight persons, and 9 psychiatric controls. The normals were younger than all the other participants and were recruited through newspaper advertisements. The anorectics and bulimics were consecutive admissions to a clinical service. Each subject was asked to judge, while wearing a bathing suit and after fasting for 12 hours, when a television image of herself truly represented her own proportions. There were ascending and descending trials in relation to the initial setting of the television image as either "too fat" or "too thin." There was also a retest after the subject had eaten a meal. The anorectic and bulimic groups overestimated their size significantly more than the normal or the psychiatric controls. The difference was more pronounced for the bulimic than for the anorectic group. Eating a meal had little effect on the body size judgments. No control judgments of nonself objects were included in the study.

The studies reviewed to this point are those that somewhat positively support the idea that anorexic women have an exaggerated concept of their body size. In some instances the support has been only partial. The remaining studies to be perused stand out as largely nonsupportive. First, Crisp and Kalucy (1974) used a modification of the Slade and Russell (1973a) body size estimation technique. It is based on judging the size of a variable strip of light on a wall rather than the size of the space between two lights. In one phase of their study, Crisp and Kalucy obtained body size judgments from four anorexic women and then repeated the measures after asking the women to "drop your guard" and admit to themselves that they had in fact starved themselves into an emaciated (smaller) state. There was no normal control group, and there were no estimates of control nonself objects. At the time of the first testing, considerable overestimation of body size (average of 65%) was found; when asked to be "less guarded", the overestimation decreased to 40%. When these individuals had, later, been restored to normal weight, their size overestimation averaged about 35%; and, when asked again to be "less guarded" their overestimation decreased to 13%. These findings are interesting, but difficult to interpret because of the absence of normal controls.

In a second phase of the study, six anorexic women and six normal women (members of nursing and occupational therapy staff) were compared in their body size judgments, just before and after eating one meal that was obviously low in carbohydrates and a second obviously high in carbohydrates. There was a significant trend for the anorexics to increase their body size judgments more than the normals after the obviously high carbohydrate meal, but not after the low carbohydrate meal. However, the size judgments obtained before neither the high nor the low carbohydrate meals differentiated the anorexics from the normals. The anorexics did not overestimate their body size more than the normals. Crisp and Kalucy (1974) were impressed with the multiple factors that influence body size estimates in the anorexic person. Thus, they were able to reduce such estimates simply by asking the anorexics to be 'less guarded" and to increase them by impressing the anorexics with the fact that they had consumed a high caloric meal.

Further perspectives on these issues were provided by Garner, Garfinkel, Stancer, and Moldofsky (1976). They studied five groups, totaling 84 females: 18 anorexics, 16 juvenile onset obese, 16 "thin normals," 18 normals of average weight, and 16 psychiatric patients (non-psychotic) of average weight and without a history of weight problems. Body size estimates were obtained with two different procedures. One was the moving light technique (Slade & Russell, 1973); the second was the anamorphic lense distorting technique developed by Glucksman and Hirsch (1969), which calls for the subject to adjust the projected photographic image of herself "so that it looks exactly the way you see yourself." Control size estimates of a vase and a "standard female figure" were also secured from all subjects.

The results from the Slade and Russell (1973a) technique indicated no essential differences in degree of overestimation among the five groups. There were also no differences for the estimates of the nonself control objects. With respect to the Glucksman and Hirsch measures, it was observed that although the anorexic and obese subjects did not differ from each other, they did significantly exceed the three control groups in degree of overestimation. However, at the same time about half the anorexics underestimated their size. The anorexics and obese were not less accurate than the controls. No differences emerged for the estimates of the non-self control objects. The Eysenck Personality Inventory had been administered to all subjects; in both the anorexic and the obese the degree of self-overestimation was positively correlated with degree of neuroticism. This was not true in the various control groups. The Rotter Locus of Control Scale had also been administered. It turned out not to be linked with the body size judgments in any of the control groups. But in the anorexic women a sense of lacking self-control was positively correlated with body size overestimation. Garner et al. (1976) were puzzled by the results they obtained from the Slade and Russell (1973a) technique contrasted to the Glucksman and Hirsch (1969) method. They wondered whether the latter did not more personally and directly (and therefore perhaps more validly) involve the subject with her body, and they finally concluded that anorexics (and the obese) do distort their body perceptions by way of unrealistic magnification. Garner et al. did not face up to the fact that many of the previous studies that had observed overestimation in anorexic persons were based on the Slade and Russell method. Therefore, their findings with this method constituted a failure to replicate.

In a later study, Button, Fransella, and Slade (1977) used the Slade and Russell (1973a) body size estimation technique to appraise 20 anorexic women and 16 "normal females, mainly occupational therapy students." The mean age in both groups was in the 23-24 range. Button et al. included in their analyses some of the data from the original Slade and Russell (1973a) study. They found that the anorexics in their study were significantly older than those in the Slade and Russell sample. In their analysis of their own size estimation data, they could not detect significant differences between the anorexics and normal controls. They did find that their anorexics overestimated their body size significantly less than did the Slade and Russell anorexics. After probing the data for an explanation of this difference, they came upon evidence that the degree of overestimation in the anorexics (who were all hospitalized) was positively correlated with how many days had passed from time of admission to the time when the size judgments were obtained, and also with weight gain since admission.

Button et al. (1977) speculated that the experience of gaining weight might somehow produce body size overestimation; and they wondered whether they might have tested their anorexic sample earlier in the hospitalization sequence (before weight gain) than had Slade and Russell. But no data were available concerning the pertinent time parameters in the Slade and Russell study. In any case, Button et al. had to square their speculation with the additional fact that some studies have found that anorexics cease to be overestimators when they attain normal weight. They speculated that there might be a curvilinear process, with early weight gain in the anorexic leading to overestimation and then a decrease in overestimation with the additional weight gain that brings the individual into the normal range of weights. Another trend they detected related to the fact that anorexic women who were vomiters were significantly more inaccurate in their body size judgments than nonvomiters. Finally, once again there proved to be a signifcant negative correlation between initial tendencies to overestimate body size and weight gain after leaving the hospital. Although the presumed difference in body size overestimation between anorexics and normals was not sustained, support did emerge for the negative prognostic value of a high degree of body size overestimation early in the anorexic's hospitalization.

Halmi, Goldberg, and Cunningham (1977) were puzzled why the original Slade and Russell (1973a) findings had run into so much contradiction in subsequent studies. They noted that the anorexics in the Slade and Russell study averaged about 20 years of age, whereas the normal controls averaged about 25, with the difference attaining almost the .05 significance level. They were struck too with the Crisp and Kalucy (1974) observation that a group of "younger" normal women overestimated their body size to the same extent as a comparable anorexic group. Therefore, they decided to study the effects of age on body size estimation. Their sample consisted of 86 normal girls distributed fairly equally at each level in the age range 10-18. Body size estimates were obtained by means of linear judgments on an apparatus similar to that devised by Shontz (1969). Judgments were rendered not only for the usual body width dimensions, but also for foot and arm length and the length of a control nonself object (block of wood).

Overestimation typified the body width judgments at every age level; and age was consistently positively correlated with degree of overestimation. Width overestimation showed its largest drop between ages 10 and 11. The body length judgments were, without exception, in the direction of under-estimation, but age and length judgments were uncorrelated. The tendency to underestimate rather than overestimate foot and arm lengths is not surprising in view of Shontz's (1969) earlier reported findings in this respect. The control nonself object was the most accurately estimated at all age levels. Halmi et al. (1977) were impressed with the fact that Elkind (1975) had found support for Piaget's (1960) observation that younger children overestimate lines in certain positions and that at later ages the overestimation declines. They suggested that the anorexics' self overestimation indicated they "regress to an earlier stage of perceptual performance" (p. 257). However, Halmi et al. found that beyond the age of 15 there was a relatively small and gradual decline in the tendency to overestimate body width dimensions. This raises a doubt as to whether age differences between anorexics and normals, who typically have been 18 or older, could play a substantial part in explaining the differences in body size overestimation that have been reported.

The pursuit of the anorexic's exclusive "body perception defect" was continued by Garfinkel, Moldofsky, Garner, Stancer, and Coscina (1978). Twenty-six anorexic women and 16 normal females were appraised. The average age in both groups was in the 20-21 year range. Their body size estimates were secured by having them adjust to actual size (via anamorphic lenses) a projected photographic image of self. Baseline estimates were secured; subjects were then asked to view themselves in a full-length mirror; and their estimates were obtained once again. It was expected that the mirror experience would increase accuracy of self-estimates. Ideal size judgments were also obtained on each occasion, and a control estimate of a nonself object (vase) was obtained at the time of the first testing.

The anorexics were inclined to overestimate their overall body size more than the normals, but the difference did not quite reach statistical signifi-cance ($p = .06$). There were no significant changes in body estimation produced in either group's looking in the mirror, and during this retest there were only chance differences between the two groups. The failure of the mirror experience to influence body size judgments corresponds well with a similar result reported by Shontz (1969). Incidentally, the normals' ideal body size was significantly thinner than the anorexics' ideal. No differences emerged in judgments with reference to the nonself object (vase).

Garfinkel et al. (1978) also studied the impact of eating an obviously high caloric versus low caloric meal on body size judgments. No significant effects could be detected. This result contradicts the earlier mentioned findings of Crisp and Kalucy (1974), who reported that an obviously high caloric meal made anorexics (but not normals) increase their overestimates of their own body width. Garfinkel et al. did conclude that their study "confirms the presence of body image distortions in some patients with anorexia nervosa" (p. 497). It is not clear how they arrived at this conclusion in view of the fact that, when body size estimates were obtained on several different occasions, in only one instance did the difference between the anorexics and normals even approach significance.[17]

In a continuation of this study, Garfinkel, Moldofsky, and Garner (1979) did a one-year follow up of 16 of the anorexic patients and 13 of the normal controls. The same basic procedure was used as already described. Each subject was seen twice, with 7 days intervening. Just prior to giving body size estimates at the first session, either an obviously high caloric or low caloric meal was eaten, and this was counterbalanced at the time of the second session. The anorexics did not significantly exceed the normals in degree of body size overestimation. The ingestion of an obviously high versus low caloric meal had no effect on the size estimates. Further, the previously described procedure of exposing the subject to a full-length mirror image of herself failed to influence the size estimates in the two groups. The anorexics showed high correlations between their test-retest size estimates, whereas the analogous correlations for the normals were consistently low. Overall, the follow-up survey affirmed the negative findings of the original study.

Probably one of the best studies, particularly in terms of sample size, was carried out by Casper, Halmi, Goldberg, Eckert, and Davis (1979). They compared 79 female anorexics with 130 normal females. Body size judgments were made on a linear scale and involved an apparatus similar to that used by Shontz (1969). Not only were the usual estimates of body width obtained, but also the length of the foot, length of arm, depth of body, and length of a nonself object (block of wood). The data revealed overestimation for most body parts[18] in both groups. However, there were no consistent significant differences between the anorexics and normals. Casper et al. concluded, on the basis of their findings and a review of previous studies, that there was no solid evidence that anorexics overestimate their body size more than normals do. They did observe that, within the anorexic group, the more the overestimation of body size, the greater the denial of the seriousness of the symptoms;

the less the weight gain during subsequent treatment; the larger the weight loss prior to beginning treatment; the less successful were previous treatment efforts; and the greater the psychosexual immaturity. They deduced that the more an anorexic woman overestimates her body size, the more she employs denial as a defense mechanism and the greater the long term gravity of her symptoms.

A study by Garner and Garfinkel (1981-82) focused on possible differences between anorexic patients who were over- and underestimators of body size. Size estimates were obtained in response to projected (via anamorphic lenses) photographs of the subjects. A variety of measures were administered to tap different levels of psychological functioning (viz., anxiety, depression, locus of control, body dissatisfaction). The data indicated that the over-estimators generally displayed more negative and psychopathological signs. They had more intense symptoms of anorexia, were more "external" (i.e., felt they had less control over their lives) on a locus of control measure, were more depressed, more anxious, and felt greater dissatisfaction. These findings are supportive of the Casper et al. (1979) observations just outlined.

Another clearly negative study was reported by Strober, Goldenberg, Green and Saxon (1979). They looked at 18 women with anorexic symptoms and 24 female controls, all of whom were psychiatric patients. Body size judgments were expressed via the Askevold (1975) technique that calls for the individual to mark with a pencil on a large sheet of paper her perceived body size dimensions (shoulders, waist, hips). Subjects were not dressed during the procedure. Estimates were secured within 3 days of admission to the hospital and again during the 6th month of hospitalization. No estimates of nonself control objects were obtained. The anorexics and normals did not differ significantly in their body size judgments on either of the two occasions they were tested. Further, even though the anorexics had returned to a normal weight by the time of their second testing, there was no significant difference between their two sets of body size judgments. The normals did not show a change either. Two other body image measures had been applied to the subjects. One was the Fisher (1970) Body Distortion Questionnaire, which calls for reports of the presence of a possible variety of body image distortions (e.g., perception of body parts as excessively small, large, deper-sonalized). The second was the Witkin et al. (1962) Sophistication of Body Concept Scale, which measures body concept differentiation as represented in the subject's drawing of the human figure. The total Body Distortion Questionnaire score was greater in the anorexics than in the controls, at both test and retest, but only the second difference was statistically significant. Analysis of individual items in the questionnaire suggested that the anorexics were particularly likely to experience sensations of body depersonalization, weakness of body boundaries, blockage of body openings, and perception of body as excessively large. Total body distortion scores decreased significantly in both anorexics and controls over the 6-month period of hospitalization. Anorexics who vomit were found to have significantly higher total body distortion scores than those who do not vomit. Strober et al. (1979) considered that the elevated body distortion scores of the anorexics supported s;peculations by Bruch (1973) and Palazzoli (1978) that the anorexic condition is rooted in body image defects. Finally, the Witkin et al. (1954) Sophistication of Body Concept Scale showed only a borderline trend for anorexics to produce less differentiated figure drawings than the controls.

Still another negative outcome was presented by Ben-Tovim, Whitehead and Crisp (1979). They used the Slade and Russell (1973a) technique to obtain size estimates of face, chest, waist, and hips. The subjects were 8 female anorexics and 11 normal weight females from a girls' day school. Judgments of nonself control objects were not secured. The data indicated no difference in body size estimation between the anorexics and the controls. Within the distribution of judgments for any particular body part (e.g., waist), there was an inverse relationship between the actual size of that part and the degree to which it was overestimated.[19] Ben-Tovim et al. noted too that Goldberg et al. (1977) had detected a similar trend. In any case, even when the estimates of the anorexics and normals were corrected for such size discrepancies, there was still an absence of significant difference in degree of overestimation.[20]

Touyz, Beumont, Collins, McCabe, and Jupp (1984) also failed to corroborate the overestimation hypothesis. They studied female anorexic patients (N = 15) and normal weight female controls (N = 15). Subjects were asked to adjust an image of self that was projected on a video monitor so that it would correctly match their own proportions. A lens system made it possible to vary the horizontal dimension of the figure on the monitor. The anorexic subjects did not differ from the controls in their degree of overestimation of their own body size. They did, however, have a significantly greater tendency to be more inaccurate in such size estimates. When asked to judge the size of an average normal weight woman, they underestimated her size significantly more than did the normals. Both the anorexic and normal subjects wished they were smaller than their actual proportions.

Overview

The original idea put forward by Slade and Russell (1973a) that women with anorexia nervosa perceive their own body as uniquely magnified in size has not really stood up well if one looks at the entire array of pertinent work. True, a few initial studies and subsequent investigations by Pierloot and Houben (1978), Garfinkel et al. (1983), and Freeman et al. (1983) have shown promise with regard to this idea. But the majority have either completely failed to demonstrate that anorexics overestimate their body size more than normal persons do or come up with equivocal findings. Hsu (1982) reached a similar negative conclusion after reviewing a portion of the literature dealing with size perception in anorexics.

However, one interesting trend with regard to the overestimation issue should be mentioned. There were three studies (Garfinkel, et al., 1978; Garner et al., 1976; Garfinkel et al., 1983) that used the anamorphic lens technique and two (Freeman et al., 1983; Touyz et al., 1984) that utilized judgments of one's overall image on a TV screen. Four of the five demonstrated that the anorexics were greater overestimators of their overall body size than were various controls. In three of the instances the differences were significant and in one attained the .06 level. It will be recalled that the anamorphic lens technique typically calls for a judgment with respect to one's overall size rather than individual body parts. Anorexic women may be inclined to exaggerate the size of their body space when they regard it as a totality. This is a lead worth pursuing. It may be that, if there is a body attitude typifying anorexics that involves a sense of one's body being inflated, it is most likely to be revealed in the context of judgments about self as a total person rather than about separate, relatively impersonal body parts.

As more basic work has been directed to understanding body size perception, we have learned that numerous conditions, aside from anorexia nervosa, are linked with overestimation of one's body size. Shontz (1969), of course, demonstrated the influence of a wide range of variables. Research with anorexics has added a few tidbits like the fact that body size overestimation tends to be particularly high in young children, negatively correlated with ego strength, and higher in those who are pregnant. There are hints that it may also be affected by whether ther subject eats a high caloric meal before rendering body size judgments; and it has been learned that simply instructing the anorexic subject to be "less guarded" may cause a reduction in estimates.

Although the findings are ambiguous and perhaps negative with regard to whether anorexics overestimate body size more than normal controls, there is consistent evidence that, *within* the anorexic group, overestimation is a meaningful parameter. In a number of studies of anorexics (Button et al., 1977; Casper et al., 1979; Garner, Olmstead, Bohr, & Garfinkel, 1982; Slade & Russell, 1973a; Wingate & Christie, 1978) degree of overestimation was found to be correlated with such variables as neuroticism, poor self-control, and distorted body experiences; at times it is also predictive of the future course of the anorexic symptoms. The greater the overestimation, the poorer the prognosis. No parallel relationship has been observed with amount of overestimation of nonself objects. Perhaps the very fact that an emaciated woman would portray herself as exaggeratedly larger than her true size signifies unusually poor judgment and by implication, a particularly unrealistic level of functioning. Perhaps it is as an index of lack of realism that body size overestimation provides prognostic information aboout the anorexic woman.

Strober (1981) examined in some detail the MMPI correlates of body size overestimation (as defined by the anamorphic lens technique) in female anorexic adolescents ($N = 65$). He discerned a significant link between body size overestimation and depression and anxiety. He administered the Fisher (1970) Body Distortion Questionnaire to the same subjects and found that degree of body image distortion was associated (as defined by the MMPI) with "atypicality, confusion, and unusual thought processes (F, Sc), hysterical tendencies (Hy), and interpersonal sensitivity, mistrust and paranoid trends (Pa)" (p. 326). But it is of particular interest that he found a significant positive correlation between body image distortion and degree of size overestimation.[21]

The failure to find a clear-cut "defect" in the anorexic's perception of her body size does not mean that there are not other forms of body image disturbance linked with anorexia nervosa. Bruch (1962) may yet be supported in her conclusion that anorexics have a "disturbance in body image of delusional proportions" (p. 188). She suggested that one of their principal difficulties may be a "disturbance in the accuracy of perception of cognitive interpretation of stimuli arising in the body, with failure to recognize signs of nutritional need . . ." (p. 189). Preliminary observations with reference to hunger experiences and interoceptive sensations in anorexics have been equivocal (Garfinkel & Garner, 1982) in their support of Bruch's speculation. However, it remains to be seen whether anorexics are typfied by other kinds of body image distortions, such as frightening fantasies about what occurs in the gastrointestinal tract or deviant ideas about the need to sacrifice the substance of one's own body in atonement for feeling hostility toward one's parents.

Some initial encouragement that anorexics do experience body image distortions comes from several studies: Strober et al. (1979) observed that anorexics obtained significantly higher total scores on the Fisher (1970) Body Distortion Questionnaire than did controls. Knight (1981) found that anorexic forms of behavior were significantly positively correlated with self-reported feelings of body incongruence. Kalliopuska (1982a) reported that anorexics produced figure drawings with significantly more distortions than did controls. Biggs, Rosen, and Summerfield (1980) discovered that anorexics exposed to brief video feedback of themselves engaged in a discussion responded with a reduction in self-esteem; normals displayed an increase in self-esteem. Joseph, Wood, and Goldberg (1982) and Garfinkel and Garner (1982) established that girls particularly vulnerable to anorexia are attracted to occupations (e.g., dancing, drama) where there is a heightened focus on the body. Interesting speculations have been offered by Story (1976) to the effect that the anorexic woman may dramatize her body as an ugly object in order to communicate to her parents how overcontrolling and deprecating they have been. Story suggested that the anorexic's portrayal of her body has elements of the ridiculous that satirize how unreasonably she feels she has been treated. Such speculations are interesting, but they have yet to be tested.[22]

THE OBESE CONDITION

The corpulent body is usually not acceptable to its owner and is even less acceptable to others. This is certainly the impression one gets from most investigators who have interviewed the obese (Kalucy & Crisp, 1974; Rand & Stunkard, 1978; Stunkard & Mendelson, 1967) and probed them with questionnaires (Blanchard & Frost, 1983; Brantley & Clifford, 1979a; Gray, 1977; Hawkins, Turell & Jackson, 1983; Hendry & Gillies, 1978; Kessler, 1978; Speno, 1981; Thomas, 1973). Horan Smyers, Dorfman, and Jenkins (1975) reported that the obese are particularly inclined to avoid looking at themselves in the mirror. Younger and Pliner (1976) demonstrated that obese people monitor their self presentation to others significantly more than do the nonobese. Many of the obese perceive their bodies as disgusting and ridiculous.[23] In contrast, there are cultures and subgroups (e.g., lower socioeconomic) in which being fat has few negative connotations. Considerable debate has occurred about whether overeating is caused by neurotic conflicts, unsatisfied oral drives, and other forms of emotional difficulty (Bruch, 1973; Buchanan, 1973; Herman & Polivy, 1975; Keith & Vandenberg, 1974). The issue is still not scientifically settled. One of the reasons for this uncertainty is that we do not know whether or how much the experience of obesity itself can induce emotional disturbance in an individual. Another complication is our increasing awareness that the obese constitute a heterogeneous group. For example, they differ in how early in life they became overweight, their sex and age, the ease with which they can lose weight, and so forth. There are parameters that probably define meaningful subgroups of the obese; and there are hints that personal maladjustment may vary within each group.

Some (e.g., Bruch, 1973) have suggested that obesity evolves in people who have not learned to respond selectively to body cues indicative of hunger, but who, instead, may be prompted to eat when they experience nonhunger cues, for example, body arousal reflecting anxiety. Presumably, their early caretakers (e.g., mother) responded to their signals of body tension in an inconsistent and confused fashion that did not foster learning how to discriminate accurately among different body cues. There are a number of studies suggesting that the obese are less accurate[24] in monitoring physiological events in their bodies than are the nonobese (Campbell, Hashim, & Van Itallie, 1971; Coddington & Bruch, 1970; Griggs & Stunkard, 1964; Orta, 1979; Stunkard & Koch, 1964). One study (Stunkard & Fox, 1971) failed to detect such a difference. In general, these findings fit well with the work of Schachter (1971) and many others who have demonstrated that the obese, in contrast to normal weight persons, are less attuned to their own internal states and, in making decisions about when and how much to eat, are more influenced by inappropriate cues from the environment.

Several studies have indicated that the obese are also unusually sensitive to cues outside themselves when making decisions about a variety of matters having nothing to do with eating. For example, their judgments about time and their responses to distraction seem to be relatively highly influenced by the external setting (Leon & Roth, 1977). However, to attribute the obese individual's overeating to neglect of appropriate body signals and focus on external cues is complicated by the fact that, as several studies (e.g., Herman & Polivy, 1975; Polivy, Herman, & Warsh, 1978) have shown, that merely experiencing a sense of oral deprivation (such as that induced by dieting) may foster an "external" orientation in normal weight persons. Because the obese so often start a new diet or try to restrain their eating habits (and therefore feel orally deprived), it is at least conceivable that their external orientation reflects, rather than leads to, their obese state. Finally, externality as a cause of obesity has been seriously criticized by Leon and Roth (1977) in view of some observations indicating that superobese persons may not be responsive to external cues as are the moderately obese.

In any case, the obvious concern of obese persons about being incongruously large has prompted studies to find out, in precise quantitative terms, just how they do perceive their size dimensions. These studies are not easy to interpret. One project, carried out by Glucksman and Hirsch (1969) at Rockefeller University had considerable impact. The Glucksman and Hirsch work involved six severely obese persons (three male, three female) who were hospitalized for a regimen of weight reduction. There was a control group of four nonobese hypercholesterolemic persons (three male, one female) also hospitalized and living under the same conditions as the obese. Over the course of 8 months, the obese lost an average of 87 pounds, while the nonobese controls maintained their weight. Size estimates were obtained from the obese subjects once weekly for 8 months. They adjusted projected images (via anamorphic lenses) of their photographs, which portrayed them as either too large or too thin, so that they would be corrected to their "real body size." Included were control tasks that involved correcting the projected image of a vase, an anonymous average weight male, and an anonymous average weight female. The nonobese controls were tested once weekly for only 6 successive weeks. It was found that as the obese lost weight they increasingly overestimated their total body size.[25] This did not occur with reference to the control stimuli (vase, anonymous male, anonymous female) and the nonobese controls did not show an increase in overestimation of their own size over time. But the obese and the nonobese did not differ significantly in their initial degree of overestimation of their own body size or of the control stimuli. Glucksman and Hirsch interpreted their data in terms of a "phantom body size" paradigm. They speculated that those who have been obese since childhood have a "body size image before weight loss" that "is relatively fixed, and cannot be altered as rapidly as the actual change in body configuration" (p. 6). In other words, the obese increasingly overestimate their size because, as they lose weight, they hold on to a phantom version of their original inflated configuration. This study did not demonstrate that the obese overestimate their body size more than the nonobese do; rather, it indicated that, when the obese lose weight, they are slow to become aware of the reduction in their body size.

In another paper, Grinker (1973) briefly summarized his comparison of the body size estimates of six persons who had been obese since childhood with five persons who became obese after attaining adulthood. The former over-estimated their size with weight loss, and the latter tended to underestimate. Grinker also compared the juvenile-onset and adult-onset groups with re-spect to whether their body size estimates would be affected by their viewing themselves in a full-length mirror just prior to making the size judgments. The juvenile-onset patients did not show any greater accuracy in their judg-ments, whereas the adult-onset patients did make more accurate judgments. No data were provided concerning statistical tests of any of the reported differences. This study suggests that the findings of the aforementioned Glucksman and Hirsch (1969) paper concerning the overestimation of body size subsequent to weight loss apply only to the juvenile-onset obese.

The results of the work with superobese persons at Rockefeller University created the impression that the obese are anomalous ("defective") in their perception of their body size and stimulated a good deal of subsequent investigation. There had been mixed results from a scattering of studies conducted prior to the 1969 work of Glucksman and Hirsch. Shipman and Sohlkhah (1967) reported that when obese ($N = 37$) and nonobese ($N = 20$) women were asked to adjust a distorting mirror so that it reflected their "actual size," the obese were less accurate and were inclined to depict themselves as "substantially broader than they are" (p. 540). Schonbuch and Schell (1967) compared male college students ($N = 60$) of various weight categories in their judgments of their body size as determined by their "selecting from a graded series of pictured physiques that one most nearly like their own" (p. 999). The overweight (and underweight) made incorrect judgments significantly more often than did the normal weight group. The obese did not, however, overestimate their size more often than the normal weight subjects. Their errors occurred in both directions. It should be noted that those labeled as obese in this study and in most of the others to be cited were less extremely overweight than the subjects in the Glucksman and Hirsch (1969) study.

Cappon and Banks (1968) surveyed the body size estimates of a largely female obese sample ($N = 23$) and a comparable sample of normal weight persons ($N = 23$). Body size estimates were obtained by asking the subjects to make linear judgments (in a darkened room) in terms of the distance between two moveable lights. The obese were significantly less accurate in their body size estimates, but there was no consistency in the direction of their error. When the subjects later examined themselves in a mirror and then repeated their size judgments, the obese became significantly more accurate, but the nonobese did not.

Meyer and Tuchelt-Gallwitz (1968) studied groups of obese ($N = 23$) and nonobese women ($N = 28$). These women examined 17 different pictures of their own faces that had been systematically "broadened" or "thinned," and picked the one that was the "real photograph." The obese and the nonobese proved not to be different in the amount or direction of their errors in identifying their true facial size.

Overall, these early studies suggested that the obese are less accurate than normal weight persons in their estimates of their body size. However, only one indicated a trend for the obese to overestimate their size. It should be added, by way of a note of caution, that none of these studies obtained judgments of nonself objects as a control for possible tendencies to be generally inaccurate in size estimates.

Studies completed since 1970 will now be reviewed. In 1973, Lasky obtained body size estimates from female college students ($N = 60$) in overweight, normal, and underweight categories. Subjects were asked to draw a picture of self, among other tasks. No differences were found among the groups for the body size judgments.[26] There was a significant trend for the overweight to draw the larger figures.[27] The groups did not differ in their ratings of degree of dissatisfaction with various parts of their bodies (Jourard-Secord, 1954, Body Cathexis Scale).

Yamokoski (1975) sought to distinguish body size perception among various subgroups of the obese. He secured estimates of body size by means of the anamorphic lens technique that involves correcting the projected distorted image of one's photograph. There were seven groups of female subjects: four had a history of obesity (juvenile-onset currently obese, juvenile-onset who have lost weight to a normal level, adult-onset currently obese, and adult-onset who have lost weight). Three groups had no history of obesity: underweight, normal weight, normal weight who feel they have difficulty in maintaining their weight. The results were mixed. Those who were currently obese overestimated their body size, but the formerly obese were not typified by the same overestimation. The juvenile-onset obese were less accurate in their body size judgments than the adult-onset obese, but there was no difference in direction of error.

In 1976, Garner, Garfinkel, Stancer, and Moldofsky used two different body size estimation techniques to compare five groups of women: juvenile-onset obese ($N = 16$), anorexics ($N = 18$), "thin normals" ($N = 16$), normals ($N = 16$), nonpsychotic psychiatric patients with no history of weight problems ($N = 16$). They employed both the anamorphic lens distortion technique and the Slade and Russell (1973a) procedure, which involves linear judgments (in a darkened room) of the distance between two moveable lights. Besides judgments of several body parts, control estimates of a vase and a standard female figure were obtained. The estimates based on the distorting lenses indicated that the obese did not differ from the anorexics, but the obese did overestimate their body size more than the other three control groups did. Estimates of nonself control objects did not differentiate the obese subjects from the controls. Body size judgments derived from the Slade and Russell technique gave largely negative results. The only significant difference was that the obese overestimated the width of their hips more than the other groups, except the psychiatric patient controls. No differences emerged for size estimates of face, chest, waist, and a control non-self object (vase).

Allebeck, Hallberg, and Espmark (1976) asked male ($N = 8$) and female ($N = 15$) superobese patients (awaiting intestinal bypass surgery) to adjust a distorted TV picture of their own head to its correct proportions. Their size judgments in this respect were compared with those of male ($N = 26$) and female ($N = 20$) normal weight controls (medical students and nurses). Control judgments of a nonself object (plastic cube) were also part of the procedure. The results indicated that, "the obese subjects tended to compress the picture vertically more than the control subjects" (p. 587). No difference was observed for the horizontal dimension or for the judgments of the non-self control object. Apparently, the obese were biased in the direction of perceiving their heads as relatively short, but were not biased in their judgments of their head width.

Kessler (1978) appraised a range of obese women ($N = 30$): mild, moderate, and massively overweight. Also included were subjects with childhood versus adult onset obesity. Normal weight women ($N = 33$) provided controls. Body size perception was approached with the Slade and Russell[28] (1973a) linear judgment technique. Control judgments of nonself objects were not obtained. No differences between the obese and normal weight subjects in size judgments emerged for the chest or waist, but the obese did significantly overestimate face and hip widths to a greater degree than the controls did. The difference between the obese and controls for all body size judgments attained only the .10 level of significance.[29] Those with juvenile onset obesity did not differ from adult-onset obese in their size judgments. It was further found that the individual obese subjects gave a wider range of size estimates for each of their body areas than did the individual controls. They seemed to be less sure of their various body widths; and it was concluded that they have a "less well articulated" concept of such areas. No correlations of significance emerged between body size judgments and various indices of degree of satisfaction with one's body (e.g., Jourard-Secord, 1954, Body Cathexis Scale).

Chwast (1978) carried out a project involving 24 superobese and 24 normal weight women. The obese were differentiated into two categories: early versus adult onset. The obese participated in a weight reduction program based on a liquid protein diet. All subjects were asked at a baseline point to estimate the overall size of their bodies and then to repeat the judgment after viewing themselves in a full-length mirror. They also estimated the sizes of two control objects: a carton and a nonobese female laboratory assistant. The size estimates were obtained by showing a graduated series of 29 rectangles, each the same height but decreasing in width. In each instance, subjects chose the rectangle that best represented the proportions of height to width of the object being judged. The instructions for self-estimation were as follows: "Pick the box (rectangle) in which your head would just touch the top, your feet just touch the bottom, and the widest part of your body with your arms at your side, would just touch the sides" (p. 49). There was a retest after approximately 17 weeks, when the obese subjects had averaged a 23% weight loss.

The obese and nonobese were found not to differ significantly in the accuracy or direction of any of their size estimates at either the original test or retest points. Judgments of self size made with and without the cues provided by viewing one's mirror image did not differ significantly. Obese subjects became significantly more accurate in their body size estimates after weight loss than they had been before such loss. There was no detectable difference between early and late obesity onset subjects with regard to their body size judgments. Also, as was true in the Kessler (1978) study cited earlier, body size judgments were not significantly related to degree of body satisfaction, which was determined from the Body-Cathexis scale that had been administered.

Chwast (1978) was emphatic that his findings contradicted those of Glucksman and Hirsch (1969). He not only criticized the Glucksman and Hirsch work for using very small samples, but added that the control groups used (cardiovascular patients) had not been tested at time intervals comparable to the obese group. Thus, there was only one data point for controls but four data points for the obese group. Noting that the Glucksman and Hirsch obese patients had been hospitalized for many months, Chwast wondered if their results might not reflect the "effects of confinement on size estimation accuracy" rather than of variables linked with obesity.

Pearlson, Flournoy, Simonson, and Slavney (1981) appraised male ($N = 16$) and female ($N = 38$) patients in a weight reduction program who were at least 21% overweight. Normal weight volunteers from the hospital staff comprised control groups (16 male, 38 female). The Slade and Russell (1973a) technique was applied to obtain size estimates of head, chest, waist, and hip widths. No estimates of control nonself objects were secured. The data indicated that the male obese did not differ significantly from the male controls in their body size judgments. However, the female obese significantly exceeded the female controls in their judgments of all four body areas that were considered. Degree of obesity within each overweight group tended to be positively correlated with degree of size overestimation but reached statistical significance only in the instance of hip judgments for the female obese. Female obese overestimated chest, waist, and hip widths to a greater degree than did the obese men. Age of onset of obesity was not significantly correlated with body size judgments. Pearlson et al. indicated that 55% of the normal control women and 31% of the normal control men had had a previous history of obesity. These previously obese individuals did not differ significantly in their body size judgments from the controls who had not earlier been obese. No links were observed between size judgments of given body area widths and how positively or negatively subjects viewed these areas. Also, the degree of overestimation of body size did not prove to be predictive of how successful subjects were in reducing their weights.

Speno (1981) appraised body size perception in three groups of women: (a) obese subjects ($N = 17$) participating in a weight reduction program; (b) subjects ($N = 17$) who were previously obese and who had maintained a satisfactory level of weight reduction for at least 6 months; (c) subjects ($N = 17$) who had never experienced any problems with being overweight. Estimates of body size were obtained for four body areas: face, chest, waist, hips. The estimates involved linear judgments similar to those in the Slade and Russell (1973a) technique. No differences in body size perception could be discerned among the various categories of subjects.

A particularly interesting project involving obese children was carried out by Leon, Bemis, Meland, and Nussbaum (1978). They obtained linear judgments of six body parts from 16 obese children, ages 8–9 and 18 obese children, ages 12–13. There were approximately equal numbers of girls and boys. Equivalent samples of normal weight children were also studied. Judgments of a nonself object (asymmetrical block of wood) were obtained too. Both the obese and the normal weight groups tended to overestimate their body size, but they did not differ from each other. However, there was a significant trend for the younger children in both groups to exceed the older ones in their degree of overestimation of their body proportions, but not of the control objects.[30]

To digress momentarily, a few words are in order about body attitudes of the obese that do not involve body size perception. Several studies have looked at the effects of weight loss on feelings about one's body. In general, whether the weight loss was induced by dieting or by intestinal bypass surgery, there seems to be a more positive evaluation of one's own body associated with it (Britton, 1981; Jupp, Collins, McCabe, Walker, & Diment, 1983; Kalucy & Crisp, 1974; Leon, 1975; Loftis, 1981; Silberfarb, Phelps, Hauri, & Solow, 1978; Solow, Silberfarb & Swift, 1974).[31] When the obese reduce their bulk, they do not seem, in general, to mourn for their lost substance. Grinker et al. (1973) reported, however, that juvenile-onset obese were more likely than adult-onset obese to perceive the effects of weight loss as having negative connotations. Numerous impressionistic statements have been made about the greater pathology associated with the juvenile-onset as compared to adult-onset obese, but there is a minimum of pertinent, solid data. Indeed, clear contradiction of the negative perspective toward the juvenile-onset obese emerged in the work of Schwebel (1978). She compared 40 juvenile-onset and 40 adult-onset obese women in terms of questionnaire measures of self-esteem, body attitude, and emotional stability. She reported that there were no differences. Further, she found that they did not differ in amount of weight lost in response to two different treatment modalities.[32] It will be recalled that Kessler (1978) could find no differences in body size perception between the two categories of obesity.

To return to the issue of body size perception, the findings since 1970 do not indicate that the obese consistently differ from normal weight subjects in their judgments fo sizes of *separate* parts of their bodies. Five of the studies (Garner et al. (1978); Kessler (1978); Lasky (1973); Leon, Bemis, Meland, & Nussbaum (1978); Speno (1981)) failed to detect significant differences in this respect; and one (Pearlson et al. (1981)) found significant results only for women and not for men. However, the two projects (Garner et al., 1978; Yamokoski, 1975) that employed the anamorphic distorting lens for judgments of total body size clearly indicated that the obese were relative overestimators.

The Garner et al. work is particularly striking because it failed to distinguish the obese from the normal weight persons when judgments were made in relation to separate body parts. Only when the anamorphic lens procedure was introduced did significant differences occur. The Chwast study, which also called for total body size estimates, did not indicate any size estimation differences between the obese and normal controls. But the method of estimating size was very different from the anamorphic procedure. It did not involve being confronted with a picture of oneself, but rather with a series of geometric forms (rectangles), varying in size, to which one had to match one's concept of one's magnitude.

How can these findings be integrated with the previously cited results from the pre-1970 studies? It will be recalled that the major trend to emerge from those studies was that the obese were less accurate than normal persons in their judgments of their body size. There was no consistent evidence of body size overestimation by the obese. However, the point has already been made that overestimation in the post-1970 studies was consistently apparent only when the anamorphic lens technique was used that involves making a judgment of total body size, rather than of separate body parts. Of the four pre-1970 studies cited only two, (Schonbuch & Schell, 1967; Shipman & Sohlkhah, 1967) called for judgments of total body size; and one (Shipman & Sohlkhah) of these reported significant overestimation by the obese. In the Schonbuch and Schell study, the obese overestimated, but not significantly more than the normal controls. The Shipman and Sohlkhah study called for judgments of one's size as depicted in a large distorting mirror. This procedure parallels the drama and intensity of the anamorphic lens technique, which also involves confronting the subject with a large and perceptually vivid representation of self. The Schonbuch and Schell study that called for total body size judgments, but which failed to elicit significant overestimation, was based on responses to ordinary sized photographs of anonymous figures varying in apparent degree of obesity. Thus, it did not even involve direct confrontation with an image of self.

OVERVIEW

Generally, there seems to be justification for concluding that the obese tend to magnify their true body magnitude, but primarily when they are judging their total body size rather than separate body sectors.[33] There is increasing reason to doubt the original Glucksman and Hirsch (1969) assertion that superobese persons, who are so grossly overweight that radical reducing procedures have been initiated, are slow to perceive a decrease in their bulk when they lose a good deal of weight. Chwast (1978) could find no evidence of such a lag and also, as described earlier, raised serious questions about the design of the Glucksman and Hirsch studies.

It may be speculated that the magnifying effect of the anamorphic technique on the judgments reflects, at least partially, the special susceptibility of the obese to external cues. Being confronted with a vivid projected image of self in a darkened room may constitute an input that is particularly impressive to the obese in its suggestion of magnification. Shontz (1969) reported that sensory experiences that increase the vividness of perceptual input increase size overestimation in normal subjects. One problem with attributing the perceptual magnification observed in the obese to their sensitivity to external cues is that they did not manifest the same magnification in relation to nonself control objects presented in the anamorphic lens context. It is relatedly pertinent that Shontz found evidence that external input influenced judgments of size of nonself objects more than it did judgments of size of one's own body. However, there is the possibility that a full-length projected image of self in a darkened room is so uniquely powerful as an external input that it exceeds the influence of a projected image of a control object like a vase. One should add that too many of the studies in the literature still fail to include control judgments of nonself objects.

Attention should also be directed to whether the juvenile-onset and the adult-onset obese differ in their body size perceptions. Although Grinker (1973) and others have emphasized the existence of such differences, the findings are equivocal. Yamokoski (1975) reported that the juvenile-onset obese were less accurate in their body size estimates than were the adult-onset obese. However, when Kessler (1978), Chwast (1978), and Pearlson et al. (1981) probed the issue in carefully designed studies, they found no differences. Of course, Yamokoski's positive results were obtained with the vivid anamorphic lens procedure, whereas Kessler and Pearlson et al. secured linear estimates of separate body parts and Chwast utilized overall body judgments made in relation to impersonal rectangles varying in size.

Can one attribute obesity to some defect in the individual's body size image? For example, do people become obese or have difficulty losing weight because they cannot conjure up realistic images of their body proportions? Perhaps they cannot make realistic judgments about whether they are becoming larger or smaller and therefore do not regulate their food intake commensurately. The available evidence does not fit with such speculation. First, there have been no consistent correlations reported in obese populations between degree of overestimation in judging one's body size and amount of overweight. Second, three studies (Pearlson et al., 1981; Yamokoski, 1975; Speno, 1981) clearly showed that persons who had been obese and were currently of normal weight did not make more total errors or errors of a particular directionality in their body size judgments than did normal weight individuals who had no history of obesity. That is, bias in body size perception did not appear to exist when the obesity itself was absent as a complicating factor. It is apropos to add that Slade (1977) discerned a significant tendency for pregnant women to overestimate the sizes of various body areas to a greater degree than do normal weight, nonpregnant women. Because pregnancy involves an enlargement of the body, one might conclude that any experience that results in persons perceiving their bodies as unusually increased in size induces an extreme "I am terribly inflated" set. This, in turn, is probably reflected in a tendency to exaggerate one's body size even beyond the actual degree of enlargement that has occurred. Analogously, it is not unreasonable to assume that when people arrive at an obese state, their view of their bodies is so encrusted with negativity that they become vulnerable to developing irrational biases about their body space. It is not surprising that the obese should have a perception of themselves as even bigger than their true proportions, if one considers that the prime message persistently delivered to them is that they are "so big and fat."

SCHIZOPHRENIC PERSONS

There has been lively debate about whether schizophrenics experience their bodies as smaller or larger than nonschizophrenics do. By 1969 there were several studies that concluded that schizophrenics are inclined to overestimate their size dimensions (Burton & Adkins, 1961; Cleveland, 1960b; Cleveland, et al,. 1962; Mermelstein, 1968; Reitman, 1962). Such overestimation was typically interpreted within a framework of boundary loss. That is, it was presumed that schizophrenia produces a decrease in the articulation of self or body boundaries and consequently evokes sensations that one is more "spread out." This view was anchored in the work of Liebert, et al. (1958), who had shown that when LSD apparently produces boundary loss in schizophrenics or normals, there is an increase in perceived body size, but not in the sizes of objects external to self.

By way of contrast, a study by Weckowicz and Sommer (1960)—among the first to be completed in this area and consequently of considerable influence—found schizophrenics to be underestimators of the size of their extremities. Weckowicz and Sommer offered two possible explanations for their finding. One alternative derived from speculations by Schilder (1950) and Federn (1952) to the effect that schizophrenics are characterized by a narrowing of the self boundary, which results in their investing less value and cathexis in the distal parts of the body. Perceiving one's extremities as small would presumably reflect a lessened investment in the periphery. A second explanation was phrased in terms of a breakdown in size constancy in schizophrenia. It was theorized that schizophrenics lose some of their capability of correcting size perceptions in relation to the distance of perceived objects from themselves, and therefore distal body parts are regarded as smaller than body parts nearer to the eyes. This second explanation was the one favored by Weckowicz and Sommer. Two investigators (Dillon, 1962a, 1962b; Fisher, 1966b) could detect no differences between schizophrenics and various controls with respect to body size estimates.

All these studies made use of either linear or configurational methods for obtaining size estimates. But another approach to the size issue was attempted by the questionnaire method (Fisher, 1964e; Fisher, 1966b; Fisher, 1970; Fisher & Seidner, 1963). Subjects were not asked to estimate the sizes of body parts, but rather to agree or disagree with a variety of statements like, "My hands feel unusually large," "My hands feel unusually small," and "My head feels unusually large." In three studies that employed this approach, schizophrenics seemed to be selectively preoccupied with sensations of body smallness and shrinkage. However, although they consistently reported more such sensations than normal subjects, they could not consistently be distinguished from hospitalized, nonpsychotic psychiatric patients. Fisher (1966b) suggested the possibility that when schizophrenics (or other psychiatric patients) give magnified body size estimates (e.g., on a linear scale), they may be doing so to compensate for underlying feelings of smallness. The feelings of smallness might reflect a diminished sense of self, a lessened sense of extension into the world. In accordance with this compensatory model, Fisher (1966b) detected a significant positive correlation in male schizophrenics between the questionnaire measure of sensations of smallness and the degree of overestimation of various body parts. But in a female schizophrenic sample the correlation was of a chance order.

When Shontz (1969) reviewed the research dealing with body size perception in schizophrenics, he concluded that the results were equivocal. He thought it was premature to say whether schizophrenics consistently display distortions in body size perception. He pointed out that not only were there contradictory findings, but also that a number of the studies had serious failures in design. For example, there were instances in which subjects had not been asked to give estimates of nonbody control objects, and hence it had not been established that observed over- or underestimation patterns were specific to body perception as such. Shontz also pointed out that in some studies (e.g., Weckowicz & Sommer, 1960) schizophrenics were more accurate than normal individuals in their body size estimates. Fisher (1970), in his analysis of the same literature, was also skeptical whether schizophrenics consistently over- or underestimate their body dimensions.

Bruyn (1975), mindful of the defects in the earlier literature, devised a study with unusually careful built-in controls to ascertain the degree to which schizophrenics differ from various other groups in their body size perception. He evaluated 20 VA in-patients diagnosed as schizophrenic, 20 VA chronically institutionalized domicilary patients who were not psychotic, 20 VA staff personnel employed at the VA center, and matched for age with the patients, and 20 college students with no history of serious psychological disturbance. All subjects estimated, by the linear judgment method, their own head width, hand length, foot length, forearm length, and waist width. They also estimated the length of five wooden rods, each corresponding to the average length (as defined by previously studied populations) of the body parts just enumerated. Judgments of body parts were made without the subjects being able to see their own bodies. Similarly, nonbody objects were evaluated by touch alone. A second, configurational method was also employed to obtain size estimates. Subjects indicated their judgments by choosing from a set of photographs of increasing size the one matching self. Sets were constructed to represent each of the five body parts and each of the five nonbody stimuli. Subjects expressed their size judgments by means of both the linear and configurational methods. Half gave their linear judgments first, and half gave their configurational judgments first. In addition, the Fisher (1970) Body Distortion Questionnaire, which inquires whether the individual is experiencing various forms of body distortions (e.g., "My legs feel unusually small") was administered.

Bruyn (1975) could not detect significant differences between the schizophrenics and the three control groups. They did not differ in size estimates based on the linear method or those derived from configurational judgments. Indeed, the schizophrenics displayed the same pattern of overestimation of head and forearm and underestimation[34] of hand and foot lengths as occurred in the controls and which has been described by Shontz (1969) in his studies as typifying normal individuals. The subjects in all groups paralleled Shontz's previous findings by overestimating the sizes of the body stimuli to a greater degree than the sizes of the nonbody stimuli. Further, as would be anticipated by Shontz's findings, the body estimates were more variable than the nonbody ones. It was found also that the Fisher (1970) Body Distortion

Questionnaire elicited a significantly greater number of reports of distorted body experiences[35] from the schizophrenics than from the controls. In any case, the major point to be derived from Bruyn's study is that the schizophrenics perceive the size dimensions of their bodies in the same fashion as normal persons do.

In recent years other pertinent studies have appeared that require analysis. Several have focused particularly on how schizophrenics perceive their own height. Hamersma and Papson (1973) obtained height estimates by asking subjects to indicate when full-length images of self, which were projected from slides on to a screen, had been adjusted to the point where they equaled their own actual heights. Subjects made similar estimates of the height of a mother figure and of themselves in relation to the mother image. Such judgments were secured from 20 chronic undifferentiated schizophrenic males and 20 normal males of comparable age, race, education, and visual status. The schizophrenics underestimated their heights significantly more than the normals. However, the schizophrenics perceived the mother figure as larger than did the normals. In addition, the schizophrenics were so influenced by the contrast produced when they viewed their own image standing next to the maternal figure that they intensified their underestimation of self height to a considerably greater degree than did the normals in this context.[36] The dwarfing effect of the maternal image was regarded as support for the theory that chronic male schizophrenics grow up in families in which mother was unusually dominant, that is, psychologically big and powerful.

In another project, Papson and Hamersma (1974) once again used the adjustment of the size of a projected image to examine estimates of self-height, height of maternal and paternal figures, and height of self in relation to the height of the maternal figure. Twenty schizophrenic males and 20 normal males were evaluated. The results indicated that schizophrenics underestimate their height significantly as compared to normals and that they overestimate the maternal figure's height. But schizophrenics do not differ from normals in estimations of the paternal figure's height.

Seruya (1977) approached the measurement of body height and of shoulder width by asking subjects to render their judgments about self and some neutral acquaintance of their choice on a linear scale. Two schizophrenic samples, each consisting of 10 males and 10 females, participated; and there was a comparable normal group. The schizophrenics underestimated self-height significantly more than the normals did. But there was an absence of real difference for the shoulder width estimates. The schizophrenics were less accurate than the normals in judging their own height, but not in their estimates of the height of another person. The schizophrenics were just as accurate as the normals in their estimates of the shoulder width of both themselves and another person.

A special feature of this study was an attempt to train the schizophrenics to achieve a more realistic concept of their body size. During a series of sessions in which they made body size estimates, they were given consistent feedback as to how accurate they were. A control group of schizophrenics had equal contact with the experimenter, but simply engaged in neutral recreational activities. The schizophrenic patients who were given training in body size judgments showed considerable improvement in the accuracy of their estimates. In addition, as compared to the controls, they became significantly less anxious, more socially responsive, and apparently less fearful of being intruded upon. The improvement in their general psychological state as a result of the training in judging body size was depicted as dramatic.

Contrary to the schizophrenics' underestimation of self height reported in the Seruya (1977) study and in the others previously cited (viz. Hamersma & Papson, 1973; Papson & Hamersma, 1974), Mermelstein[37] (1968) observed a significant trend toward overestimation in his experiment involving 20 poor premorbid, nonparanoid male schizophrenics and 20 normal male controls. Height estimates were obtained in a dark room by judging the vertical level of an horizontal luminous rod. Subjects in the study also judged head width and hand length in terms of horizontal distances between two luminous rods. The schizophrenics significantly exceeded the normals in their head and hand length estimates. But, surprisingly, the schizophrenics were more accurate in their estimates than were the normals. When the schizophrenics were exposed to a series of sessions in which they could observe videotape recordings of themselves that provided the opportunity for them to examine their bodies from different perspectives, their height and head estimates became significantly smaller. There was no effect on hand length. The normal subjects who were exposed to the videotape experience were significantly inclined to increase their height, head, and hand estimates. This contrasts with the decrease in such estimates that appeared in the schizophrenic sample.

Franco (1973) used an unusual method for getting at perceived body size in a sample of schizophrenics (18 male, 7 female) and a normal control group of equal size. He adapted the "Small Ames Room" apparatus to this purpose. The Ames Room was originally constructed to incorporate a variety of visual distortions, but when the room is viewed monocularly its dimensions appear to be normal. The distortions built into the Ames Room are such that "as objects are moved along the real wall they appear to grow and shrink depending on whether they are moved to the right or left" (p. 31). Franco asked his subjects to view the interior of the Ames Room in which a standard full–length human cut–out figure was fastened on the left side of the rear wall. The subject's own full–length picture had been transformed into a cut–out and mounted on a track so that it could be moved back and forth in the right–left dimension. Subjects were able, by means of a dial, to move the cut–out version of their own body on the track until it appeared to be equal to the standard figure.

The experimenter knew at which point on the track the retinal images of the standard figure and the subject's pictured form were actually equal. Deviations from this point could be fairly precisely quantified.

Franco (1973) reported that the schizophrenics were less accurate than the normals in judging when their own pictures were equivalent in size to the standard. The direction of the errors made by the schizophrenics indicated that they perceived their self-representations as relatively smaller than did the normals. They underestimated the overall sizes of their own pictured bodies. Franco had predicted that the amount of distortion in the schizophrenics' body size estimates would be positively correlated with an index that presumably measured how much inconstancy and incongruity they were experiencing in their current life roles. He assumed that the greater the self inconstancy people bring to a perceptual situation the more likely they are to distort it. Role inconsistency was measured in terms of the difference between the life activities the schizophrenics felt they should be able to engage in successfully and those they felt they actually could successfully cope with currently. Franco found, as predicted, that the greater the role incongruity, the greater the size judgment errors.

Demick and Wapner (1980) used size estimates of the head to test a theory concerning the effects of a real-life stress on the body boundaries of schizophrenics. They appraised a sample of 10 chronic institutionalized schizophrenics during a 2-month period surrounding their relocation. It was hypothesized that the schizophrenics would perceive the move as threatening and therefore would experience a diffusion of body boundaries. It was also anticipated that the boundary diffusion could be detected by securing estimates of head size. Previous sensori-tonic studies had suggested that when body boundaries decrease in articulation, there is a corresponding increase in perceived head size. It had been shown, for example, that primitivizing agents like LSD, which presumably weaken the individual's boundaries, increase apparent head size (Liebert, Werner & Wapner, 1958). Demick and Wapner obtained head size estimates (by a linear method) not only from the schizophrenics but also from 10 "antisocial personalities" and 12 normal control employees in the hospital. The schizophrenic group overestimated their head width more on the test occasion immediately preceding and the one immediately following the relocation than on the test occasions 1 month before and 1 month after the move. The "antisocial group" showed a reverse size estimation pattern; and the normal controls were characterized by a linear decrease in head overestimation over the series of four judgments. These results seemed congruent with the prediction that the trauma of the relocation would particularly weaken the boundaries of the schizophrenics.

Overview

It is doubtful that a general statement can validly be made that schizophrenic persons typically over- or underestimate their own body size dimensions. There is also no evidence that they are consistently inaccurate in their body size judgments. Bruyn (1975) indicated that they are similar to normal controls in overestimating some body parts (e.g., head) and underestimating others (e.g., hand length). Further, like normals, they render size judgments differently in response to body as compared to nonbody stimuli. There is little reason to assume they differ from normals in their perceptions of the sizes of specific parts of their bodies. As Shontz (1969) pointed out, the pre-1969 studies dealing with this issue were marked by inconsistency and in some instances by the absence of necessary controls. Although these studies weakly suggested that schizophrenics might be overestimators of body size, in view of what we have learned since 1969, that notion can probably be dismissed.

However, that is not the end of the matter. If one examines the studies that have been reviewed above, one cannot but be impressed with the fact that in three of the four (viz., Hamersma & Papson, 1973; Papson & Hamersma, 1974; Seruya, 1977) in which estimates of one's height were obtained, the schizophrenics consistently underestimated their true height as compared to normals. The schizophrenics perceived their overall height as being relatively smaller. Interestingly, they did not demonstrate such underestimation when judging the heights of other people. In one of the studies (Mermelstein, 1968) the schizophrenics were significant overestimators of their own height. There were also two studies prior to 1969 in which schizophrenics were asked to judge their heights (Fisher, 1966b; Reitman, 1962). In the Reitman study the schizophrenics overestimated their heights as compared to controls, whereas in the Fisher study the schizophrenics did not differ from the controls.

It should be added that in one other study cited above (Franco, 1973) in which schizophrenics were asked not to judge their height, but rather the overall size of their pictured body, they were underestimators. They perceived full-length pictures of themselves, in the context of the Ames Distorted Room, as smaller than a standard picture. Such findings take on meaning if one recapitulates as follows: in four studies (Franco, 1973; Hamersma & Papson, 1973; Papson & Hamersma, 1974; Seruya, 1977) schizophrenics were inclined to judge their total size as being relatively small. In two studies (Mermelstein, 1968; Reitman, 1962) they were overestimators, and in one (Fisher, 1966b) no bias was displayed. In other words, either significant under- or overestimation occurred in six of the seven studies in which overall size was estimated. In five of the six in which such bias was shown, the experimental context was unusually unstructured, dramatic, and probably conveyed a sense of strangeness. Thus, in four instances, the estimates were obtained in the dark, either by adjusting luminous rods or altering the dimensions of life-size representations of oneself projected on a screen. In another instance, the estimates were made in the context of the unreal ambiance of the Ames Distorted Room. However, the one study (Fisher, 1966b) that found no bias in schizophrenics' height judgments took place in a lighted room and involved simple linear judgments.

There seems to be fair justification for concluding that schizophrenics either minimize or magnify their overall size (principally as defined by height) in unstructured contexts that have unreal connotations.[38] It may be that such contexts are particularly stressful, or perhaps their ambiguity encourages the projection of special underlying size feelings.[39]

When schizophrenics judge the dimensions of isolated parts of their bodies, their perceptions do not differ significantly from normal patterns. This is true even when they make their estimates in unusual settings like dark rooms. However, if, in analogous contexts, their attention is called to the overall size of their bodies, selective under- or overestimation seems to be mobilized.[40] One will recall that an analogous distinction between judging parts versus the total body emerged in the research dealing with body size overestimation in anorexic women. Why should this be so? A plausible explanation is that confrontation with one's total body is more ego involving than merely responding to a part of it. Perhaps one can be more detached about a part. The total body has an immediate "I" quality, with basic identity connotations. Therefore, it may trigger especially intense reactions. It may call forth defenses or release unconscious feelings about self.[41] It is possible that in underestimating their height schizophrenics are expressing feelings of being small, down, and inferior. One could also speculate that they overestimate their heights to compensatorily deny sensations of powerlessness.[42] Everything that has just been said about the schizophrenics' size estimates may not be unique to schizophrenics and may, in fact, appply also to non-psychotic psychiatric patients. As earlier noted, since 1969 all the studies concerned with height estimates included only normal controls and made no use of nonpsychotic psychiatric patient controls.[43]

FURTHER SPECULATIONS

Ten years ago it was widely believed that overestimation of the size of one's body had negative, even pathological, implications. Overestimation was said to be linked to schizophrenia, and there was a widely accepted, although vague, notion that overestimation was a manifestation of poorly articulated body boundaries. Presumably, experiencing one's boundaries as indistinct made one more likely to feel "spread out" and therefore larger than one really was. We now know this idea to be fallacious as a generality.[40] Indeed, it has become apparent that normal people are generally inclined to overestimate a number of their body dimensions. The association of pathology with overestimation was fostered not only by some of the early studies of size perception in schizophrenics, but also by reports in the sensori-tonic literature that primitivizing agents (e.g., LSD) produced a sense of body enlargement.

We have gradually learned that size overestimation has multiple meanings. This should have been obvious from some of the earliest sensori-tonic experiments. While they demonstrated that primitivizing conditions resulted in sensations of being more spread out (enlarged), they also showed that a body part, such as the arm, felt lengthened (larger) if it was holding a tool or if it was pointing toward a meaningful target. Also, the body felt taller under conditions of success as compared to failure. This material should have suggested that feeling larger can issue too from a sense of being effective and goal oriented. A variety of conditions have, in some contexts, been observed to increase body size overestimation:

1. Attaching great significance to a body area because of its valued function (Furlong, 1977).
2. Being obese (e.g., Garner et al., 1976).
3. Becoming pregnant (Slade, 1977).
4. Ingesting an obviously high caloric meal (Crisp & Kalucy, 1974).
5. Compensating for feelings of being psychologically small (Fisher, 1964c).
6. Being young and immature (Halmi et al., 1977).
7. Inducing a primitivized level of functioning, e.g., due to ingesting LSD (Liebert et al., 1958).

There are many factors that may induce the sensation of being larger than one actually is. They range from the prosaic feeling that one has eaten too much to the special symbolic importance ascribed to a body area. People show moderate to high stability in their body size estimates (Shontz, 1969). Long-term experiences and attitudes seem to be basic to many body size feelings. However, salient changes in one's state (such as becoming pregnant) may be superimposed on habitual size experiences and result in new, significantly exaggerated perceptions.[41] There is suggestive evidence that exaggerated body size judgments (whether over- or underestimation) often express a defensive reaction to gross body changes. They might be described as defensive statements reflecting a feeling that all is not as it should be. They may be statements of surprise, alarm, concern about a sense of unacceptable transformation.

A number of scattered findings bear on such a perspective. It will be recalled that Glucksman and Hirsch (1969) claimed superobese persons continue to portray themselves in their formerly expanded form even after they lose considerable weight. They were said to persist in the old perception rather than assimilating the new, drastically changed version of self that dieting had produced. This could be regarded as a way of holding on to a longstanding, accustomed state of self that is being too rapidly altered. An interesting analogy to such behavior may be found in studies that demonstrate that individuals viewing their body through distorting lenses are particularly likely to see as least distorted those areas about which they entertain the greatest anxiety (Fisher, 1970; Fisher, 1973a; Fisher & Fisher, 1974; Fisher & Richter, 1969; Magee & Fisher, 1971).

In another vein, the Slade (1977) study indicated that the early body changes linked with pregnancy bring with them a sense of the body's being even larger than the actual enlargement that occurs. But, interestingly, at a later stage in the pregnancy, when body enlargement becomes quite extreme, the exaggerated overestimation of one's body dimensions disappears. It is as if the initial pregnancy changes are too abrupt and therefore are perceived as being of greater magnitude than they really are; but, once adaptation to the size shift takes hold, the even larger body changes of later pregnancy are perceived realistically. It is important to add that a woman's history of weight loss and gain prior to the pregnancy plays a detectable role in how she judges her expanding body. If she has had a relatively unchanging body weight and therefore is unaccustomed to significant alteration in her body size, she is likely to overestimate the ballooning effect of her pregnancy to a greater degree than do those women who are accustomed to body change because they often fluctuate in weight. Apparently, having had practice in frequently experiencing weight shifts mediates and diminishes the abrupt impact of the pregnancy size changes. Still another pertinent illustration comes from Slade and Russell (1973a), who observed that a sample of anorexic women who had overestimated their size while they were severely underweight pretty much ceased to do so when they attained normal weight. Their overestimation might be regarded as a defensive reaction (e.g., "I wish I were larger" or "I could not possibly have wasted away that much") to the radical body image change implied by their emaciated bodies. When their bodies were no longer emaciated, the defensive need to perceive them as larger than they actually were dissipated.

At another level, one might also speculate that the over- and underestimation of total body size observed in schizophrenic persons represents a statement of incongruity or surprise about self. Perhaps there is a sense of not being psychologically the "right size" (e.g., "I am inferior and insignificant"), which gets expressed in body terms. An example of such translation of feeling about self into body imagery was provided by the Wapner, Werner, and Krus (1956) and by the Shaffer (1964) demonstrations that a mood of failure (inferiority) can eventuate in a feeling that one's body is diminished in size. Other studies have suggested that sensations of having lost articulated identity (ego diffusion) may be converted into feelings of body size increase (e.g., in head width). Similarly, Furlong (1977) found that the more normal women felt doubt about their womanliness, the greater was their overestimation of their waist width. There was a very specific restatement of their self-doubt into biased perception of the waist area. Feelings of doubt about self were depicted in body imagery. In the spectrum of examples cited, various forms of feelings of incongruity about self, whether they involve body appearance or social identity, seem to color one's perception of one's size dimensions.

There are studies that indicate a special relationship between psychological disturbance and degree of body size overestimation in persons whose bodies are actually severely obese or underweight (anorexic). Slade and Russell (1973a) reported, in their previously described study, that the lower an anorexic woman's ego strength, the more she overestimates her body size. This was not true for a normal weight control group. Relatedly, Garner et al. (1976) noted, in both obese and anorexic samples, that neuroticism (as defined by the Eysenck Personality Inventory) was positively correlated with body size overestimation. However, an equivalent correlation did not appear in normal controls. Further, several studies have observed that the more anorexic patients exaggerate their body size, the more severe are their clinical symptoms. It appears that when persons embark on a course of converting their body into an extreme example of largeness or smallness the extremeness of the process is somehow linked to degree of psychological disturbance. The inclination to express psychological disturbance in body size terms, which is revealed in obesity or anorexia, is also manifested in certain aspects of their body size judgments.

Why should people be particularly inclined to portray their disturbance in body size metaphors, as it were? Why should the "body big" or the "body small" become associated with disturbed feelings? We obviously do not have a good empirical explanation. However, there are findings suggesting that bigness and smallness are linked to issues of power versus weakness (e.g., Fisher, 1964e; Fisher & Fisher, 1981) and it may be speculated that some individuals respond to feelings that they are losing the power to cope with life problems by acting them out in body terms. They may either dramatically decrease their body size, as the anorexic does as a direct statement of the sense of diminished significance in the world, or they may heap on the pounds in an attempt to attain a compensatory bigness that denies the sense of psychological shrinkage. Indeed, there are clinical observations (e.g., Minuchin, Rosman, & Baker, 1978) suggesting that the anorexic does feel unusually weak, controlled, and powerless. Many studies have found the obese to be inclined toward field dependence and also oriented to guidance from external cues. This implies a feeling of powerlessness, of not being capable of autonomy and requiring special bolstering from "out there."

Although a variety of interesting findings have issued from studies of body size perception, it has become apparent that they cannot be wrapped up in a neat package. There is really no general theory to explain the diversity of results in normal, anorexic, obese, and schizophrenic persons. As already noted, multiple, often unrelated, variables shape the judgment of the size of a particular body part at a given point in time. There is little likelihood that we will ever be able to arrive at broad generalities about what over- or underestimation of the size of the total body or any of its parts signifies. However, two particularly basic findings have emerged from the body perception literature: (a) the size attributes of the human body are experienced as being distinctive from those of other objects in the world; (b) the sizes ascribed to body areas may be influenced by values and intentions. These observations help to establish that the body space possesses unique perceptual properties that, at least in part, reflect an individual's psychological orientation. There has been little research effort to determine if body size estimates are related to general personality traits. The few more recent efforts in this direction (e.g., Furlong, 1977; Shontz, 1969) have not been encouraging, although they focused on the correlates of estimates for separate body parts rather than the body as a whole. Several older studies (e.g., Epstein, 1957; Fisher, 1964e; Fish, 1960) have found that total height estimates are significantly linked with personality variables. It may be that the biases displayed in judging one's total body size are more intertwined with the personality domain than are those involving separate body parts. This may be one reason why the judgments only of total body size, rather than of specific body parts, distinguished the obese and also schizophrenics from normal controls.

Most lacking in the size perception literature are systematic experiments designed to determine how various psychodynamic variables affect perception of the sizes of specific body parts and of the total body. Little has been done, for example, that parallels the work of Shaffer (1964), which examined the effects of failure on perceived body height. One could systematically explore the impact of failure or success on the perceived size of separate body parts. Does failure at an intellectual task have a greater diminishing effect on the perceived size of the head, the designated center of intellectuality, than it does on leg size, which has minimal intellectual connotations? Does failure at an athletic activity have just the inverse effects on the apparent sizes of head and legs? Or one could study the impact of creating anxiety about specific body areas on their perceived size. Does watching a film about the amputation of an arm selectively affect the experienced size of one's own arm? Does exposure to material about facial injury affect the apparent width of the facial area? There are numerous other dimensions worth exploring. It would be interesting, for example, to determine whether the sizes of one's body parts seem to vary with how much attention is focused on them, the degree to which they apparently match or deviate from ideal standards of appearance, and the extent to which they are sites of pain or discomfort. A systematic program of such studies might provide us with models of how various emotional states and attitudes find expression in body size terms. We would also be in a better position to determine whether the size experiences linked with some parts of one's body have specific emotional counterparts. Indeed, we would probably arrive at a clearer view of whether there is any promise at all in trying to link perceived size of specific body parts, as contrasted to the apparent size of one's total body, with personality and psychodynamic vectors.

NOTES

[1] The sensori-tonic theory predicts that increasing boundary articulation of a body area will result in that area's being experienced as smaller, and the opposite effect is predicted when boundary articulation is decreased.

[2] Other kinds of size specificity have been reported also. For example, Nash (1969a) found that the distances from the navel to the feet and from the crotch to the feet are typically underestimated. Hester (1970) reported that the upper arm is usually underestimated.

The best validated observation concerning size specificity is that head size is consistently overestimated at all age levels. Gellert (1975) demonstrated this phenomenon in children as young as 5 years of age, and it has also been demonstrated in adults of various ages (Fisher, 1970).

[3] Koff and Kiekhofer (1978), with a sample of 30 children (grades 1, 3, and 5), examined their linear judgments of the sizes of several parts of their own body and of the body of the experimenter, and also the sizes of nonself objects. They concluded:

> The results indicate that children are capable of relatively accurate body-part size estimation and that the skills necessary for this task appear to be established by age 6. For both personal and experimenter's body parts, hand length was estimated most veridically, and head width, forearm length, and hips estimated least veridically. . . . The striking consistency in the degree of veridicality of judgments among both children and adults, and the similarity in the children's judgments of personal and experimenter's body parts size, despite absolute size differences and different measurement conditions, suggest that body size judgments are perhaps more reflective of cognitive than perceptual processes. This notion receives support from the observation that non-body objects were judged more veridically than were body parts, a result reported for adults as well. . . . The correspondence between the children's and the adults' patterns of errors, coupled with the findings that adults consistently misjudge the sizes of certain body parts, suggests that the tendencies observed among the adults may have been established at an earlier stage of development, and reflect relatively stable and longstanding cognitive predispositions. (p. 1049)

[4] Shontz (1969) regards the configural method as being more sensitive than the linear method to personality processes. Thus, configuration techniques more clearly differentiate the body size judgments of normals from those of schizophrenics.

[5] Ruggieri and Valeri (1981a) have, in addition, shown that there may be individual differences in the size properties ascribed to body areas at right versus left body sites. Persons may consistently perceive body sites on the left side as larger or smaller than

corresponding sites on the right side. Ruggieri and Valeri (1981b) observed too that shifts in right-left size perception may occur as a function of changes in the body (e.g., menstruation).

⁶But it should be noted that one previous study (Barton, 1964) found that hemiplegics judge the paralyzed arm to be longer than the nonparalyzed arm.

⁷Fuhrer and Cowan (1967) reported that when persons actively moved certain body parts (e.g., arm), they were inclined to judge them as relatively larger than when they did not move them.

⁸There are several reports of sex differences in perceived self-height in children, but they are contradictory. For example, Gellert and Stern (1964) found that, whereas boys do not consistently over- or underestimate their personal height, girls are consistent overestimators. Doering (1974) reported that, in contrast, boys overestimate their height, whereas girls are "consistently accurate."

⁹Schlachter (1971) observed a significant relationship (in 200 female subjects) between anxiety level and error in estimating shoulder width. This is another instance in which body size perception is linked to a personality variable.

¹⁰The women seeking cosmetic surgery were also found not to have neuroticism scores (as measured by Gryzier's (1956) Dynamic Personality Scale) outside the normal range.

⁹Nash (1958) observed a significant trend for the degree of masculinity ascribed to various body areas to be positively correlated with the actual sizes of those areas. There may be a fundamental link, in the body realm, between size and meaning that precedes other linkages that evolve in relation to the function of a body part or the significance ascribed to it symbolically.

¹²There is no evidence, however, that the size ascribed to various body areas is generally correlated with how satisfied or dissatisfied the individual is with such areas (Fisher, 1970). But, paradoxically, Berkowitz (1980) has shown that a mother's degree of dissatisfaction with her body may possibly have repercussions in the accuracy with which she estimates the body size of her children.

¹³Several studies have shown that males whose size has been seriously inhibited as the result of hormonal deficiencies react to their smallness in a more emotionally distressed fashion than do females with the same problem (e.g., Brust, Ford, & Rimoin, 1976).

¹⁴Gellert and Stern (1964) found that boys aged 8-12 tended to be significantly more accurate than girls in linear estimates of self height. This sex difference held true when a configurational technique was used to measure ability to detect size disproportion of various body parts presented in standard drawings with defined disproportions. Cremer (1970) too found a significant trend for boys to be a bit more accurate than girls when expressing body size judgments in terms of the size dimensions assigned to drawings of human figures.

¹⁵Askevold (1975) originally used his technique to study 15 anorexics, 7 obese persons, and 20 normal controls (physiotherapists). He did not analyze his findings statistically but offered the impressionistic opinion that anorexic patients are inclined to overestimate their body size.

Koski, Kumento, and Valve (1979) reported that measurements taken with the Askevold technique indicated that diabetic children underestimated their body size to a significantly greater extent than did nondiabetic controls.

[16] The Fisher-Cleveland Barrier and Penetration scores were not significantly correlated with degree of body size overestimation or judgmental variability.

[17] Garfinkel et al. (1979) also established that anorexic subjects did not show a normal aversion to sucrose after a 400-K cal load. Further, the greater the anorexic's overestimation of her body size, the less the sucrose aversion she manifested. An analysis of sensations after eating indicated that anorexics felt fuller before eating than the normals. They also reported more postprandial bloating, nausea, and thoughts of food. These findings faintly suggest that the anorexic may experience sensations associated with eating differently than normals do. Garfinkel (1974) presented some earlier exploratory observations, based on questionnaire data, that implied there is a "disturbance in the experience of satiety, but not of hunger, in anorexia nervosa" (p. 312).

Garfinkel and Garner (1982) also reviewed several studies that imply that anorexic subjects may be less accurate in judging interoceptive sensations than are normal controls. They remarked: "several lines of experimental inquiry have suggested that patients with anorexia may misperceive internal experiences, particularly related to satiety. It is not clear whether these perceptual disturbances are determinants or byproducts of the syndrome" (p. 155).

[18] However, there was underestimation by the anorexics for two body areas, viz., length of foot and arm. These findings are congruent with Shontz's (1969) reports and support the view that over- and underestimation are, at least partially, a function of which specific body area is involved. If earlier researchers, like Slade and Russell (1973a) had been aware of this and had included a wider range of body size estimates in their studies, the stereotype might not have so easily developed that anorexics simply overestimate their body size.

[19] Shontz (1969) did not observe such a relationship in his extensive studies of normal college students; neither did Fuhrer and Cowan (1967). However, Furlong (1977) did find judgmental errors to be influenced by variations in the size of the specific body part.

[20] Percival (1982) used the Askevold (1975) technique to obtain body size estimates from college girls with "subclinical" anorexia problems and found that they did not differ in their estimates from control subjects.

[21] Personal communication from Strober.

[22] Women with bulimic symptoms have shown a tendency to rate their body less favorably than normal controls (Katzman & Wolchik, 1984) and a slight trend to overestimate their body size (Gray, 1983). Only judgments of body size pertaining to 1 of 3 different body parts significantly exceeded those of controls in degree of overestimation.

[23] However, there are scattered studies in which the obese have not described their bodies more negatively than normal weight persons do (e.g., Leon & Chamberlain, 1973). Also, Katz (1969) observed that obese black women took a significantly more favorable attitude toward their obesity than did white obese women.

Although Lasky (1973) found that overweight college students showed an elevated amount of anxious body concern, as defined by the Secord (1953) Homonym Test (which presumably taps into a more unconscious level of response), Kessler (1978) did not confirm this observation.

[24] Interestingly, Gorchynski (1973) has shown that the obese (and also those who

are markedly underweight) are significantly less accurate than normal weight subjects in estimating the weights of others.

[25] As reported in another study involving these obese subjects (Glucksman, Hirsch, McCully, Barron, & Knittle, 1968), some discomfort was expressed about the change in body size resulting from weight loss. Also, there was a trend for figure drawings produced subsequent to weight loss to be larger than those drawn before weight loss.

[26] This summary was based on an abstract and certain details were not available, such as the possible use of control judgments involving nonself objects.

[27] Inconsistent results have emerged with regard to the size of figure drawings produced by the obese. For example, contrary to Lasky's findings, Meeker (1978) observed that these obese women drew shorter figures than normal weight women. Nathan (1973) could find no evidence that obese children produce either unusually large or small figure drawings. She did find that their drawings were less differentiated, and thus matches a similar observation by Gottesfeld (1962) concerning figure drawings by super-obese adults. Nathan thought her findings were indicative of unusual immaturity in the body image of the obese.

[28] Slade and Russell (1973a) observed a trend for them to overestimate their body width. However, this was an impressionistic report, and no statistical evidence was presented.

[29] Kessler (1978) pointed out that Garner et al. (1976) similarly found no differences in average body size estimates of various body areas between obese and normal weight persons, but that they did observe that the former overestimated hip size more than the latter.

[30] Measures of body boundary articulation, viz., Fisher-Cleveland (1968) Barrier and Penetration scores, were secured from all subjects by means of the Holtzman, Thorpe, Swartz, and Herron (1961) Ink Blots. No differences in boundary definiteness between the obese and normal weight children could be detected. However, Geiger (1978) reported that obese children in the 9–12 age range have "weak body boundary conceptions" as defined by the Barrier score.

[31] The Britton (1981) study found that women who had lost weight during a behavioral modification treatment program showed, in pre- to post-testing, that they felt more positively about their body, were more accurate in identifying their own true proportions in photographs, and were more accurate in verbally estimating the sizes of several different body parts. There were, however, no significant correlations between amount of weight loss and changes in the body image measures. Britton attempted to facilitate the behavioral weight loss program by providing subjects with special body image experiences (e.g., repeatedly viewing oneself in a mirror that narrowed or widened one's apparent size). She found that subjects who had the mirror exposures did not lose any more weight than did control subjects without such exposures.

Collins, McCabe, Jupp, and Sutton (1983) observed that women ($N = 68$) who had lost weight in a weight reduction program became more accurate in their body size judgments (of video-image representations of the total body). Such an increase in accuracy was also observed in the Chwast (1978) study.

[32] More will be said with regard to juvenile- versus adult-onset obesity in the section dealing with body boundaries.

[33] Two studies have suggested that when the obese have a chance to view them-

selves in a mirror prior to making estimates of their body size, their estimates are influenced by the experience. Cappon and Banks (1968) found that obese subjects became more accurate in their linear size judgments, whereas normals did not. Grinker (1973) reported that mirror exposure resulted in the adult-onset obese's becoming more accurate in their size judgments; this was not true for the juvenile-onset obese. These findings contrast with Shontz's (1969) observations that the body size judgments of normal subjects do not seem to be significantly influenced by visual information about their own bodies. As noted, Cappon and Banks did, indeed, support this lack of effect of visual input on normal subjects. Finally, Garfinkel et al. (1978) found no effects of mirror information on the size estimates of normal and anorexic samples. One wonders whether the greater impact of mirror information on the obese reflects their greater susceptibility to external input.

[34] The schizophrenics and the college students were significantly more inclined than the other groups to overestimate head and forearm and underestimate hand and foot lengths. If the schizophrenics had been compared with the domiciliary and VA normal personnel only for hand and foot lengths the schizophrenics would have appeared to be underestimators of body size. It will be recalled that Weckowicz and Sommer (1960) arrived at just such a conclusion on the basis of the hand and foot estimates they secured from their schizophrenic sample. This points up the importance of using a range of body sites in studies of body size perception. Some sites may elicit underestimation, whereas others may trigger the opposite tendency.

[35] No attempt was made by Bruyn (1975) to analyze whether the groups differed with respect to subjective sensations of body shrinkage or magnification.

[36] In another study using the same methodology, Hamersma and Deboer (1973) observed that sociopaths overestimate their height to a greater degree than do normal subjects; such overestimation continued even in the context of comparison with the image of a female authority figure or that of a male authority.

[37] Even though this study was completed in 1968, it is included in the present analysis because it was missed in the previous Fisher (1970) review.

[38] All the height estimate studies carried out since 1969 have compared schizophrenics with normal subjects. However, in almost all previous studies in which schizophrenics estimated the size of body parts, their performance was compared to that of nonpsychotic psychiatric patients. Differences in results pertaining to schizophrenics' size estimates of body parts as compared to their estimates of total height may reflect the use of psychiatric controls as comparisons in the first instance and normal controls in the second. One should hasten to add that Bruyn's (1975) definitive study of schizophrenics' judgments of the sizes of body parts made use of both normal and nonnormal controls. The possibility that schizophrenics do not differ from nonpsychotic hospitalized psychiatric patients in their height estimates cannot be discounted until the completion of studies comparing the two groups.

[39] The studies cited have not demonstrated that schizophrenics are consistently inclined to over- or underestimate the overall sizes of nonself control persons and objects. However, there is a considerable literature (Asarnow & Mann, 1978; Cromwell, 1972; Kopfstein & Neale, 1971; Neale, Held, & Cromwell, 1969; Strauss, Foureman, & Parwatikar, 1974) suggesting that different types of schizophrenics may display contrasting size biases in their judgments. For example, paranoids and acute good premorbids have been observed in some instances to underestimate sizes of objects, and the opposite has been noted for acute poor premorbids. However, such

size biases are apparently fragile and may be affected by such factors as the sequences in which stimuli are presented, the degree of threat of stimuli, and so forth. Schizophrenics and normals do not seem to differ in their ability to estimate the sizes of nonself objects accurately.

[40] Wittreich (1959) reported that, when schizophrenics who are wearing aniseikonic lenses, view themselves in a mirror, they see more distortions of their overall size and shape than they do of specific parts of their bodies.

[41] Epstein (1955) and Sugarman (in Ittelson & Kutash, 1961) have described especially extreme compensatory responses by schizophrenics to representations of self (e.g., own voice played backward, figure drawing) in a context where the did not recognize these representations.

[42] A distinction between the level of ego involvement elicited by size judgments of parts of one's body as compared to one's total body may clarify certain aspects of the literature concerned with the personality correlates of body size estimates in normal persons. Shontz (1969) could find no consistent personality correlates of estimates of the sizes of *parts* of one's body. However, others like Fisher (1964e) and Epstein (1957) have found significant relationships between overall height estimates and personality variables.

[43] A number of studies have found that schizophrenics and other classes of psychiatric patients produce human figure drawings whose overall height is smaller than drawings by various normal control groups (e.g., Clodfelder & Craddick, 1970; Cvetkovic, 1979; Roback & Webersinn, 1966). Other studies have not detected such a difference (Roback, 1968; Swensen, 1968). The matter awaits further research. However, even if clear differences between schizophrenics and other groups could be demonstrated with respect to figure drawing size, there would still remain the question of what they mean. Some studies have shown a positive relationship between figure drawing size and self esteem (e.g., Delatte, Jr., and Hendrickson, 1982; Ludwig, 1969); happy mood (Viney, Aitkin & Floyd, 1974); and absence of a sense of stress (Cooper & Caston, 1969). On the other hand numerous other studies have failed to demonstrate such relationships (Bennett, 1964; Gray & Pepitone, 1964; Prytula, Phelps, & Morrissey, 1978; Prytula & Thompson, 1973).

[40] It will be recalled that Pierloot and Houben (1978) found no relationship between boundary articulation, as measured by the Fisher and Cleveland (1968) Barrier and Penetration scores, and degree of body size overestimation.

[41] The potential instability of body size perception is highlighted by Barber and DeMoor's (1972) observation that people begin to experience changes in body size when they merely sit quietly with their eyes closed.

5 Stressful Body States in Normal Persons

Existence inevitably brings with it threats to one's body—there is always the possibility of illness, disease, and injury. Numerous studies have documented the universal concern about suffering body damage. A significant component of normal "nervousness" and fearfulness has been shown to involve fears of bodily harm (Costello, 1982; Strahan, 1974). It is common for themes of body destruction and mutilation to appear in the spontaneous verbalizations of both adults and children (Fisher, 1970). People must learn to cope not only with actual body damage but also with its unpredictable imminence. The extreme threat represented by body dysfunction is dramatized by the fact that it is not uncommon for people to delay seeking medical consultation for somatic symptoms that are obviously serious (e.g., Andrew, 1972; Hammerschlag, Fisher, DeCosse, & Kaplan, 1964).[1] In addition, there is the need to adapt to the long-term decline in the body due to aging. Stresses with direct body-image implications are a normal part of life. This chapter is devoted to cataloguing these stresses and analyzing what is known about how people defend against them. Fisher (1970) evaluated the pertinent literature in this area that had appeared prior to 1970. The present review considers the findings that have emerged since then. Such key questions as the following will be asked of the available data: Is the impact of body damage on the body image directly proportional to the amount of damage? Which dimensions of the body image are most sensitive to body damage and threat? What defense strategies are most commonly employed to cope with body damage? Are there significant sex differences in coping strategies?

THE THREAT OF SURGERY

It does not require much documentation that the need to undergo surgery induces serious alarm. Fisher (1970) reviewed a number of studies indicating disturbance incited by the prospect of surgery could be detected in conscious self-reports, in projective test responses, and in dream imagery. There was evidence that even minor surgical procedures mobilized concerns about body damage that were out of proportion to the real nature of the threat. Janis (1958) proposed, on the basis of a survey of surgical patients and the illness experiences of college students, that persons typified by either little or very high preoperative anxiety are those most likely to develop emotional disturbance during or after the surgical stress; whereas those with a moderate amount of anxiety previous to surgery were said to make the best adjustment. Janis indicated that those low in preoperative anxiety would not be sufficiently concerned or aroused to undertake preparatory cognitive rehearsal of coping strategies to meet the threat of surgery and so would react more negatively to the surgery experience. Fisher could not find consistent support for Janis' curvilinear model in the research literature available at that time. He also called attention to several other, less salient matters. For example, he reported that the Ego Strength scale developed by Barron (1953) showed unusual promise in predicting postsurgical behavior. He was impressed too with the number of reports indicating that female children were less threatened by surgical procedures than were male children. This sex difference was congruent with data from other sources (Fisher, 1970) suggesting that females exceed males in their degree of body security.

Since 1970 studies have been launched to find out more about the pattern of anxiety associated with the entire process of submitting to surgery. It has been observed that anxiety (usually as defined by a state anxiety[2] questionnaire) typically is at a high point in adults just before surgery and declines in the immediate postoperative period (e.g., Auerbach, 1973; Martinez-Urrutia, 1975; Spielberger, Auerbach, Wadsworth, Dunn, & Taulbee, 1973; Wolfer & Davis, 1970). This has also been shown in studies of children undergoing surgery (e.g., Burstein & Meichenbaum, 1979). An interesting qualitative analysis of preoperation anxiety has been presented by Bodley, Jones, & Mather (1974) who studied 28 patients (male and female) about to undergo surgery. Using the Kelly (1955) grid technique,[3] they were able to isolate some of the major elements of preoperation anxiety: fear of death, concern about the separation from home and family associated with hospitalization, fear of mutilation, possible loss of control due to the anesthetic, and concern about the pain that will be experienced.[4]

It is apropos to mention also the work of Green (1976), who closely sampled the behavior of eight boys (ages 14–17) hospitalized for emergency appendectomies. Counts were made of how often the boys mentioned their bodies, and such body references were, in turn, categorized. The frequency of body references was very high immediately after the surgery but peaked about two days later. Then, it declined slightly but consistently throughout the remaining period of hospitalization. The statements of body concern fell primarily into six categories: capability, endurance, intactness, impairment, improvement, uncertainty. Green noted with respect to the postsurgical period: "The patterns indicated during the five day hospitalization were: realizing they were alive and the surgery was over, period of stabilization of acquainting self with body as ill and wounded, increasing control of self and body, increasing acquaintance and control of self in the environment, and anticipated socialization in familiar environments" (p. 129). She also had some interesting comments about the specific nature of body perception in the surgical patient (p. 123):

The intensity of the boys' attention toward their injured parts and the continual change in their physical state during recovery, demanded that they view their bodies as objects to the extent that they could not see themselves as whole persons with any degree of positive continuity. There were so many changes that the boys were forced to deal with minute details of body experiences. The boys' overall perceptions of their physical selves following surgery were: partial or segmented definitions of self, loss of the usual sense of self, and negative value of self as subject and self as object. In addition, they perceived that none of the body rhythms that integrated their body experiences were operating in usual or useful patterns. The boys' situation demanded that they be aware of a strangely different self, of others, and of things, almost constantly. (p. 123)

A study by Johnston (1980), which measured state anxiety at various pre- and postsurgery points in several samples of patients totaling 136 (male and female), disagreed with the view that anxiety simply declines from pre to postsurgery. In some samples anxiety was actually higher in the post- than in the presurgical period. In one particular sample, maximum anxiety was, on the average, attained not on the day of surgery but two days earlier, when hospitalization had not yet occurred. Johnston suggested that the discrepancy between her findings and those of other investigators was due to such deficiencies in the latter as sampling for too limited time periods or delaying measurement of anxiety in the postsurgical phase until recovery was well advanced. However, inasmuch as so many reasonably good studies have detected a decrease in anxiety from pre- to postsurgery, one has to be skeptical about Johnston's claims.

Considerable attention has been focused on Janis' (1958) original hypothesis that either very low or high anxiety in surgical patients prior to surgery is predictive of high emotional disturbance after surgery. Most of the studies since 1970 that have set out to test this curvilinear hypothesis have not found support for it. Johnson, Leventhal, and Dabbs, Jr. (1971) studied anxiety and mood levels in 62 female surgical patients on the morning of surgery and then evaluated pain, mood, and analgesic usage postoperatively. The data supported a linear rather than a curvilinear model. There were significant trends for those most anxious preoperatively to be also those most troubled postoperatively. Similarly, Sime (1976) discovered in a sample of female surgical patients ($N = 57$) that there was a significant linear relationship between preoperative fear scores and several postoperative indices of difficulty: length of hospitalization, number of sedatives and analgesics, and negative postoperative affect. Wolfer and Davis (1970) could not discern a curvilinear relationship (in samples of 76 female and 67 male patients) between preoperative self-rated fear anxiety and such postoperative measures as fear-anxiety, anger, depression and complaints.[5] Instead, the significant correlations that did appear were linear. Further, Volicer (1978) observed (in a sample of 252 male and female surgical patients) linear rather than curvilinear links between preoperative measures (e.g., Hospital Stress Rating Scale) and indices of recovery. Johnston and Carpenter (1980) in a well designed study of 73 female surgical patients were particularly interested in testing the Janis model. They found that preoperative anxiety had a weak linear rather than curvilinear relationship with postoperative anxiety. No support was observed for the Janis assumption that postoperative anger is likely to be especially high in patients with low preoperative anxiety. Mild support for the Janis model did come from the greater likelihood that patients with low preoperative anxiety would show poor postoperative recovery rates (defined by variables like amount of pain and ability to resume normal functioning), as compared with patients who displayed moderate anxiety preoperatively. However, Johnston and Carpenter concluded (p. 366): "In view of the weight of evidence failing to support Janis'[6] model, this finding would require replication to be of practical or theoretical significance" (p. 366).

A few studies have come up with data that are in part congruent with Janis' views. Auerbach (1973) obtained from 56 male surgical patients three sets of measures of anxiety and emotional responses to being hospitalized: 24 hours prior to, 48 hours after, and 6 days after surgery. Contrary to the Janis formulation, he found a significant positive linear correlation between pre-operative anxiety and indices of emotional disturbance postoperatively, but he also observed one pattern that was supportive of Janis. When he categorized the patients into low, medium, and high preoperative anxiety groups according to the degree to which their preoperative anxiety was higher than their "normal" baseline level (defined by the anxiety score 6 days after surgery), the middle group was significantly less disturbed by the hospitalization experience than was either the low or the high group. However, this pattern emerged for only one of four measures of emotional adjustment to the hospitalization.

Burstein and Meichenbaum (1979) explored the relationships of children's ($N = 10$ male, 10 female) level of anxiety,[7] defensiveness, and play patterns 1 week prior to, during, and 1 week after hospitalization for minor surgery. There was a clear trend for the children to be dichotomized into those who directly confronted the "work of worrying" called for by the surgery experience and those who were "highly defensive" in their avoidance of the anxiety linked to the experience. Defensiveness was not correlated with the children's level of anxiety before or during hospitalization; but it was significantly and positively correlated with their degree of anxiety following discharge from the hospital. This finding was interpreted as supporting Janis' formulation. Burstein and Meichenbaum noted:

> The parallels between the present results and Janis' study are striking. In both studies high defensiveness was associated with a minimized tendency to be involved with stress-related themes prior to hospitalization. This anticipatory

cognitive rehearsal is seen as crucial to the development of effective reassurance and coping mechanisms. Hence, high defensive patients not engaged in
the work of worrying experienced more postsurgery emotional disturbance in
Janis' study and higher posthospitalization anxiety level in the present study.
(p. 127)

However, the authors also recognize that their data were discrepant with
Janis' position "in that no curvilinear relationship was found between pre-
hospital anxiety level and posthospital distress" (p. 127).

Vernon and Bigelow (1974) attempted a direct test of Janis' model by
reducing it to a series of hypotheses. They reasoned that, if the model is valid,
persons receiving accurate information concerning their impending surgery
should experience "anticipatory fear and the work of worrying, which leads
to the development of accurate expectations—the knowledge of specific
problems and reassurances—which has the result of reducing the incidence
of hostility and depression during stress impact" (p. 51). They studied 40 male
surgical patients. Twenty were exposed to information concerning the nature
of the experiences they would have as the result of surgery; the 20 controls
did not receive such information. Various questionnaires were administered
to measure subjects' anxiety and hostility levels pre- and postsurgery. Analysis of the data did not reveal any differences in anticipatory fear between the
experimental and control subjects. There was, however, a significant trend for
the experimental subjects to be more aware than the controls of specific
difficulties that might be associated with their surgery. Further, the experimental subjects had lower levels of postoperative hostility than the controls,
but the difference did not quite attain statistical significance. Vernon and
Bigelow suggested that their findings supported Janis' insofar as they indicated that the experimentals were more aware than the controls of specific
problems and difficulties linked with the surgery and that the experimentals
were slightly more prone to episodes of postoperative anger. But they added:

However, the data failed to support an important aspect of Janis' theory. The
data provided no support for the notion that anticipatory fear and worry are
essential parts of the process by which preparation helps people reduce the
impact of stress. First, the informed patients did not differ from the uninformed
patients in the most straightforward and direct measure of worry (i.e., the self-
ratings of preoperative fear on the day before surgery). Second, the incidence of
postoperative anger[8] was unrelated to the incidence of problem-oriented preoperative opinions. . . . That is, postoperative anger was as common among
patients whose experiences focused on problems and difficulties as it was
among patients whose opinions were thoroughly optimistic. (p. 57)

It seems fair to say that the studies just perused largely do not confirm the
Janis model.[9] Some of the findings do confirm Janis, only in a partial,
incomplete fashion. There seems to be more validity in the linear model that

predicts a positive correlation between one's degree of disturbance prior to and after surgery. Overall, little or no effort has been devoted to probing the body image alterations resulting from the experience of being surgically "opened up." We do not have more than an inkling of how various dimensions of the body image are affected. Further analysis of this topic is provided in a later chapter, in which the boundary meanings of surgery are considered.

TRANSPLANTING AND REMOVING BODY PARTS

Transplants

Surgeons have become increasingly versatile in reshaping the body. Whereas they previously devoted themselves largely to removing diseased body parts, they are now adept at introducing "new" replacement organs into the body. They transplant hearts, kidneys, and lungs and implant pacemakers and a variety of other devices. There is some suggestion that surgery that inserts new parts into the body may elicit defensive reactions very different from those linked to surgery that simply removes or amputates a body substance. A number of clinically oriented studies of transplant patients (Abram & Buchanan, 1976; Basch, 1973; Castelnuovo-Tedesco, 1973; Crombez & Lefebvre, 1972; Viederman, 1974) have focused on the difficulties involved in accepting and making a part of oneself organs that originally belonged to someone else.

There are conflicting opinions about how serious a problem this is. Some (e.g., Simmons, Klein, & Simmons, 1977) suggest that the whole issue has been exaggerated. Others (e.g., Crombez & Lefebvre, 1972) see it as significantly involved in just about all instances of organ transplantation. The speculation is that when a transplanted organ is placed inside the body it creates problems of self-differentiation. Presumably, the self-delineation that is normally attained is threatened by the transplant because one may feel "fused" with it and confuse one's own identity with that of the person from whom the transplanted organ was obtained. There are cited in the literature dramatic instances (e.g., Castelnuovo-Tedesco, 1973) in which kidney transplant patients have developed delusional alterations in identity that seem to be linked to the origins of the transplant. There have even been clinical observations asserting that there are fewer signs of psychological disturbance when transplants come from anonymous "cadavers" than when they have been offered by members of one's own family (Abram & Buchanan, 1976). Presumably, the possibility of "fusion" with a family member would be greater than with an anonymous donor.

Attempts have been made to discern "stages" in the process of psychologically assimilating the organ transplant. Muslin (1971) depicted the internalization" of a new kidney as involving three phases: experienced as a "foreign object," "partial incorporation," and "complete incorporation." Others (e.g., Basch, 1973; Graham, 1981) emphasize the individuality of psychological adaptation to the transplant, with some individuals almost immediately making it a part of self, and others requiring an extended time period. One observer has expressed doubt that the introduction of a new organ such as a kidney[10] alters the body image (Viederman, 1974):

> I too started with the assumption that there would be modifications of the body image. To my surprise, patients rarely reported a sense of change inside the body except to speak of the form of the kidney which is palpable from the outside. . . . given the fact that the aspect of the self representation which we call body image is primarily an experiential phenomenon . . . it would be unlikely that any coherent *sense* of the organization of the inside would occur. Our knowledge of the inside is basically cognitive (intellectual) rather than experienced in a coherent sensory way with form, limits, surfaces. In my view there is no internal body image although, of course, there is a potential richness of fantasy about the insides. Except for the scarring and the lump, the body image is rarely dynamically affected by the operation. (p. 289)

These various speculations are simply speculations. There have been only a few even quasiempirical studies of the body image effects of transplant surgery. Three projects (Graham, 1981; Schwitters, 1975; Simmons et al., 1977) have called for interviewing or obtaining questionnaire responses from transplant patients both before and after surgery and have involved a certain degree of quantitative analysis of the data. Generally, these studies found that conscious confusion about identity was a very infrequent result of introducing the foreign organ. Indeed, they all observed considerable improvement in psychological state postsurgery. Indices of improvement diversely involved MMPI scores, self-concept ratings, and human figure drawings. The Graham study, which was an intensive evaluation of 10 kidney transplant patients and which made use not only of interview material but also of the Rorschach test and the Draw-A-Person Test, concluded there was a dramatic improvement in the figure drawings from pre- to postsurgery. This was impressionistically considered to be indicative of increased body image security.

A few exploratory attempts have been made to determine the effects of implanting cardiac pacemakers (Blacher & Basch, 1970; Dlin, 1966; Dlin, Fischer, & Huddell, 1968; Romirowsky, 1978). Most are of the impressionistic clinical variety. They have, in some instances, uncovered interesting qualitative material about fantasies that are fostered by the implantation. Blacher and Basch interviewed 50 pacemaker patients and found considerable concern about the pacemaker's representing self-submission to a machine. One patient said, "I am not a person; I'm really a robot run by a generator." Few of the patients expressed their concern so explicitly. There were also fantasies about being "different" and "damaged" and about the impact of the pacemaker on various body functions (e.g., sexual). About a third of the patients adopted a denying, repressive attitude toward the implications of the pacemaker. Romirowsky (1978) administered a number of psychological tests (e.g., IPAT Anxiety Scale, Rosenzweig Picture Frustration Study for Assessing Reaction to Frustration) to 35 males about a year after pacemaker implantation and to 35 males one year after coronary bypass surgery. The pacemaker patients were found to be significantly more anxious and less expressive of aggressive feelings. They were also more concerned with the difficulties of "continued living."

Various interesting observations have been published concerning the feelings of organ donors (e.g., Abram & Buchanan, 1976; Fellner & Marshall, 1968; Eisendrath, Guttmann & Murray, 1969; Kemph, 1966). A number of clinically oriented studies have suggested that donors are highly ambivalent toward, and quite traumatized by, the entire experience of giving up a part of themselves. Kemph (1966) noted:

> The donor tended to withdraw emotionally and appear harassed as the operative date approached. The loss of a part of his body was rapidly becoming a reality. Previously he felt compensated for the altruistic sacrifice he was making, but when surgery was imminent he realized more fully the significance of losing an organ through major surgery in terms of narcissistic threat, fear of damage to sexual organs, and the vital dangers of major surgery. (p. 628)

More positive appraisals typify most of the other studies (Abram & Buchanan, 1976) that are less clinically oriented. Indeed, Marshall and Fellner (1977) concluded after a long-term systematic follow up of 12 kidney donors that "The donation has had a considerable positive, long-lasting impact upon (their) lives. The idea that donors 'lose a kidney but get nothing in return' is untenable" (p. 576). True, a few of the donors felt that the loss of their kidney had had serious negative consequences, but they were exceptions. Many of the donors seemed to derive satisfaction from the extraordinarily positive responses their sacrifice had aroused in other family members and also from the fact of being able to see self as having behaved in an heroically altruistic fashion. Incidentally, there has also been a good deal of exploration of the variables that are associated with being a blood donor (e.g., Burnett, 1981; Oborne & Bradley, 1975; Oswalt & Napoliello, 1974). Although the findings are not consistent, there are suggestions that those who do volunteer to give their blood are relatively better educated,[11] more religious, and more humanitarian in orientation than those who do not volunteer. Curious tidbits have also emerged. For example, Burnett (1981) found that blood donors have lower self-esteem and are more concerned about their health than are nondonors. He speculated that the act of donating blood might actually represent an attempt to win approval and thereby to bolster self-esteem.

PHANTOM EXPERIENCES FOLLOWING ORGAN LOSS

Surgery that results in a loss of a body part is usually accompanied by an illusory experience that the missing part is still there. An amputated arm or leg is replaced by a phantom representation of it. The phantom representation may include paresthesias of different intensities; often involves only parts of the missing member; and with time may be characterized by a "telescoping" process in which the illusory part seems to shrink into the stump and finally disappears. Loss of limbs and projecting body parts is particularly likely to stimulate phantom sensations, but there is evidence that surgically removed internal organs may also reappear as phantoms (Dorpat, 1971).[12] Fisher (1970) summarized the major findings concerning phantom phenomena that had appeared up to 1970. A fundamental disagreement has persisted as to whether phantoms are tied primarily to peripheral[13] or to central factors. It has been theorized, on the one hand, that phantoms are primarily a reflection of irritants and sensations arising in the stump. But others have taken the view that phantoms are the result of a central process that simply maintains an image of one's body as it was prior to the loss of a part. One of the chief arguments in favor of the central theory is that, if a body part is congenitally missing or if its loss occurs very gradually, as is the case with absorption of digits in persons with leprosy, phantom sensations fail to appear. Simmel (1956) published studies that seemed to affirm this perspective. The underlying idea was that if the missing body part was never integrated into the body image or if it was so gradually eliminated from the body image that its loss had minimal impact, there was no basis for a compensatory or stabilizing phantom. However, a number of findings suggest that phantoms can be experienced by those who have suffered a congenital loss of a limb and also by those, like lepers, who have lost body parts gradually (e.g., Poeck, 1964–65; Price, 1976; Vetter & Weinstein, 1967). There are two varieties of central theories of phantom formation. One approach (e.g., Simmel, 1956) perceives the central mechanism as a cognitive one that simply involves the persistence of a body scheme that lags behind the alteration associated with amputation. The more psychodynamic perspective (e.g., Murphy, 1957) regards the phantom as a form of symbolic denial and mourning for the lost (body) object (Bloom & Snyder, 1976; Szasz, 1957).

As analysis of the conditions affecting the appearance of the phantom has gone forward, it has become apparent that both oversimplified peripheral and central theories are inadequate. Many variables have now been shown to be involved in the appearance versus nonappearance of body phantoms. Their complexity points up the complexity of those factors that probably contribute to the phantom experience.

Almagor, Jaffe, and Lomranz (1978) explored the relationship between limb dominance and frequency of phantom limb sensations in 20 male homologous limb double amputees. As predicted, phantom sensations were reported to be significantly greater in the dominant limb. This finding was interpreted as providing support for Simmel's (1959) view that there is a relation between the likelihood of appearance of phantom limb sensations and the amount of previous kinesthetic input from that limb. Presumably the greater the past kinesthetic experience the more articulated and intense would be the central representation of the limb and therefore the greater the disparity between that representation and the actual input from the amputated part. Almagor et al. noted that this finding was congruent with earlier observations that there is a strong relation between degree of representation of a body area in the cortex of the paraplegic and the occurrence of phantom sensations in that area. No correlation was observed between frequency of phantom sensations and how well subjects had "accepted" their disabilities, as defined by a questionnaire.

There have been several studies of breast phantoms in women with mastectomies.[14] Weinstein, Vetter, and Sersen (1970) reported that of 203 women they interviewed who had had mastectomies,[15] 33% experienced phantom breast sensations. The average for several previous studies was approximately the same. The percentages are much, almost universally, higher for parts such as legs and arms.[16] For those with left mastectomy, the incidence of phantom was significantly higher in younger women. Further, premenopausal women were in general characterized by a greater incident of breast phantoms than were the postmenopausal. Weinstein et al. speculated that some factor like reduction in sex hormones might play a role in the lower incidence of phantoms in the postmenopausal. However, as will be seen, there has also been speculation that breasts have greater importance for the identity of the younger, often more sexually active women in whom, therefore, breast loss evokes a stronger defensive response, presumably in the form of phantom representations. The incidence of phantoms was not significantly related to how aware a woman said she was of the absence of her breast, the actual size of her breasts, or whether she had ever breast fed.

Cofer (1980) probed the factors that contribute to the development of breast phantoms in 61 mastectomy patients. She administered the Wechsler Adult Intelligence Scale; two personality tests (Adjective Check List [Gough & Heilbrun, 1965] and Fundamental Interpersonal Relations Orientation Scale-Behavior [Schutz, 1967]); measures of creativity; a body image questionnaire derived from Berscheid et al. (1973); and an index of conjugate lateral eye movement directionality. The measure of intelligence was included because Simmel (1966) had observed a tendency for women of higher intelligence to have greater probability of developing a phantom following mastectomy. A measure of creativity was used because Simmel had impressionistically noted that it probably requires a sensitive tuning to one's own body to detect the relatively weak level of phantom sensations. Inasmuch as there are suggestions that sensitivity to one's own body is linked positively with originality, Cofer decided to use originality as an indirect index of bodily sensitivity. Finally, the direction of eye movements was measured to ascertain degree of right versus left cerebral dominance. Cofer's interest in this matter was stimulated by reports by Weinstein et al. (1970) that brain damage on the right side of the brain could delay the appearance of phantoms in damaged limbs. Thirty-eight of the 61 subjects experienced breast phantoms. Those with phantoms were significantly younger than those without phantoms. This observation has not only been duplicated by Weinstein et al., but also by others (Jamison, Wellisch, Katz, & Passnau, 1979; Jarvis, 1967; & Simmel, 1966). Cofer found too that women with breast phantoms were more likely to be married. She put these two sets of findings together and concluded that the phantom must serve a compensatory purpose: "In a culture which extolls the breast as a primary source of feminine identification and sexual attractiveness, the loss of a breast may well be deemed catastrophic by younger and married women who desire or are involved in intimate sexual relationships. For these women, the phantom breast may well represent the psychological denial of the loss of this highly symbolic organ" (p. 36).

Three personality variables derived from the Adjective Check List (Gough & Heilbrun, 1965) were significantly associated with phantom breast. Those with phantoms were higher on Affiliation and Nurturance and lower on Intraception. Cofer interpreted this pattern of differences as follows: "This suggests that while women experiencing phantoms tend to be involved in numerous personal relationships and exhibit behavior which is emotionally supportive to others, they do not attempt to develop insight into their own or others' behavior" (p. 40). The other personality measure used (FIRO-B) did not differentiate the two groups. Relatedly, Jamison et al. (1979) could not distinguish breast phantom women in terms of their scores on the Eysenck Personality Inventory. It is noteworthy that, contrary to Simmel's original findings, Cofer did not detect any differences in intelligence between the phantom and non-phantom women. Further, no differences were observed in measures of originality and, by implication, sensitivity to one's own body. However, it is doubtful that a measure of originality can be considered an adequate index of sensitivity to one's own body experiences. Cofer also did not find any differences in the directionality of lateral eye movements in phantom and nonphantom groups and, therefore, presumably in their patterns of cerebral dominance. No differences emerged between the phantom and non-phantom groups with respect to self-concept or overall satisfaction with one's body. Finally, phantoms were significantly more likely to occur the longer a woman knew prior to surgery that she would definitely lose a breast.

Jamison et al. (1979) appraised 41 women who had undergone mastectomy and reported that 22 had experienced some form of phantom breast sensation. A major finding was that those in the phantom group were significantly inclined to see themselves as getting inadequate emotional support. They perceived themselves as having relatively poor relationships with their husband and receiving poor emotional support from their surgeon. Also, they rated themselves as adjusting to the surgery relatively poorly at an emotional level. The appearance of the phantom seemed somehow to be linked to a sense of going through the mastectomy experience without adequate support from the primary figures in one's life. There were also quite a number of negative findings. The phantom experience was not correlated with such variables as race, religion, marital status, number of children, scores on a marital adjustment test, locus of control, sexual adjustment, and, as already mentioned, scores from the Eysenck Personality Inventory.

A certain percentage of phantoms that appear following amputation are felt as painful.[17] Reports of the frequency of phantom pain have varied widely. Ewalt, Randal, and Morris (1947) estimated that it involved about 1% of amputees, whereas Riddoch (1941) thought the percentage was as high as 50%. Cofer (1980) reported that half the women in her mastectomy group who developed a breast phantom also had pain apparently emanating from it. She discovered that there were correlations between occurrence of the painful phantom and a number of variables with obvious psychological implications. Painful phantoms were more likely to occur in those who knew someone who had undergone mastectomy. Kolb (1959) too observed that amputees with painful phantoms were particularly likely to live in close association with an amputee before their own loss occurred. Cofer found further that painful breast phantoms were positively linked with such factors as age, being divorced, and feeling pessimistic. Other investigators have documented correlations between painful phantoms and various indices of personality and psychopathology. For example, Parkes (1973) noted that, in a sample of 37 male and 9 female amputees, painful phantoms were correlated with "compulsive self reliance", being unemployed, and being ill for an extended period. Morgenstern (1970) detected, in a comparison of 123 amputees with phantom pain and 41 without pain, that the former were older, were more likely to be retired from work, were more depressed, and obtained higher neuroticism scores on a personality inventory.

Such observations suggest that the painful phantom has its roots to some degree in psychological disturbance. However, Melzack (1971), conceding that psychological factors may be significant, cautioned that psychological explanations cannot explain the sudden relief in phantom pain often produced by nerve blocks. He doubted that emotional factors are the major cause of phantom pain and proposed instead the following explanatory model:

> Briefly, the model proposes that a portion of the brainstem reticular formation acts as a *central biasing mechanism* by exerting a tonic inhibitory influence, or bias, on transmission at all synaptic levels of the somatic projection system. When a large proportion of sensory fibers is destroyed by amputation of a limb, thereby decreasing the amount of input into the reticular formation, the inhib-

itory influence decreases. This results in self-sustaining activity at all neural levels that can be triggered repeatedly by the remaining fibers. Pain occurs when the output of the self-sustaining neuron pools reaches or exceeds a critical level.[18] (p. 415)

A similar negative attitude toward the role of psychological or psychodynamic factors in the simple occurrence of phantoms has been voiced by Weinstein (1969). He favored a central theory attributing "the presence of the phantom to activity within the cortical projection areas which subserved the missing or differentiated bodily parts. Such activity is hypothesized as occurring spontaneously in some states, or through excitatory process from neighboring projection or other cortices . . ." (p. 81). He cited the following to support this antipsychodynamic position:

1. The frequency, vividness, and duration of the amputation phantom has in several studies proven to be directly correlated with the actual size of the cortical sensory homunculus (the cortical representation of bodily parts).
2. Studies of mastectomy patients indicate that only about a third develop phantoms and this "does not appear to lend support to a 'need' or 'fantasy' theory" (p. 92).
3. Although studies indicate that women value their breasts more than other body parts such as the thumb, phantoms are much more likely to appear after removal of the thumb than the breast. Indeed, one survey found a nonsignificant correlation between the subjective importance assigned to various body parts and the likelihood of their becoming sites for phantom sensations. In a paraplegic sample, there was a significant negative correlation between these two parameters.

The points made by Weinstein are cogent, but they go too far. The role of psychodynamic vectors in phantom phenomena cannot be dismissed. Their degree of importance is not yet clear, but they obviously contribute significantly. How else can one explain the correlations that have been demonstrated between the occurrence of phantoms and such variables as degree of dissatisfaction with amount of support received from the primary figures in one's life, personality traits (e.g., Affiliation), and marital status? Psychodynamic influences seem to be particularly prominent in the development of painful phantoms. It is possible that psychodynamic variables play a larger or smaller role in phantom phenomena depending on the body part involved. Phantoms are just about universal for amputated limbs and appear no matter what the individual variations in psychological state. In contrast, phantoms appear in only about a third of women with mastectomies, and there is considerable evidence that these women differ psychologically from those who do not experience phantoms. The occurrence of the breast phantom may be particularly incited in those who experience the breast loss as a threat to their most important social relationships. Perhaps the origin of the phantom can be radically different for some body sites as compared to others. It is possible that the determinants of phantoms shortly after amputation differ from those that become influential after a longer time. Further, if one considers the ubiquity of sex differences in body image functioning, there may even be important divergences in what triggers the phantom in males and in females.

BURNS

Dramatic, traumatic attacks on the body result from severe burns. Individuals with extensive burns not only experience an extended period of extreme pain and threat of death, but also ultimately end up with gross forms of disfigurement. A number of clinical observations have detailed the psychological distress of burn patients (e.g., Andreasen & Norris, 1972; Andreasen, Noyes, Hartford, Brodland, & Proctor, 1972; Breslin, 1975; Solnit & Priel, 1975; Vigliano, Hart, & Singer, 1964). A few studies have more systematically examined the psychological consequences of suffering burn damage. Ronnebeck (1972) analyzed self-reports of activities engaged in during a 4-week period by 22 facially disfigured teenagers and a matched, nondisfigured control group. Surprisingly, males with burns were found to be more adversely affected than were females with burns. The adverse effect was defined particularly in terms of inhibiting venturesome movement out into the environment. In view of the importance of attractiveness in the female role, one might have expected facial disfigurement to have more of an inhibiting effect on girls than on boys.

Johnson (1977) focused on the body image alterations produced by burns. He obtained self-ratings of body esteem from burn patients ($N = 40$) within 2 weeks of their hospitalization. He demonstrated that: (a) patients with burns to more than 50% of the body had lower body esteem than did those with burns to less than 50% of the body; (b) patients with burns to the face or hands had lower body esteem than did those with burns to the trunk or extremities; (c) female patients with burns had lower body esteem than did male patients with equivalent burns. This last finding appears to contradict the sex difference cited earlier in the context of the Ronnebeck (1972) study. However, whereas the Johnson study involved adults, the Ronnebeck project included only teen-aged subjects.

Mlott, Lira, and Miller (1977) administered the MMPI and the verbal subtests of an intelligence test fo 16 male and 9 female burn patients on two occasions (on hospital admission and approximately 1 year after discharge). All patients had burns that covered 25%–30% of the body surface. The composite MMPI profiles were essentially normal at the time of both administrations. On retest, the females showed a significant tendency toward greater social orientation and gregariousness. Some small increments in intelligence test scores were noted. Mlott, et al. interpreted their data as indicating that previous studies had exaggerated the severity of the psychological deterioration resulting from severe burns. They speculated that they had found less drastic disturbance than previous studies for several reasons: (a) they appraised adult burn patients, whereas several of the most drastic negative reports in the literature had involved children; (b) some of the more negative studies have involved not only patients with burns more extensive than 30% of the body surface, but also patients with poorer premorbid adjustments than typified by those in the by Mlott et al. study; and (c) an unusually large amount of psychological support was provided to the patients in the Mlott et al. study. The relative lack of disturbance reported by Mlott et al. raises the possibility that more impressionistic observations have simply exaggerated and overgeneralized dramatic negative effects in individual patients.

In a related vein, Andreasen and Norris (1972) interviewed 11 men and 9 women with average total body surface burns of 37%. They also administered the MMPI. Only two of the patients were characterized by serious deviance in their MMPI profiles. Seventy percent were found to be adjusting well at least 1 year after hospitalization. The other 30% were said to have mild or moderate problems. Those who had severe facial scarring gradually became desensitized to the reactions of others. There was a tendency to minimize to oneself the seriousness of the scarring. Seven of the 20 patients rated themselves as having less of a deformity than did the rater who interviewed them. Andreasen and Norris commented: "By the time progressive desensitization is completed the patient has learned to conceptualize his identity primarily on the basis of internal or nonphysical values, and the body image is blurred, ignored, or denied" (p. 358).

MENSTRUATION AND PREGNANCY

Women experience stressful bodily changes as a result of both the menstrual cycle and pregnancy. We know that many women perceive menstrual bleeding as threatening, and we also know that the gross body alterations that accompany pregnancy can be alarming. Fisher (1973c) has analyzed some of the body threats implicit in these phenomena. He noted: "The body threatening significance of menstruation, both as a symbol of future dangers linked with pregnancy and as an immediate process involving blood flow from a body orifice" is "a cause for disturbance and anxiety in menstruating women" (p. 120). With respect to pregnancy Fisher remarked:

> In several different ways the body changes initiated by pregnancy seem to raise significant adjustment problems. There is, first of all, the slowly initiated

but then sharply accelerated increase in body size and change in body shape that accompany the development of the fetus. This is climaxed by a precipitous reversal when the body shrinks in size at the time of delivery. . . . Pregnancy body changes are threatening because they signal a biological process that can, in reality, lead to serious illness and even death. (pp. 133–134)

Menstruation

The few scattered research reports dealing with the body image aspects of menstruation suggest that the actual experience of menstruating has an impact on the body image. In a previously described study by Thorbeck (1978) it was shown that young girls (age 13), who were menstruating at the time, drew human figures that were less differentiated, as defined by the Witkin et al. (1962) criteria, than were those drawn by girls not menstruating. Further, Fisher and Richter (1969) demonstrated in two studies that, when women in various stages of the menstrual cycle were asked to report changes produced in their mirror images as a function of viewing them through aniseikonic lenses, there was a significant trend for those who were closest to menstruating to manifest the greatest resistance to perceiving any changes in the pelvic region. Previous studies have shown that the greater the anxiety aroused by a target stimulus, the less likely it is to be perceived as altered when viewed through aniseikonic lenses. It appeared that there was a specific intensification of anxiety concerning the pelvis resulting from increased imminence of the menstrual flow. However, DiNardo (1974) found that when women ($N = 60$) in different phases of the menstrual cycle were asked to rate various of their body parts on Semantic Differential continua, there was no relationship between the imminence of menstruation and how positively or negatively their ratings were.[19] The DiNardo data were based on ratings susceptible to social desirability effects, whereas the Fisher and Richter and also the Thorbeck data derived from measures much less likely to be shaped by social desirability response sets.

There are findings bearing on the relationship of how secure women feel about their body space and their perception of their menstrual experiences. DiNardo (1974) observed that the more positively women rated their bodies, the lower the degree of menstrual discomfort they reported. Haft (1973) discerned no significant relationships in early adolescent girls between Semantic Differential ratings of their own bodies and indices of menstrual discomfort. But she did report that the more positive were ratings of one's own body, the more positively was the term "menstruation" rated. Relatedly, but at quite another level, Osofsky and Fisher (1967) observed in a sample ($N = 66$) of student nurses that the more secure their body boundaries the less likely they were to develop amenorrhea in a stressful life situation.[20] Although the data are minimal, they do point to a promising link between feeling that one's body is secure and being able to experience menstruation as relatively non-threatening.[21]

Pregnancy

Considerable effort has been devoted to tracking the alterations in body perception that take place during the pregnancy cycle. There have been both detailed studies of individual pregnant women and more conventional large-scale appraisals making use of tests and questionnaires. Jamieson (1980) has provided accounts of pregnancy experiences that he derived from exhaustive observations of 10 married women pregnant for the first time. Each woman was interviewed in her 9th month of pregnancy, again shortly after delivery, and finally 2 to 3 months postpartum. Jamieson emphasized that the purpose of his study was to understand individual patterns rather than to arrive at "average" conceptualizations. After analyzing the verbalizations of the women in his study, he concluded that not only was there a heightened sense of body vulnerability during pregnancy, but also, at times, a feeling that one's body has superlarge qualities that render it potentially powerful and even destructively so. He added: "Present evidence suggests that fear of body damage is far from being a unidimensional variable in pregnant women. We must at least make the distinction between concerns which seriously implicate the women's basic sense of body structure and those which are more peripheral and fleeting" (p. 85). As he probed the sources of body anxiety during pregnancy, he felt that those women who were least anxious had a previous history of being able to use their body effectively and of having experienced it as competent, capable, and strong. He speculated that body competence was, in turn, linked with having achieved a relatively unconflicted identification with one's mother.

Leifer (1977) interviewed and evaluated 19 first-time pregnant women at seven different points during their pregnancy (beginning in the 1st trimester and concluding 7 months postpartum). She reported

> there is a progressive increase in negative feeling about the pregnant appearance. In the postpartum more women felt negatively about their appearance than at any time during pregnancy. . . . Themes that emerged from the interviews indicated that women who had positive feelings expressed considerable pride in their pregnant appearance, enjoyed the attention of other people, and were intensely involved in the bodily changes that were occurring. For many, looking pregnant evoked an enhanced sense of womanliness and a pride in being fertile. However, the marked alterations in appearance which occurred by the last trimester evoked dissatisfaction with appearance even for these women. . . . In the later stages of pregnancy the occurrence of minor bodily changes, such as stretch marks in the skin and increased breast size, often heightened their fears of damage to the body and their concerns over loss

of sexual attractiveness. An important factor contributing to negative feelings by the third trimester was the increased size of the body. Concern with weight became more prevalent, and many women experienced a sense of loss of control over their bodies. For many, the body seemed ego-alien. (p. 71)

In another study, involving multiple observations and testings of 64 pregnant women and their families (at several points in the pregnancy and delivery sequence), Shereshefsky, Plotsky, and Lockman (1973) noted:

All the women reacted to physical aspects and changes, some with eagerness to 'show' early and with pleasure in their new bodily appearance, others with more mixed feelings. Many of the women seemed to be continuously aware of their bodily processes even before quickening and fetal activity brought special reminders. . . . Bewilderment at what was going on internally was a common reaction, and even otherwise knowledgeable young women at times showed confusion at frequency of urination, breast enlargement, or the need for frequent napping. (p. 77)

Further, Shereshefsky et al. found that: "Reactions to quickening sometimes revealed how uncertain the women had been that the pregnancy was real. . . . For the most part, the women reacted with an admixture of relief at the relative certainty and excitement and gratification at the newness of the experience" (p. 79). With respect to quickening sensations Leifer (1977) said: "After experiencing the fetal movements (the 'quickening') there was decreased concern concerning miscarriage. Many women now expressed concern regarding the normalcy of the fetus.[22] The quickening intensified these fears, since the fetus was now perceived as a living organism. In the last trimester, self-concern became more salient, and anxieties about delivery, fear of death . . . were commonly expressed" (p. 73). These word pictures of body pregnancy experiences are mentioned by way of introduction to accounts of more quantitative studies that follow.

There is little doubt that women perceive their bodies as considerably transformed by pregnancy, but it is not at all clear how they feel about the change. A number of clinical observers (e.g., Deutsch, 1944–1945) have described pregnancy as a time of crisis and disturbance. However, Fisher (1973c) showed in a review of the pertinent research literature that it is still an unsettled matter whether pregnant women are in general more anxious or upset than the nonpregnant. At the same time, the aforementioned several descriptions of pregnancy-induced body alterations do suggest that the alterations of pregnancy may have threatening connotations. Recall that terms like "fear of body damage" and "concern over loss of sexual attractiveness" were mentioned. Although conceivably women can adapt to threatening bodily changes without gross increases in anxiety, the literature on how women perceive their radical shifts in body shape and size during pregnancy contains scattered reports based on figure drawings that suggest that pregnant women are somehow uncomfortable with their bodies.

Soichet (1972) evaluated figure drawings obtained from 360 women during the first trimester of pregnancy and impressionistically concluded that an unusual number manifested signs of distortion and disturbance. Tolor and Digrazia (1977) collected figure drawings from 216 pregnant women representing each of the trimesters and 6 weeks postpartum. The drawings were scored by three raters for specific items (e.g., body distorted or intact, drawing large or small). No figure drawing differences were detected in relation to the phase of pregnancy. But, when compared with drawings obtained from nonpregnant gynecological patients ($N = 76$), the pregnant women's drawings were significantly more often judged to be distorted, small in size, nude, and unusually emphatic in depicting the sex organs. This was interpreted to mean that pregnant women have deviant and disturbed body image experiences. Viney, Aitkin, and Floyd (1974), in a study of the figure drawings of 32 married and 15 unmarried pregnant women (6 months into pregnancy) and those of 30 unmarried, nonpregnant women, could detect no differences among the groups in drawing size, but they did not analyze any of the other variables that were appraised by Soichet or Tolor and Digrazia.

Shane and Linn (1977) administered a modified version of the Jourard-Secord Body Cathexis scale to 38 couples in a childbirth education course during the seventh month of pregnancy. Each wife and husband rated the wife's body. The wives were also asked to judge how their husband would rate them. The husbands' ratings were significantly more positive than the wives'. Further, the wives expected the husbands' ratings to be more negative than they actually were. The data indicated that the women had a negative attitude toward their own pregnant forms.

Carty (1970) interviewed 40 women in varying stages of pregnancy or in the postpartum period concerning how they felt about the body changes that had occurred. She totaled the positive and negative statements made and converted them into a 5-point scale of total degree of satisfaction-dissatisfaction. She discovered that more than half of the women were either somewhat dissatisfied or completely dissatisfied with their pregnant bodies. Interestingly, this dissatisfaction was equal or more extreme in four women in the sample who were in the postpartum phase. Carty said of the postpartum subjects: "These women were prone to think that once the baby was born, their nice, flat stomach would soon come back. Dissatisfaction was openly expressed when they found the abdomen was a little big and lacked muscle tone" (p. 41).

In the earlier referred to Liefer (1977) study, a 10-item version of the Jourard-Secord Body Cathexis scale was administered to 19 first-time pregnant women on four different occasions: during the 1st trimester, when the woman was asked to respond as she would have before pregnancy, in the 2nd and 3rd trimesters, and at 2 months postpartum. There was a significant trend for the body changes of pregnancy to evoke negative feelings. Leifer found a particularly heightened degree of body dissatisfaction during the postpartum period.

A different picture emerged when Watts (1980) administered the Body Cathexis scale to 28 married women (pregnant for the first time) in their 3rd trimester of pregnancy and again 4 months after delivery. No differences in degree of body satisfaction between the two time phases could be detected. The same measure was taken on the husbands of these women, and their scores also failed to change. A control group of 16 nonpregnant women (and their husbands) were included; their scores did not differ significantly from those of the pregnant women. Incidentally, the body satisfaction scores of the women proved to be positively and significantly correlated with their income, occupation, and education levels.

As earlier described, Slade (1977) studied body size perception in 40 women (including both first and second or more pregnancies) who were about 4 months pregnant. They were asked to estimate the size of face, chest, waist, and hips by setting an interval between two moveable lights. Sixteen of the women were retested when they were 8 months pregnant. Control groups of normal women ($N = 20$) and those with anorexia nervosa ($N = 14$) were also included. At the 4-month point, the pregnant women overestimated their body size significantly more than the normals, but significantly less then the anorexia patients. Overestimation by the pregnant women was particularly pronounced for the waist. On retest at 8 months, the pregnant women overestimated their body dimensions significantly less than at 4 months. Slade suggested that this represented a "positive adaptation" to their change in body size.[23] Overall, the findings document a tendency for pregnant women to exaggerate unrealistically the increase in their body size. One assumes this plays some role in the somewhat negative body appraisals they manifested in the several studies just enumerated.

Detailed probes have been made of the factors mediating alterations in body perception in the pregnant at an overall level and also at specific intervals during the pregnancy sequence. Let us sift through the observations that have accumulated. Venezia (1972) was interested in the relationship of personality to shifts in body attitudes during pregnancy. He asked 40 pregnant women (all had had at least one previous child) to rate their bodies on Semantic Differential scales during the 3rd trimester and 6 weeks after delivery. He also had them fill out the Eysenck Personality Inventory and a measure of attitudes toward pregnancy. Women who were more extraverted perceived their bodies significantly more negatively during pregnancy than did those less extraverted. There were no overall shifts in body ratings from the 3rd trimester to the postdelivery point. Attitudes toward pregnancy were not correlated with the body ratings.

Gordon (1976) studied 138 first-time pregnant women. The Jourard-Secord

Body Cathexis scale was administered, and some measures of anxiety were secured. Data were also collected concerning maladaptive physiological responses during pregnancy and delivery. Body satisfaction was negatively and significantly correlated with anxiety level. The relationship between body satisfaction and the presence-absence of maladaptive physiological responses was generally not significant.

Belson (1977) measured body attitudes in 50 women (first pregnancy) with the Jourard-Secord (1955) scale. Shame about being pregnant was ascertained by analysis (based on the Gottschalk-Gleser Content Analysis Scale, (1969) of a taped response to the request to talk for 5 minutes concerning how one feels about being looked at while pregnant. Subjects rated their bodies for degree of satisfaction in terms of both their pregnant condition and their prepregnant state (as they could recall it); the less favorable their body evaluations during pregnancy as compared to prepregnancy, the significantly greater was the shame expressed. Body attitudes at either of these points alone were not significantly correlated with pregnancy shame.

Uddenberg and Hakanson (1972) explored the distribution of body anxiety in 45 pregnant women during the 2nd trimester. They mapped this distribution by asking subjects to view themselves in a mirror while wearing aniseikonic lenses and to judge the degree to which various body areas appeared to be changed as the result of the lens effects. Previous research had demonstrated that the greater the anxiety associated with a body area (or any perceptual target), the less altered it was considered to be when viewed aniseikonically. When degree of conflict about reproductive functions was determined from interview responses, it proved to be significantly positively correlated with resistance to perceiving the pelvic region as aniseikonically changed. Relatedly, women with sexual adaptation difficulties were able to see few aniseikonic pelvic alterations. But, interestingly, when the women were explicitly asked for their attitudes toward pregnancy, the formal statements they made were not correlated with the aniseikonic indices. Apparently, social desirability effects intervened. This study suggests that the pelvic region may become a focus for those pregnant women with heightened anxieties about pregnancy and sexuality.[24]

Several attempts have been made to determine not only whether the amount of distortion in body experience is greater in the pregnant than in the nonpregnant, but also how feelings of body distortion fluctuate over the course of the pregnancy. Three studies have employed the Fisher (1973c) Body Distortion Questionnaire for such determinations. This questionnaire consists of 82 items to which the subject responds with either Yes, No, or Undecided. A total distortion score is derived equal to the number of items marked Yes or Undecided. A variety of subscale scores that pertain to specific types of body image distortion can also be derived; more will be said about them shortly.

Karmel (1975) studied 32 pregnant women who were tested twice, first in the 3rd trimester and again 6 weeks postpartum. A control group of 28 nonpregnant women without children were retested equivalently. The pregnant women reported significantly more distorted body experiences than did the nonpregnant,[25] but showed a significant drop in distortion from the 3rd trimester to the postpartum phase. Four subscales of the Body Distortion Questionnaire (viz., Large, Boundary Loss, Blocked Openings, Skin Sensations) declined significantly for the same period.

When Fisher (1973c) administered the Body Distortion Questionnaire to 42 women who were, on the average, in their 6th month of pregnancy (most for the first time), he found a significant decrease in distortion scores from the pregnancy to the postpartum period. However, he did not find that pregnant women had significantly higher distortion scores than have typified nonpregnant female samples. Shane (1977) evaluated a sample of 30 white, 41 Cuban, and 55 black women (first time pregnant) at several points during the pregnancy sequence: 4 months, 9 months, and 6 weeks postpartum. The Body Distortion Questionnaire was administered at each point. Total distortion scores were significantly higher at all points during the pregnancy than in nonpregnant women. There was an absence of significant change in the total distortion score from the 4th to the 9th month. From the 9th month to postpartum the total distortion scores decreased significantly.

The results derived from the separate subscales of the Body Distortion Questionnaire indicate that from the 4th to the 9th months there is a significant increase in the sensation that one's body is growing larger. From the 9th month to postpartum sensations of largeness decrease and smallness sensations increase significantly. A subcategory involving sensations that the openings of one's body are blocked decreases significantly. Further, boundary loss sensations and unusual skin sensations decrease significantly.

The Fisher (1970) Body Focus Questionnaire was also administered in two of the three studies just enumerated (viz., Karmel (1975); Shane (1977)). This questionnaire measures how much attention persons are focusing on each of a number of major body areas. It calls for making 108 paired comparison judgments. In each instance persons indicate which of two body parts they are most aware at that moment. There are scales of items that embrace such body areas as the arms, legs, heart, stomach, and so forth. Certain aspects of the findings linked to the Body Focus Questionnaire are considered in more detail at a later point. However, note that Shane detected a significant increase in stomach and in mouth awareness from the 1st trimester to the 3rd.[26] She also observed a significant decrease in stomach awareness from the 9th month to the postpartum period. Mouth awareness did not decline in a parallel fashion. Karmel too observed a decline in stomach awareness from the 3rd trimester to the postpartum period.

Several salient trends emerge from the material that has been reviewed. First, two of three studies that employed the Fisher Body Distortion Questionnaire indicated that pregnant women experience their bodies in a more distorted fashion than do nonpregnant women. The pregnant women were more likely to see themselves as unusually altered. Several other studies, variously involving figure drawings and body size judgments, have similarly suggested a pattern of distorted body perception in pregnant women. It is pertinent to this matter that all three investigations that made use of the Body Distortion Questionnaire observed a significant decrease in distorted body perceptions in the postpartum phase as compared to the last trimester of pregnancy.[27] The Shane (1977) and the Karmel (1975) studies concurred in defining the decrease as occurring largely in relation to four specific types of body distortions (viz., Large, Blocked Openings, Boundary Loss, Skin Sensations). Fisher (1973c), however, found a decrease only in Blocked Openings and an increase in Small sensations. It is reasonable to conclude that women do find that pregnancy produces changes[28] in their body image that have an "I am strangely altered" quality[29] and that, as suggested by several studies (Carty, 1970; Leifer, 1977), frequently take on negative connotations in the context of such variables as attractiveness and vulnerability to body damage. It is surprising that in the Shane study a significant increase in body distortions could not be detected between the 1st and last trimester of pregnancy, which is, after all, a period of marked transformation in the pregnant body. But in this period there was a significant and logical increase in specific sensations of growing large. The Shane study documented a significant increase in the amount of attention focused on the stomach area during the same time period. Not surprisingly, it is the stomach region that seems to attract the greatest increase in attention from self during pregnancy.

We know relatively little about the factors that mediate how negatively a woman views her pregnant body. The Venezia (1972) study did suggest that extraverted women were more likely than the introverted to feel dissatisfied about their pregnancy alterations. Also, the Uddenberg and Hakanson (1972) study, which employed aniseikonic lenses, suggested that a previous history of being conflicted about one's sexual or reproductive role could intensify anxiety about certain areas of the pregnant body. The Shane (1977) study uncovered cultural differences (e.g., being black versus being Cuban or white) that affect the degree and timing of distorted body experiences during the course of pregnancy. The Jamieson (1980) study speculated that concern about body damage is likely to be least in those pregnant women who have a previous history of using the body effectively and competently. These several observations are too disparate and tentative to provide a solid basis for any conclusions. However, they provide interesting leads that should be pursued.

GROWING OLD

What shall I do with this absurdity—
O heart, O troubled heart—this caricature,
Decrepit age that has been tied to me
As to a dog's tail? (Yeats)

It is a common notion in our culture that aging is a trying submission to the deterioration of one's body. Presumably, as people see the body growing old, they are upset by what they behold. Aging appears to be a threat to the integrity of the existing body image. One writer has detailed some of the major body changes that are inflicted on the aged (Murray, 1972):

> The decline of physical powers . . . will be more strongly felt in the late sixties and thereafter. This heightens fears of incapacitation and the nothingness of death. When the older person looks at himself in the mirror, what does he see? He may not see what others see; he may not like what he does see. He looks different now. Eyeglasses and a hearing aid; wrinkles and pigment changes in the skin; gray, sparse hair; the discolored or irregular teeth. . . . The gait becomes stiff and tottering; joints stiffen; strength in the arms and hands as well as the other muscles is decreasing. . . . The enlarged knuckles and misshapen hands, the bunions on the feet and horny nails may interfere with activity and cause the person to feel ugly. (p. 625)

In the context of the typically negative version of the elderly person's body, one would expect to find abundant evidence that those who are old perceive their bodies negatively. There is also a good deal of common sense lore suggesting the same thing. However, the pertinent scientific literature paints quite a mixed picture. It is true that several studies have shown the presence of negative body experiences in the aged. Leon, Gillum, Gillum and Gouze (1979) evaluated a group of men ($N = 132$) who had been followed over a 30-year period from middle age to old age. The MMPI was administered at four different times during this period. The data demonstrated a significant increase in somatic concerns and physical complaints as the subjects entered old age. Schwab and Harmeling (1968) studied 124 male and female patients admitted to a medical hospital. The patients rated their degree of satisfaction with a variety of their body parts and functions. There was a low (but significant) positive correlation (.28) between age and expressed body dissatisfaction in the male group, but a complete absence of such a relationship in the females. Plutchik, Conte, Weiner and Teresi (1978) examined the figure drawings of 75 normal adults (college students), 30 adult psychiatric inpatients, 29 normally functioning senior citizens, and 33 elderly inpatients in a mental hospital. Subjects were asked to draw a nude male and a nude female. The drawings were scored for a variety of emotional indicators that work by Koppitz (1968) suggests are indicative of anxiety and disturbed functioning. There was a significant trend, with increasing age, for figure drawings to get smaller, to become less sexually differentiated, and to be typified by more "body image disturbance." Note, though, that the difference between the aged and younger subjects for "body image disturbance" was less than 1 point on a 5-point scale. Well-functioning elderly could not be distinguished from elderly psychiatric patients, whereas the young college students showed significantly fewer signs of disturbance in their figure drawings than did the relatively young psychiatric inpatients.

A few other studies (e.g., Lorge, Tuckman, & Dunn, 1954) of figure drawings of the elderly have suggested that their body representations are poorly executed, but others have refuted this idea (Davis, 1960; Tuckman, Lorge, & Zeman, 1961). Negative findings with regard to the aged have emerged too from the work of sensori-tonic researchers (Wapner & Werner, 1965a). It has been dependably shown that when persons over 60 are asked to adjust a luminous rod to the vertical while their bodies are tilted, they respond by displacing the vertical toward the direction of tilt. This displacement is the opposite of that found in young and middle-aged adults, but is a reversion to what typifies young children. The sensori-tonic studies hint that the elderly undergo some kind of regression in how they adapt to shifts in the spatial position of the body.

A larger number of studies have not discerned elevated body image disturbance or dysfunction among the elderly. Fisher (1959a) investigated the degree of body boundary definiteness (as defined by the Fisher-Cleveland Barrier and Penetration scores) in 40 elderly subjects (median age 67). They were compared with 32 younger persons (median age 36), who had been chosen on a matching basis from their own immediate families. No boundary differences could be shown to exist between the elderly and younger groups.[30] Inasmuch as boundary definiteness has been shown to be linked with a sense of body security, the aged were not more insecure than the younger persons about their body space. Although this finding was originally interpreted as support for the idea that boundary differentiation is relatively independent of the state of the body itself, it was difficult to reconcile with commonsense notions about the impact of aging. However, the data that have accumulated since then render it more and more reasonable.

As earlier described, Berscheid et al. (1973) appraised responses to a "body image" questionnaire that readers of *Psychology Today* were invited to fill out. Over 60,000 people responded, and 2,000 questionnaires that duplicated national age and sex distributions were chosen for analysis. The questionnaire asked for ratings of degree of satisfaction with 25 different aspects of one's body. No differences could be detected as a function of age. Older persons (e.g., 45 and over) did not express more body dissatisfaction than did the younger. Only with respect to their teeth did the older express more negativity, but the younger were more dissatisfied with their complexions. Also, as earlier mentioned, Schwartz (1982) found subjects over age 55 to be more like younger subjects in body satisfaction ratings than different.

Christensen (1978) analyzed the quality of the aging experience by intensively investigating the feelings and impressions of three men and three women who were over 65, healthy, and functioning well. He concluded that older people do not inwardly feel different or old. Their sense of aging arises primarily from their dealings with others who give them "You are old" signals. Also, physical health was found to play a significant role in one's sense of aging.

Goodrich (1973) administered a Gerontological Apperception Test to 96 males and females 65 and over. He analyzed their responses to determine how positive or negative their attitudes were toward aging and found that these attitudes were mediated by socio-economic and sex variables. Persons in the upper socio-economic classes[31] were significantly more positive toward the process of growing old than were those in the lower classes. The former portrayed old age in a largely optimistic fashion. The upper class males were significantly more optimistic than were the upper class females.[32] A number of studies have reported that older age groups are inclined to have more positive self-feelings than younger groups (e.g., Grant, 1967; Gurin, Veroff, & Feld, 1960; Parker & Kleiner, 1966).[33]

What do we find when we focus on studies specifically concerned with body perception in the aged? Two researchers (Back & Gergen, 1968; Gergen & Back, 1966) observed a number of years ago what they called "aging and the paradox of somatic concern." They explored a variety of statistics concerning the amounts of money and energy people devote to their own bodies at different age levels. They showed that the elderly were relatively low in their expenditures for clothing, in their frequency of seeking medical consultation and special health aids, and in their expenditures for items like cosmetics and hair preparations that are intended to improve bodily appearance. They also cited data indicating that when people were asked whether they would like to change their bodily features (e.g., weight, height), the elderly were least likely to want such change. Gergen and Back (1966) commented:

> The results seem to indicate that passage through the life cycle is highly associated with a lessened concern with one's body. . . . The most intriguing . . . aspect of the . . . findings is the implicit contradiction of commonsense expectations. Compensation for bodily deficiencies is a widespread phenomenon. The existence of entire business enterprises devoted to such activities as creating garments which emphasize or conceal parts of the body, producing cosmetics which conceal skin blemishes . . . is ample evidence of this fact. And yet, why should persons who are most in need of such compensatory measures tend to be the ones who adopt them least? (pp. 318–319)

They tried to answer this question by speculating that aging results in the constriction of one's "life space." They suggested (Back & Gergen, 1968): "When the environment offers few alternatives and little time for action the need for bodily care is to some extent obviated" (p. 246). That is, the aged individual who finds that at his or her stage in life the possibilities for action and energy output have been markedly reduced can presumably afford to be less concerned about the body as an effective agent.[34]

As mentioned, Plutchik et al. (1971, 1973a, 1973b) have provided us with particularly direct information about body image attitudes in the aged. They launched a project that diversely involved: (a) 29 senior citizens (16 male, 13 female) who were in their late 60s and 70s and who attended a community center for recreation purposes; (b) 20 residents (4 male, 16 female) of a Jewish home and hospital for elderly people (none with severe medical problems); (c) 20 female geriatric ex-mental patients who were living in a special residence home and who had had a diagnosis of psychosis; (d) 20 psychotic geriatric patients (11 male, 9 female) randomly selected from the geriatric wards of a state hospital; (e) 35 schizophrenic patients (17 male, 18 female) in a state hospital who were in their 30s and 40s; (f) 36 college students (22 male, 14 female) in their early 20s. Questionnaires were administered to these subjects to tap such variables as body satisfaction, body appearance, and body worries and discomforts.

Plutchik et al. (1971) reported the results of responses to inquiries concerned particularly with body worries and body discomfort. The nonpsychotic elderly subjects did not report more bodily discomfort than did the younger normal subjects. Plutchik et al. concluded: "It appears not to be the case, therefore, that the older one gets the more disturbed, distorted, or regressed is one's body image" (p. 349). Body discomfort and distortion proved to be significantly linked to psychological disturbance rather than age. This relationship was present primarily in the female samples. Females in general, reported more body discomfort than did males. Kelly (1978) administered the Plutchik et al. body worries and discomfort questionnaire to a sample of retired nuns ($N = 68$) and found no greater negative body feelings in those above the group's median age of 77 than in those below the median.

In another study Plutchik et al. (1973a) described their findings when the same subjects just mentioned were asked to rate their head on a series of Semantic Differential continua. The elderly subjects did not judge their head to be less good or potent or active than did the younger subjects. Most of the differences detected were in the direction of psychotic patients' perceiving the head more negatively. No gross sex differences were noted in the nonpsychotic samples.

Plutchik, Conte, and Bakur-Weiner (1973b) asked the same subjects to imagine that they had "lost" a number of specific body parts (e.g., eye, ear, nose, arm, foot) and then to imagine what monetary compensation they would request from an insurance company for each part. No relationship could be discerned between age and the value placed on any separate part or the total of parts. Interestingly, males generally placed a greater dollar value on their body parts than did the females. Psychiatric patients placed significantly lower values on their parts than did the non-psychiatric groups. The legs, eyes, and arms were generally considered to be of greatest value and the fingers and toes of least importance.

Body image attitudes in the aged were sampled by Phillips (1979), who administered the Fisher (1970) Body Distortion Questionnaire to 108 persons (54 men, 54 women) whose average age was about 70 years (range 60-87). The Body Distortion Questionnaire calls for reports of the degree to which one has experienced a variety of different forms of body distortion (e.g., feelings of depersonalization, sensations of body largeness or smallness, concern about body boundary loss). The values obtained by Phillips indicated that the total amount of body distortion in the aged subjects was not higher than that typifying a variety of younger normal groups studied by Fisher (1970). On the contrary, both the male and female aged obtained significantly lower distortion scores than do younger subjects. Phillips detected a significant inclination for the aged females to report significantly fewer distorted skin sensations than did the aged males. Phillips tried to link the total number and kinds of body distortions with the degree of spatial distance subjects preferred in their social relationships but found no significant correlations. Apropos of the matter of body distortion, one should also note that Furlong (1977) did not find a decline in accuracy of body size perception in women as they moved into their 50s and 60s.

McLean (1978) probed body and clothing satisfaction in 242 women distributed into seven groups varying in age from 20 to 89. The women were all living independently and actively participating in community affairs. They responded to the Body Cathexis Scale and to a Clothing Satisfaction scale. A trend appeared for those in the two youngest groups (ages 20-39) to express more body dissatisfaction than the women in the two oldest groups (70-89). However, overall, body satisfaction was not significantly associated with age. Essentially, the same results emerged with reference to satisfaction with one's clothing. McLean offered the following tentative explanation for the findings: "It was surmised that inability of the younger groups to attain the desired goal of the 'ideal figure' might account for a lower level of satisfaction, whereas the maintenance of physical capabilities by the older groups which allowed continued participation in activities could result in greater satisfaction" (p. 105).

There is no question that advanced age brings with it body infirmity and a decline in attractiveness as conventionally defined. At the same time, the available scientific data do not indicate a corresponding decline in self-appraisal or body satisfaction. It is also impressive that there is no increase in conscious death anxiety (e.g., Colon, 1981; Conte, Weiner, & Plutchik, 1982) attributable to aging. Both structured questionnaire responses and projective test responses have largely failed to establish a relationship between advanced aging and negative body feelings. Back and Gergen (1968) sought to explain this phenomenon by proposing that the limited "life space" of the older person makes fewer demands on the body as an effective instrument and therefore permits a relatively high level of body satisfaction. This remains a possibility that needs further testing. It is possible also that the extremely negative picture of body aging that is current in our culture is largely in the eye of the younger beholder. Younger observers (Goldman & Goldman, 1981) may react with alarm to the typical signs of old age as they encounter them in others because they portray transformations that could potentially occur in themselves. Suddenly the younger person is confronted with an image of what he or she could become. However, the aged person arrives at natural body transformations over a period of many years and has the opportunity to assimilate them gradually. From the "inside" perspective of the aged, being old may "feel" quite different. It is also possible that an increase in repressive defenses vis-a-vis one's body accompanies aging. This would parallel the observations (Fisher, 1970) that most people who develop body defects learn to adapt to them and to minimize their threatening connotations.

LONG-TERM BODY INCAPACITATION

Adults

What happens when a person experiences permanent incapacitation of an important body system or function? What are the body image implications of becoming a paraplegic or suffering heart damage that severely restricts activity or being a seriously affected diabetic? There is a vast literature concerned with the general psychological impact of somatic incapacitation. It is not the purpose of the present review to examine that literature, but rather to concentrate on information that has specific body image implications. In 1970 Fisher commented with regard to the "body disablement" literature then available: "Severe body disablement sometimes produces surprisingly little apparent effect upon the body concept. Whether this is partially a function of the insensitivity of the measuring devices remains to be seen. But it is probably even more a reflection of the ability of the individual to deny a transformation which is too threatening to acknowledge" (p. 79).

Let us appraise what has emerged from pertinent studies that have appeared subsequently. Shontz (1977), after an extensive review of the disability literature, concluded that the psychological consequences of body disablement were not proportional to the seriousness of the associated body damage. Indeed, he felt that the psychological impact of a body alteration was more likely to be linked to how suddenly it had occurred rather than to its severity. He commented that "negative emotional experiences . . . are sometimes associated with improvement in somatic status as well as with the onset of disability or disease" (p. 345).

Scattered studies have indicated that the process of experiencing certain forms of body disability registers perceptually and emotionally. Podietz (1974), applying a sensori-tonic perspective, examined the effects of idiopathic scoliosis (curvature of the spine) on the inclination of 82 adolescents to rotate the axis of a copied design away from the actual axis of the design as depicted on a stimulus card. He discovered that the degree of design rotation exhibited by the scolosis patients was significantly greater than that characterizing a normal group. Scoliotics do seem to translate their own distorted posture into a distortion of the position of objects in extrapersonal space. Similar spatial distortions have been reported in patients with paralysis of one side of the body (Fisher, 1970). Of related interest, Rustad (1975) observed, as predicted by sensori-tonic theory, that the greater the motor disablement of individuals, e.g., as defined by being a quadraplegic ($N = 29$) versus being a paraplegic ($N = 29$), the more they engaged in fantasy activity. Jasnos and Hakmiller (1975), in a study of 29 males with spinal damage, confirmed the results of previous work by Hohmann (1966), which established that the higher the level at which transection occurs in those with spinal injuries, the greater the loss in the intensity of their affective experiences. Presumably, the higher the level of the spinal transection, the more there is restriction of afferent return from peripheral physiological changes.[36] In this instance, the nature of the body disablement seems to alter the emotional texture of experience.[37]

The body image implications of spinal injury have received a fair amount of attention. Nelson and Gruver (1978) appraised three groups: hospitalized male spinal-cord injured patients ($N = 14$); hospitalized male tuberculosis patients ($N = 14$); and nonhospitalized, nondisabled males ($N = 14$). The subjects were administered the Draw-A-Person Test, and no differences could be detected between those with spinal injuries and the controls with reference to six Draw-A-Person scores that included an index of "body vulnerability." The paraplegics also did not differ from the controls on self-ratings of self-esteem. Mayer and Eisenberg (1982b) administered the Tennessee Self Concept Scale (based on self-ratings) to 45 spinal-cord-injured patients (males) and found that one of the derived scores ("physical self-esteem") was significantly lower in this group than in three different control groups (viz., unusually well-adjusted normals; normals with average adjustment; and psychiatric patients). Interestingly, although the spinal-cord patients were lower on physical self-esteem than all the controls, they were not lower than the psychiatric controls on a general index of self-esteem based on self-ratings.

Further data concerning this matter come from an investigation of paraplegics reported by Genskow (1967). He appraised three groups: 35 male college students who were paraplegics, 34 nondisabled college males, and 18 male paraplegics with no college experience. A large battery of procedures was administered: Draw-A-Person, Secord Homonym Test; Jourard and Secord Self Cathexis and Body Cathexis scales; Semantic Differential ratings of self and body; and several personality measures. Complex arrays of data emerged. Those pertinent to the present context may be summarized as follows:

1. The paraplegics evidenced significantly more body anxiety than did the nondisabled, as defined by self-ratings. However, there were no differences as defined by the Homonym test.

2. The paraplegics (via Semantic Differential ratings) judged their bodies to be significantly less potent, active, and positive than did the nondisabled.

3. Body esteem and self-esteem ratings were significantly positively correlated, but, contrary to prediction, the relationship was not lower in the paraplegics than in the nondisabled.

4. Nonbody concepts were rated higher than body concepts in all groups. However, the paraplegics exceeded the nondisabled in this respect.

5. There was an interesting trend for the paraplegics' Semantic Differential ratings of their figure drawings to be more like their ratings of "least liked" aspects of their own bodies, whereas the nondisabled ratings of the drawings were more like ratings of "my body." It appeared that the paraplegics were more likely to project negative body feelings in their figure drawings. A trend was also found in the paraplegics for degree of disturbance in their figure drawings to be positively correlated with how positively they rated their body on the Semantic Differential. This was not true in the nondisabled. One could interpret this finding to mean that the paraplegics were more inclined to make their conscious self-ratings in a more compensatory or denying fashion.

6. The figure drawings of the paraplegics could not be distinguished from those of the nondisabled.

Manganyi (1972) compared the figure drawings of 40 black male paraplegics in a South African hospital with those of 39 black normal controls. Using Witkin's et al. (1954) Sophistication-of-Body-Concept scoring technique, he could not detect a significant difference in the drawings. The Manganyi study and the forementioned Genskow (1967) and Nelson and Gruver (1978) studies concur that the paraplegics cannot be identified by the characteristics of their figure drawings.[38] An older study, by Wachs and Zaks (1960), also failed to demonstrate that figure drawings could distinguish between spinal injured patients and ambulatory patients with chronic diseases.[39] However, the accumulated data do indicate that when asked to rate their body paraplegics depict it relatively negatively.

One of the most novel and important investigations of body attitudes in the physically disabled was carried out by Ringe (1980). It involved 30 physically disabled (16 men, 14 women) and 30 able bodied (16 men, 14 women) college students. The disabled groups included those who were amputees, deaf, blind, paraplegic, and severely arthritic. Subjects were asked to rate 28 different body parts and concepts on Semantic Differential continua developed by Kurtz (1969). They also filled out a self-rating self-esteem scale. No differences emerged between the disabled and the able bodied in their Semantic Differential body ratings, and likewise there were no differences in general self-esteem. However, when the body ratings were factor analyzed, quite different item clusters appeared in the disabled as contrasted with the control group. The physically disabled were typified by four factors: facial appearance, lower extremities and mobility, body size and shape, and the manner in which a person walks. These clusters related to specific body parts or functions. In contrast, the clusters for the controls were more general and consisted of many body parts or constructs not linked by function or body area (viz., general body, body size and shape, body outline). Ringe (1980) said: "Whereas the physically disabled sample clearly viewed their bodies in a highly differentiated manner, the able-bodied expressed a more holistic gestalt" (p. 51). It is possible that the more differentiated pattern displayed by the disabled represents a defensive effort to localize the sphere of influence of any disabled body parts. That is, instead of conceiving of one's body as a total object that has good-bad or active-passive qualities and which therefore could, in an overall sense, be identified with an undesirable body defect, it is divided into zones whose boundaries limit the spread of effect from any one zone.[40]

It is apparent from the several studies reviewed above that one cannot easily generalize about whether adult disabled persons have low body esteem or distorted body perception. Figure drawing indices have revealed no consistent differences between the disabled and controls; although self-ratings in two of three studies have revealed more negative self-evaluations of body in disabled than in the nondisabled. The significant results emerged particularly in the comparisons involving paraplegics. Obviously, the data are too sparse and inconsistent to permit any reliable conclusions. However, the Ringe (1980) findings suggest that there are strategies the disabled can adopt that localize the impact of a body defect and limit the degree to which it affects one's general level of body esteem. Indeed, these strategies may actually block or eliminate the process of formulating an overall evaluation of one's own body.

Children and Adolescents

There is some evidence that children and adolescents whose bodies are severely impaired manifest more signs of maladjustment than do their nonimpaired peers (e.g., Harper, 1978; Harper & Richman, 1978; Steinhausen, 1981). However, there are also studies that fail to confirm this idea (e.g., Fisk, 1981; Kellerman, Zeltzer, Ellenberg, Dash, & Rigler, 1980). Similar conflicting observations have been made with regard to disabled adults (e.g., Cook, 1979; Viney & Westbrook, 1981). It is not surprising, then, that one is confronted with inconsistencies in the literature concerned with the impact of body disability upon the body image of children and adolescents.[41]

Fisher (1970) appraised the literature available up to 1970 concerning the body image alterations linked with body disablement in children. Most published studies were of the clinical anecdotal variety; he was able to find only a limited number of objective studies, and the results of those were usually on the negative side. One investigation (Offord & Aponte, 1967) could not significantly distinguish the figure drawings of Inside-of-the-Body drawings of children with congenital heart disease from those of a normal control group. Poeck and Orgass (1964), using a special battery of body image measures (e.g., identifying parts of one's body, making right-left distinctions), failed to differentiate a group of largely congenitally blind children from normal controls. Silverstein and Robinson (1956) did not find anything distinctive about the figure drawings of children disabled by polio. Similar negative findings with regard to figure drawings of disabled children were presented by Sims (1951), Corah and Corah (1963), Johnson and Wawrzaszek (1961), and Centers and Centers (1963). One study, by Wysocki and Whitney (1965), did show that the figure drawings of crippled children had significantly more areas of "insult" than those of normal children.

Since 1970 the figure drawing technique has almost ceased to be used in studies of body disabled children. However, certain variants of the technique have been applied. Weininger, Rotenberg, and Henry (1972) asked children to construct a human figure by means of a series of plastic parts and forms. Three groups of subjects participated: institutionalized spina bifida cases (N = 8), spina bifida cases living at home (N = 8), and normal nonhandicapped children living at home (N = 8). There were five girls and three boys in each group. The human figures constructed were scored for size and relative proportions of parts and also examined for omissions. No significant differences could be shown between the spina bifida children living at home and the nonhandicapped children. But the institutionalized children depicted the human figure as small, out of proportion, and with parts missing significantly more often than did either of the other two groups. The body experiences that typify a spina bifida were not sufficient to result in a distorted figure construction; only when the child had to undergo institutionalization did figure distortion occur. Weininger et al. conjectured that institutionalized children are exposed to experiences that make them withdraw, encapsulate themselves, and narrow their life space. The narrowing process was said to be reflected in the smallness of the figures they created.

Kinsbourne and Lempert (1980) had nine congenitally blind children and nine sighted children model a human figure with plasticene. There were five girls and four boys in each group. The blind children were tested once, and the controls were tested once with vision and once while blindfolded. The figures produced by the children were scored for several indices of realism. Sighted subjects, whether blindfolded or not, shaped the figures significantly more realistically than did the blind subjects. There was a trend for the blind to render the arms disproportionately long and wide. It was concluded that: "The pattern of results suggests that the congenitally blind build up a defective representation of the human body" (p. 36). It is apropos to note that Witkin, Birnbaum, Lomonaco, Lehr, and Herman (1968) discovered that human figures modeled with clay by blind children were significantly less differentiated and articulated than figures fashioned by sighted children. However, Witkin et al. found only a low nonsignificant correlation between articulation ratings of the clay figures and analogous ratings of figure drawings in the sighted sample.

Fraiberg and Adelson's (1973) detailed observations of blind babies are said to illustrate the difficulties of the congenitally blind in developing a sense of "I" and an integrated body scheme. They remarked: "The blind child has no sensory mode available to him which will immediately replicate his own body or body parts. The blind child is obliged to constitute a body image from the components of non-visual experiences available to him, not one of which will give him, through objective reference, the sum of his parts (p. 559). But neither Cratty and Sams (1968) nor Walker (1973) could find in the existing literature any clear evidence that blind children are particularly inferior in tasks calling for identification of body parts, discriminating right and left, and executing specific body movements. One can say only that when blind chldren are called upon to depict a human figure, they exhibit less realism and less differentiation than do the sighted.

A few other scattered studies have been published that relate to the body image of disabled children.[42] Sullivan (1979a, 1979b) obtained questionnaire replies from 105 female diabetic adolescents (ages 12-16) concerning their adjustment to their diabetes. One of six different adjustments areas covered by the questionnaire dealt with "body image concerns." Degree of body image concern had low significant relationships with several other scores indicative of difficulty in adapting to being a diabetic. It was the only score that was significantly related to age of onset of diabetes. The earlier the diabetes had occurred, the less was the reported body image anxiety.

Brantley and Clifford (1979A) secured the Witkin et al. (1954) rod-and-frame measure of field independence from 44 (20 male, 24 female) children with cleft palates and 61 normal controls (30 male, 31 female). The cleft palate children were significantly more field dependent.

Landon, Rosenfeld, Northcraft, and Lewiston (1980) evaluated the self-image of adolescents with cystic fibrosis. A questionnaire that taps several different dimensions of the self-image was administered to three classes of subjects: cystic fibrosis males ($N = 16$), cystic fibrosis females ($N = 8$), and several types of normal control groups. Subjects were all roughly in the 12-19 age range. The cystic fibrosis males had significantly higher scores indicative of negative body attitudes than did the subjects in the control group. However, no such differences appeared when the cystic fibrosis females were compared with their controls. One should also mention that Boyle, di Sant'Agnese, Sack, Millican, and Kulczycki (1976) analyzed impressionistically the figure drawings of 27 (18 male, 9 female) cystic fibrosis patients (13-30 years of age) and concluded that they evidenced a striking "denial of sexual differentiation."

Fisk (1981) used a variety of techniques to explore the body image attitudes of children ($N = 20$) with gross congenital facial deformities. The children ranged in age from 4 to 7. They were compared with a normal control group ($N = 20$). The body image measures that were employed were as follows: (a) children's figure drawings and drawings of the self; (b) analysis of the children's instructions to an artist as to how to draw their picture; (c) reactions of the children to four dolls depicting different kinds of body defects. Objective scoring systems were derived for each measure to depict apparent selectivity and concern with reference to the theme of body defect. None of the body image measures distinguished the facially deformed from the controls. An exploratory technique was also devised to determine if the parents of the deformed subjects displayed unusually anxious or defensive behavior with respect to their children's being photographed. Unusual defensiveness could not be demonstrated.

Uelmen (1978) obtained Semantic Differential type ratings of a series of silhouettes varying in degree of incapacitation: normal person, person in a wheelchair, person with crutches, person without arms. These ratings were secured during a summer camp session for developmentally physically handicapped children and adults (ages 7–45). There were 315 males and 285 females. It was assumed that the ratings of the silhouettes would provide meaningful information about how the subjects felt about their own disabled bodies. Analysis of the data indicated that the nature of the subject's own disabilities did not influence the ratings. Their disabilities were categorized in terms of whether they involved limited use of the arms, need for assistance with walking, use of a wheelchair, no visible disability, or none of these categories. Age also proved not to be significantly linked with ratings of the silhouettes. Further, no sex differences could be detected. Although the normal silhouette was evaluated more positively than were the disabled figures, the wheelchair and crutches figures were reacted to in a relatively positive fashion. The figure without arms was perceived most negatively. In view of past studies that have found correlations between Semantic Differential body ratings and age and sex, the absence of such correlations in the present study led Uelmen to speculate that body image formation in those who are disabled may differ from the pattern characterizing the nondisabled.

The aforementioned findings are vague and inconclusive. There are hints of the negative impact of body disablement in males with cystic fibrosis, but not in females (Landon et al., 1980). Children with cleft palates are inclined to be field dependent (less differentiated) (Brantley & Clifford, 1979a). Blind children make models of the human figure that are less differentiated than are those of the sighted (Kinsbourne & Lempert, 1980). At the same time, there is an array of past studies, cited earlier, based on figure drawings that have failed to register body image disturbances that might possibly be linked to diverse body pathologies like polio and heart disease. In the same vein, noninstitutionalized children with spina bifida cannot be distinguished from normal children by their human figure constructions (Weininger et al., 1972). Children with facial deformities (Fisk, 1981) cannot be differentiated from normal controls with respect to their figure drawings and a variety of other body image measures. Finally, even the occurrence of body image distortions in the blind has been challenged (e.g., Walker, 1973). The methods used to find out if children and adolescents with serious body disabilities suffer gross body image distortions have come up with little substantial evidence of such distortions.

BODY IMAGE AND ATTITUDES TOWARD THE DISABLED

This is an appropriate context in which to consider the reactions evoked in persons by interactions with those whose bodies are crippled or disabled. There is little doubt that the mere sight of a crippled or mutilated body is stressful to many people. Ample evidence of this reaction comes from Siller, Chipman, Ferguson, and Vann (1967), who interviewed nondisabled persons about how they feel in the presence of those with disabilities. In accounting for their uneasiness, the nondisabled offer many explanations: "gut reaction" aversion, fear that it could happen to oneself, empathic suffering by identifying with the disabled one, discomfort at being in the presence of someone who "looks different", and so forth. The anxiety evoked by the image of disability has also been revealed in perceptual and physiological indices. Noble, Price, and Gilder (1954) and Wittreich and Radcliffe (1955) have shown that an amputee viewed through aniseikonic lenses is perceived as less distorted than a normal figure. This phenomenon has been attributed to the fact that the greater one's anxiety about a stimulus viewed aniseikonically, the more one tries to stabilize the perceptual field in which it is embedded by excluding the lens induced distortions.

Congruent with many previous studies (e.g., Billings, 1963; Richardson & Royce, 1968), Richardson (1970) has accumulated data showing that negative responses to body disability occur at ages 5 and 6. Weinberg (1978) found bias against those with orthopedic disabilities in children even as early as age 4. In the Richardson study hundreds of children (ages 5–12) were asked to rank-order six pictures of children in terms of how much they "liked" them. The pictures were identical except that five of the pictured children had obvious physical handicaps (e.g., crutches and brace on leg, left arm missing) and one did not. At every age level except kindergarten, the child without the handicap was liked better than the handicapped ones.[43] Degree of rejection of the disabled increased with age. The same negative response to the disabled child was manifested by the parents of the children who participated in the investigation. The girls who were studied were particularly likely to be negative toward pictured figures that had cosmetic defects (viz., facial disfigurement), whereas the boys were most negative toward figures with "functional handicaps" (viz., child with crutch and leg brace, child in wheelchair, child with hand amputation).

Previous work has shown the same sex difference pattern (Chigier &

Chigier, 1968; Richardson, Goodman, Hastorf, & Dornbusch, 1961). There were suggestions in the Richardson data that from the age of 9 females were generally more influenced in their preferences by the presence of body defects than were the males. Richardson speculated: "The greater importance for females of physical appearance in judging others may be related to the greater role that physical appearance plays in social life and marriage for females than for males" (p. 213). Richardson speculated that the general negative impact of the pictured figures portraying physical defects might, to an important degree, be due to the fact that "discrepancy from the familiar may well arouse anxiety and fear and lead to dislike" (p. 212). That is, a figure with a body defect could be disturbing simply as a function of its departure from what one ordinarily expects. Richardson pointed out that Kagan had observed that babies as young as 8 months showed anxiety when responding to a model human face on which the parts were disarranged but did not display anxiety when reacting to a model of a normal face.

One particularly well-done study undertook to find out more about the role of novelty in the negative responses evoked by physical disability. Langer, Fiske, Taylor, and Chanowitz (1976) reasoned that if novelty and unexpected difference are major components in the negative avoidant responses of the nondisabled to the disabled, it should be possible to decrease the avoidant behavior by giving the nondisabled a preliminary opportunity to become acquainted with the disabled, to scan them until they are no longer an unexpected novelty. In an experiment involving 36 females and 36 males, they permitted some subjects to view an apparently crippled, pregnant, or normal woman prior to meeting her; other subjects did not have a prior opportunity to decrease the novelty of the person as a stimulus. Those with the chance for preliminary scanning later sat significantly closer to the women with the body "defect" than did those who lacked the preliminary scanning experience. When subjects did not have the chance for preliminary scanning, they sat significantly closer to the normal than to the body deviant woman. However, this difference was not apparent for subjects who engaged in preliminary scanning. Langer et al. pointed out that any theory suggesting that the nondisabled avoid the bodily deviant because of disgust or fear would have to explain why getting a good look at the disabled in advance apparently renders them less threatening. To bolster their case, they cite previous work in which not only was no derogation of the physically stigmatized by nondisabled persons observed, but a contrary tendency to evaluate the stigmatized ones favorably was found (Kleck, 1968). At this point it is apropos to call attention to a study by Mitchell (1975). He divided a sample of college students ($N = 279$) into two groups. One viewed a videotaped recording of a counselor seated in a wheelchair during a session with a client. The second viewed a similar recording, but the counselor's wheelchair could not be seen. The counselor in the wheelchair was perceived significantly more favorably than when apparently not in a wheelchair, with respect to empathic understanding, positive regard, and congruence. Incidentally, the subjects had filled out a body cathexis scale and there was no relationship between their body esteem and their ratings of the counselor in the wheelchair. In any case, explanation is required for the preference for the apparently disabled counselor, the mere sight of whom is supposed to evoke negative feelings.

Other studies have highlighted the fact that the disabled can evoke apparently positive responses. For example, Bolstad (1974) reported, on the basis of observation of family behavior in the home, that orthopedically handicapped children were not treated in a more negative or deprecating fashion by their parents than were their nondisabled sibs. Zahn (1973) concluded after a study of 2454 randomly selected applicants for disability benefits that "sickness or disability are associated with better interpersonal relations" and "among the younger age group the visibly impaired tend to get along better in interpersonal relations than did the non-visibly impaired" (p. 115). It is becoming apparent that how the physically disabled are perceived is considerably more complex than has been supposed. True, the sight of a crippled body stirs anxiety in the nondisabled observer. Perhaps, though, it may also stir sympathetic identification, guilty overcompensatory niceness, and even fascinated preoccupation with the threat portrayed.

There is a long list of variables mediating how negatively or positively individual persons react to the sight of the defective body. English (1971a) and Yuker, Block, and Younng (1966) have extracted evidence from the literature that such reactions are influenced by demographic variables such as education, sex, occupation,[44] religion, and socio-economic status. In addition, personality and attitudinal factors like aggression, intraception, anxiety, internal-external locus of control,[45] and ethnocentrism have proven to be significant mediators.[46] The details of the literature concerned with such mediating variables will not be reviewed here. They are intriguing, but not directly pertinent to the task of analyzing the role of body image in shaping attitudes toward body defect and disablement. In 1970 Fisher was able to find only a few studies (e.g., Epstein & Shontz, 1962; Jabin, 1965; Masson, 1963) that dealt with this matter. These studies suggested in a weak fashion that those who feel negatively about their own bodies tend to feel negatively about the bodies of the disabled.

One study that Fisher overlooked in his original review was by Siller et al. (1967). It involved 65 high school and college students (27 males, 38 females). Their attitudes toward the disabled were measured with several different techniques. A wide range of personality measures was administered, including three with specific body image significance: (a) Rorschach indices developed by Landis (1963) that tap degree of boundary permeability and impermeability and bear some resemblance to the Fisher-Cleveland (1968) Barrier and Penetration scores that measure body boundary articulation; (b) a Thematic Apperception Test index developed by Schwartz (1955) to evaluate Castration Anxiety; (c) a Draw-A-Person measure that is vaguely defined as tapping several dimensions like integration and sexual differentiation. All these indices demonstrated small but significant correlations with specific aspects of attitudes toward the disabled. More favorable attitudes were linked with low boundary permeability, low castration anxiety, and superior Draw-A-Person qualities. That is, a more positive orientation to the disabled seemed to be linked to more stable, secure body image attributes.

The possible influence of boundary security on attitudes toward the disabled was affirmed in a study by Reisfeld (1984). He appraised 298 children, ages 8–15. Their attitudes toward the disabled were measured with a Semantic Differential technique. Barrier scores were obtained by means of the Holtzman Inkblots. When analyses of the data were undertaken that partialed out the effects of age, sex, and their interaction, is was found that the higher the children's Barrier scores, the more likely the children were to recognize appearance differences in the disabled and to express positive attitudes with respect to potential intimate relationships with them.

Reinforcement of the findings pertaining to castration anxiety has been provided by Fine (1978). He asked 83 boys and 42 girls (ages 3-5) to apply adjectives to pictures of children, some of normal appearance and some portrayed as physically deviant (missing an arm). He selected out 20 children (13 boys, 7 girls) who proved, as defined by their age and their selectively high frequently of application of negative adjectives to the disabled figures, to be early discriminators of body deviance. He also administered a children's Thematic Apperception Test to all the subjects and had the projective stories scored for the presence of castration imagery (e.g., damage to or loss of body parts). Analysis of the data indicated, as predicted, that castration anxiety was significantly higher in the early discriminators than in the remainder of the sample. Also, there was a significant positive correlation in the total sample between degree of negative evaluation of physical deviance and the castration anxiety scores.

Further reinforcement of the castration anxiety findings has come from the work of Follansbee (1981). She studied 100 male college students and measured their level of castration anxiety by means of a quantitative scoring system applied to TAT stories they wrote. After being exposed to a stressful film, half of the group responded to a questionnaire that measured attitudes toward disability. The other half did so after a neutral activity. It was predicted that the castration film would increase negativity of attitudes toward the disabled. The data did not support the prediction. However, it was found (at a significant level) that the greater the degree of castration anxiety, as defined by the TAT, the more unfavorable were the attitudes toward the disabled. Incidentally, a measure of maturity of object representation derived from a quantitative analysis of several of each subject's dreams was negatively related to unfavorableness toward the disabled.

Cassell (1974) conceptualized persons as differing in the degree to which they feel threatened by the possibility of being personally disabled and devised an Attitudes Toward Personal Disability Scale to measure this parameter. He was able to establish in a sample of 162 college students that the greater such a sense of personal threat, the more negative were attitudes toward other persons with disabilities. He also found evidence that humor about body disablement served defensive functions for those both high and low in their fear of personal disablement. In situations where there was exposure to stimuli with body disablement connotations, those persons most anxious about personally becoming disabled reacted most positively to humor depicting body threat. Apparently, the humor serves to defend against the threat.

Gladstone (1976) tested the hypothesis that the more intense are persons' fears of danger to the self, the more rejecting they would be of the physically handicapped. A total of 163 college students (78 male, 85 female) were evaluated. Their defense styles were measured by means of a Defense Mechanisms Inventory. In addition, their tolerance for pain was ascertained in relation to their responses to pressure applied by means of a blood pressure cuff. When anxiety about threat was determined in terms of "defensiveness," as defined by the Defense Mechanisms Inventory, it was found to be significantly positively linked with difficulty in tolerating pain and with negativity toward the disabled. Unusual inclinations to use defense mechanisms based on turning aggression either outward or inward were positively and significantly linked with bias against the disabled. However, degree of pain tolerance was not predictive of attitudes toward the disabled.

Henry (1976) explored the hypothesis that evaluative attitudes toward one's own physique and the importance attached to one's own physical appearance interact to shape attitudes toward disabled persons. A questionnaire was designed to measure valuing processes toward three aspects of self: own physical appearance, own intelligence, own work performance. These three aspects proved to be significantly interrelated, and the possibility was raised that this relationship was due to a social desirability attitude. The greater the apparent preoccupation of individuals with how their self attributes compared with those of other persons, the more negative they were toward the cosmetically disabled. But the greater the inclination to value self attributes for their own sake without utilizing a standard, the more positive individuals were toward the disabled.

Relatedly, Cormack (1966) tested the hypothesis that the greater the discomfort persons manifest with regard to their body, the more negative are their attitudes toward the visibly disabled. The subjects were 194 male and 124 female college students. Their degree of body discomfort ("body dissonance") was assayed by comparing their actual and their ideal body evaluations. The discomfort index proved to be significantly positively correlated with degree of negativity toward the disabled as derived from a questionnaire (Attitude Toward Cripples).

Although the findings are still sparse, they do reinforce the impression that some of the variance in negative responses to the disabled derives from how secure one feels about one's own body. It appears that a sense of body vulnerability induces sensitivity about phenomena that dramatize the susceptibility of the body to damage. The sight of another person with a crippled or defective body arouses alarm and seems to result in a defensive, rejecting attitude toward that body. However, the magnitude of this effect is probably quite small and overshadowed by variables like education, sex, and amount of personal contact with the disabled.

OVERVIEW

We have examined the body image literature to ascertain what is known about the impact of a variety of body stressors that people normally encounter in the course of living. The pertinent literature is often disappointing. In some instances, there are only a few contradictory sets of findings, and all too often measures were employed simply because they are conveniently easy to administer. However, this is not an atypical state of affairs in almost any literature review one undertakes. In any case, it is surprising how little attention has been paid the body image aspects of such universally important phenomena as aging and long-term body incapacitation. In the instance of aging, there are literally only a half dozen or so efforts that deserve to be called research investigations. The need for a program of inquiry in this area is obvious.

When the body is severely breached, pain and other negative sensations are aroused that alter the usual "feel" of the body milieu. The body suddenly feels different and takes on a new relationship to self. Observers of surgical patients have noted that these individuals become uncertain about their bodies and fear loss of control. Of special interest is that the intensity of the sensations and anxiety linked to the threatened or disabled body region results in a segmentation of body perception.[47] One body region seems to become extraordinarily prominent, and other regions are atypically subordinated. Green (1976) stated that a great deal of the postoperative energy of boys hospitalized for appendectomies went into coping with feelings of body strangeness and trying to restore a sense of body wholeness as represented by the somatic experiential pattern that existed prior to body deformation. One has to learn to make sense of the sick or wounded body. There is evidence that the degree of difficulty one has in coping with negative body alterations can be predicted from one's usual level of body security and the intensity of one's anticipatory anxiety about the alterations.

It is not easy to generalize about the data that have been reviewed across the multiple categories of body stress. Perhaps the major impression to emerge is that the body image is a sturdy structure. People seem to adapt well to extreme forms of body disablement, disfigurement, and change. It is difficult to detect body image alterations even in persons with crippling body defects. Denial and repression seem to be major defenses in restoring body image equilibrium after severe body damage has occurred. Use of denial has been particularly well documented in the case of patients with disfiguring burns. One is reminded too of Polivy's (1977) surprising observation that women who suffer a mastectomy do not manifest any immediate decline in body esteem, but do some time later. Their immediate response is to act as if the body were still intact. Some people with body injuries struggle and have difficulties for a considerable time as they try to reintegrate. Phantom experiences linked to loss of body parts may reflect just such defensive efforts. Thus, there are suggestions that women who perceive the loss of a breast as especially threatening to certain of their relationships are likely to experience a breast phantom, that is, to perceive themselves as if they had not been deprived of the breast. In some instances the phantom persists for a long period and takes on an insistent, even painful quality. It is difficult to avoid the impression that this phenomenon represents, in part, an effort at magical denial and substitution. The possibility has been raised that body areas may actually differ in the degree to which they lend themselves to the expression of psychological defenses via phantom representations. Extremities—the arms and legs—may be less available for psychologically based phantom depictions than are body areas like the breasts.

Additional comment should be made about body image adaptation to body injury that involves isolating or zoning off the affected part. It will be recalled that Ringe (1980) found that persons with serious body disablements were more likely than the normal uninjured to conceptualize their bodies in terms of bounded functional zones. Several other studies have shown that although self-esteem is significantly positively correlated with body esteem in the uninjured, it has only chance correlations in seriously disabled samples. It appears that the disabled exclude the negative body elements from their overall evaluations of self and therefore isolate them. Surprisingly pertinent to this issue is the fact that body attitudes are tied to attitudes toward others whose bodies are disabled. Persons who seem not to be comfortable with their own bodies are particularly likely to be negative toward those with disabled bodies. This phenomenon may be a defensive effort to deny one's own body negativity and to put it off on other convenient body targets. Such a projection strategy could be said to exclude and minimize the salience of one's own body in the context of the highlighted badness of the bodies of those with obvious body defects. A related phenomenon has been described by Fisher (1978c), who found that those who experience their own bodies as dirty and anally contaminated are particularly likely to appraise the identity of the black person in negative terms. Indirectly pertinent to this issue is recent research showing that persons who use denying defenses cope better with the stress of surgery than do those who are sensitizers. There is a paradoxical realism in the use of denial to defend against one's own body defects. After all, body defects and required body revisions simply confront one as unavoidable threats. Perhaps the most realistic thing to do is to minimize their prominence and try to exclude them from one's perception of self.

Certain of the questions addressed at the beginning of this chapter can be answered from the available literature while others cannot. One question that was raised was whether the disturbance produced in the body image by body damage is proportional to the amount of damage. The answer is probably no. It has not been possible to show that people with extreme forms of body disablement, like quadraplegia or grossly disfiguring burns, evidence more body image disturbance than do persons with lesser disabilities. Shontz (1977) arrived at a similar conclusion; he could find no evidence that the psychological consequences of body disablement are proportional to the associated body damage. Some studies (e.g., MacGregor et al., 1953) have even hinted that people with borderline defects are more disturbed about their appearance than are those with obvious defects. The presence of an obvious defect may somehow hasten or even facilitate the process of adaptation. The ambiguity of a borderline body defect may paradoxically intensify attention upon one's own body in order to define how apparent the defect is and whether it is of real consequence. But people with obvious defects can perhaps move at once to institute containing strategies.

A second question posed initially was whether certain dimensions of the body image are more vulnerable to the impact of body damage than are others. A meaningful answer cannot be provided. This is simply due to the fact that no systematic attempts have been made to look at multiple aspects of the body image in those with body defects. Most studies have relied on one or two measures at most. In those few instances where comparisons can be made of studies that have looked at a particular body defect by means of different body image measures the results are difficult to interpret because there are confounding differences related to duration of body disablement, sex composition of the samples, and the context in which the subjects were evaluated.

A third question was whether there are consistent sex differences in mode of adaptation to body stress. No such consistencies have appeared. In his 1970 review of the pertinent literature, Fisher thought there was evidence that females adapted better to body stress than males. However, this has not been supported by studies of surgery, aging, or severe body disablement. Shifting and incongruent findings have emerged. Women have been observed in several studies (Yuker et al., 1966) to be less unfavorable in their responses to the disabled than are men. This has been ascribed to the greater inclination of women to be nurturant and sympathetic with those who are suffering or in need of help.

As one wanders through the research literature concerned with the effects of body stressors, one sees again and again how little energy has gone into examining body image aspects. Since 1970 few studies have been directly concerned with body image variables within each of the topic areas reviewed. It is true that in one or two areas, for example, the impact of body disability on children, there have been as many as fifteen papers. However, few or no body image investigations have been completed with respect to the stresses resulting from surgery or being severely burned or receiving an organ transplant. Further, body image probes of phantom phenomena have been confined largely to the one category of breast phantoms.

Even where body image dimensions have been explored, one cannot help being puzzled by the choice of measurement techniques. As indicated earlier, it often seems that the choice was dictated primarily by the ease or simplicity of administration. The favorites are brief questionnaires that presumably tap "body esteem," Semantic Differential ratings of body parts, and the Draw-A-Person Test. Seldom are more complex procedures—body size estimation, aniseikonic perception of one's mirror image, or judging one's bodily position in space—employed. Yet such procedures would seem to hold promise of teasing out the body image changes that occur as the body is threatened. For example, previous work (Fink & Shontz, 1960) has suggested that injured body areas may appear to change in size; and it would certainly be interesting to explore whether body areas that have been the site of surgery change in their perceived size characteristics. Similarly, in view of the proven sensitivity of aniseikonic lens perception of one's mirror image to the effects of bodily injury and threat (Fisher & Richter, 1969; Magee & Fisher, 1971), it would appear to be ideal for investigating the localized buildups of anxiety in body regions that have suffered disfigurement or surgical revision. We need to apply a variety of such measurement techniques to get at the full complexity of the effects of stress on body perception. Only then will we be able to construct body image models that go beyond one-dimensional simplicity.

NOTES

[1] Body image attitudes have been implicated in patient delay in seeking treatment and in noncompliance with treatment. For example, Bille (1975) demonstrated that patients who had suffered a myocardial infarction showed a significant positive correlation between favorable body feeling (as defined by the Jourard-Secord Body Cathexis scale) and compliance with posthospital prescriptions.

[2] Trait anxiety, in contrast to state anxiety, has consistently been observed not to be affected by the surgical experience.

[3] Anxiety linked with hospitalization is mediated by a considerable array of variables. It varies not only with parameters like age and sex, but also with the seriousness of the illness and the size of the hospital in which treatment occurs. Lucente and Fleck (1972) reported that anxiety was higher in hospitalized female patients than in male patients, higher in hospitalized blacks than in whites, higher in

patients in university hospitals than in small community hospitals, and so forth. Tsushima (1968) found that Italian patients reported more preoperative signs of emotional tension than did Irish patients.

[4] Feldman (1975) illustrated with a case presentation the potential value of the repertory grid technique for exploring body attitudes.

[5] Female patients tended to be more anxious preoperatively than did the males. However, not only were there gross differences in the types of surgery performed on the two sexes, but there were uncontrolled differences in how long they had been in the hospital before they rated their degree of anxiety.

[6] Johnson (1973) studied the effects of various forms of preparatory information on the distress levels of college students who later submitted to a pain-inducing procedure. He concluded that Janis' (1958) assumption "that an optimum amount of fear before the threatening event results in low distress during the encounter with the event does not explain the findings in these experiments. The messages about what to expect did not differentially affect fear levels in either experiment" (p. 271).

[7] No sex differences in anxiety were observed. Generally, since 1970 the few studies comparing surgical anxiety in males and females have found either a slightly greater level in females or no differences at all.

[8] Wilson (1982) reported that women who were inclined to be aggressive (as defined by their responses to a defense mechanism inventory) manifested more postoperative difficulties than did relatively nonaggressive women.

[9] After reanalyzing Janis' (1958) data, Vernon and Bigelow (1974) expressed skepticism about whether his original deductions concerning the curvilinear anxiety model were justified.

[10] Body image disturbance has been observed in patients undergoing kidney dialysis (Basch, Brown, & Cantor, 1981; Pollak, 1980). However, the measurement techniques employed have been relatively crude.

[11] Similarly, Cleveland and Johnson (1970) reported that persons who indicated, in response to a questionnaire, that they would in the future be willing to be organ donors had significantly higher educational levels than those unwilling to do so. Also, Claxton (1974) could detect no correlation between favoring organ donation and death anxiety.

[12] Marbach (1978) has even described a "phantom bite syndrome," which refers to an illusory perfect dental bite that people feel they have lost and seek to recover by frequent consultations with dentists.

[13] As summarized by Fisher (1970), such factors as cephalocauded location or sensory sensitivity of a stump may influence the appearance and also the disappearance of the phantom.

[14] Sands (1981) did not discern a significant relationship between self-ratings of body satisfaction and alertness to the possible signs of breast cancer (as represented by regular self-examination).

[15] A number of studies have focused on the psychological effects of mastectomy (e.g., DeSantis, 1979; J. M. Goin & M. K. Goin, 1981; Long, 1975; McDonough, 1979; Polivy, 1977; Ray, 1977; Ryan, 1978). They, of course, universally found that the removal of a breast is extremely disturbing, often more seriously threatening than other forms of surgery. Polivy (1977) discerned a particularly interesting pattern in the adaptation of women to breast removal, compared with women with negative breast biopsies and another group of women admitted to the hospital for noncancerous

surgery. She administered the Berscheid et al. (1973) measure of body satisfaction (among other measures) 1 day before surgery, 6 days after surgery, and 6 to 11 months later. Her findings indicated that immediately after surgery there was no change in mastectomy patients' body esteem. However, considerably later, a significant decline in body esteem occurred. This contrasted with a tendency for the negative biopsy patients to show body esteem decline only immediately after the biopsy procedure and for the general surgical patients to exhibit no change. The results were interpreted to mean that the mastectomy patients had maximum need to deny any changes in their bodies immediately after surgery but that "over time . . . this denial is broken down by the reality of the loss, and self-image reflects this" (p. 86). Partially supportive of Polivy was Long's (1975) observation of an increase rather than a decrease in esteem 2 weeks following mastectomy in 26 women. But Ryan (1978) and McDonough (1979) could not confirm a pattern of delayed decline in feelings about self and body in mastectomy patients. Cofer (1980), who used the same Berscheid et al. (1973) measure of body image that Polivy employed, found that approximately 5 years after mastectomy her subjects could not be distinguished from normal controls. The issue of how mastectomy patients adapt to their breast loss over time remains open to further investigation.

Daoud (1976) probed the impact of the loss of the uterus as the result of hysterectomy. He found a significantly lowered level of body satisfaction up to 14 weeks after the loss. There was also a considerable elevation of depression during this same period. Anxious awareness of the body (as defined by the Secord Homonym Test) was at its highest point just before surgery and declined progressively postoperatively.

[16]Generally, the occurrence of phantom sensations is considerably less for nonskeletal amputated body parts such as testis (22%) or penis (58%) than for amputated limbs (Weinstein et al., 1970).

[17]Little is known about the link between body image and pain. It has been shown that persons with well-articulated body boundaries have a relatively high tolerance for pain (Nichols & Tursky, 1967). Also, Armentrout (1979) discerned significantly lower ratings of body esteem in hospitalized patients with chronic pain than in hospitalized patients without a chronic pain problem. Attempts to relate pain tolerance to field independence and to hypochrondriacal tendencies (Dworkin, 1969) have not been promising, and there have as yet been no consistent demonstrations of correlations between pain experiences and personality variables (Bond, 1973; Davidson & Bobey, 1970; Davidson & McDougall, 1969b; Lynn & Eysenck, 1961; Parbrook, Dalrymple, & Steel, 1973; Schalling, 1971; Timmermans & Sternbach, 1974).

[18]Melzack and Bromage (1973) have artifically produced phantom-like experiences by inducing anesthetic block of the sensory and motor nerves of the arm. The perceived positions of the phantoms were analogous to those often ascribed to the arm after amputation or paraplegia. It is pertinent that Gross, Webb, and Melzack (1974) found that, when subjects were asked to identify the apparent position of their hand and arm, which were concealed from view, the "upper limb" is systematically perceived to be closer to the midline of the body on the right-left dimension, and closer to the body on the near-far dimension than it really is" (p. 346). The pertinence lies in the fact that just such "biases" are often found in the positions attributed to the phantom arm. Gross et al. also reported that the sensory qualities (e.g., heavy, warm,

tingling) ascribed to the concealed arm resemble those apparently linked with phantoms.

[19] There are equivocal data concerning the effects upon the body image of transition from the premenarcheal to postmenarcheal development phase. Two previously cited studies (Koff et al., 1978; Rierdan & Koff, 1980a) detected a significant trend for figure drawings to become more sexually differentiated as girls made this transition. But Thorbeck (1978) failed to find differences in the Witkin et al. (1954) Articulation of Body Concept score for girls in pre versus postmenarcheal categories.

[20] The relationship between body boundary articulation and menstrual experiences is explored in detail in a later chapter.

[21] Fisher (1973c) has reviewed data suggesting the possibility that the repetitive menstrual experience may have stabilizing effects.

[22] Gillman (1973) has shown that the manifest content of the dreams of pregnant women reflects their heightened concern about potential harm to the fetus.

[23] Fawcett (1976), using a relatively gross estimation method, found that not only did pregnant women show a decrease in their perceived body size from the last trimester to the postpartum period, but this was also true of their husbands' self perceptions. The implication is, of course, that husbands somehow share in the body changes experienced by their wives during the pregnancy sequence. No changes were detected in the figure drawings (as defined by the Witkin, et al., 1954, Articulation-of-Body-Concept Scale) of either the wives or husbands in the course of this sequence.

[24] Several studies suggest that body image variables, such as degree of body satisfaction, may play a role in choice of contraceptives (Drucker, 1975; Young, 1981). But McCormick (1978) reported no difference between pill and diaphragm users with respect to body anxiety (as defined by interview ratings) and body awareness (as defined by the Secord Homonym Test). She also detected no relationship between Homonym scores and number of side effects associated with the pill.

[25] Kirschner (1975) discovered that pregnant women who differ with regard to whether they choose or do not choose to receive Lamaze (natural childbirth) training for the delivery also differ in degree of anxious body concern. Body anxiety was measured with the Homonym Test of Body Cathexis (Secord, 1953). Choosers of the training received Homonym scores in the middle range, which is said to be linked with a "healthier moderate level of body concern" (p. 94).

[26] Harris (1979) reported a number of cultural differences with respect to changes in Body Distortion Questionnaire scores during and after pregnancy. That is, she observed differences among black, Cuban, and white subjects. For example, whereas total body distortions reported by the Cubans and blacks peaked at 9 months, they were unusually low at that point for the whites.

[27] These findings seem to contradict three previously cited studies, two (Carty, 1970; Leifer, 1977) that reported a relatively high degree of body dissatisfaction in the postpartum period and one (Venezia, 1972) that could discern no change in body satisfaction from the 3rd trimester to postdelivery. It is obvious that having distorted body experiences does not necessarily lead to body dissatisfaction. Likewise, body dissatisfaction can occur in the absence of distorted body experiences. Thus, it is possible that a pregnant woman could realistically perceive a variety of unusual alterations in her body but simply assimilate these alterations into her identification with the role of being pregnant and not feel markedly anxious or dissatisfied about

them. With regard to the body dissatisfaction that is apparently common in the postpartum period, Fisher (1973c) has suggested that it may be, in part, a reaction to the abruptness of the change in body size and shape resulting from the delivery of the baby. Perhaps any sudden gross body change is viewed negatively, even if it has positive enhancing connotations.

[28] There are changes in the body image boundary linked with pregnancy that are discussed at a later point.

[29] Greenberg and Fisher (1983) have also demonstrated a significant increase in phallic imagery in pregnant women.

[30] Hayslip, Jr. (1982) found in a sample of men and women (N = 104) who ranged in age from 54 to 94 that those above the age of 67 obtained significantly lower Barrier scores than did those below that median. It is possible, then, that some decline in Barrier occurs once persons enter their 70s, 80s, and 90s.

[31] Kaplan and Pokorny (1970) reported that positive self-feelings in the aged are particularly enhanced in situations where stress and life demands decrease in intensity.

[32] Howe (1973) found complex sex differences in both evaluation of self and one's body in persons along the age continuum. Such sex differences have also been described by Back (1971).

[33] Herzog, Rodgers, and Woodworth (1982) have analyzed a considerable amount of old and new data concerning the apparent increase in "subjective well being" that accompanies aging. They indicated that this was, indeed, a solid phenomenon. They granted that it might be, in part, an artifact of a tendency on the part of the elderly to give "socially desirable" or "acquiescent" responses to questionnaires. However, they concluded that it is probably more strongly a reflection of the "diminishing stress in later years that presumably results from fewer major life events such as marriage or divorce, change of job or residence, birth of a child, loss of spouse or friend, or unemployment" (p. 37). They also found evidence that elderly persons' greater religiosity and longer period of familiarity with their environment contributed to higher level of satisfaction and comfort. Interestingly, they discovered that illness was just as upsetting to younger persons as to the aged. They concluded: "Health satisfaction has little impact on the subjective well-being of the older age group despite many suggestions in the literature . . . indicating that this is an important determinant of subjective well-being for older people" (p. 89).

[34] Kaplan (1971) measured feelings of self-derogation in 500 individuals varying in age and discovered that those in their 50s who were most extensively involved with the environment were not most self-derogatory. Indeed, he found just the reverse to be true. In a sample of 60-year-olds, there was no relationship at all between degree of environmental involvement and feelings of self-derogation. Such data do, of course, raise questions about the Back and Gergen (1968) perspective.

[35] His perspective has been disputed by Weiss, Fishman, and Krause (1971), who reported that above-knee amputees (N = 56) were more negatively affected psychologically than were below-knee amputees (N = 44). Inasmuch as above-knee amputation represents the more severe form of disablement, they considered that their findings demonstrated a link between degree of disablement and negative psychological consequences. Some studies (e.g., Barton & Cattell, 1972) have shown that those who endure a major long-term illness do evidence personality changes.

[36] Cassell (1976) analyzed the recorded language of patient-doctor interactions and

concluded that there is a tendency for both physician and patient to depersonalize affected body areas.

[37] Fisher (1972) demonstrated that the specific site of body injury or disablement may selectively affective perception of dynamic themes linked with such sites. More is said concerning this finding at a later point.

[38] There have been contradictory reports as to whether figure drawings are, in general, sensitive to body defects. After a review of the literature up to 1970, Fisher (1970) concluded that figure drawings are not usually sensitive indicators of the presence of real body distortions. In 1972, Johnson observed that although patients with paralysis due to poliomyelitis draw smaller figures than did controls, their drawings were not characterized by more distortions. However, Genskow (1967) did not find that patients paralyzed by poliomyelitis produced unusually small figure drawings. Brumback, Bertorini, and Liberman (1978) found only borderline trends for patients with neuromuscular diseases to produce Inside-of-the-Body drawings that differed from those obtained from normal subjects. Dines (1982) reported no significant differences between the figure drawings of adolescent amputees and those of normal controls.

[39] Arnhoff and Mehl (1963) reported that paraplegics were significantly less accurate than normal controls in estimating their shoulder width. Arnhoff and Mehl observed too that paraplegics did not differ from normals in accuracy of estimating the width of a wheelchair. However, the former overestimated, whereas the latter underestimated, the wheelchair size. It is tangentially pertinent that Antler, Lee, Zaretsky, Pezenik, and Halberstam (1969) found in a sample of rehabilitation patients (including a number of paraplegics) that the greater the body impairment, the less positive was the attitude toward the wheelchair. These findings suggest the possibility that body image attitudes may spread to include the appliances patients use to compensate for their disablement. Hartung (1974) found body image changes in disabled persons as a function of substituting one type of brace for another.

[40] Wittreich (cited in Fisher & Cleveland, 1968) found that when schizophrenics and normal controls were asked to view themselves in a mirror while wearing aniseikonic lenses, the former were inclined to see overall lens-induced changes in their appearance, whereas the latter tended to see changes in localized body areas. This analog is obviously reversed in its directionality, but it does point up possible variations in the degree to which "zoning" of body areas may occur in adapting to different kinds of threats and disruptions.

[41] Nash (1982) has studied in considerable detail how normal children respond to pictures of distorted figures that are blends of human and animal forms ("hybrids"). He has analyzed the various cognitive strategies used to deal with the contradictions posed by such distorted (malformed) figures.

[42] Surprisingly, although there have been a number of studies (e.g., Darling, 1979;Decarie, 1969; McFie & Robertson, 1973) of children with severe body defects due to their mothers having taken Thalidomide during pregnancy, no systematic observations have been made of the impact of the defects upon the body image.

[43] Katz, Katz, and Cohen (1976) have published a contradictory finding. They evaluated responses of white children (kindergarten and 4th grade) to white and black examiners portrayed as disabled or nondisabled. Although the responses were influenced by the racial identity of the examiner, they were not significantly affected by whether or not the examiner was disabled. Of course, the Richardson (1970) study

differed from this study in many ways, including the fact that the Richardson subjects responded to the stimulus of disabled and nondisabled children, whereas the Katz et al. subjects responded to the stimulus of disabled and nondisabled adults.

[44] English and Oberle (1971) discovered that persons in occupations that place a high emphasis on physique are strongly rejecting of the physically disabled. For example, female flight attendants (who are identified with body glamour) were significantly more rejecting of the disabled than were typists.

[45] MacDonald and Hall (1971) discuss and support the hypothesis that physical disabilities would be particularly threatening to externals, "as such disabilities might be viewed negatively by the social agents upon whom they depend" (p. 338).

[46] Interesting information is also available concerning factors that mediate the response of the disabled to the negative behavior displayed toward them by the nondisabled (Grand, 1972).

[47] Freud (1959) referred to the hypercathexis of injured body areas.

6 Pathological Phenomena

There are conditions that produce severe behavioral disturbance and disorganization. For example, brain damage or schizophrenia may induce radical breakdown and regression. In this chapter, we focus on the body image phenomena observed in such extreme forms of pathology. We consider not only the changes in body image accompanying disorganization but also those resulting from therapeutic procedures intended to produce reintegration.

BRAIN DYSFUNCTION

Brain damage can dismember the body image in extravagant ways. The degree of primitivization it can induce at times goes far beyond that resulting from any other type of pathology. As described elsewhere (Fisher & Cleveland, 1968), it was the very extremeness of certain body image distortions linked to brain damage that stimulated the earliest interest in body image phenomena among neurologists such as Bonnier, Pick, Head, and Schilder. Paul Schilder (1950), who is recognized as one of the prime energizers of the 20th century studies of body experience, entered this domain by way of his neurological observations. The primitivization resulting from brain damage can be so extreme that afflicted persons deny the very existence of a body part, or are unable to identify the boundaries of the body, or lose the ability to differentiate the right and left body sides. Neurologists have worked hard to develop classificatory schemes that logically group the body image symptoms of the brain damaged. Their major classifications (e.g., Frederiks, 1969) relate variously to denial of body weakness or defect (anosognosia), loss of perception and recognition of one side of the body (hemiosomatognosia), inability to name body parts (autotopagnosia), absence of normal reaction to pain while elementary sensations continue to register (asymbolia for pain), perception of body parts as abnormally large or small (macro- and microsomatognosia), and seeing a literal double of oneself (autoscopia).[1]

Localization of the Body Scheme

One of the major themes in the literature of body image distortions in the brain damaged relates to whether body image functions are localized in a unitary fashion in specific brain locales. There has been considerable disagreement about this issue of localization (Critchley, 1953b; Frederiks,[2] 1969; Weinstein, Lyerly, Cole, & Ozer, 1966). More specific information has emerged from a study by Erwin and Rosenbaum (1979). They administered a questionnaire (based on the Fisher Body Distortion Questionnaire) that measured body image disturbance in four groups: schizophrenics (10 male, 5 female), normals (10 male, 5 female), persons with focal parietal damage (7 male, 8 female), and persons with brain damage in other than parietal region (10 male, 5 female). They observed no differences in number of body image distortions between those organics with focal parietal damage and those with other than parietal damage. However, they did find that, regardless of the specific location of lesions, subjects with right hemisphere damage had significantly higher body image distortions scores than did subjects with left hemisphere damage. This is one of the first systematic studies to demonstrate that body image distortions (aside from anosognosia) are particularly likely to be linked to damage in the right hemisphere. Erwin and Rosenbaum found also that brain-damaged patients generally reported a significantly lower number of body image distortions than did the schizophrenics. Surprisingly, the brain damaged could not be significantly distinguished from the normals. This is a finding that invites verification because it flies in the face of many clinical reports.

The question of localization has been dramatized in a long time dispute about the so-called Gerstmann syndrome. Gerstmann (1942) published an account of an unusual cluster of symptoms in a woman with brain damage. This woman was unable to recognize her own fingers. There was also right-left disorientation, especially for parts of her own body and for the bodies of others, and she had difficulty completing arithmetical calculations and writing spontaneously. Gerstmann concluded that the cluster represented a specific body schema disorder. He attributed the disorder to a lesion of the left angular gyrus in its transition to the second occipital convolution. His formulation had considerable impact in seeming to establish a neurologically defined syndrome that could be tied to the concept of a body scheme. The Gerstmann syndrome and the associated idea that aspects of the body scheme are localized in specific brain areas have stirred severe criticism[3] (e.g., Benton, 1977; Critchley, 1953a; Poeck & Orgass, 1966).

One of the most negative evaluations is found in a critique by Poeck and Orgass (1971). They reviewed the available literature and concluded, in essence, that the Gerstmann syndrome is a fiction. Indeed, they concluded that all the syndromes said to define a specific defect in the body image are illusory. In the case of the Gerstmann syndrome, they pointed out that the available data indicated a very low correlation among the four defects presumably defining that syndrome. They doubted that there was justification for even putting them together in a common cluster. Poeck and Orgass analyzed previously reported cases of various kinds of disturbances of the body schema (e.g., finger agnosia, autotopagnosia) and decided they really were reflections of more generalized brain defects[4] rather than a particular species of body scheme defect. They stated:

> Under the heading of body schema disturbances, there have been grouped together a great number of very heterogeneous symptoms. It was shown that each of the classical disturbances of the body scheme is much more readily explained as being the consequence of other neuropsychological syndromes which are obviously better defined. This holds true for autotopagnosia as well as for finger agnosia and right-left disorientation. In most of the relevant cases these disturbances can be explained as aphasic symptoms. (p. 274)

However, the literature contains a number of cases in which the Gerstmann syndrome does occur in the absence of aphasia (Kinsbourne & Warrington, 1962; Roeltgen, Sevush, & Heilman, 1983; Strub & Geschwind, 1974). It is obviously premature to dismiss the possibility that localized brain lesions may selectively produce defects related primarily to the perception of one's own body.

Anosognosia

The term anosognosia refers to a type of body scheme distortion in which one literally denies the parts of one's body. In a milder form, the distortion may involve the feeling that one's body part is not connected to one's body, but, at a more serious extreme, it takes the form of complete denial of the existence of the part (Friedlander, 1967). Anosognosia is particularly common in people who have suffered hemiplegia as the result of brain damage (Nathanson, Bergman, & Gordon, 1952; Weinstein & Kahn, 1955). It seems to be considerably more common in left than in right hemiplegia (Cutting, 1978). Previous studies estimated that anosognosia in left hemiplegics occurs in about 30–50% of such cases (Cutting, 1978). Interestingly, Weinstein and Kahn found that anosognosia was probably the result of an interaction between the brain damage involved and certain body attitudes that existed prior to the brain damage. They noted: "The outstanding characteristic of patients in this group concerned their attitudes toward illness and the mode in which they had been expressed. All had previously shown a marked trend to deny the existence of illness. They appeared to have regarded ill health as an imperfection of weakness or disgrace. Illness seemed to have meant a loss of esteem and adequacy" (p. 73).

A study by Jaffe and Slote (1958) showed that interpersonal factors play a role in the hemiplegic's display of anosognosia. Jaffe and Slote elicited differential degrees of denial of illness as a function of whether the person interviewing patients encouraged them either to minimize or to exaggerate their symptoms.

Sullivan (1969) created an experimental situation in which normal nonbrain-injured persons resorted to adaptive strategies that resembled the "denial of illness" characterizing patients with anosognosia. He studied 30 college students (sex unspecified) who were asked to insert their hand into a glove in an apparatus and to draw a line. Without their knowledge, the situation was manipulated so that they were actually watching someone else's gloved hand. As they watched this hand, gross discrepancies arose between the kinesthetic cues they were getting from their own hand and the visual cues they were receiving from the hand they mistakenly assumed to be their own. Under the impact of these discrepancies, a number of the subjects began to evolve anosognosic-like response (e.g., "I'm looking at my hand but it doesn't belong to me"). Sullivan speculated that the dynamics of the hemiplegic's anosognosia might have an analogous origin:

> The neglect of movement cues and the reliance on visual cues observed with these subjects in response to an experimental illusion suggests that stroke patients who experience an alteration in sensory processing may adapt in a similar manner. For example, it would appear likely that the stroke patient would go through an initial period of attempting to verify and explain current percepts on the basis of previous sensory experience. Prior to the stroke the sensory information attended to was veridical . . . visual sensations were matched to movement-tactile impressions of the same perceptual field. After the stroke, sensory integration of visual and movement-tactile modalities may be grossly impaired but, solely on the basis of previous experience, the patient would be likely to assume that the sensory modes still provided veridical information. Consequently, before the patient would relinquish the assumption of veridical perception he would have to test out various percepts. In terms of the present findings, the patient would be likely to rely initially on the visual system during that testing out period. Thus, if he were to *see* that a limb or body area was intact he might not believe that it was impaired. (p. 76)

The material just reviewed suggests that, strange as anosognosia in the brain damaged may appear to be, analogous, though much less extreme, behaviors can be detected in normal persons exposed to experiences that introduce confusion and conflict into their body perceptions. Additionally, it is clear that even the degree of anosognosia displayed by the brain damaged is partially a function of psychological variables like their premorbid attitudes toward body disablement and their perception of how much others in their world are receptive to such symptomatology.

Hemiplegia

Several studies have presented evidence that hemiplegic patients perform in a relatively inferior fashion when asked to make body judgments. Reviewed by Fisher (1970), data from Shontz (1956), Fink and Shontz (1960), Birch, Proctor, and Bortner (1961a, 1961b), and Barton (1964) point in this direction.

It has variously been demonstrated that hemiplegics have special difficulty in identifying parts of their body, in estimating distances on their body, in locating points on their body surface, and in perceiving the position of their body in space. Little or no research pertinent to this matter has been published beyond the studies cited earlier, although Cardone and Olson (1969) did present some relevant data. They exposed hemiplegics ($N = 15$, 10 female, 5 male) and normals (10 males) to a mirror that distorted their appearance. As the experimenter altered the mirror, they were to indicate when various of their body parts "look exactly as they would in an ordinary mirror." The hemiplegics proved to be just as accurate as the controls in recognizing their true mirror image. Interestingly, the hemiplegics were significantly less accurate in judging the true mirror image of non-self objects. This study did not support the tenor of the previous research, which detected significant disturbance in the hemiplegic's body scheme. However the distorted mirror technique employed by Cardone and Olson has not been well validated; and the sample involved was quite small.

It is surprising how little experimental research has been carried out in recent years that deals with the effects of brain damage on body perception. Most of the recent literature involves qualitative descriptions of clinical cases in which symptoms of body image distortion do or do not appear as a consequence of lesions in specific brain locales. Clearly, an important area of research is being seriously neglected.

MENTAL RETARDATION

The mentally retarded, severely limited in their intellectual functioning, are less capable of complex and differentiated behavior than are persons of normal intelligence. Considerable interest has been shown in how body perception is affected in the mentally deficient. Shontz (1969) reported that they differ from normals in their body size judgments. They do not seem to discriminate, as normals do, between judgments involving their own body parts and those involving nonself objects. Other research indicates that they differ from the nonretarded in their tendency to introduce more distortions and omissions and less detail into their figure drawings (Maloney & Glasser, 1982; Wysocki & Wysocki, 1973); in being less accurate and stable in identifying their own image in a distorting mirror (Vinter, Mounoud, & Husain, 1983); in making more errors in right-left discriminations and finger localization (Benton, 1959); and in being less accurate in tactile localization and imitation of hand gestures (Clapp, 1969). As earlier noted, retarded children are also delayed in learning to recognize their own mirror image (Hill & Tomlin, 1981). The evidence is fairly strong that the retarded encounter special difficulties in coping with and integrating their body experiences.

Conflicting data can be found with regard to whether special training procedures can improve the accuracy and complexity of body perception in the retarded. A number of studies have described positive results (e.g., Daw, 1964; Edgar, Ball, McIntyre, & Shotwell, 1969; Franklin, 1979; Maloney, Ball, & Edgar, 1970; Maloney & Payne, 1970; Ohwaki, 1976). But other studies have been negative (e.g., Foley, 1975; Kavaler, 1974; Ratliff, 1975; R. E. Richardson, 1970; Shuman-Carpenter, 1977). While there are no obvious differences in the methodologies of the positive and negative studies, it is interesting that the negative ones not only were more recently carried out but also involve considerably larger numbers of subjects. One would be inclined to give greater weight to these more recent investigations.

NEUROSIS AND PSYCHOSIS

Just as the unusual body image distortions resulting from brain damage recruited early interest in body image phenomena, so did the sometimes flamboyant body experiences of neurotics and schizophrenics call attention to this realm. The literature abounds with dramatic case histories in which disturbed individuals variously reported feelings of body deterioration, sensations of body parts growing larger or smaller, and perceptions of alterations in one's sexual attributes. Fisher (1970) and Fisher and Cleveland (1968) have presented full accounts of this clinical literature. Let us now review some of the more empirical data that have accumulated since 1970 concerning body perception in persons with serious psychological problems.

Depersonalization

One of the most widely studied forms of disturbed body perception is depersonalization. Although the meaning of the term depersonalization originally had to do with a feeling of loss of ego, it has more and more come to refer to a state in which people regard the self, and particularly their body, as a foreign object. They are estranged from their own corporeal base and do not experience it as belonging to self. There are often parallel feelings of being without volition. Depersonalization may vary from a momentary experience to a chronic one. Many theorists and clinicians have speculated about the etiology and significance of depersonalization. An overview of these speculations has been provided by Fisher (1970). They diversely attribute depersonalization to loss of love, inability to invest libido in the world or in one's own body, difficulty in coping with rage, the need to mediate very opposing identifications, and so forth. Psychoanalytic theories of depersonalization are of three general types (Cattell, 1966):

1. One orientation attributes depersonalization primarily to denial. Presumably it is a defense mechanism to deny "forbidden" urges (e.g., sadistic-aggressive impulses.)

2. Another view focuses on depersonalization as an expression of intra-psychic conflict and splitting. The split is said to be within the ego or between the ego and superego. There is presumably a disharmony between inter-nalized identifications or values, and one part is defensively dissociated.

3. A third perspective links depersonalization to a lack of meaningfulness in self-perception. Feelings about self that are distorted or unstable or discre-pant with important frames of reference about the world lead to disturbances in identity and orientation reality, and these result in depersonalization phenomena.

As of 1970, not a great deal was known empirically about the nature of depersonalization. It had been shown (Dixon, 1963; Fisher, 1964c; Roberts, 1960; Sedman, 1966) that feelings of depersonalization were quite common not only in psychiatric patients[5] but also in normal persons.[6] It appeared that as many as 50% of normal college students had been through episodes of depersonalization. However, there were suggestions (not well validated) that the depersonalization in the normal individual was less intense and of shorter duration than that occurring in psychiatric patients. No clear connection had been demonstrated between depersonalization and specific personality traits (e.g., extraversion-introversion or clinical syndromes).

Since 1970 there has been only modest progress in exploring deper-sonalization issues. Psychiatric patients in whom depersonalization is a prominent symptom have been compared by several investigators with other types of patients, and somewhat confusing, often negative, results have emerged with reference to background variables and responses to a range of tests. In 1965 and 1969 Cappon and Banks had reported somewhat negatively that groups of psychiatric patients with outstanding symptoms of deper-sonalization could not be distinguished from controls in terms of body perception tests (e.g., body size estimation or body orientation judgments) and also tests of time and length estimation. Let us scan a number of the pertinent studies that have appeared since 1970. Sedman (1972) compared patients reporting depersonalization as a prominent symptom with anxious patients and with a group of depressed patients who did not report deper-sonalization symptoms. There were 6 males and 12 females in each of the three samples. A battery of tests and questionnaires was administered to each subject; it included: (a) psychomotor tasks; (b) self-reports of alterations in thinking, affect, and body image; (c) personality measures (e.g., introversion-extraversion, neuroticism); (d) measure of anxiety, depression and hysteroid-obsessive tendencies.

Few differences could be detected between the depersonalized subjects and those in the two control groups. There were significant trends for the depersonalized to describe themselves as having more difficulties in thinking, more problems in maintaining self-control, and more sensations of body image disturbance. The depersonalized subjects were also as depressed as the depressed sample, but significantly less anxious than the anxious sample.

Negative results considerably outweighed the positive ones. There was little or no clarification of the possible origins of depersonalization.

Myers and Grant (1972) studied 339 female and 552 male English college students who described any depersonalization episodes they might have experienced in the past. Twelve percent of the females and 6% of the males convincingly described such episodes. The females who had experienced depersonalization manifested more disturbance than did controls on a questionnaire tapping emotional disturbance. This was not true for the depersonalized males. However, these males were more neurotic, as defined by Eysenck's personality inventory, than were controls. But, strangely, the females did not evidence significantly elevated neuroticism scores. Agoraphobic symptoms were significantly more common in females with depersonalization than in controls, but no such association appeared in the males. Males with depersonalization experiences exceeded controls in the degree to which they reported past episodes of *déja vu.* Myers and Grant tried speculatively to evolve a theory to explain the link between depersonalization and *déja vu:* "Are *déja vu* and depersonalization part of a system which minimizes fear by redressing certain fear-inspiring qualities of sensory information? . . . On this basis *déja vu* would result from redressing frightening unfamiliarity; the unreality feelings of depersonalization would have a comparable relationship with frightening familiarity . . ." (p. 62).

Fleiss, Gurland, and Goldberg (1975) administered a 700-item structured mental state interview to 866 hospitalized adult mental patients in New York and London. The data from the first 500 patients were factor analyzed and a cross validation was undertaken with the remaining 366 patients. One of the numerous factors that emerged was labeled "depersonalization-derealization." It included such items as not feeling like a real person or feeling unreal when looking in the mirror. Scores based on this factor did not consistently differentiate between psychotics and nonpsychotics. Indeed, they did not correlate with any diagnostic classifications, which affirms a similar observation by Tucker, Harrow and Quinlan (1973). About 15% of all the patients reported having experienced depersonalization or derealization during the month before admission.[7] No sex differences were detected, but there was a significant trend for younger patients to exceed older ones with respect to such experiences. The absence of sex differences has been reported by others. (e.g., Brauer, Harrow, & Tucker, 1970; Freeman & Melges, 1977; Tucker et al., 1973). The relatively greater occurrence of depersonalization in younger persons has been affirmed by Brauer, et al. and Tucker, et al. but was not observed by Freeman and Melges (1977). However, the last mentioned study was based on a much smaller sample than the others cited.

Brauer, Harrow and Tucker (1970) administered to 85 hospitalized psychiatric patients a questionnaire that measured depersonalization. Responses to a number of other inventories and questionnaires were obtained. Depersonalization was found to be significantly positively correlated with visual and auditory hallucinations, with measures of cyclothymia, and with trait anxiety. As in the aforementioned Myers and Grant (1972) study, it was also positively correlated with a tendency to have *déja vu* experiences. Congruent with earlier cited work, it was not consistently correlated with introversion, although there were borderline positive trends. It was significantly and positively linked with a cluster of symptoms characteristic of depression, such as guilt, withdrawal, feelings of "deadness," anomie, frustration, and poor self-esteem, but not with immediate degree of depressed mood or motor retardation. It was positively and significantly correlated with questionnaire measures of increased body awareness and increased restless body movement. Brauer et al. note: "The patients with depersonalization were likely to interpret external stimuli as affecting their bodies rather than their emotions or intrapsychic feelings; this was particularly true of the way they perceived the effects of the hospital milieu. They felt that psychotropic drugs, particularly phenothiazines, increased their feelings of depersonalization" (p. 513). Brauer et al. stated in terms of an overall analysis of their data: "We can attempt to characterize the type of patients who most often experience depersonalization as young, frequently anxious, introverted patients with mood swings" (p. 513). They were impressed with the inclination of depersonalized patients to focus their attention on inner experiences and at the same time to have special difficulties in processing and synthesizing incoming stimuli that may have led to self-perceived changes in the self.

Tucker et al. (1973) used a questionnaire to evaluate depersonalization in 155 hospitalized psychiatric patients (59 male, 96 female). In addition, a variety of self-report and observer-derived information was compiled. A small but significant negative correlation was found between a measure of social desirability and the tendency to report depersonalization symptoms. Depersonalization proved to be significantly positively linked with a "dysphoric" orientation that embraced depressive affect, thought and motor retardation, negative self-image, and anomie. But it was not linked with having a primary depressive diagnosis. The Rorschach Inkblot test had been administered to the patients. Inkblot indices of "disorganized thinking" and difficulty in maintaining boundaries between concepts that were derived from it proved to be positively and significantly correlated with depersonalization. A previous study, by Shorvon (1946), had also suggested a positive correlation between depersonalization and Rorschach signs of pathological thinking. In the same vein, Tucker et al. detected a significant positive relationship between depersonalization and schizophrenic disorganization. The Fisher and Cleveland (1968) Barrier and Penetration scores (measures of body boundary articulation), which were derived from the inkblot responses by Tucker et al., were not significantly correlated with depersonalization. Depersonalization was found to be significantly and positively correlated with anxiety and negatively with measures of suspiciousness and paranoia. Anxiety has been linked to depersonalization in a number of previous studies (Dixon, 1963; Harper & Roth, 1962; Noyes, Hoenk, Kuperman, & Slymen, 1977; Roth, 1959, 1960). Tucker et al. concluded: "The picture of the patient who experiences depersonalization is that of a person with chronic anxiety, persistent depressed affect, and some degree of psychopathological thinking" (p. 705).

Freeman and Melges (1977) focused on possible relationships between depersonalization and temporal disintegration. Thirty-seven hospitalized psychiatric patients (20 female, 17 male) responded to a series of questions read to them that dealt with self-estrangement (e.g., "I feel like a stranger to myself") and disturbance in temporal perception (e.g., "My past and future seem to have collapsed into the present, and it is difficult for me to tell them apart"). The depersonalization and time disturbance measures were substantially positively correlated. The patients had also been asked to respond to questions about their perceptions of their body boundaries (e.g., "My body boundaries feel fluid and changing"). Degree of body image disturbance was positively and significantly correlated with body depersonalization and time disturbance. Freeman and Melges commented "that the fragmentation of personal time is closely related to the experience of the self as strange and unreal. These findings are in accord with Erikson's formulation that discontinuity and the lack of the feeling of 'self-sameness' over time are basic to the experience of the self as unreal" (p. 681).

Comment. The studies just reviewed do not provide much satisfying information about the etiology of depersonalization or its possible adaptive functions. One learns simply that psychiatric patients with prominent symptoms of depersonalization are particularly inclined to be anxious, to feel dysphoric, to view self negatively, to have problems in maintaining logical modes of thinking, and to experience time continuity as disrupted. Depersonalization cannot be linked to a specific diagnostic syndrome or to a particular personality constellation. It can be said only that psychiatric patients with marked depersonalization are also particularly distressed in a number of ways. But, depersonalization also occurs fairly frequently in normal individuals confronted by threatening stress. It is a mode of reaction that is not unique to highly maladapted people. There is a temptation to interpret depersonalization as essentially a means for dampening the intensity of bodily feelings[8] and sensations that are difficult to tolerate. The normal individual who has just had a catastrophic automobile accident and feels depersonalized may be seeking to mute overwhelmingly threatening bodily sensations. Similarly, the psychiatric patient who is experiencing threatening unpleasant internal affects or negative fantasies about the body may need to pull away from such highly charged regions.

In future studies of depersonalization we need to extract more detailed information about the experience, especially at the level of body perception. For example, instead of merely determining whether depersonalization is present and how intense it is, we should also ascertain the degree to which each of the major parts of the body feels "strange" and "not like my own." We may discover that certain body areas (e.g., the hands) are more susceptible to depersonalization than are other areas (e.g., the face). We may learn too that patterns of susceptibility differ as a function of diagnosis, sex, age, and degree of psychological disorganization. Depersonalization in the schizophrenic may involve different parts of the body than does depersonalization in a normal individual. If differences of this sort could be isolated, they would increase the likelihood of teasing out etiological relationships. Consider the possibility that persons with certain focal conflicts could be shown to be more likely to depersonalize particular body parts as compared to others. This would be an important step in clarifying the defensive functions of depersonalization. From a body image perspective, it would be interesting too to explore certain other leads suggested by the studies just reviewed, e.g., Freeman and Melges' (1977) observation that depersonalization is higher in persons particularly concerned about loss of body boundaries or the Brauer et al. (1970) report that people inclined to depersonalize are especially sensitive to their own body sensations. Few of the studies in the literature have attended to the role of body image variables in the development of depersonalization. Although, as noted, there is dispute (Sedman, 1970) about the importance of body image concepts in explaining depersonalization phenomena, such concepts should be applied in future exploratory studies to see where they will lead.

Hypochondriasis

The term hypochondriasis has been around for a long time, but only as late as the 19th century did it acquire its present meaning of being morbidly preoccupied with one's health (Kenyon, 1976). It refers to an unreasonable feeling that one is sick. It may involve perception of a completely healthy body area as impaired, or it may represent the exaggeration of minor impairment. Extensive reviews of the concept have been provided by Kenyon (1965, 1976) and Ladee (1966). Fisher (1970) summarized the literature up to 1970 that was pertinent to the body image aspects of hypochondriasis. He pointed out that psychoanalytic formulations frequently attributed hypochondriasis to withdrawal of libido from objects and its concentration on organs of one's own body. This was said to lead to an unconscious "genitalization" of such organs, and this, in turn, could afford symbolic forms of gratification for various fantasies. Some analysts linked hypochondriacal focus on specific organs with castration anxiety (Deutsch & Murphy, 1955; Fenichel, 1945). Speculation abounded, but empirical data were sparse. A few studies established that the MMPI Hypochondriasis scale was positively linked with other indices of somatic concern (Endicott & Endicott, 1963; Popplestone & Van Every, 1963). Also, Grayden (1958) found modest empirical support for Alexander's (1948) theory that neurotic hypochondriasis may be traced to a dynamic constellation in which persons feel rejected by others, turn compensatorily to bestow upon their own body the outside interest they have lost, and at the same time are disturbed by newly mobilized hostile feelings that create a need to suffer. People are presumed to find in the hypochondriacal symptom a means for focusing attention upon their body and also for suffering and assuaging guilt.

More recently, Kenyon (1976) analyzed published reports concerning the relative frequencies of hypochondriacal symptoms in various subgroups. He concluded that the following were inclined to be more prone to such symptoms: males, lower social classes, the very young, the old, Jews, and medical students. However, these conclusions remain in dispute (Ford, 1983). Little real evidence is available that hypochondriasis is tied to any particular diagnostic category. It has been observed in every diagnostic subgroup, including patients with brain damage. Some clinical speculations persist that it is particularly associated with depressive and obsessive-compulsive tendencies. An earlier study by Kenyon (1964) that involved 512 English psychiatric patients with hypochondriacal complaints found three areas of the body to be the most common discomfort sites: head and neck, abdomen, chest. Expressed by body system, the sites were musculo-skeletal, gastro-intestinal, and CNS (headaches included). About 16% of the symptoms were predominantly unilateral, and of these 73% were left sided.[9] Estimates of the frequency of hypochondriasis in those who present themselves for medical treatment range from 3% to 14% (Ford, 1983).

Smith, Snyder, and Perkins (1983) tested the hypothesis that hypochondriacal individuals use reports of physical illness and symptoms as a strategy to control evaluations of their performance in settings where they are being judged. Fifty-two women with high and 57 with low MMPI Hypochondriasis scores participated in the study. There was a complex experimental design, but essentially the subjects were divided into those who reported their current and past physical symptoms in a context where they felt they were being evaluated and those who did so in an apparently nonevaluative situation. The results indicated: "Hypochondriacal subjects reported more physical illness and symptoms in an evaluative situation in which poor health could serve as an excuse for poor performance than in both an evaluative setting in which poor health was precluded as an excuse and a non-evaluative setting. Nonhypochondriacal subjects did not evidence this strategic pattern of reporting illness and symptoms" (p. 793).

Bianchi[10] (1971) carried out a particularly perceptive analysis of 30 psychiatric patients (20 female, 10 male) with clear-cut, persistent, unfounded fears that they were suffering from a physical illness or disease. He compared them with 30 matched psychiatric controls who lacked such fears. All were inpatients and the majority had diagnoses of depression (nonpsychotic). Concern about having cancer and heart disease predominated in the hypochondriacal group. A large number of measures was obtained from the subjects: psychiatric interview data (coded and quantified), sensation thresholds and pain tolerance, biographical material, Rorschach inkblot responses, and various physiological indices. The findings indicated that the hypochondriacal patients had experienced relatively more disease and deaths among their own family members than had the controls, and Bianchi wondered whether this might not be an important anlage for developing anxiety about bodily functioning. It was also noted that the hypochondriacal were more likely to have been treated as weak and sickly during childhood; to have been more maternally overprotected and babied; and to have been the youngest sibling.

Bianchi (1971) considered these data to indicate that the hypochondriacal had, from an early age, been given the message they lacked bodily strength and were unusually vulnerable to body damage. Their heightened sensitivity to their body experiences was affirmed by the fact that they had a significantly lower threshold for detecting sensations produced by an electrical current and for reporting that the current was painful. There were data indicating too that the hypochondriacal felt more guilty[11], inhibited anger more, and felt more self-pity. Bianchi pointed out that the heightened sensitivity they displayed to the electrical current matched previous reports.

Solon et al. (cited by Bianchi, 1971) found that in normal women there was a significant positive correlation between MMPI Hypochondriasis scores and augmenting stimuli as defined by the Petrie (1967) technique. Bianchi remarked that Petrie had found those who augmented or exaggerated body stimuli to be particularly concerned about eating proper nutritionally valuable foods. Bianchi found in his own sample an analogous significant trend for the hypochondriacal to take vitamins as a way of insuring proper nutrition. Two major points can be extracted from Bianchi's study. First, the hypochondriacal were probably treated as bodily weak and vulnerable by their parents in early childhood. Second, they are apparently particularly sensitive to their own bodily experiences.

Several other studies have come up with findings pertinent to these two points. With respect to the role of parental babying and overprotectiveness in fostering sensations of body weakness, consider the following. Parker and Lipscombe (1980) examined in 64 female and 36 male patients, who had come to see physicians in general practice, the relationship between hypochondriasis (as measured by a questionnaire) and self-reported recall of how much care and overprotection one's parents provided during childhood. They found that: "subjects who scored high on hypochondriasis were distinguished by scoring their fathers as overprotective and their mothers as caring and, when ill, remembering their mothers as highly likely to call the doctor and both parents as evidencing sympathy at that time" (p. 362). They considered three possible levels of explanation for the findings. First, it is possible that children with hypochondriacal and dependent tendencies are particularly inclined to seek attachment and therefore to stimulate their parents to display more caring and protective behavior. Second, there might be a genetic disposition to high anxiety in the family, and this would not only motivate the child to be especially anxious about his body but also stimulate the parents to act anxiously protective. Third: "It is conceivable that parents who overprotect a child and/or respond selectively with greater over-solicitude to a child's illness, promote a sense of vulnerability and insecurity in their child. . . . By responding to the illness as if it were a 'real physical' illness of some severity and requiring external medical help, they encourage a somatic interpretation of stress symptoms, thus promoting any hypo-chondriacal tendency" (p. 362). This last explanation seems to have been the favored one.

In a related vein, Baker and Merskey (1982) appraised 20 psychiatric patients (15 female, 5 male) with clear hypochondriacal features and 20 psychiatric patients (15 female, 5 male) without such features. They evaluated the subjects' attitudes toward their parents with the same questionnaire that was employed in the just referred to Parker and Lipscombe (1980) study. The hypochondriacal subjects reported that their mothers were significantly more often overprotective than did the controls. There was a similar trend with regard to paternal overprotectiveness, but it was not significant. Baker and Merskey pointed out that previous researchers, such as Zborowski (1952), Levy (1932), and Katzenelbogen (1942) likewise had been impressed with a link between being overly responsive to, and concerned about, one's body and having an overprotective mother.[12]

The hypochondriac's enhanced sensitivity to body experience noted earlier by Bianchi (1971) has been directly or indirectly probed by others. Tyrer, Lee, and Alexander (1980) examined awareness of pulse rate in three psychiatric samples: hypochondriasis (8 male, 10 female), anxiety neurosis (10 male, 13 female), phobia (7 male, 12 female). To evaluate how accurately subjects could judge their own heart rate, they were shown two films that varied in degree of excitement and were asked to judge their heart rate levels during various phases of the films. Their judgments were then compared with actual heart rates. Interestingly, the hypochondriacal and anxious groups showed higher correlations (.50 and .29 respectively) between judged and actual heart rate than did the phobic group ($r = -.04$). This was true even though the phobics had a higher mean heart rate. Tyrer et al. thought that, in view of the very low correlations between judged and actual heart rates observed in normal subjects by previous investigators and in view of the relatively high correlation they found in the hypochondriacal sample, the somatic preoc-cupation of hypochondriacal individuals "is explicable if their level of bodily awareness is postulated to be abnormally sensitive, so that they are troubled by symptoms from essentially normal physiological activity" (p. 173).

In another instance, Hanback and Revelle (1978) showed that normal subjects (18 female, 25 male), classified as to degree of hypochondriasis by their responses to a questionnaire based largely on the MMPI Hypochondriasis scale, also differed in their perceptual sensitivity. The sensitivity measures were based on thresholds for detecting two-flash fusion and faint auditory signals. Subjects with high hypochondriasis scores were significantly more sensitive to the visual (two flash fusion) stimuli than were low scorers. However, they did not differ for auditory sensitivity. In the hypochondriasis scale, a cluster of items that directly involved body awareness and concern about health was the major source of the correlation between the total hypochondriasis score and the two-flash fusion threshold. Previous studies had shown sensitivity to two-flash fusion to be greater as a function of elevated arousal, and Hanback and Revelle considered their results to mean that hypochondriasis is linked to being in a state of intensified arousal. Of course, their data did not demonstrate a direct relationship between hypochondriasis and sensitivity to one's own body sensations, but only to a sensitivity to visual stimuli.

A study by Palmer and Broverman (1969) is indirectly pertinent to this issue. They approached hypochondriasis from the perspective of a dimension they called "automatization." This dimension refers to the degree to which persons have automatized or overlearned simple, everyday repetitive behaviors. Palmer and Broverman predicted that the more poorly one automatizes body behaviors, the greater the hypochondriacal symptomatology one will experience. They reasoned "that diffuse somatic complaints of nonspecific origin are in part a reflection of poorly automatized motor or somatic functioning . . . that inefficient, poorly automatized bodily functioning would engender greater experience of subjective bodily distress" (p. 594). Presumably, the less automatized functioning of the body would result in an enhanced awareness of it as a negative object. In two different samples (60 male college students and 30 male medical patients) measures of hypochondriasis computed largely from items in the MMPI Hypochondriasis scale were significantly negatively related to automatization scores (based on ability to perform tasks like naming repeated objects or reading color names). The findings of this study plus those of Tyrer et al. (1980) and Hanback and Revelle (1978) are, at the least, suggestive that the hypochondriacal are inclined to a heightened sensory awareness of the body and perhaps even to a heightened sensitivity to nonbody inputs.

It is noteworthy how little research has directly addressed the relationship between hypochondriasis and body image variables.[13] Only two studies could be located in the literature. One (Hardy, 1982) concerned patients (11 women, 2 men) who had dermatological symptoms but no evidence of significant dermatological pathology. There were two control groups: matched patients with psoriasis and matched persons without any somatic symptoms. All subjects responded to a repertory grid designed by Feldman (1975) for examining an individual's body imagery. The grid consisted of 14 elements (e.g., face, mouth) and eight constructs (e.g., acceptable-unacceptable, sexually attractive-sexually unattractive). The results were meager.

Basically, it turned out the hypochondriacal patients were less satisfied with their body than the nonsymptomatic, normal subjects but not less so than the psoriatics. In another study, Miller, Murphy and Buss (1981) administered to 275 males and 353 females a newly devised questionnaire designed to measure "body consciousness" and also a modified version of the MMPI Hypochondriasis scale. No correlations of significance were obtained between the measures.

Concerning the role of hypochondriasis in mediating the apparent effects of other variables upon the body, two studies have shown such mediating effects. Stone and Neale (1981) established that the correlation between life events and the development of somatic symptoms is smaller in those with high hypochondriasis scores than in those with low scores. They attributed this to the greater symptom reporting inaccuracy of those who are strongly hypochondriacal. Wright, Kane, Olsen, and Smith (1977) observed a similar inaccuracy in the reporting of pulmonary symptoms by mine workers high in hypochondriasis. It appears that researchers who are interested in obtaining symptom reports should correct for the hypochondriacal set that introduces inaccuracies.

Comment. The research concerned with hypochondriasis that has appeared since 1970 is not abundant, but it does provide some new empirical leads. It highlights the possibility that hypochondriacal persons scan the environment with heightened sensitivity and perhaps as a result also experience their body sensations in a magnified fashion, lending itself to distortion and a sense of discomfort. Petrie (1967) reported that those who seem preoccupied with their health are inclined to be augmenters rather than reducers of sensory input. Barskey (1979) and Barsky and Klerman (1983) too concluded, after a survey of the literature dealing with somatizers, that the typical hypochondriacal individual is often one who amplifies bodily sensations.

There are suggestions that the anxious way in which the hypochondriacal tune into their body space may stem in part from having had parents who acted in an "overprotective" fashion and who communicated the idea that the human body is weak and vulnerable. The parents' overprotecting attitude toward the child's body may have become a paradigm for how that child should address his or her own body. But it is a paradox that the very same sensitivity that leads to alarming, false interpretations of certain classes of body events may also heighten accuracy in perceiving other classes. As noted, Bianchi (1971) detected in hypochondriacal patients a particularly high level of accuracy in judging their own heart rate. This paradox is intriguing. It reminds one that, although a good deal of the research dealing with the impact of being exposed to one's mirror image has shown that it stirs guilt and self-disapproval, evidence has also emerged that it increases the accuracy of perception of certain bodily events. Is it possible that the chronic close scrutiny of one's own body required for a high level of informed and accurate awareness of what is.going on there is usually avoided by most people and typifies only those who have unusual motivations, such as fear of getting hurt or guilt about body experiences? It may not be adaptive to tune in too sensitively to one's own body, simply because this creates the potentiality for the eventual distorted magnification of some categories of body experience to an hypochondriacal level. The "normal" pattern may require that one maintain a somewhat repressive and distanced attitude toward one's own body experiences.

Schizophrenia

As indicated by Fisher and Cleveland (1958) and Fisher (1970), there is a good deal of ambiguity about whether schizophrenia is linked with deviant amounts or specific forms of body image distortion. At the time of Fisher's review in 1970 the following was the state of our knowledge in this area:

1. There were many clinical anecdotal reports that portrayed schizophrenics as frequently having bizarre experiences of body change and transformation (e.g., in sexual identity). However, when Fisher (1970) and Fisher and Seidner (1963) undertook studies that systematically inventoried body image distortions in schizophrenic, neurotic, and normal samples, it was possible to demonstrate only that the schizophrenics and neurotics had more such distortions than normals. The schizophrenics could not be distinguished from neurotics.

2. Considerable controversy prevailed as to whether schizophrenics were inclined to overestimate the size of their body parts. Many studies did report overestimation (e.g., Cleveland, 1960b; Cleveland, Fisher, Reitman, & Rothaus, 1962); but others did not (e.g., Dillon, 1962b; Weckowicz & Sommer, 1960). Fisher (1970) and Fisher and Seidner (1963) discovered that, when asked to describe their subjective experiences of body size, schizophrenics reported elevated feelings of corporeal smallness. Although they had more feelings of being small than normals did, they did not differ from neurotics in this respect. As indicated in a previous chapter, the more recent research literature does not substantiate a trend for schizophrenics to overestimate the size of specific parts of their body. They are inclined to over- or underestimate their total body size only when judgments are rendered in an unstructured context that presumably encourages projection of unconscious feelings. But it is still unclear whether schizophrenics differ consistently from neurotic (nonpsychotic) psychiatric patients in this respect.

3. Wapner (1961a, 1961b) showed that there were apparently differences in the way schizophrenics and normals judged their body position in space. When normals were tilted in a dark room and asked to adjust a luminous rod to the vertical, they shifted the apparent vertical in a direction opposite to that of their own body tilt. When asked to adjust a luminous rod so as to align

it with their own body tilt, they overestimated the amount of tilt. Schizophrenics showed the opposite pattern. They were inclined to shift the apparent vertical toward the direction of their body tilt, and they were less likely to overestimate their own degree of tilt. This was interpreted to mean that schizophrenics experience less of a polarity than do normals between self and object. The evidence for this difference was fairly solid. However, the Wapner studies did not include samples of nonpsychotic psychiatric patients (neurotics); hence, the question could be raised whether the phenomena observed were specifically linked with psychosis, as such, or whether they might be byproducts of other factors such as hospitalization or having experienced certain forms of psychiatric treatment. It is of related interest that Witkin and his associates (1954, 1962) were not able to demonstrate consistent differences between schizophrenics and normals in ability to judge accurately the position of true vertical in a darkened room. Evidence even appeared that paranoid schizophrenics could perform more accurately than normal subjects.

4. There were scattered hints that schizophrenics might respond in a special fashion if confronted with self-representations. Epstein (1955) observed that, when schizophrenics encountered samples of self (e.g., their own voice played backwards) without being aware that they were doing so, they rated them relatively more favorably than normal controls did in judging their self-representations. Epstein thought this indicated that the schizophrenics had a greater defensive need to enhance themselves and unconsciously used the opportunity provided by the experimental situation to do so. But Sugarman (1961) failed to obtain analogous results when he compared schizophrenics and normals in their unconscious reactions to self-representations. Thomas and Stasiak (1964) detected a difference in the eye movements of schizophrenics and normals as they perused pictures of self and others. When viewing their own pictures, the schizophrenics focused more on their body than on their head, and the pattern was reversed for the normals. This was interpreted to mean that the schizophrenics might be trying to shut out awareness of the information conveyed by their own faces.

5. Another interesting lead related to the possible deviance or confusion in the schizophrenics' perception of the masculine versus feminine properties of their own body. McClelland and Watt (1968) detected evidence that: "some part of the schizophrenic woman's unconscious self-image is insensitive and more masculine, whereas some part of the schizophrenic man's self-image is sensitive and more feminine" (p. 235). They concluded this from data based on subjects' degree of satisfaction-dissatisfaction with various of their body parts that had been classified as masculine (e.g., elbow, fingers) versus feminine (e.g., lips, skin).

6. Finally, schizophrenics were observed to require a larger *buffer zone* around their body than did normals. Horowitz, Duff, and Stratton (1964)

noted that when approaching various objects and persons in an unstructured setting, schizophrenics maintained a greater distance than did normal controls. Horowitz et al. considered this buffer space to be part of the body image. One cannot be too impressed with the differences that had been described by 1970. Where they did apparently exist, they were small, were not well cross-validated, and in some instances had not been put to the test of a full range of necessary control groups. They were certainly not of the spectacular quality that had been suggested by dramatic clinical reports.

Are There Typical Schizophrenic Distortions? With this review as a framework, let us appraise what has been reported in the more recent literature. Both positive and negative findings can be discerned. We will first look at what has appeared on the positive side.

Veatch (1969)[14] administered a number of body image and self-concept measures to four male samples: normals, anxiety reactions, paranoid schizophrenics, nonparanoid schizophrenics. There were 15 subjects in each sample. They responded to the following tests: a modified version of the Bills, Vance, and McLean (1951) Index of Adjustment and Values, which measures self-concept; a modified form of a body percept scale developed by Zion (1963), which calls for subjects to describe their body (Body Description) and their degree of acceptance of it (Body Acceptance) by rating the applicability of a series of adjectives; the Secord and Jourard (1953) Self Cathexis and Body Cathexis measures; and the Miskimins (1968) Self Goal–Other Discrepancy Scale that taps self-concept parameters.

Veatch (1969) found, as predicted, that the body image measures did, overall, distinguish the various diagnostic groups better than the self-concept indices. The self-concept measures did as well as the body image measures only in showing that the nonparanoid schizophrenic patients perceive themselves more negatively than the normals. Interestingly, whereas the Zion self-descriptive body image measure significantly distinguished the normals from the nonparanoid schizophrenics, the Secord and Jourard Body Cathexis score failed to do so. One of the Zion scores also showed paranoid schizophrenics to feel more negatively toward their body than normals, but none of the other body image measures was similarly differentiating. Although self-concept measures could not differentiate paranoid from nonparanoid schizophrenics, both the Secord and Jourard Body Cathexis score and one of the Zion body perception scores (Body-Ideal–Body Discrepancy) indicated a significantly more favorable body attitude in the paranoid group. The Zion Body Description score also indicated that the anxiety subjects were significantly less positive toward their body than the normals. But what is of special importance is that the anxiety sample could not be differentiated from either of the schizophrenic samples. In summary, although the body image measures were able, in an overall sense, to separate the various diagnostic categories, the anxiety sample could not be specifically distinguished from the two schizophrenic samples. That is, a neurotic group could not be differentiated from the schizophrenics.

As described earlier, Erwin and Rosenbaum (1979) administered a Body-Image Disturbance Questionnaire, based on the Fisher (1970) and the Rosenbaum, Cohen, Luby, Gottlieb, and Yelen (1959) measures of distorted body experiences, to four groups: schizophrenics, normals, and two samples of persons with organic brain damage. They found an overall significant trend for the schizophrenics to report more distorted body experiences than did any of the other groups. None of the normal or brain damaged samples could be distinguished from each other. Fisher (1970) too had found that distorted body experiences were higher in schizophrenics than in normals. However, he also found that schizophrenics did not exceed neurotics in this respect. In the present study, there was an absence of a neurotic group, and so the two sets of data cannot be compared. Obviously, the possibility exists that, if neurotics had been included in the Erwin and Rosenbaum study, they would not have differed from the schizophrenics. It is surprising that the schizophrenics reported more body distortions than the brain damaged, who represented a broad spectrum of this category. Such a comparison, not previously available in the literature, calls for additional exploration.

Rosenberg and Tucker (1979) came up with some data indirectly pertinent to the matter of body image distortion in schizophrenics when they undertook a computer analysis of the content categories characterizing the verbal productions of 26 schizophrenics (15 male, 11 female) and 27 nonschizophrenics (14 male, 13 female). All subjects were psychiatric inpatients, and the nonschizophrenics included 13 with neurotic and psychotic depression diagnoses and 14 with personality disorders. The verbal productions of the subjects were obtained by means of a standardized 15-minute interview during the 1st and 7th weeks of their hospitalization. A number of differences were demonstrated in the verbal themes typifying the schizophrenics versus nonschizophrenics. There was a significant trend for the schizophrenics to verbalize more about body parts and to obtain higher scores on a factor emphasizing a focus on death and medical pathology. These differences could be interpreted as meaning that the schizophrenics were "leaking" more anxiety about their body into their interview statements. There was a significant drop in themes of body anxiety in the schizophrenics at the time of their second interview, when clinical improvement had occurred.

It is also of import that, at the time of the first interview, there were significant reversals for the schizophrenics (especially the females) in verbal content categories linked to sex role. That is, the schizophrenics were inclined to verbal productions more typical of the opposite sex than of their own. For example, female schizophrenics utilized a relatively large number of words having to do with exerting control and power, which appear more typically in the verbalizations of normal males. This reversal is pertinent to observations of McClelland and Watt (1968) and of Holzberg and Plummer (cited by McClelland and Watt), which suggested reversals in schizophrenics' feelings about masculine versus feminine parts of their body. However, skepticism is in order in view of two later studies. One, by Ecker, Levine, and Zigler (1973) involving 40 schizophrenics (20 male, 20 female) and 20 normals (10 male, 10 female), found no differences between schizophrenics and normals in how they rated the masculine and feminine parts of their body. Ecker et al. speculated that their results differed from those of McClelland and Watt because the latter had derived from schizophrenics hospitalized for long durations (10 years), whereas their schizophrenic subjects had been hospitalized for only a few months. This suggests that either the reversal in attitude toward masculine and feminine body parts is increased by being hospitalized or it is most likely to occur in schizophrenics so disorganized as to require lengthy hospitalization.

The other pertinent study conducted by Elfert in 1971, is mentioned by LaTorre (1976). Elfert found that outpatient male and female schizophrenics and neurotics did not differ significantly in their evaluations of male and female body parts. Nonhospitalized schizophrenics could not be distinguished from a neurotic group. The data just reviewed are obviously in disagreement. But a few of the observations are sufficiently promising to suggest it would be worthwhile to look more systematically into whether schizophrenics adopt unusual attitudes toward the sexual features of their bodies.

Attempts have been made with other techniques to tap body image variables that could evaluate masculine versus feminine parameters in schizophrenics. Much of this work has been summarized by LaTorre (1976). He reviewed a number of projects in which efforts were made to find deviations in the way schizophrenics represent masculine and feminine attributes in their figure drawings.[15] Although he concluded there was an apparent trend for schizophrenics to be deviant, the evidence is hardly impressive. There are simply too many studies that have found no trace of such deviation. LaTorre also reviewed a number of studies in which the Franck-Rosen Drawing Completion Test was used to explore possible disturbances in gender identity in schizophrenics, and the findings were largely negative. The overall information that is available concerning possible deviations in the way schizophrenics experience the sexual attributes of their bodies does not lend itself to a clear interpretation and does not appear to be especially promising.

A few probes have been made to detect body image deviations in schizophrenic children. They have focused on right-left awareness. Walker and Birch (1970) examined 80 hospitalized male children schizophrenics (age range 8–11). These children were compared with 69 normal children. Among other measures, the ability to identify the right and left aspects of one's body was evaluated. The schizophrenic children were significantly less accurate in making the right-left judgments and were also less clear in the development of hand preference. Curcio (1974) duplicated the Walker and Birch findings when he studied 36 boys and 36 girls (ages 7–15) who were hospitalized and diagnosed as childhood schizophrenics. He too found that when the children's ability to identify their right versus left body parts was compared with that of the same normal group used by Walker and Birch, the schizophrenics were significantly inferior.

Controversy has surrounded the suggestion that schizophrenics suffer from a *proprioceptive dysfunction,* which represents a deficiency in ability to process proprioceptive sensations from one's own body. There has been a good deal of past clinical speculation about such proprioceptive impairment. Both Rado (1953) and Meehl (1962) thought it was typical of schizophrenics. The empirical investigations that have looked into this matter have given conflicting results. Systematic study began with the work of a group at the Lafayette Clinic in Detroit, Michigan. They were impressed with the fact that, when they administered to normal subjects a drug (Sernyl) that blocks proprioceptive signals, this seemed to trigger errors in symbolic thinking similar to those characterizing schizophrenics (Cohen, Rosenbaum, Luby, & Gottlieb, 1962). Also, since proprioceptive deficit is characteristic of people who have sustained damage to the parietal region of the brain, they speculated that parietal dysfunction might somehow play a role in the pathology of schizophrenia. Several studies were undertaken to explore the nature of proprioceptive deficit in schizophrenics and persons with parietal damage.

In addition to the Erwin and Rosenbaum (1979) study already described, there were others by Ritzler and Rosenbaum (1974), Rosenbaum, Ebner, and Ritzler (1966), and Rosenbaum, Flenning, and Rosen (1965). In these studies, a modified method of limits was employed to evaluate performance on a weight discrimination task. It was reported that schizophrenics did about as well as normals when called upon to discriminate heavy weights (400–gram standard), but they did not discriminate light weights (40–gram standard) as accurately as normals. In view of the fact that light weights provide less proprioceptive feedback than heavy weights, the results were interpreted to mean that schizophrenics display proprioceptive deficit.

However, subsequent work has not been confirmatory. Ritzler (1977) observed that proprioceptive deficit could be found not only in schizophrenics but also in nonschizophrenic psychotics (manic depressive, depressive, amphetamine induced). In addition, he failed to observe a deficit in a sample of paranoid schizophrenics. It was his impression that "when the proprioceptive performance of schizophrenics was compared to that of nonschizophrenic patients, the results indicated that a proprioceptive deficit—while apparent for the most severely disordered patients—was not unique to schizophrenia" (p. 509). In another study, Leventhal, Schuck, Clemons, and Cox (1982) were unable to detect a proprioceptive deficit when they compared weight judgment performances of outpatient (rather than hospitalized) paranoid schizophrenics, outpatient nonparanoid schizophrenics, outpatient psychiatric patients, and aged normals. They speculated on the basis of their data that it could be long-term hospitalization rather than schizophrenia, as such, that produced what was previously regarded as a unique proprioceptive deficit in schizophrenic subjects. It is apparent from such work that any study that specifies unique body image deficits in hospitalized schizophrenics without employing other types of hospitalized psychiatric patients as controls should not be taken seriously.[16]

A measure of "body-image aberration" was developed by Chapman, Chapman, and Raulin (1978). They constructed a 25-item questionnaire scale that taps five categories of body experiences: unclear body boundaries (e.g., "Sometimes I have had the feeling that I am united with an object near me"); feelings of unreality or estrangement of parts of one's body (e.g., "I have sometimes felt that some part of my body no longer belongs to me"); feelings of deterioration of one's body (e.g., "I have sometimes had the feeling my body is decaying inside"); perceptions of change in size, proportions, or spatial relationships of one's body parts (e.g., "Occasionally it has seemed as if my body has taken on the appearance of another person's body"). They compared the questionnaire responses of the following samples: 66 male hospitalized schizophrenics, 20 male nonpsychotic clients (largely college students) attending a university psychology clinic, 100 male normals obtained at shopping centers and fire stations, 718 normal female college students, and 631 male normal college students. The mean body image aberration score of the schizophrenics was 5.71. Surprisingly, scores within the schizophrenic group were negatively correlated with months since first hospitalization. Chapman et al. said of this: "Apparently the experience of body-image aberration occurs more in the early stages of the illness and the symptoms are forgotten or eclipsed by more serious disorders as the illness progresses" (p. 403). For the noncollege normal controls, the mean Body Image Aberration score was 3.71, significantly lower than the mean for the schizophrenics. For the nonpsychotic outpatients, the mean score was 3.80, which was significantly lower than the mean of the schizophrenics. However, the mean scores of the male and female college students were respectively 4.55 and 5.56, which did not differ significantly from the mean of the schizophrenics. Fisher (1970) too had noted that his questionnaire measure of body distortion elicited from college students unusually high scores that overlapped a good deal with those of schizophrenics; normal subjects who were not college students obtained considerably lower body distortion scores.

Chapman et al. (1978) reported minimal correlations between their Body-Image Aberration scores and the following: social desirability, acquiescence, age, education (in the noncollege samples), and father's social class. A 7-item scale said to tap general perceptual alterations other than in the body (e.g., "Sometimes when I look at things like tables and chairs, they seem strange") correlated highly with the Body-Image Aberration scores in all of the samples. Chapman et al. interpreted this to mean "that body-image aberration is an aspect of a broader perceptual dysfunction" (p. 405). Of course, it is conceivable that the broader perceptual distortions are somehow a derivative of distorted experiences in the body space. It is a matter of concern that Chapman et al. did not compare the schizophrenics with other control groups embracing different categories of hospitalized psychiatric patients. There is also the puzzling fact that normal college students' scores could not be distinguished from those of the schizophrenics. This suggests that the distortions reported by the schizophrenics are not unique.

Research with a special version of the Body-Image Aberration Scale that also includes the seven items dealing with general perceptual distortions has been carried out. This scale is called the Perceptual Aberration Scale. It has been shown that college students who obtain high scores on this scale also show deviant logic in their Rorschach responses (Edell & Chapman, 1979); report a relatively large number of psychotic-like experiences (Chapman, Edell, & Chapman, 1980); behave relatively inappropriately in social situations (Numbers & Chapman, 1982); and perform relatively poorly on a word-communication task (Martin & Chapman, 1982). One investigator even found that high scorers exhibit an electrocortical pattern said to be associated with psychopathology (Lutzenberger, Elbert, Rockstroh, Birbaumer, & Stegagno, 1981). Chapman and his colleagues believe that high scorers are particularly vulnerable to the development of schizophrenia. However, this has yet to be proven.

Other scattered attempts have been made to explore body image parameters in relation to schizophrenia. Wilps, Jr. (1972) made use of a body-distorting mirror to examine possible differences in body perception between normals (36 males) and chronic hospitalized schizophrenics (36 males) and .also to test several hypotheses about the effects of induced muscular sensations upon body perception. The mirror duplicated one that has been used in previous studies by Orbach, Traub, and Olson (1966) and Cardone and Olson (1969). Subjects are presented with a distorted mirror image of self; and, as the concave or convex distortions are gradually reduced, the subjects indicate at what point the mirror image becomes most true to life. A series of trials is administered. In the present experiment subjects also made judgments about the mirror images of two nonself objects, one a simple rectangular form and the other a rectangular form of considerable more complexity because its sides were elaborately scalloped and indented with bilaterally symmetrical ornaments. The mirror judgments were scored for their degree of realism and for their clarity (as defined by range). Experimental subjects responded to the mirror task first, so that a baseline measure could be obtained, and then again after 4 minutes of *kinesthetic arousal*, which involved such activities as holding the arms and legs extended horizontally or applying a vibrator to the neck and shoulders. These tasks were derived from a study by Van De Mark and Neuringer (1969), which had demonstrated that such kinesthetic arousal increased body boundary articulation as measured by the Fisher-Cleveland (1958) Barrier score.

Wilps, Jr. (1972) intended to test the sensitivity of the Mirror Distortion technique to a parameter that had already been shown to be effective in influencing another type of body image measure. He also asked subjects to draw same and opposite sex figures before and after the kinesthetic arousal task. The drawings were scored in terms of the Witkin et al. (1962) Sophistication-of-Body-Concept Scale. This provided an opportunity to determine if "kinesthetic arousal" would affect still another body image measure. Half the schizophrenic sample and half the normal sample went through the experimental procedure. The other half of each sample went through the same procedure, except that, instead of intervening kinesthetic arousal, there was a neutral condition that involved such activities as listening to taped music and looking at a modern painting. The schizophrenics were found to be significantly less accurate and less clear in their mirror judgments of self than were the normals. However, they were also significantly less accurate in their judgments of the nonself objects. Thus, they did not display a specific body image deficit, as such. Further, the schizophrenics produced significantly more "primitive" drawings than the normals. The kinesthetic arousal condition did not affect mirror or figure drawing scores to any greater degree than did the neutral condition. Neither measure was sensitive to the impact of the arousal in the body's muscle sheath. Wilps, Jr. was particularly impressed that, when subjects were asked to evaluate the distortions produced by the mirror in different areas of the body (e.g., head, legs), their judgments were not highly correlated. That is, there seemed to be considerable differentiation with respect to how they dealt with the major body regions. This raised the possibility that there might be "independence of various parts of the body in the total body image" (p. 69). Shontz (1969) discerned a similar independence with reference to how the sizes of different regions of the body were perceived. While certain regions might be consistently overestimated, others were just as consistently underestimated. More is said at a later point concerning this matter.

Dimond and Hirt (1974) compared semantic differential ratings of 21 body-products (e.g., feces, vomit, saliva) by hospitalized schizophrenics ($N = 25$), paraplegics ($N = 25$), and normals ($N = 25$). No differences in ratings could be discerned. Ross, Hirt and Kurtz (1968) had previously reported remarkable consistency across diverse samples of people in their attitudes toward a range of body products. The findings just described for the schizophrenic sample supported their findings. Dimond and Hirt (1973) also reported that, when the Secord Homonym Test was administered to the same samples described in the body-products study, the schizophrenics' scores could not be distinguished from those of the normals. But the parapelgics exhibited significantly higher body awareness scores than the normals and a borderline higher level than the schizophrenics. It is of related interest that Puente and Morrisey (1981) did not discern a difference when a Self-Consciousness Scale developed by Fenigstein, Scheier, and Buss (1975) was administered to 10 long-term and 10 short-term schizophrenics, 10 sociopaths, and 10 normal subjects. The Self Consciousness Scale, which relates to self awareness, does have some body connotations.

A series of investigations was concerned with the *body buffer zone*. This term was originated by Horowitz, Duff & Stratton (1964), who proposed that persons conceive of a certain area of space contiguous to their body as particularly their own. They presumably may have varied feelings and attitudes about the size, shape, and vulnerability to penetration of this space. As earlier mentioned, Horowitz et al. found that schizophrenics have an unusually large buffer zone. That is, schizophrenics try to maintain a large space between their own body and the bodies of others. There have been numerous reports that people who are significantly maladjusted seek to establish a relatively large buffer zone (Evans & Howard, 1973), but several reports have not discerned such a relationship (Blumenthal & Meltzoff, 1967; Dosey & Meisels, 1969; Meisels & Canter, 1970). In any case, it is doubtful that a large body buffer zone is unique to schizophrenia. Kinzel (1970) observed that nonpsychotic prisoners who were extremely pugnacious and aggressive had highly expanded buffer zones. Tolor and Donnon (1969) found, paradoxically, that schizophrenics who had been hospitalized an average of 11 years displayed a relatively greater interest in social closeness than did psychiatric patients hospitalized only briefly. The problem of studying the buffer zone has been complicated by the fact that it apparently varies as a function of whether it involves the front or the back of the individual's body (Kinzel, 1970).

Comment. The literature concerned with body perception in schizophrenics has been consistently disappointing. Most of the interesting past leads have not worn well with time. As already described, little remains of earlier assertions that schizophrenics are typified by a major body image defect that manifests itself in an overestimation of body size. It is true that, in certain limited contexts in which judgments of total body size are involved, schizophrenics are inclined either to overestimate or to underestimate their actual size. But they are no less accurate than normals in their size judgments. The McClelland and Watt (1968) conclusions that schizophrenic males and females show sex reversal in their body attitudes have been contradicted by subsequent studies. Similarly, the initially promising leads concerning "kinesthetic deficit" in schizophrenics that came from the group at the Lafayette Clinic have not been supported by a number of investigators. Even where, in a few instances, questionnaire measures of experienced body image distortion have revealed differences between schizophrenics and normals, they have not been able to differentiate schizophrenics from other diagnostic groups; and, in fact, they have been shown to be vulnerable to serious criticism because they have not controlled for the effects of hospitalization itself. The same criticism about lack of control for the effects of hospitalization can be applied to the Wapner and Werner (1965a) observations about the regressive manner in which schizophrenics judge the vertical when their bodies are tilted. It is also true that early reports about the large body buffer zone of the schizophrenic have turned out to be oversimplified. Indeed, it is not at all clear that the schizophrenic's buffer zone differs from that of other psychiatric diagnostic groups.

One category of finding stands in contrast to the negative ones just cited. Two studies have reported that schizophrenic children have unusual difficulty in making right-left body discriminations. It is not clear what this means. Childhood schizophrenia is probably a different species from adult schizophrenia, and its etiology may be more directly linked to brain damage. In any case, it can be said unequivocally at this point that there is no solid evidence that adult schizophrenics experience their bodies in any unique fashion or that they suffer from some extraordinary "body image deficit." Why empirical studies fail to verify the flamboyant body image dramas that abound in so many clinical vignettes about schizophrenics remains a mystery. In many case history reports schizophrenics are said to verbalize fantasies about body transformation and distortion. Possibly such published vignettes represent the select minority of instances in which extreme body image distortions were present, and clinicians were sufficiently impressed to seek publication. Possibly, too, there has been an underestimation of how often dramatic body image distortions occur in neurotics and even in normal subjects. Chapman et al. (1978) and Fisher (1970) have reported that college students entertain a surprisingly large number of unusual body fantasies.

Other Maladaptive Syndromes

It is not much of a task to peruse the several investigations that have in recent years examined the relationships between body image parameters and other forms of maladaptive behavior besides schizophrenia. Let us first review a few studies pertaining to depression. Teri (1982) measured depressive feelings in 340 females and 228 males (14–17 age range) by means of the Beck (1967) Depression Inventory. She also evaluated self-concept, body image attitudes, and other parameters by means of the Offer Self-Image Questionnaire (Offer, 1969; Offer & Howard, 1972). In addition, a variety of demographic information and a measure of assertiveness were obtained. The data indicated that, of all the variables, the best predictor of depression in this adolescent sample was the Offer body and self-image index, which taps feelings of awkwardness and discomfort with one's body. Those reporting greatest comfort with their body were likely to be low in depression.

Relatedly, Marsella, Shizuru, Brennan, and Kameoka (1981) appraised depression (by means of the Zung, 1972, Self-Report Depression Scale) in several samples of college students at the University of Hawaii: Japanese-American (47 male, 23 female), Chinese-American (24 male, 36 female), Caucasion-American (47 male, 49 female). A Body Image Satisfaction scale developed by the authors was administered. Subjects were asked to rate their degree of satisfaction with 17 different body areas. When they were split into high and low levels of depression, it was found that the relatively non-depressed were significantly more satisfied with their bodies. Analyses were undertaken to determine if there were differences between the depressed and nondepressed with respect to dissatisfaction with specific body areas. Chinese males showed strong continuity for areas of body dissatisfaction across the depressed and nondepressed categories. In the case of the Chinese females, dissatisfaction with waist and hips was continuous for the two groups, but the depressed were more dissatisfied with their weight and nose and the nondepressed with their breasts and complexion. Japanese-American males displayed continuity across the depressed and nondepressed groups for dissatisfaction with height, waist, and complexion; but height was a source of particular dissatisfaction for the depressed. As for Japanese-American females, the continuity between depressed and nondepressed groups involved dissatisfaction with hips, weight, and waist, but there was increased dissatisfaction with complexion and breasts in the depressed. The Caucasian-American male depressed group was characterized by unusually high dissatisfaction with nose, neck, complexion, and chest, whereas the nondepressed were particularly dissatisfied with weight, posture, height and hair. Elevated dissatisfaction with only complexion was observed in the depressed female Caucasian-Americans. Males in general were significantly more likely than females to be dissatisfied with ears, neck, and height; females, with hips and body hair. Marsella et al. summarized their overall findings as follows:

> Chinese-American males showed increased body-image dissatisfaction with "physique" variables (e.g., height, hips, shoulders) when depressed; Chinese-American females showed increased dissatisfaction with "facial" and "figure" variables (e.g., head, lips, ears, nose, weight). With the exception of complexion, Japanese-American males also showed increased body-image dissatisfaction with "physique" variables as a function of depression, while Japanese-American females primarily showed increased dissatisfaction with "facial" variables. Both Caucasian-American males and females demonstrated increased body-image dissatisfaction with "facial" variables. (p. 368)

Marsella et al. noted that depression introduces new areas of body dissatisfaction for some, merely exacerbates existing dissatisfaction for others, and in some instances has little impact on body dissatisfaction. It is of interest that there were such variations as a function of ethnic background.

Buxant (1976) set out to determine if there were body image differences between female hospitalized neurotics ($N = 25$) and normal female controls ($N = 25$). The neurotic group consisted of 16 women diagnosed as depressives and 9 as hysterics. The study was carried out in Belgium. The following body image procedures were employed: Secord and Jourard Body Cathexis Scale, the Fisher (1970) Body Distortion Questionnaire, and the Fisher (1970) measure of body awareness (Body Prominence). In this last measure, subjects list 20 things they are aware or conscious of, and the listed themes are scored for references to the body. In addition to the body image techniques, questionnaires were administered that evaluated degree of anxiety and depression and also preference for specific mechanisms of defense (e.g., projection, regression).

The neurotics were found to have significantly higher total Body Distortion Questionnaire scores than the normals. They were particularly high on feelings that one's body is dirty and alien and that one's body openings are blocked. They were also significantly less satisfied with their body, as defined by the Body Cathexis scores. No differences in Body Prominence could be ascertained. Differences between the depressives and hysterics (in the neurotic sample) for Body Cathexis and Body Prominence did not attain significance. However, hysterics indicated a significantly higher degree of concern about boundary loss (as defined by the Fisher Body Distortion Questionnaire) than did the depressives. There was a significant trend in the neurotic group for those who experienced elevated body anxiety to use denial, projection, and regression as defense mechanisms. Also, in the neurotic group, Body Prominence was significantly positively correlated with general anxiety, negatively with the defense mechanism of denial, and negatively with sensations of body largeness. No relationship of significance appeared in the normal group between Body Prominence and the other measures. It is important to keep in mind that the two groups studied differed not only in degree of pathology, but also in the fact that one was hospitalized and one was not.

Two studies have observed a link between body image variables and addictive behavior. Weathers and Billingsley (1982) were struck by earlier findings of low body esteem in female alcoholics.[17] They examined body esteem (by means of the Secord-Jourard Body Cathexis Scale) in 20 addicted women (10 alcoholic, 10 opiate addicts) and 20 nonaddicted women in treatment for emotional difficulties. The addicted women had significantly more negative body attitudes than the nonaddicted. But the finding seems incongruent with a report by Brehm and Back (1968), who investigated the factors that increase the likelihood that one will use drugs to change oneself. The subjects were 147 college students who indicated how positively they felt about taking a variety of drugs and who also responded to a questionnaire that measured physical anxiety as well as social and ego anxiety. There was a significant trend for those most positive about drug usage to have low physical anxiety. Although these findings seem to contradict the Weathers and Billingsley study just cited, in the first instance the subjects were college students without clinical pathology, and in the second instance they were serious addicts who were relatively disabled. College students who are willing to experiment with drugs may be so inclined partially because they have relatively low fear about incurring body damage.

Miscellaneous other studies touch on the relationship of body image to various deviant behaviors. They need only be mentioned. Crowe (1972) found increased signs of body image disturbance in the figure drawings of hyperkinetic children. But Gounard and Pray (1975) did not discern such disturbance in the figure drawings of learning disabled children. Prytula, Wellford, and DeMonbreun (1979) noted that homosexual males had relatively high levels of dissatisfaction with their body. Sobel (1976) found in a sample of male adolescents that the more negative their attitudes toward homosexuality the more positive they were toward their own body.

BODY ORIENTED THERAPY MODES

There seems to be a growing interest in the possibility of using body experience for therapeutic purposes. Speculation abounds about the value of focusing on the body as part of the psychotherapeutic process (e.g., Brown, 1973; Chaiklin & Chaiklin, 1982; Dublin, 1981; Ehrlich, 1970; Horner, 1973; Redfearn, 1970; Weiner, 1974). It is said that most psychotherapeutic approaches are too verbally oriented and do not deal with attitudes and inhibitions that are primarily coded as body experiences. Ehrlich (1970) remarks:

> Traditionally psychotherapists define their work in terms of the verbal encounter between patient and therapist. The mainstream of analytic writing since Freud has consistently placed enormous faith in the power of the word to set man free; that is, verbal insight or intellectual understanding is thought to be liberating . . . Body awareness has the potential for transforming self. Sensory and kinesthetic awareness is a rich, untapped source of nonverbal communication if both patient and therapist are sensitive to the infinite number of subtle ways in which inner feelings are expressed in posture, facial expression, breathing, gait, voice—indeed, in all expressive movements including the basic activities of standing, walking, sitting and lying. Discovering the language of the body—which is not an easy task—entails a heightened awareness of proprioceptive sensations. This experience can serve as a vivid anchoring point to a reality, allowing for the kind of direct perception that leads to accurate self-knowledge. (p. 181)

Body oriented therapy systems have been formulated by a number of past clinicians: Reich (1949), Lowen (1967), Perls, Hefferline, and Goodman (1951), Braatoy (1954), Des Lauriers (1962). The details of these systems need not be reviewed here. Although such systems had been widely applied, little is known empirically about their effectiveness or in what ways, if any, they alter the body image. In fact, the scientific literature dealing with relationships between therapy and body image is relatively sparse. Fisher (1970) and Fisher and Cleveland (1958) reviewed earlier available data concerning the effects of therapeutic maneuvers upon the body boundary. They found a few positive and encouraging results. Fisher and Cleveland reported that, when boundary articulation was measured (by means of Barrier and Penetration scores) pre- and posttreatment in persons judged to have improved during long-term individual or group therapy,[18] a significant increase in boundary articulation was detected. Cleveland (1960a) described augmented boundary definiteness (as defined by the Penetration score) in schizophrenics who showed clinical improvement. However, Cardone (1967) failed to observe analogous boundary changes in a group of schizophrenics he followed. It is also of tangential pertinence that McGlothin, Cohen, and McGlothin (1966) detected in normal subjects, who systematically experienced the effects of LSD, an increase in ability to tolerate stress that was paralleled by an increase in boundary articulation (as defined by the Barrier score).

Several investigators began in the 1960s to explore empirically the use of body oriented therapies with schizophrenics (Goertzel, May, Salkin, & Schoop, 1965; May, Wexler, Salkin, & Schoop, 1963; Salkin & May, 1967). They reported significant improvement in schizophrenics who participated in sessions in which they were made more body aware and more boundary aware and were provided with movement experiences that clarified the meanings of various modes of body expression. The results, while significant, were neither dramatic nor spectacular. There were also a few studies that reported improvement in schizophrenics as the result of sensory deprivation experiences that presumably fostered more realistic body boundaries (Azima & Cramer, 1956; Cooper, Adams, & Cohen, 1965). Apparently this work did not stir much interest. Only a smattering of pertinent studies involving schizophrenics followed. There were exploratory attempts to use videotape self-confrontation as a means of intensifying and altering body perceptions in schizophrenics (e.g., Berger, 1970; Boyd & Sisney, 1967; Braucht, 1970; Mermelstein, 1968; Spiro & Silverman, 1969) and some reported preliminary promising results. However, two more recent studies[19] involving videotape self-confrontation turned out rather negatively. They are worth detailed attention.

Berman (1972) exposed hospitalized male schizophrenics ($N = 15$) to a series of videotaping sessions in which they talked about themselves, performed exercises, and identified various aspects of their own bodies. Immediately after each taping session, subjects viewed a replay of the videotape sequence and were asked about their reactions. Rorschach protocols were obtained from them prior to the first videotape session and following the last videotape session. A control group of male schizophrenics ($N = 15$) was similarly tested and retested. However, after they performed the same exercises and body identification tasks as the experimental subjects, they watched replays of commercial television programs rather than videotapes of their own performance. There were also 15 normal subjects who underwent the same procedure as the experimental subjects. The schizophrenics exposed to videotape self-confrontation did not show any significant pre- to postsession changes, as defined by Rorschach measures of ego strength and primary process thinking. But the normal subjects showed a significant decline in "less-well-controlled primary process thinking" and a significant increase in ego strength. Berman was not able to explain why the results were more positive for the normals than for the schizophrenics.

Muzekari, Weinman, and Kreiger (1973) explored the effects of three different treatments on schizophrenic subjects: (1) *Physical self-experiential,* which involved 24 group sessions "intended to provide the chronic psychotic with experience in defining, and establishing awareness of, his body as distinct from others and the environment. Videotape feedback was utilized within the sessions and was primarily directed toward further facilitating the patient's awareness of his body" (p. 421). (2) *Emotional self-experiential,* which likewise consisted of 24 group sessions with videotape feedback that emphasized the expression and recognition of appropriate emotions in relation to various situations. (3) *Social interaction,* which consisted of sessions designed to demonstrate that social experiences can be satisfying and to provide a repertoire of techniques for relating to people. Six males and six female hospitalized patients participated in each of the treatment conditions. Pre- and posttreatment measures were obtained regarding self-concept, clinical status, and social awareness. The results indicated that neither of the self-confrontation techniques was effective. Indeed, the self-concept scores of the patients in the self-confrontation conditions tended to decline, whereas those of the patients receiving the social interaction treatment rose. Muzekari et al. speculated that, for the chronic schizophrenic: "stark confrontation with the realities of his appearance and the evident deficits in his functioning, as highlighted by videotape feedback, constituted a negative experience" (p. 425).

Two studies employing body techniques other than videotape self-confrontation have reported positive results in treating schizophrenics. Seruya (1977) instituted a project designed to test the proposition that training schizophrenics to perceive their body size more veridically would have a positive therapeutic effect. The design involved two groups of 20 schizophrenic subjects each. The experimental subjects were exposed to a series of sessions in which they were given practice in learning to estimate their body height and width more accurately. The control subjects were given a choice of doing a variety of neutral recreational tasks. Pre- and postmeasures were obtained on all subjects with respect to state and trait anxiety and distancing from others as defined by a drawing task. Also, posttest data were obtained with regard to distancing and spontaneous social response in a special social interaction situation. The schizophrenics receiving treatment evidenced a significantly greater reduction in both state and trait anxiety than did the schizophrenic controls. The former were less likely posttreatment to take a distancing attitude as defined by circle drawing representations of self, a friend, and a stranger in the context of defining how close to self one would want these people be in an ordinary social situation. In addition, the treated schizophrenics demonstrated significantly more closeness and social spontaneity (e.g., as evidenced by eye contact and smiling) in special posttreatment social situations. Seruya concluded that during the experimental treatment the "patient's body image boundaries were being restored" and this, in turn, led to improved ability to relate to others and to greater comfort with self.

Also on the positive side, Rosenthal and Beutell (1981) reported a preliminary study in which they obtained figure drawings from nine chronic schizophrenics (4 female, 5 male) at a day care center before starting a therapeutic body movement program that focused on different aspects of the body. Sessions took place once a week for 10 weeks. A second set of figure drawings was obtained upon completion of the movement exercise series. Significantly less disturbance was present in the second than in the first drawings. However, there was no control group, and therefore the meaning of the findings cannot be judged.

Aside from the Seruya (1977) study, the results just reviewed are not particularly impressive with reference to treating schizophrenics by means of body oriented techniques. This is not surprising in view of the fact that psychotherapeutic procedures, in general, have been shown to have little impact on schizophrenic symptomatology. The therapeutic effects achieved by Seruya verge on the dramatic if one considers that they resulted from relatively brief training procedures intended to make body size perception more realistic. If they could be replicated, this would suggest that confusion about the spatial proportions of one's body plays a role in schizophrenic disturbance.

Examples may be found in the literature of body oriented therapeutic techniques that have helped nonpsychotic individuals. Dosamantes-Alperson and Merrill (1980) studied 28 normal college students (26 female, 2 male) exposed to Experiential Movement Psychotherapy, which "focuses on the client's subjective experiencing as s/he converts an inner sensation to overt physical movement, and transforms this movement into visual and verbal symbols" (p. 63). Subjects met twice weekly for a total of 16 sessions. They were shown how to experience contrasting sensations in particular body areas, muscular tension-relaxation, and the transformation of inner-directed movement into images and thoughts. The following measures were taken pre- and posttherapy: Secord-Jourard Body-Cathexis Scale, a measure of the subject's expressive movement range, and a questionnaire designed to tap such dimensions as inner-directedness, spontaneity, and self-acceptance. Two control groups were included. One ($N = 17$) consisted of college students who participated in a program of ballet training; a second ($N = 7$) involved college students who were on a waiting list to enroll in the Experiential Movement Psychotherapy program. The experimental subjects improved significantly more than the controls on a number of the measures. They displayed a greater increment of feeling satisfaction with their bodies; their body movements became more light, confident, and explorative; and they shifted to being more inner-directed, more sensitive to their own needs, and more accepting of themselves.

De Chiara (1982) applied an "art program" designed to strengthen the body image to 10 learning disabled children, ages 8–11 (3 girls, 7 boys). This program involved sessions three times a week, for a total of 22. The body image enhancing procedures diversely called for acquainting oneself with individual body parts and their functions, engaging in body expressive activities, and becoming familiar with one's own appearance and contours. Pre- and posttests were given: Draw-A-Person, a manikin assembly task, a measure of ability to imitate postures, and an evaluation of ability to identify one's body parts. A control group of 10 children (1 girl, 9 boys) participated in a regular classroom program but not in the body image oriented activities. The experimental subjects improved significantly more than the controls in their self-identification of body parts, in their ability to imitate postures, and in the developmental complexity of their figure drawings; but no significant differences emerged for the other body image measures. De Chiara considered that her results indicated positive therapeutic effects for the treatment program.[20]

Djalali (1978) evaluated the effectiveness of Bioenergetic Body Therapy in treating drug addicts. A 24-hour marathon group session was run with 13 addicts (9 male, 4 female). The subjects were asked to focus on their relationship to their body. A second addict group ($N = 13$) was involved in a purely verbal form of therapy, and a control group of addicts received no treatment. Pre- and postsession measures were taken at a number of different levels (body awareness, boundary articulation, self-ratings of self and body). Both the Bioenergetic and verbal therapy groups displayed significantly greater improvement than the no-treatment controls. They moved in the direction of greater body image security and more positive evaluations of self and body. The Bioenergetic group tended to show more improvement than the verbal therapy group, but the differences were small.

Wright (1981) explored the effects of a body therapy on muscle tension (Muscle Action Potential), on self-ratings of one's body, and on a questionnaire measure of openness to intimacy. The subjects were 30 persons enrolled in 3–day Neo-Reichian[21] Bodywork workshops. The therapist used Bioenergetic exercises, which focused on breathing "to loosen muscular armoring and free the energy flow in the body." One sample was evaluated pre- and posttherapy. A second sample of subjects was evaluated before and after a period in which they were waiting for therapy and then again before and after actually receiving therapy. Body esteem increased significantly in the treated versus delayed treatment subjects for several days after therapy was completed, but 2 months later this effect had dissipated. Overall, the therapy also had a significant effect in reducing muscle tension. No significant differences were found with regard to openness to experience. It was considered that the Neo-Reichian therapy had shown itself to have a positive therapeutic impact.

Further on the positive side, several studies have reported that Structural Integration therapy has therapeutic effects. This therapy, more popularly known as "Rolfing," is based on the assumption that posture is behavior and that most people suffer from body imbalances and displacements that interfere with free physical movement and emotional expression. Rolfing involves the use of deep massage and manipulation of body tissue in order to restore muscular balance and integration. Townsend (1976) found that an experimental group (16 males, 22 females) significantly exceeded a control group (13 males, 15 females) in showing increases (as defined by a questionnaire) in self-regard, ability to maintain meaningful relationships, and ability to accept feelings of aggression. Dickerson (1978) made use of three groups: persons receiving a series of Rolfing sessions, control participants in a 10-week jogging program, and nontreated controls. Both personality and body image questionnaires were administered pre-, post-, and after 8 months. Analysis of the data was complicated by the fact that the groups differed significantly for some of the pretests, though they did not differ in terms of their self-ratings of their bodies. The Rolfing group showed significantly more improvement than the other groups with reference to body image ratings, both at the immediate post-period and 8 months later.

Beckett (1974) obtained pre- and post-questionnaire measures from 27 persons exposed to a series of Rolfing sessions, 28 persons exposed to traditional psychotherapy, and 35 controls who received no therapy. Both the Rolfed and the conventional psychotherapy groups showed significantly more improvement than the controls, but these two groups did not differ from each other. Pratt (1974) reported that 24 patients who received Rolfing evidenced significant improvement in terms of pre- to post- self-ratings. However, there was no control group. Adair-Leland (1980) reported mixed results in a study of 14 persons who experienced Rolfing, 17 persons involved in a Yoga therapy program, and 18 controls who received no treatment. A variety of pre- and post-measures (e.g., body awareness, embedded figures, ink blots, self-ratings) were administered. As compared to the controls, the Rolfed subjects showed significant improvement only for self-evaluations. The Rolfed subjects did not differ significantly from the subjects involved in Yoga therapy. (More is said later concerning the negative results obtained with the other measures that were employed in this study).

Long (1977) studied the effects of Rolfing on 14 subjects and compared these effects with the impact of Gestalt therapy on 10 subjects and the changes in a control group (N = 14) receiving no treatment. Pre- and postmeasures were taken: self ratings, ink blots, figure drawings. Also, spontaneous accounts of therapy effects were obtained. There were trends for the Rolfed and Gestalt groups to show significant increases in positive feelings about self. However, findings for the other measures were largely nonsignificant. Lieber (1975) examined the effect of Rolfing on postural alignment and self-esteem (as measured by the Tennessee Self Concept Scale). No control group was employed. Self-esteem shifted significantly in a positive direction from pre- to posttesting. The improvement in postural alignment was of borderline significance. Overall, Lieber was not impressed with the size of the changes that had occurred. In another study, Carrera (1974) found that observers could do significantly better than chance in differentiating videotaped movement segments of Rolfed versus unRolfed subjects. However, he was unimpressed with the magnitude of correct identification.

On the more negative side, with regard to body therapies, Houde and Tetreau (1981) reported that a "bioenergetic," bodily oriented therapeutic approach not only did not result in positive change in a group of normal subjects, but instead increased their anxiety level.[22]

A number of studies have simply looked at the impact of various psychotherapeutic procedures on body perception. The psychotherapeutic approaches diversely involve Gestalt therapy, Yoga, group interaction, and sexual enhancement workshops. The measures of body perception have typically been based on self-ratings of body satisfaction. Several of the studies have described the development of more favorable body attitudes as a result of exposure to therapy (Johnson, 1974; Livingston, 1976; Thompson, 1978; Zamarin, 1976). Several found no effects (e.g., Brenner, 1978; O'Dell & Seiler, 1975). There were no obviously identifiable variables that distinguished the studies in which body perception was or was not altered.

OVERVIEW

Without question, certain forms of pathology can eventuate in deviant modes of body perception. Certainly the anosognosia displayed by a brain injured individual represents an extreme form of disturbance in body experience. Fairly good findings exist too that the mentally retarded are delayed in mirror recognition of self and do not manage certain distinctions between body and nonbody stimuli that are typically made by persons of average intelligence. There is, though, nothing in the literature that convincingly shows that schizophrenics entertain unique numbers or types of body image distortions. Although the matter is not fully settled, the burden of proof rests on those who would declare that schizophrenia is fraught with a dramatic breakdown in the organization of the body image. It is interesting in this respect that in 1970, when Fisher reviewed the data bearing on whether schizophrenics display unusual disturbance in their body boundaries, his conclusion was in the negative. One recalls too that Witkin and his associates (1954, 1962) could not show that schizophrenics as a group make excessive errors in using their bodies as a frame of reference for judging the position of vertical when external cues are either eliminated or misleading. Like so many defects that have in the past been attributed to schizophrenia, the "fragmented body image" may turn out to be illusory.

Some of the findings that have been cited suggest that hospitalization itself may have an effect on the body image. There have been instances in which supposed body image defects in schizophrenic subjects disappeared when controls for being hospitalized were instituted. How might hospitalization affect body perception? First, just living within the environs of a hospital, with its connotations of illness and death, could intensify feelings of body vulnerability. Also, being in a psychiatric hospital often results in limitations on motility; there are rules that confine patients to a limited space. This might possibly lead to either increased or decreased kinesthetic sensations or affect an individual's degree of preoccupation with such sensations. Feelings about body boundary articulation could thereby be altered (Fisher, 1970). Finally, it is likely that hospitalized patients are subject to relatively high doses of medication and perhaps are required to submit to body intrusive medical procedures. Such variables might be expected to create novel and often puzzling body experiences that can not quickly be assimilated. In short, hospitalization not only arouses a medley of new body experiences but places the body in a position of apparent jeopardy.

Although the work reviewed in this chapter has not revealed specific forms of body image deficit linked to particular psychopathological syndromes, it has pointed up some ways in which people can be uncomfortable with their body. Depersonalization seems to represent a degree of discomfort that calls for shutting out the reality of one's own body space. Paradoxically, there are suggestions that those who manifest depersonalization are actually unusually sensitive to body sensations and are particularly inclined to translate events into body terms. Brauer et al. (1970) found that psychiatric patients with prominent symptoms of depersonalization were prone to interpret external stimuli as affecting their bodies rather than their emotions or intrapsychic feelings. Depersonalization may well represent an attempt to balance or compensate for too much body sensitivity. Hypochondriacal individuals too are obviously overly responsive vis-a-vis body events. They seem to perceive the body as undependable and have learned from their parents that it must be faithfully monitored and nurtured if it is to survive. Unlike those who depersonalize, they rely on a sensitized defense system. They do, indeed, show a heightened sensitivity not only to body sensations but also to visual stimuli (Hanbeck & Revelle, 1978). It would not be surprising if future work revealed basic similarities in the concerns and conflicts of hypochondriacs and those who depersonalize. Although schizophrenics do not appear to be either deviantly attentive or inattentive to their body experiences, there is evidence that they are somehow uncomfortable with their size (as may also be true of neurotics). Fisher (1970) has shown that schizophrenics are concerned with feelings of bodily smallness. In addition, several studies indicate that schizophrenics tend either to over- or underestimate their total body size in unstructured contexts that encourage projective judgments. These two sets of findings suggest that they are not at ease with regard to their relative magnitude in the world. However, their degree of deviance in this respect does not appear to be of major or dramatic proportions.

The literature dealing with the use of body oriented techniques in treatment modes is thought provoking. The more recent studies employing videotape self-confrontation (viz., Berman, 1972; Muzekari et al., 1973) in a quasipsychotherapeutic context have been completely ineffective with schizophrenics. A few earlier videotape studies involving schizophrenics did demonstrate some significant therapeutic effects, but they were small and unimpressive. However, a promising lead comes from the Seruya's (1977) work, which focused directly on helping schizophrenic patients to arrive at veridical perceptions of their body size. There was no psychotherapeutic context, and a specific class of body experiences was the center of the therapeutic strategy. Seruya reported considerable success with this approach. Several other projects (viz., de Chiara, 1982; Djalali, 1978; Dosamentes-Alperson & Merrill, 1980) that achieved therapeutic success with nonpsychotics were aimed at giving patients a direct better knowledge and understanding of their body experiences. Further, several studies reporting some success with the application of Rolfing to a nonclinical population were completely nonverbal in character and involved direct massage to the body. Fisher (1970) described studies in which schizophrenics were able to increase their body boundary articulation simply by activating and focusing attention on their musculature. It might be worthwhile to develop systematic, body oriented procedures that would focus primarily on improving accurate awareness of major classes of body experience. The therapeutic efficacy of such procedures could be evaluated in relation to their success at different points on a continuum of psychological disturbance. A few of the major classes of body perception worth exploring are:

1. Ability to judge kinesthetic sensations
2. Facility in perceiving changes in internal organs such as the heart
3. Accuracy in perceiving touch stimuli on the skin in various spatial sectors of the body (e.g., front and back, upper and lower, right and left)

The question is whether fostering more veridical perception of such levels of body experience would enhance the individual's ability to cope with anxiety and to think more realistically. The findings of Seruya and others just cited empirically raise just such a possibility. However, one must keep in mind that few, if any, differences in body image functioning have been solidly demonstrated to exist among persons with different degrees of psychopathology. One may ask, then, why procedures that apparently enhance the accuracy and focused quality of body perception should be therapeutic? No compelling answers come to mind. Of course, one has to reckon with the possibility that there are body perception defects in those with serious psychopathology and that they are not being detected by our current, rather crude measurement techniques. Presumably, such defects would hamper adaptation, and correcting them would be therapeutic. The fanciful thought also comes to mind that directly body oriented techniques might be successful because it is special and reassuring for people to find themselves relating to an authority figure who approvingly assigns their body a central place in the transactions that occur. Perhaps this reassurance satisfies longstanding fantasies about closeness[23] that are phrased in the images of early relationships with parents, who, after all, focus on and nurture the child's body.

NOTES

[1] Damas-Mora, Jenner, and Eacott (1980) recently reviewed what is known about autoscopia.

[2] Frederiks (1969) states that distortions in body perception are particularly likely to be associated with damage in the "somesthetic afferent system, the thalamus and the parietal lobe" (p. 211).

[3] There has also been debate as to whether a Gerstmann-like syndrome exists in children with reading and writing difficulties (Pirozzolo & Rayner, 1978; Spellacy & Peter, 1978). Note too that Silverman (1979) has reported that nonbrain-injured field dependent persons display defects in the performance of certain tasks (e.g., laterality judgments) that suggest the presence of a "subclinical" Gerstmann syndrome.

[4] Schwartz and Halpern (1973) found in a small sample of aphasics ($N = 5$) that disturbance in dealing with body stimuli was positively linked with degree of body impairment but not with amount of speech disturbance.

[5] Depersonalization has been observed in every category of psychiatric patients and in persons with brain damage. It occurs too as the result of sleep deprivation, hallucinogenic drugs, sensory deprivation, fatigue, use of marijuana, and facing life threatening danger (Melges, Tinklenberg, Hollister, & Gillespie, 1970; Noyes, Jr. & Kletti, 1976; Sedman, 1972; Szymanski, 1981). It has also been linked to self-mutilating behavior (e.g., Bach-Y-Rita, 1974; Pao, 1969).

[6] In 1984 Trueman reported that 34% of a sample of normal male and female college students ($N = 388$) indicated (in reply to a questionnaire) that they had had definite depersonalization experiences.

[7] Contrastingly, Brauer, Harrow, and Tucker (1970) observed depersonalization symptoms in 80% of a diverse psychiatric sample. It is obviously an unsettled question as to how common depersonalization experiences are in patients with severe neurotic and psychotic symptoms. Also, little is known about the average duration of depersonalization episodes.

[8]Sedman (1970) has been critical of those who portray depersonalization as a disturbance of the body image. He bases his objection on the failure of Cappon and Banks (1961, 1965) to find specific body image distortions in psychiatric patients with prominent depersonalization, as well as on Fisher's (1964c) report that psychiatric patients and normals do not differ on a body image measure of depersonalization. However, it is difficult to see how distorted body perception can be ruled out when a primary part of depersonalization is the complaint "My body feels strange." Note too that Sedman (1972) actually observed body image disturbance in one sample of patients with prominent depersonalization. Body image correlates of depersonalization have also been described by Brauer et al. (1970) and Freeman and Melges (1977). Note further that certain phenomenological and existential theories of depersonalization link it to a sense of not having the power to initiate action that can purposefully shape events and insure personal autonomy (Weckowicz, 1970). The role ascribed to action in this context has obvious implications for the body, which is, after all, the source of action.

[9]A number of factor analyses of measures of hypochondriasis have been carried out. Several were based on the MMPI (McKinley & Hathaway, 1940) Hypochondriasis scale (e.g., Comrey, 1957; Hanbeck and Revelle, 1978; O'Connor & Stefic, 1959). Others were based on quanitified interview and test variables (Bianchi, 1973) and specially devised questionnaire items (Pilowsky, 1967). The various factor analyses conjured up rather different lists of factors, although they all produced at least one that roughly referred to body preoccupation.

[10]Bianchi (1973) also published a later paper in which the data of this study were subjected to a factor analysis. One factor he noted "probably represents a distinct hypochondriacal syndrome, the component with its highest loading on 'unnecessary' operations, psychogenic pain, somatic preoccupation and being female. Its other sizeable loadings are on much family illness, low sensation threshold, poor prognosis, and life defeats. Much family illness is an important variable" (p. 546).

[11]The finding with regard to guilt affirms Grayden's (1958) study in which, as hypothesized by Alexander (1948), guilt was found to be significantly elevated in the hypochrondriacal.

[12]Nuller (1982) reported that psychiatric patients with prominent symptoms of depersonalization often during childhood had a constant fear of losing their parents.

[13]Berger (1977) reported significant correlations between hyypochondriasis (as defined by the MMPI) and selective participation in certain types of sports. For example, athletes participating in "high harm" sports were more hypochondriacal than those in "low harm" sports. The possibility was considered that "hypochondriac individuals may choose to participate in high harm sports . . . as a means of 'working out' their concern of harm or danger" (p. 204).

[14]This 1969 study was not available in the original Fisher (1970) review.

[15]Scattered attempts to use figure drawing indices to identify schizophrenics or to discriminate levels of schizophrenic symptomatology continue to appear in the literature. They usually come up with either negative results (e.g., Cancro, 1971; Cvetkovic, 1979) or relatively inconsequential findings (e.g., Kokonis, 1972).

[16]Pitblado, Shapiro, and Petrides (1980) found that hospitalized schizophrenics displayed a small deficit in use of proprioceptive cues when adapting to prismatic displacement. But this was based entirely on a comparison with normal subjects; no other psychiatric groups were included as controls.

[17] Cleveland and Sikes (1966) also reported the presence of elevated body image disturbance in male alcoholics.

[18] Two studies (Bauste, 1971; Livingston, 1976) have shown, interestingly, that a brief period of group interaction with persons who are supportive and friendly produces significant increases in feelings of body satisfaction.

[19] Several other studies that used self-image confrontation and that have been published since 1970 will not be reviewed either because they failed to employ elementary controls or did not specify the degree of pathology of the subjects (e.g., Griffiths & Hinkson, 1973; Spire, 1973).

[20] Sensori-motor training procedures have been reported to produce "positive" changes in the figure drawings of young children (e.g., Matthews, 1971; Sunal, 1976). However, negative results have also been reported (Bennett, 1980; Shuman-Carpenter, 1977).

[21] Interestingly, studies (Dudas, 1980; Kerberg, 1976) have begun to appear which support some of Reich's (1949) and Lowen's (1971) concepts concerning "bioenergetic body types."

[22] Heide and Borkovec (1983) found evidence that therapeutic procedures designed to produce body relaxation may instead arouse anxiety in a significant proportion of persons.

[23] The therapeutic effects of procedures that foster a sense of closeness to one's parents have been described by Silverman, Lachmann, and Milich (1982).

7

Integrative Conclusions

Major segments of the literature of body image phenomena published since 1969 have been reviewed. Although analyses of the material presented have been provided within each chapter, it would be well at this point to look back and consider larger trends. One cannot help but exclaim again about the luxuriant growth of inquiry into body image matters. Body image concepts have established outposts in all the behavioral science territories. Social psychologists particularly have shown a surge of interest in the role of the body in social interactions. Few aspects of persons' adaptations are not at least indirectly influenced by how the body domain is experienced. As already described, body image measures have been linked with an impressive list of variables and there has been much innovative fashioning of sophisticated techniques for measuring body attitudes. Recent years have seen the development of new indices diversely based on responses to lens distortions, mirror exposure, selective memory tasks, tachistoscopic input, feedback of body events, manipulation of body attention patterns, and so forth. Paul Schilder (1950) would be pleasantly surprised if he could witness the escalation of creative activity energized by his speculations about the "image and appearance" of the body.

The diversity of the phenomena associated with body perception is wondrous to behold. It is sensible to look for some broader integrative notions in this diversity. What kinds of generalized functions, defenses, and adaptations can one discern? Obviously, there is a basic class of body perception phenomena that pertain to monitoring such body sensations as temperature, position in space, pain, discomfort, thirst, hunger, sphincter tension, and so forth.[1] Many of these sensory categories have been intensively studied, but only a few (e.g., position in space, hunger) have been seriously examined within the context of body image concepts. Much of the body image literature has focused on body experiences that lie more within a realm that is delimited by terms like identity, personality, ego defenses, and psychodynamic functions. It is true, though, that important data relevant to such terms have been obtained from the study of such dimensions as perceived body size and position in space, which, at first sight, would appear not to be promising in this respect. What major categories pertaining to body image functions and dynamics can one discern?

1. A number of studies have shown that people ascribe to their body properties that parallel the psychological impact of events they are currently

encountering. Various examples may be cited. It will be recalled that Shaffer (1964) observed that children made to experience failure perceive themselves as relatively shorter—the failure brings with it a shrinkage in perceived body height. Relatedly, it has been reported (Ford, 1977) that the presence of an authority figure who has the status of a superior figure may increase feelings of body smallness in a subordinate. Indeed, reports from sensori-tonic researchers (Fisher, 1970) indicate there is a constant process of feeling that one's body is growing larger or smaller as different life conditions are encountered. Pennebaker (1982) has shown that the presence in the environment of stimuli referring to illness may trigger the interpretation "My own body is impaired or sick."

Degree of satisfaction-dissatisfaction with one's body appears, in certain contexts, to fluctuate as a function of how negative one's life circumstances are (Goldberg & Folkins, 1974; Kurtz & Hirt, 1970). Of course, people constantly observe changes in their body and emotional states as different situations are encountered. Parallels exist also between long-term psychological attitudes and particular patterns of body perception. Consider the following examples. Overall amount of body satisfaction has been shown in a number of studies to be positively correlated with one's general level of self esteem (Jourard & Secord, 1955). The degree of overestimation of the size of one's head parallels the intensity of one's investment in intellectual and educational activities (Furlong, 1977). Body image differentiation, as defined by the Witkin et al. (1962) measures, has been tied to numerous personality variables like autonomy, suggestibility, and sociability. Fisher and Cleveland (1958) and Fisher (1970) have detailed significant correlations between the state of the body boundary and such variables as achievement motivation, suggestibility, and vocational interests. People who are authoritarian in their life orientation are inclined to avoid awareness of their own body (Bookbinder, 1963). Other relationships analogous to those just cited could be detailed. How is one to interpret the body image equivalents of situational experiences or psychological attitudes? At one extreme, they can be regarded as epiphenomena, as echoes. However, the available data do not support this as a reasonable position. Evidence is accumulating for the quite opposed view that the body image equivalents serve important signal functions, helping to organize information and render decisions. More concerning this matter will be said later. But, in any case, the immediate point is that one of the apparent potentials of the body image is to represent in body experience terms what is being perceived and coded at other levels of psychological feeling and attitude.

2. It is impressive how much of the body image literature is taken up with issues of anxiety and defense (Fisher, 1970). People spend a lot of time and energy pondering potential threats to their body space. We know that children's stories, especially those produced by boys, are full of themes of body damage. There is widespread anxiety about illness and medical procedures,

and one expression of it is the irrational delay that frequently occurs before people seek medical consultation for somatic symptoms. Fear of body damage has also been documented in dreams, projective responses, figure drawings, and various questionnaires. Much of the past research dealing with body perception is concerned with the strategies and defenses people adopt to cope with their body concerns. Let us analyze these strategies.

One of the prime ways of managing body anxiety is by *denial*. A multitude of illustrations of this mechanism have been documented. One immediately thinks of the studies that have looked at misidentification of one's own voice. Gur and Sackeim (1979) and Sackeim and Gur (1978) showed that persons who are exposed to a failure experience have increased difficulty in correctly recognizing recordings of their voice. Presumably, the negative feelings induced by failure imbue one's self-representations with negativity and they are selectively tuned out. Relatedly, Gellert et al. (1971) observed that obese children, who it is known regard their own appearance negatively, have significantly more difficulty in identifying their own picture than do nonobese children. Similar denial is portrayed in the Andreason and Norris (1972) report that patients with disfiguring burns rate themselves as relatively more attractive than do observers. Also, female children have been noted (Landon, et al., 1980), despite severe body symptoms (e.g., cystic fibrosis), to deny that they have any more body dissatisfaction than normal, nonsymptomatic children. In the same vein, one would classify depersonalization as a repressive, denying mode of confronting one's body. The point has already been made that people seem, in general, to shut out many body aspects. Not only do they exhibit unexpected difficulties in identifying full-face pictures of themselves, but they also make surprisingly inaccurate judgments about such body variables as the size of various parts and the intensity of arousal of internal organs. One is struck with the paradox that such shutting out represents the polar opposite of what is unique about body perception. The body is the only perceived object that is apprehended also at the level of being "inside" it. There seem to be strong tendencies to avoid this "inside" prerogative. Of course, the obverse, namely heightened sensitivity to one's body, occurs too, as is apparent in the case of hypochondriacal individuals. One may observe such sensitivity in persons who are sick or who are required to undergo drastic medical procedures or who have been exposed to self referring stimuli like their own mirror image. Note that a sensitized attitude toward one's body may have both negative repercussions (as in the case of hypochondriasis) and positive ones. The positive effects may take the form of simply being able to detect more realistically what is happening within one's body; for example, drug effects (Gibbons et al., 1979) or intensity of specific emotional sensations (Pryor, et al., 1977).

The literature that has been reviewed suggests that another way of dealing with body anxiety is by rigidly *holding on* to the immediate structure of the body image. That is, the more threatened persons feel about potential danger to a given part of their body, the more they may seek to stabilize that part perceptually. They defend against the threat of potentially dangerous alteration in the body region by imposing a "no change" condition upon it. Uddenberg and Hakanson (1972) found that the greater the anxiety women felt about sexuality, the less they were able to see change in the pelvic region of their body (a site obviously equated with sexual functions) when they viewed it in a mirror through aniseikonic lenses. As noted, research data indicate that the more anxiety a perceptual target evokes, the less likely it is to appear as altered when looked at through aniseikonic lenses, which create the potentiality for experiencing alteration. Other studies (e.g., Fisher & Richter, 1969) have verified the Uddenberg and Hakanson observation that this mechanism may apply to the perception of one's own body. Berscheid et al. (1973) discovered that body esteem declines when a number of significant body changes impinge on persons within a period of time. People are inclined to construct tightly routinized ways of dealing with their body, and one may assume this has comforting, reassuring intent. Body functions are usually scheduled and regularized, and there are innumerable body rituals (e.g., mode of dress, specific exercises) that are performed probably to maintain a note of body constancy. One previously cited study (Mandell, 1979) presented evidence that as children mature they find the maintenance of body constancy to be of increasing importance.

Still another denying mode of defense is represented by the process of body *segmentation*. Studies of surgical patients (e.g., Green, 1976) hint that they seek to narrow the variability of their body experiences by segmenting the body and focusing on a restricted part of it. The most telling data on this point have derived from Ringe's (1980) work, in which he found that various physically disabled persons organize their body perceptions around restricted body parts and functions, whereas nondisabled subjects view their body in a more general or total fashion. One may deduce that the disabled defensively try to isolate the influence of the disabled body part, to narrow and exclude its role in the body image. The disabled could be thought of as minimizing the negative body part by sealing it off in a separate region. It is apropos to call attention to a related sealing off process in which the body, as a psychological object, is kept out of decisions about self. Previous work by Mayer and Eisenberg (1982b) and West (1973) demonstrated that in disabled persons the correlations between measures of body satisfaction and self esteem are negligible, whereas in the nondisabled the correlations are typically substantial. This suggests, of course, that disabled persons, who are confronted with their body as a negative or unpleasant stimulus, have adapted by excluding it from the calculus that determines self-esteem.

The earlier described research dealing with transitional objects highlighted the fact that children frequently comfort themselves in stress situations by rubbing something like a blanket or a soft toy against their body. It was proposed that rubbing represents an attempt to cope with anxiety by bolstering one's body image boundaries. Input into the body surface could help to highlight the skin and therefore to intensify the articulation of the boundary sheath of the body. Such self-reinforcement of boundaries may be a significant way of coping with concern about intrusion upon one's body. Adults too have a repertoire of self-administered techniques for reinforcing boundary security. They may diversely rub lotions into their skin, take long, tingling showers, or wear clothing with special qualities of tightness and/or texture. Fisher (1970) has previously presented data indicating that schizophrenic women use self-touching as an important means for reinforcing their boundaries, and Compton (1964) reported that they also use certain types of highly visible clothing for the same purpose.

Misattribution seems to be useful for buffering disturbing body feelings. A considerable literature has accumulated that indicates that one class of body feelings may be mistakenly linked to another. For example, the tension of the insomniac was in one experiment (Storms & Nisbett, 1970) relieved by creating the impression that it was due to a substance (placebo) that had been ingested. In another study (Ross et al., 1969), anxiety about a threatening stimulus was relieved by persuading subjects to attribute their arousal to another less threatening stimulus. It has also been possible to intensify certain arousal states (e.g., anger) by feeding into them a quite different form of arousal (e.g., due to exercise). One may reasonably assume that people learn to use misattribution as a means of coping with body feelings that are too disturbing. That is, they probably learn how to create special arousal states that will cover up others that are less acceptable. Unpleasant sensations associated with feelings of body vulnerability might be dealt with by displacing them onto the discomfort created by exhausting work. Or other unpleasant body perceptions might be displaced onto the negative sensations produced by practices like overeating, smoking, or taking various drugs. Misattribution may very well represent a more important body image defense strategy than has been realized.

It is pertinent to such modes of defense that people may ward off body anxiety by seeking distractors in the nonbody space. If people feel anxious about their body, they may distract themselves by focusing on things "out there." It is well documented that there are large individual differences in habitual levels of awareness of one's body as against other objects (Fisher, 1970; Miller et al., 1981). This may be due, in part, to differences in the degree to which people adopt a "looking away" from the body defense strategy. Pennebaker (1982) has shown beautifully that anxiety about one's body is minimized if one is in a setting where there are distracting stimuli. He described an experiment in which he measured the body complaints of joggers who ran in a monotonous uninteresting environment, as compared to one with stimulating distracting variability. The level of body complaints was significantly lower in the distracting setting. It is known too that body pain is minimized when external distractors are available.

Projection is another noteworthy means of coping with body image anxiety, as has been especially evident in studies of response to persons with body defects. It is well established that the sight of another individual whose body is distorted or different elicits a sense of threat. People seem to react as if the perceived body distortion augured the possibility of a similar distortion arising in one's own body. Several investigators (e.g., Fine, 1978) have shown a relationship between certain types of body anxiety and the degree to which one feels negatively about persons whose bodies are crippled or damaged. The relationship suggests that the body anxiety is dealt with by projecting it in the form of negativity onto the image of the damaged one "out there." The process might be paraphrased: "There is nothing wrong with my body. It is that other person's body which is terribly wrong and unpleasant to look at." Fisher (1978c) has even found that bias against the skin of blacks is linked with how dirty (black) people perceive their own body to be. Another form of projection of one's body has been depicted by Gur and Sackeim (1979). They discovered that persons who are given a success experience, and who therefore are presumably highly positive toward the self as an object, are unusually likely to misidentify tachistoscopically exposed pictures of others as being their own. They attribute their own body features to the representations of others. In the proper ambiguous context, they impose their self-representations on nonbody space. Fisher (1970) has proposed that there is a general readiness for people to project body feelings into ambiguous stimuli like inkblots. He presented evidence that intensity of awareness of one's stomach significantly predicts how many responses with oral connotations will be given in the context of interpreting inkblots. Similarly, there is good evidence that feelings about the boundary regions of one's body are readily translated into the properties ascribed to the peripheries of inkblot images. It may turn out that projection and outward attribution of one's bodily images represent a major mechanism for maintaining body image equilibrium.

One of the more extreme forms of body image defense is represented by *illusory additions to the body*. There seem to be situations in which conjuring up illusory images about one's body has protective value. It has been proposed by some theorists that the phantom limb phenomenon represents an effort at restitution for a lost body member. In the case of the breast phantom, it has been shown that the probability of occurrence of the phantom is significantly increased in women who lack supportive social ties (Jamison et al., 1979). It is as if the illusory breast represents an effort at compensation for overall feelings of lack and loss. Reduplication (Weinstein & Kahn, 1955) is an analogous phenomenon. It involves the delusion that one has more than the usual number of a given body part (e.g., two heads or three hands). Typically, the reduplicated part is one that has been incapacitated, and the reduplication can easily be interpreted within a loss paradigm. It is possible that illusory restitutions occur widely in a variety of more realistic ways. Greenberg and Fisher (1980a) have shown that normal women may, in certain stress conditions, unconsciously fantasy the possession of a phallic-like attachment to the body, which has reassuring value. Self-comforting restitution may be at work too when persons unrealistically add inches to their perceived stature or magnify the assumed size of some body part or organ. Of course, the most common mode of adding to one's body is by means of clothing and decorative elaborations that convey messages about size, sex, power, and so forth (Fisher, 1973b).

At this point it is not feasible to define the relative frequencies with which the various defenses against body anxiety just enumerated are employed. Probably there are large individual differences in this regard. A question that comes to mind is the amount of overlap between the defense mechanisms one deploys in coping with problems arising out of interpersonal relationships and those brought into action when one's own body is the central focus. It may well be that as one moves closer to the experiential setting of one's own body, special defense mechanisms are called into play. There are hints that repression and denial may be especially prominent in managing body anxieties. Is it conceivable too that different defense mechanisms would come to the fore as a function of anxieties linked to specific body regions? Perhaps it is easier to use denying forms of defense when anxiety relates to the relatively inaccessible interior of the body than when it concerns the visible body surface. Would not the lower part of the body, with its sexual and anal connotations, call for different defense strategies than the intellectualized head? Perhaps it is easier to rigidify the perception of body areas that are relatively fixed in their form and function as compared to areas that are less so. It might be more difficult to rigidify one's perception of the hand, with its constantly changing shapes, sizes, and functions, than to rigidify one's perception of a part like the nose, which is fixed. Just as Shontz (1969) discovered that different body parts lend themselves to over- versus underestimation of their size, so might they elicit differential protective strategies. In view of the consistent sex differences that have appeared at almost every level of body image research, one should consider the additional possibility that males and females differ with respect to the major defenses they employ in coping with body anxiety.

3. A third broad function of the body image seems to be to provide organized information and standards that will facilitate decision making. Many of these functions are obvious. For example, a clear definition of the spatial dimensions of one's body frames the entire process of establishing spatial coordinates. People learn relatively early to identify the right–left, front–back, and up–down dimensions of their body, and these become reference points for locating objects in space. The body coordinates are basic in labeling spatial positions. Relatedly, clear notions of one's size dimensions undoubtedly facilitate all sorts of decisions in which one has to occupy spaces of different magnitudes. Or a clear awareness of one's physical strength makes it easier to decide whether one can accomplish specific tasks.

The literature that has been reviewed throws some light on how organized body perceptions may facilitate decisions relating to more complex phenomena like interpersonal relationships.

One of the prime ways in which this occurs is by building into the body image a repertoire of signals defining what is culturally acceptable or nonacceptable. These signals can stimulate or inhibit action. Many social markers or injunctions are normally represented in the values ascribed to the body. As described, children learn quite early what is desirable with reference to body appearance. They learn that obesity is bad or that certain types of facial features are unattractive. They develop body standards against which they compare their own bodies and in so doing make implicit decisions about their acceptability, their likelihood of establishing ties with other persons varying in attractiveness. They learn, in body terms, that deviance beyond a certain extreme is unacceptable. They carry with them body-phrased images that keep telling them where they stand in a number of social hierarchies. At another level, they may have learned to experience guilt about the functioning of certain body organs and this serves as a persistent signal that activities connected with such organs should be avoided. Body markers like skin color or particular ethnic features can spell out complicated scripts about one's role in different social encounters. The acceptance of parental injunctions about the weakness of one's body may create a life-long attraction to pathways that meander toward becoming the hypochondriac.

As documented later, Fisher (1970) has shown that specific values are assigned to assorted body locales and these values shape behavior. He has demonstrated that increasing a person's awareness of a particular body area may selectively influence attitudes associated with that area. Illustratively, the back of the body has been found to be linked with feelings about being anally bad, that is, being dirty and messy. The greater the awareness one has of one's back, the more one is concerned about possibly losing control and making a dirty mess. A vibrator placed on a subject's back to increase back awareness has a selective impact on the subject's ability to learn and recall words differing in degree of reference to dirt and mess themes. The vibrator input to the back produces a significantly greater increase of memory for such words than does a control vibrator placed on the arm. This is cited as an example of how a component of the body image may guide responses to a class of stimuli. Fisher (1970) has presented evidence that similar selective memory phenomena can be obtained by changing the subject's experience of other components of the body image (e.g., eye awareness or mouth awareness).

4. In surveying the strategies and modes characterizing body perception, one has to conclude that the act of focusing on one's own body initiates processes that differ from those typical of the perception of nonself objects. This has become apparent on a number of levels.

First, there is the extensive work of Shontz (1969) and others indicating that size judgments of one's own body are distinctive. It will be recalled that judgments of body size were, in contrast to judgments of nonself objects, less accurate, more variable, more influenced by starting position, less altered by extraneous sensory input, and so forth. Although such differences were shown to be a matter of degree and to decrease significantly when the control judgments involved the bodies of other persons (rather than inanimate objects), there still remained an identifiable special patterning in the size perceptions of one's own body.

Second, there is at times a remarkable degree of inaccuracy in observing events in certain areas of the body, especially in view of the amount of past opportunity to become familiar with, and develop expertise in the observation of, those areas. For example, evidence has piled up indicating an amazing lack of accuracy in judging one's own heart rate. But it is doubtful that there would be a comparable error rate in reporting on analogous change events in nonself objects that had been long available for inspection.

It has also been established (Fisher, 1970) that persons who are, without their conscious awareness, exposed to pictures of self (e.g., shadow profiles) or similar representations (recordings of their voice) respond with more extremeness (usually more favorably) than they do to similar depictions of other persons. A more intense ego-involved reaction is triggered when the stimulus involves one's own body territory.

There is reason to believe that body perception is more likely to arouse guilt than are most other classes of perception. This has been shown in an array of studies dealing with the effects of being exposed to one's own mirror image. It has also become apparent in studies that have found that becoming ill or bodily disabled often arouses an inordinate quantity of guilt in the person involved. Obviously, too, there is a good deal of sociological and anthropological data linking body ceremonies and rituals to guilt about sexual, oral, and anal functions (Blacking, 1977; Vlahos, 1979).

Introducing one's body into a perceptual situation creates at times distinctive attitudes and tensions. Sensori-tonic researchers (Glick,1964) have demonstrated that, when subjects look at stimuli in the context of their possible relationship to one's body, the stimuli take on "closeness" qualities that differ from those whose link to the presence of one's body is minimized. Mandell (1979) has relatedly demonstrated that when lens-induced distortions involve one's body, they are adapted to differently than when they involve nonself objects.

Considerably more sex differences characterize body perception than does the perception of nonbody objects. They have to do with much more than the obvious contrasts of unlike body structures. As already enumerated, sex differences in body perception have been variously detected with reference to accuracy of body size judgments, adaptation to body tilt, changes in perceived body size subsequent to failure, ability to profit from training to improve accuracy of reports concerning activity of internal organs, and certain modes of conceptualizing right-left coordinates. As is described at a later point, there are also sex differences in body boundary definiteness, values ascribed to body locales, and the stability of body attention patterns. By way of contrast, few if any, consistent sex differences have been described in relation to perceiving nonself objects.

5. The centrality of the size dimension in body image functioning cannot be too strongly understood. Feelings about body size seem to penetrate every aspect of body perception. We know that obesity is one of the earliest and most widely perceived signs of body unacceptability. Feelings about the proper size of the total body and also of particular body parts play a major role in how satisfied one is with one's body. Tremendous significance is ascribed to being the right height or not having overabundant hips or having breasts of sufficient proportions. We learn too that the perceived sizes of different body parts change as they are used or not used, as they are in active versus passive roles, as they function in different environmental contexts varying in apparent security and spatial quality.

One of the principal languages of body image change is enunciated in size terms. There seems to be a continuous registry of apparent alterations in body magnitude in reaction to the flow of events. Body size judgments have been shown to be influenced by multiple variables—mood, failure versus success, state of the body boundaries, amount of attention focused on self, presence or absence of authority figures, and so forth. Differences in the sexual identification of the body are also typically depicted in size imagery. There are even hints that deviant psychological states may somehow induce extremes in perceived body size. This was apparently the case in several studies that looked at body size perception in schizophrenics. Although perception of the size of nonself objects varies at times as a function of the values assigned to those objects, it seems to vary less frequently than in the perception of one's own body. It will be an intriguing task to discover why size has become such an important medium of expression in the body domain. Is this a reflection of the special importance of size and the associated concept of power in Western culture? One wonders if there are cultures in which one would find grossly less preoccupation with size in body imagery?

6. Little has emerged from the literature reviewed that would permit one to pinpoint the role of body image variables in the development of disturbed behaviors. It is potentially of great value to acquire information about how body perception mediates or reflects gross deviations in adaptation. In fact, it has been difficult to find any consistent signs of body image disturbance in seriously maladjusted persons. There are hints here and there of difficulties in body perception that accompany syndromes like anorexia nervosa, schizophrenia, and neurosis. Persons with those difficulties report significantly

more distorted body experiences than do normal controls. However, it is not yet clear that the differences are independent of the effects of simply being hospitalized for a period of time. Similar caution should apply to accepting other observations, such as the apparent tendency for anorexic and obese persons to misinterpret stomach sensations or the inclination of the obese to overestimate their total size. What is impressive is the minimal amount of distortion in body perception that occurs even in those who have suffered gross breakdowns in body form and function or who have become psychologically incapacitated. It has been an horrendous task to find even small dependable indications that the severely emaciated, noneating anorexic woman has deviant modes of perceiving her own body. This is similarly true with respect to the person with a massively superobese body. It remains to be seen whether new, more sensitive measures of body perception will prove to be more able to distinguish such apparently deviant persons.

7. Although some reference to this matter has already been made, it needs to be reiterated that most of the adult body image modes appear relatively early developmentally. It is surprising to find that very young children are using the same standards as adults in their body evaluations. As noted, children as young as 3 and 4 already apply criteria similar to those of adults when deciding what is bodily attractive (Story, 1979). Witkin et al. (1954) reported that body concept differentiation, as defined both by the rod and frame measure and the figure drawing index, pretty well reaches its adult level by age 14. The adult mode of compensatorily shifting the position of vertical opposite to the direction of tilt is well established in female children by the age of 12 and in males by the age of 16. One finds a similar early appearance of the adult pattern of overestimating one's degree of lateral tilt in space. By the age of 6 or 7 children are reasonably accurate in estimating their body size. The ability to use one's body in making judgments about right versus left coordinates reaches adult proficiency by age 10 or 11.[2] It is perhaps a reasonable finding that children so early in life arrive at a state of body image maturation. Presumably this derives from the body's being so central in all adaptive behavior and so important in the parent-child relationship. Even the body transformations that accompany puberty seem not to alter body image measures in any radical fashion. Those alterations in the body image that have been reported as a function of sexual maturation (e.g., onset of menstruation) are small and have not stood up well to cross-validation. There seem to be relatively early definitions of various dimensions of the body image, and interestingly, they persist into old age, despite the gross body changes that occur.

Looking back on the body image research of the last decade or so, one learns how little has been done with respect to the effects of illness and various medical and surgical procedures. The natural deviations and pathology that lead to drastic body transformations represent extraordinary body image experiments that can obviously never be duplicated in the laboratory. People are exposed to experiences in which they diversely lose important parts of their body, find their body surfaces breached, encounter threats to their sexual identity, suddenly suffer loss of motor functions, or are changed into disfigured objects. Important information may be assumed to emerge from the measurement of the body image changes resulting from such traumas. However, little in the way of systematic pertinent research has been carried out. One finds, for example, that the body image effects of organ transplantation have hardly been looked at; nor have most other forms of surgery, including plastic reconstructive procedures. We also know little about the effects on body perception of relatively simple phenomena like feeling sick, being hospitalized, suffering a penetrating wound, being in pain, wearing a cast, having a tooth extracted, receiving an injection, undergoing a routine physical examination, and so forth. If we understood the body feelings linked to these phenomena, we would be in a better position to comprehend the often irrational behaviors of people when they discover that all is not well within their body. To explore these body feelings, we need to go beyond common sense inquiries about discomfort and changes in self-evalua-tion. We should bring to bear measurement techniques that will provide more sophisticated information, such as how much affected parts of the body have changed in perceptual vividness or whether they have become more or less resistant to perceptual alteration. We need to know which body image defense mechanisms (e.g., denial, segmentation) are selectively triggered. There is a big research gap that needs to be filled.

Another sector in which there has been a lack of creative investigation is the socialization experiences that contribute to different patterns of body perception. Few efforts have been made to link persons' body image modes to their relationships with their parents. A survey of the literature discloses only scattered reports that are relevant. Witkin et al. (1962) intensively examined the attributes of the mothers of field independent versus field dependent children. However, this work was done many years ago and involves a parameter that Witkin et al. came to regard less and less as falling primarily into a body image category. Fisher and Cleveland (1958) and Fisher (1970) devoted a good deal of effort to probing the socialization experiences that affect body boundary definiteness; but their findings, while promising, were relatively meager.

There is little beyond the few major efforts just cited. There have been only a handful of small-scale studies of how parental and other socialization variables may play a role in offsprings' hypochondriacal attitudes, level of dental anxiety, interest in athletics, and phantom limb experiences. We know absolutely nothing about the involvement of parental attitudes in such basic phenomena as how people perceive their body size, how they respond to the threat of surgery, how quickly and well they learn the spatial coordinates of their body, how important it is for them to wear particular clothing styles, and so forth. Without information about the socialization roots of body image behavior, we are left with abstracted bits whose adaptive significances re-main obscure. Inasmuch as parents' interactions with their child are mediated strongly by the child's body functions, especially in the early years, there can be no doubt that there are meaningful ties between persons' body attitudes and the history of children's transactions with their caretakers.

In all fairness it must be said that information about how people organize their body perceptions has shown real growth. There are a number of areas in which we now have solid knowledge. What is missing are unifying concepts. We lack a picture of how the parts interlock. This is not surprising in view of the relatively brief period in which sustained serious body image research has flourished. What sorts of unifying concepts should we be seeking? First, we need to develop some paradigms about how body perception and percep-tion of nonself objects interrelate. We do not know how the matrix of body awareness regulates other perceptual inputs. We have interesting hints that it may facilitate or inhibit other classes of input. The work of Duval and Wicklund (1972) is cogently suggestive in this respect. Second, we need some integrative ideas about how the organization of the body image meshes with major dimensions of personality functioning. How does a personality vector like achievement drive relate to the body image? Does a certain mode of body perception provide an anlage for an achievement orientation? Do the requirements of an achievement role call for fantasy "shaping" of one's body in specific ways? Do high achievers have to portray their body space as large and well armored (possessing highly articulated boundaries) in order to feel capable of mastering the obstacles certain to be encountered on an achieving trajectory? Do introverts and extraverts have to conjure up different body concepts in order to create a meaningful world picture for themselves? Perhaps the extravert has to minimize the body as a force in the larger perceptual field, with the introvert needing to maximize its presence. Third, we need to arrive at some generalities about how the body as a psychological frame of reference helps to organize information and feed it into decision processes. Can persistent high or low awareness of a specific body area render a person selectively ready to use information pertinent to that area when arriving at decisions? Previous work on the judgmental effects of feedback of false body information (e.g., Valins, 1966) indicates potential profit in contemplating this matter.

NOTES

[1] Certain body image adaptations derive from the sheer physical topography of the body. Some parts of the body are small, and some are large; some are easily perceived, and some are not; some have lower sensitivity thresholds than others; and so forth. Even within the normal range, the mere degree of departure of the size of a body part from the norm may influence its prominence. Being unusually obese or thin

creates a special judgmental framework (Gorchynski, 1973). Just by being large a body part tends to take on masculine connotations (Nash, 1958). The sizes of large body parts are underestimated and those of smaller ones overestimated (Ben-Tovim, et al., 1979). The amazing complexity of the body experiential field itself must create a need for special integrative mechanisms.

[2] Even specific levels of body anxiety that characterize individuals at an early age persist into adulthood (Kagan & Moss, 1962).